IIAS/ISEAS Series on Asia

Asia in Europe, Europe in Asia

Edited by

Srilata Ravi • Mario Rutten • Beng-Lan Goh

International Institute for Asian Studies,
The Netherlands

Institute of Southeast Asian Studies,
Singapore

First published in Singapore in 2004 as a co-publication by
ISEAS Publications
Institute of Southeast Asian Studies
30 Heng Mui Keng Terrace
Pasir Panjang
Singapore 119614

E-mail: publish@iseas.edu.sg
Website: <http://bookshop.iseas.edu.sg>

First published in Europe in 2004 as a co-publication by
International Institute for Asian Studies
P.O. Box 9515
2300 RA Leiden
The Netherlands

E-mail: iias@let.leidenuniv.nl
Website: <http://iias.leidenuniv.nl>

The responsibility for facts and opinions in this publication rests exclusively with the authors and their interpretations do not necessarily reflect the views or the policies of ISEAS or IIAS or their supporters.

ISEAS Library Cataloguing-in-Publication Data

Asia in Europe, Europe in Asia / edited by Srilata Ravi, Mario Rutten and Beng-Lan Goh.
   1.   Asia—Civilization—Western influences.
   2.   Asia—Relations—Europe.
   3.   Europe—Relations—Asia.
   4.   Asia, Southeastern—Relations—Europe.
   5.   Europe—Relations—Asia, Southeastern.
   I.   Ravi, Srilata, 1960-
   II.   Rutten, Mario.
   III. Goh, Beng-Lan.
DS33.4 E8A832   2004

ISBN 981-230-206-9 (soft cover)
ISBN 981-230-208-5 (hard cover)

Typeset by International Typesetters Pte Ltd
Printed in Singapore by Seng Lee Press

Contents

Acknowledgements

We are grateful for the generous research grant received from the Faculty of Arts and Social Sciences, National University of Singapore, which enabled us to bring together scholars from Europe and Asia from different disciplinary backgrounds at a workshop, "Asia in Europe, Europe in Asia" held at Singapore in December 2001. The present volume brings together a selection of the revised papers presented at the workshop. The editors would wish to extend their gratitude to the publishers, the Institute of Southeast Asian Studies, Singapore (ISEAS), for their meticulous preparing and editing of the final manuscript. We would also like to thank the International Institute for Asian Studies (IIAS) in Leiden/Amsterdam for their support.

Srilata Ravi, Mario Rutten and Beng-Lan Goh

1

Introduction

Srilata Ravi, Beng-Lan Goh and Mario Rutten

It has been more than fifty years since the processes of decolonization changed the political, economic and cultural landscape in Asia and its relations with its former European colonizers. For a long time, academic discussions on Europe and Asia have focused on the political implications of their colonial histories. More recently, debates have centred on contemporary aspects of the Europe-Asia partnership in terms of international relations and economic linkages.[1] In all these discussions, relations between Asia and Europe have been predominantly studied in hegemonic terms, with Europe as the dominant political and economic and cultural centre. This centre-periphery conception of Europe-Asia relations has contributed to the establishment of seemingly unproblematic notions of a clear divide between two monolithic regions. Nevertheless such conceptions of Europe and Asia have come under increasing scrutiny given recent material realities of globalization.

Global movements of capital, knowledge and people have shown us that social spaces and cultures cannot exist next to each other as areas with boundaries around, but have to be viewed as articulated moments in a network of relations and understandings. The present volume contributes to this scrutiny by providing a critique of Europe-Asia relations from a multi-disciplinary angle. Its aims are to interrogate the dominant conceptions of Europe-Asia and to delineate the underlying complexities of the linkages between the two. To complement the predominantly political and economic interest in the Europe-Asia relationship, this volume focuses on the academic, social and cultural relations that bring Europe and Asia together, from both contemporary and historical perspectives.

The use of the terms 'Europe' and 'Asia' merits qualification. European political and cultural landscapes have undergone vast changes since World War II. More recently, the establishment of the European Union, the fall of the Berlin Wall and the succeeding reintegration processes set in motion have completely transformed the map of Europe. On the other hand, the more restrictive idea of the Far East has given way to amorphous politico-economic constructs like East Asia (China, Japan and Korea), South Asia (the Indian subcontinent and her neighbours) and Southeast Asia (a Cold War construct).

Hence we are aware that the usage of the terms 'Europe' and 'Asia' could be problematic in that they are both ideological constructs notwithstanding their associated geographical realities. While deconstruction of these terms is currently popular in academic debates, it is practical to retain their usage as they retain rhetorical power in shaping today's world. On another note, in the current world order dominated by America, the re-establishment of Europe and Asia as an academic question could also appear irrelevant. For the purposes of this volume we adopt a historical definition of America as an extension of Europe given their intertwined histories. It is often forgotten that the discovery of America in 1492 made it a part of Imperial Europe and that it was World War I that saw its rise as a distinctive political power (Mignolo 2000). In fact, its global dominance was finally consolidated only after World War II. Therefore our choice of the term 'Europe' is to capture the origins of a global power that can be traced back to the expansion of mercantile trade which eventually led to colonialism and the rise of Europe as a dominant world power. Our employment of the term Europe applies to both this history of dominance as well as the power/knowledge processes associated with European dominance.

As for the term 'Asia', we work with its rhetorical definition as the ideological Other of Europe with the aim of tracing the power of this imagining as well as unsettling its basic premises. Hence our use of these terms enables us to trace their performative power as discursive constructs and at the same time to unsettle the underlying assumptions of these imaginaries at specific locations across space and time.

It would then be imperative in this context to take Said's critique of West-East relations as a starting point in our volume (Said 1991). As we know, Said's theory of Orientalism was drawn on Foucault's notion of power-discourse that posits the East as a construction of the West to uncover the power patterns that have defined the relations between Europe and Asia; the Western self is also constituted in the process. *Orientalism* argues that a complex set of representations was fabricated, which for the West became the Orient and provided the basis for imperial rule. As such, Orientalism is not just an idea or system of knowledge but is complicit with the exercise of power that defined notions of relations between Europe and Asia. While Said's thesis establishes European hegemony and seeks to deconstruct it, he is also seen as unselfconsciously operating within European cultural heritage by attributing Europe/West as the only source of power and totality in shaping the non-West.

The authors in this volume interrogate prevailing conceptions of the East-West interaction in diverse ways in order to present the complexities of local histories, ideas and agencies in both Europe and Asia. Satish Saberwal's contribution discusses the encounters between Asian and European civilizations in the domains of modes of knowing, technology, organizational forms, and values. Concentrating on India and China, Saberwal shows that in this encounter, alien technologies and organizational forms (such as the state, schools, railways, printing, even elected governments) close to colonial designs were imposed relatively speedily while alternate modes of knowing and values emerged as incidental outcomes in the course of coping with career paths of new technologies and institutional forms in the wider colonial ambience. According to Saberwal, the Asian encounter of things European shows that although 'Europe' and 'Asia' may be counterposed geographically, in cultural and civilizational terms, the counterposing may be problematic. He argues that while there is some form of historic cultural unity to Europe, Asia has been clearly multi-civilizational, something which has been further enhanced in the course of its encounter with things European in the domains of modes of knowing, technology, organizational forms, and values.

Despite this multi-civilizational character of Asia, the concept of an Asian entity has taken strong root over time. This concept of Asia is derived from the European conceptions of the Greater traditions of the East, notably the Middle East, India and China-Japan. From these 'greater' traditions are derived the 'smaller' ones such as Southeast Asia, which refers to the region south of China and east of India. Subsequently, these regions became associated with academic areas of study during the Cold War.

The history of Southeast Asia as a field of study is critically described by Henk Schulte Nordholt in his contribution to this volume. According to him, Southeast Asia is in many respects a region by default, while Southeast Asian studies have been framed by a postcolonial predicament. Nordholt's essay shows how foreign institutions and scholars have, to a large extent, determined the research agenda of Southeast Asian studies, a situation that would have been unthinkable in the South Asian context. In line with this argument, the contribution by Syed Farid Alatas explores the possibilities of a reversal of this academic dependency. According to Alatas, one practice that would auger well for the emergence of alternative discourses is to lessen reliance on European or American standards that may not be appropriate and at the same time work towards the upgrading of local publication capabilities. He emphasizes, however, that such a development of local publications can only work if as much credit is given for locally published works by evaluators, and promotion and tenure committees, as it is for international publications.

As shown in these two chapters on Southeast Asian studies, knowledge about Asian regions has traditionally been framed within a temporal hierarchy with Europe as the definitive normative against which the Greater Eastern Traditions are understood, while the latter in turn become the norm from which meanings of the Little Traditions are derived. In such a context, it is not surprising to find that the polity and culture of the 'little', if not 'tribal', societies of Southeast Asia have been predominantly shaped by a discourse on Hindu-Buddhist and Sinic influences. Another example of the power of Orientalist knowledge is found in the Indological discourse produced during colonial rule. Indological discourse assumes that the institution of caste is at the essence of Hindu civilization. Such a discourse dismisses the importance of ancient Indian political institutions like kinship. When conceptualized in this way, caste is seen as both cause and effect of India's low political and economic development and its repeated failure to resist foreign invasion. As such, it became natural for European scholars and administrators to justify their actions on behalf of the Indians.

While Said's *Orientalism* lays bare the power relations inherent to representational formations, it exposes at the same time Europe's reciprocal dependence on those whom it subordinated. Said himself in *Culture and Imperialism*, and more recently Anne Laura Stoler, have shown that the colonies were seen as laboratories in which ideological and disciplinary regimes were developed before being brought back home to regulate metropolitan society (Said 1993; Stoler 1992). Arguably, Europe and its others were co-produced in and through their unequal interactions. In discursive practice this implies that Europe, while constructing its Other as an object of thought, was in fact constructing itself as a subject.

Homi Bhabha's theory and concept of hybridity represents the (post)colonial co-production of Europe and its Others (Bhabha 1994). Bhabha regards colonial discourse as one that goes beyond unilateral projection to open reciprocal complexities in the colonial encounter. He notes the ambivalence in colonial discourse which strove on the one hand to domesticate and assimilate the native but which on the other felt "disavowed" by the partial resemblance of the "product". Recently there has been a substantial body of work that takes into account issues concerning gender and sexuality. The female dimension of the imperial project examined by both Western and Asian scholars has enhanced our understanding of the complexities and ambiguities that have defined (post)colonial encounters (Mani 1998; Spivak 1987; Ong and Peletz 1995).

This reciprocal complexity of the Asia-Europe relationship in the postcolonial period is visible in the two contributions by Beng-Lan Goh and Mario Rutten to this volume. Together, they discuss two concepts that are important to the understanding of the Europe-Asia social and cultural interface in the postcolonial era: modernity and entrepreneurship. In her contribution, Goh shows how the implicit notion of historical progress is present in the common definition of modernity that is based on a unilinear unfolding of time and experience whereby the Western mode of time and being is the norm against which all other experiences are judged. Her essay explores displacements opened up by recent re-thinking about Western and non-Western experiences of the modern that provide ways out of the East-West binary and its associated unequal relations in the conceptualization of modernity. Through the discussion of recent examples, Goh shows how such an approach poses a challenge to understanding the modern imaginaries and transformations in Southeast Asian societies in autonomous terms rather than resorting to invidious or derivative distinctions from that of the West. The multiple formulations of modernity suggest that modernity is not necessarily only a Western phenomenon but that there are a variety of forms and meanings of the modern that are produced, imbued with local meanings, and contested in these societies.

In his comparative essay on the study of entrepreneurship in Asia and Europe, Mario Rutten argues that the widespread use of European concepts to characterize Asian entrepreneurship is often based on assumptions about the early industrialists in Europe that are highly questionable. Entrepreneurs in Asia are usually considered to be deformed, pseudo-, or non-genuine capitalists. Underlying these common views of Asian entrepreneurs is a notion of the emergence of the first industrial capitalists in Europe that is frequently invoked as model or paradigm for the behaviour of the entrepreneurs in Asia today. The validity of this model or paradigm, however, has been seldom questioned within the realm of Asian studies. Rutten critically examines some historical findings on the emergence of the early industrialists in Europe. Based on this discussion, he questions the perceptions of differences between Asian and Western patterns of entrepreneurship. He shows that, partly because scholars studying Asian society have seldom made use of new insights by European economic historians to update their notions on the early industrialists in Europe, our view on the emergence of the entrepreneurial class in Asia has been partly a distorted one.

Said's ground-breaking theory that showed that the power/knowledge processes representing the world reside in the West also opened enquiry into the possibility of other forms of knowledge beyond the West. Indeed, attempts to recover what has been labelled as subaltern or indigenous knowledge are evidence of this endeavour. The Subaltern Studies project consists of breaking up notions of a unitary India into a multiplicity of unstable identities which are the effects of changing power relationships. The concerted poststructuralist assault on Reason, Progress, and Nation probably finds its culmination in Dipesh Chakrabarty's project of "provincializing Europe" (Chakrabarty 2000). The pessimistic nature of this thesis, which attests that history is inescapably Eurocentric, also evokes the problem of "exteriority" or how to recover "subalternity from between the lines of colonial and nationalist discourse" and to claim for the once-colonized "our freedom of imagination".

Nevertheless the subaltern projects remain unresolved, by and large because these theoretical projects fall into the trap of locating power bases only in the West. On another note, historical and cultural realities continue to show Europe's hegemonic position vis à vis Asia. In response, recent studies have made some theoretical headway. Critics like Walter Mignolo acknowledge the persistent power of Europe but insist that it is the encounter between Europe and the Rest of the World that becomes sites for the release of "local" knowledge. Using the progressive idea of "border thinking", Mignolo suggests that European hegemony is always in co-existence with local forms of knowledge. He argues for the simultaneity of the production of knowledge thus opening the possibilities of other forms of knowledge beyond Eurocentrism. While Mignolo's study is that of a Latin American critic of Eurocentrism, the conclusions drawn are applicable in the Europe/Asian contexts as they provide epistemological grounds to place local Asian knowledge in a coeval position of power with that of Europe. Such theoretical developments show that universal knowledge is not constituted by the West alone. Rather, knowledge is formed as a result of an interaction between the different imaginaries and practices of Western and non-Western societies. Such a perspective allows the autonomy of thoughts and actions of non-Western societies in contributing to the making of universal knowledge.

This multiple interaction between Asia and Europe in the field of knowledge is clearly visible in the three contributions to this volume that discuss the actual historical contacts in various domains: archaeology in Thailand, seismology in Japan, and health in India and Britain. In his essay on the history of archaeology in modern Siam, Maurizio Peleggi focuses on the material and discursive practices (surveying, collecting, classification and periodization) as well as the institutions and historical actors that participated in this endeavour between the 1860s and 1920s. Both the culmination of several decades of royal antiquarian pursuits and the response to the establishment of the Siam Society by a group of expatriates in 1904, the founding of the Archaeological Society signalled the intention of investigating systematically the realm's historical landscape in the wake of its territorial and cartographic configuration as a modern state at the turn of the nineteenth and twentieth centuries. For from being the autarchic endeavour purported by some, Peleggi shows that the production of archaeological knowledge in modern Siam was heavily dependent on Western scholarship and ideas that combined pursuing the cues of royal antiquarianism with seconding the nationalist quest for origins.

In the case of seismology, Gregory Clancey shows in his contribution to this volume how the act of framing an 'earthquake problem' in Meji Japan was done by Westerners hired to teach and research other science topics in Japanese academic institutions. At a time when the Japanese government invested in a model of planned science and technology transfer from the West to Japan, a branch of 'Western learning' could develop spontaneously in Japan and eventually be exported abroad as a Japanese speciality. In this way, the peculiar trajectory of seismology is an interesting addition to the debate on Asia-Europe interaction in the field of science and technology.

This also applies to Vineeta Sinha's chapter on British colonial rhetoric in India and the realities of healing practices and health conditions in nineteenth century Britain. The rhetoric of British colonialism required and produced somewhat glowing images of 'home' that were defined in stark contrast to the inhospitable conditions in the colonies. In colonial health discussions, narratives of scientizing and civilizing 'native' populations were expressed through the assumed superior status of modern medicine rather than reflecting actual medical practices or sanitary conditions 'back home'. Through the use of historical data, Vineeta Sinha shows that the selection of modern medicine as the representative of Western/European medicine, as evident in colonial rhetoric, was in the first instance ideological more than anything else and that there are disjunctures between the claims made on behalf of modern medicine and the realities of its achievements in managing day-to-day health conditions in nineteenth century Britain. The constructed images of health and healing practices prevalent at 'home' in colonial health descriptions were at odds with the realities of actual conditions. The larger implication is that the health and sanitary scenarios at 'home' and in the colonies in the nineteenth century might have been more similar than different.

It may be appropriate at this point to relate these ideas to empirical realities concerning the question of social and cultural relations between Asia and Europe. Our central concern is to expose the interactions as well as transgressions of flows and production of cultural knowledge and social practices that are often obliterated in dominant conceptions of Asia-Europe relations. In this context, one of the most crucial factors is the question concerning Nationalism and Identities. Given the colonial experience, the problem of nationalism in Asia is often framed within the context of anti-colonial sentiments. The question of the coloniality of nationalist discourses has been well researched with ample examples of colonial acts of violence on local identities and the insidious reproduction of colonial images in attempts to recuperate cultural authenticity in the postcolonial era. What have received lesser attention are the sites of autonomous practice and imagining at the local level during both colonial and postcolonial eras and the types of agency and power hierarchy that made them possible. In addition, the problematic of nationalism and identities is not one that is merely confined to the postcolonies. Rather, in the contemporary globalized world, European nations are equally beset by the question of the impact of Asian minority cultures on the construction of European national identities.

These various sociocultural aspects of the interaction between Asia and Europe are at the heart of the contributions by Van Nguyen-Marshall and Mario Rutten in the volume. Through a discussion of Vietnamese literature on poverty of the 1930s and 1940s, Van Nguyen-Marshall shows how novels and short stories on poverty reflected Western educated Vietnamese intellectuals' preoccupation with social and moral problems associated with colonialism and global capitalism. These Vietnamese intellectuals clearly saw themselves as beneficiaries of Western modernity in terms of scientific and technological advances as well as intellectual influences. It is also clear that they were painfully aware of the separation between them and the majority of the people of their country. This bi-cultural heritage shaped the writers' understanding and portrayal of poverty as a national problem in colonial Vietnam and turned Vietnamese literature on poverty in the 1930s and 1940s into a vehicle for social criticism and indirectly for anti-colonial expressions.

Mario Rutten and Pravin J. Patel's chapter focuses on the growing presence of migrants of Asian origin in Britain. It discusses the social linkages between Indian migrants in Europe and their family members in Asia. To an increasing extent, this community of Indians abroad has become a transnational community that maintains frequent long-distance family linkages with their home region in India. Marriage arrangements, kinship networks, frequent visits, property, remittances and religious affiliations keep many of the migrants in London well-linked to villages in India, resulting in a two-way flow of people, capital and ideas between Asia and Europe. These linkages between India and Britain, however, are not static or without problems. Based on intensive fieldwork in Asia and Europe, Rutten and Patel show that there are differences of opinion between the Indian migrants in London and their relatives in India on the nature of their relationship and on the type of help rendered.

The last two chapters of the volume deal with Western cultural productions in the Vietnamese context. The contribution by John Kleinen examines the representations of Asians, in particular of Vietnamese, by Western, American filmmakers of Vietnam War movies. While the themes in these films changed from general war movies, through the depiction of bloodthirsty veterans and patriots, towards the view of the victimized servicemen, the representation of the Vietnamese did not change dramatically. Vietnamese soldiers and civilians are portrayed as cunning, cruel, even sadistic, ambivalent and irresponsible. This latent and manifest Orientalism in American movies about the Vietnam War are clear manifestations of a discourse which had broader consequences for the way Asians have been depicted. Where earlier movies showed a worldview in which the Asian participants are reduced to simple pawns in a chess game between the superpowers, the post-1975 'Vietnam syndrome' genre betrayed a stereotype which reified the Vietnamese as devious and unchanging. From a more manifest Orientalism in the earlier films, symbolized by stereotypes of the 'Yellow Peril', it changed into more latent representations of Orientalism in the so-called anti-war movies.

The second contribution that deals with Western cultural production in the Vietnamese context is the essay by Srilata Ravi on the construction and reassessment of mixed-race (Franco-Vietnamese) consciousness in European literature. In this essay, she explores how métissage represented/self-represented in a variety of different Francophone discourses (colonial, literary and popular) set specifically in a Franco-Asian context. The cultural or racial métis/métisse is neither a mere apology of colonization nor a site of unproblematic multicuturalism.

Métissage represents a colonial encounter that, in its violence, created hybridization which cannot be erased. At a time when mixed race identity is more a norm than an exception, this final chapter of the volume argues that a positive reconstruction of mixed race identities needs to be developed in postcolonial cultures.

The originality of this book lies in its multidisciplinary approach to the question of Asia-Europe and in its emphasis on the multifaceted complexity of the relationship between these two regions. The chapters in this volume are informed by a combination of perspectives from the Social Sciences and Humanities. The authors are specialists on Asia and Europe and come from different disciplinary backgrounds: history, sociology, anthropology and cultural studies. Together this book therefore presents a unique combination of the study of contemporary and historical practices between Asia and Europe and brings forth some of the latest thinking on the subject. It brings together the diversity of local histories, ideas and agencies in both Europe and Asia into a universal project of knowledge and action formation in order to reveal their constitutive interaction and contribution to the making of the world we are in.

Notes

[1]   See, for example, Yeo and Latif (2000), *Asia and Europe*; Wiessala (2002), *The European Union and Asian Countries*; Dunning (2000), *Regions, Globalization and the Knowledge-Based Economy*; Van Mierlo (1996), *Europe and Asia*; Fieldhouse (1999), *The West and the Third World*; and Birch et al. (2001), *Cultural Politics in a Global Age*.

References

Bhaba, Homi. 1994. *The Location of Culture*. London and New York: Routledge.

Birch, David, Tony Schirato and Sanjay Srivastava. 2001. *Asia: Cultural Politics in a Global Age*. Crows Nest: Allen & Unwin.

Chakrabarty, Dipesh. 2000. *Provincializing Europe: Postcolonial Thought and Historical Difference*. Princeton, NJ: Princeton University Press.

Dunning, John H., ed. 2000. *Regions, Globalization, and the Knowledge-based Economy*. Oxford and New York: Oxford University Press.

Mani, Lata. 1998. *Contentious Traditions: The Debate on Sati in Colonial India*. Berkeley: University of California Press.

Mignolo, Walter D. 2000. *Local Histories/Global Designs: Coloniality, Subaltern Knowledges and Border Thinking*. Princeton, NJ: Princeton University Press.

Ong, Aihwa and Michael G. Peletz, eds. 1995. *Bewitching Women, Pious Men: Gender and Body Politics in Southeast Asia*. Berkeley: University of California Press.

Said, Edward. 1991. *Orientalism*. London: Penguin Books.

———, 1992. *Culture and Imperialism*. London: Vintage.

Spivak, Gayatri Chakravorty. 1987. *In Other Worlds: Essays in Cultural Politics*. New York: Methuen.

Stoker, Laura Ann. 1992. "Rethinking Colonial Categories: European Communities and the Boundaries of Rule". In *In Colonialism and Culture*, edited by Nicholas Dirks. Ann Arbor: University of Michigan Press.

Van Mierlo, Hans. 1996. *Europe and Asia: Towards a New Partnership*. Leiden: International Institute for Asian Studies.

Wiessala, Georg. 2002. *The European Union and Asian Countries*. London and New York: Sheffield Academic Press.

Yeo Lay Hwee and Asad Latif, eds. 2000. *Asia and Europe: Essays and Speeches by Tommy Koh*. Singapore: World Scientific Publishing and Asia-Europe Foundation.

Part I

Academic Discourses and Concepts

2

Civilizational Encounters: Europe in Asia

Satish Saberwal

When we think of the encounter between Asia and Europe, we are aware of a lack of balance between the two entities. 'Europe' and 'Asia' may be counterposed geographically; but in cultural and civilizational terms, the counterposing is problematical. There is a historic cultural unity to Europe, due largely to the influence of the Roman Catholic Church during the Middle Ages, which has no counterpart in Asia. By the mid-12th century, the Cistercian order of monks regularly held annual meetings in central France, its monasteries' abbots, or their representatives, travelling there from the far ends of Europe—Ireland, Sweden, Greece, Portugal. For near comparisons in Asia, we would have to think of similar gatherings within China, within the world of Islam in West and Central Asia, or within India. Asia has been multi-civilizational.

China and India had a thin link in Buddhism; as did India and Southeast Asia in Hinduism. Islam spread through India and Southeast Asia rather swiftly, but the regions under its sway have been too disparate, and its institutional impulses too diffuse, to achieve the kind of shared 'personality' that Europe came to acquire. What gives Asia its unity, perhaps, is its

common experience of Europe as an expansive—indeed aggressive—
civilization; but that experience we have shared with Africa and with the
pre-Columban Americas and Australia too. On the other hand, between
Asia and Europe, there had been contacts much earlier, as with the Arabs
in Spain, or Marco Polo in China at the Mongol court; and these contacts
were profoundly consequential in shaping the course of history.

This essay considers only the period after Vasco da Gama. For all of
us in Asia, Europe's expansion, and its more recent withdrawal from
colonies, have had significant consequences in the making of the present.
The record of the encounter between Asians and Europeans over these
five centuries is a priceless resource, for, on our shrinking planet, such
cultural encounters are becoming denser and more frequent than ever
before. It is through reviewing past experience that we can learn to form
judgements about such civilizational interfaces, and to make informed
choices for the future.

There is a daunting diversity to Asia—and to Europe's presence in
Asia. Yet we need handles with which to make sense of that diversity,
and to appraise the major lines of influence. The consequences of
Europe's expansion arose initially from the commercial, political, and
similar frameworks, like the 'colonial mode of production', created by
colonial powers for their own purposes. These have often had
devastating consequences, and it has been common to blame
colonialism, and the West generally, for nearly all our maladies. Some
of the colonial frameworks—say the educational institutions for training
low cost local manpower for operating the colonial regime—had
unintended consequences: some indigenes were able to scan, more or
less intimately, spacious European cafeterias of ideas—of technologies,
of epistemologies, and so forth; and they were exposed, too, to European
modes of institutional designs. The European repertoire on offer has
included powerful resources with which to reconstitute our societies,
to set them on relatively steady courses. Whether it is the disruptions
that prevailed, or the effective reintegration of our societies into new
keys, has depended, partly, on the kinds of skill, imagination, and
organizing drives which our ancestors, and we, have brought to those
stocks of ideas—in the West, and indeed elsewhere within Asia and in
the past of our own particular societies.

Europeans and Asians have influenced and challenged, attracted
and repelled, each other in a great variety of ways. The following

consideration of what Asians have done with things European will take five steps. It opens with a brief review of the capabilities that Europe had already achieved in the Middle Ages. We in Asia have tended not to take Europe's historical experience seriously. We begin to notice Europe from the Renaissance—15th and 16th centuries—as if Europe had really been born at that time! To try to correct this misconception I wish to indicate briefly why I think Europe in the Middle Ages deserves our most serious attention.

The Asian response to things European may, in turn, be examined in terms of four domains. I shall begin with modes of knowing, that is, epistemologies, and here I shall stress the consequences of a stringent recourse to the empirical attitude. Among the most potent of these consequences have been the waves of transformation within technology, triggering waves of change in societies hosting these technologies. Societies are able to maintain themselves in order, amidst the technological and other vicissitudes, by virtue of their organizational frameworks, or institutional forms—which may be seen as a kind of social technology. Underpinning all the other domains are values; and we need to remember the symbiosis between institutions and values. Institutions embody, are made possible by, values; but institutions also bear witness to the values embodied in them—serving thereby to propagate these values (Saberwal 1995, ch. 9).

For each domain—modes of knowing, technology, organizational forms, and values—I shall begin with brief comments on what had been the principal tendencies in India and China—the two regions with which I have some familiarity—and then indicate the larger social spinoffs from the encounter with Europe, concentrating on India. We shall see that the four domains—modes of knowing and the rest—are analytic separations, with large mutual implications. Furthermore, in each domain, the new has jostled with the old, there has been much mixing and matching, and the flow of time has been loaded, as always, with the detritus of unintended consequences. I need hardly mention the kaleidoscopic nature of the analytic frame: its configurations would change sharply as one takes it from Kyoto to Shanghai, Jakarta, Tashkent, or Tehran.

The Church and its Institutions

Tenth century Europe was not much different from other agrarian civilizations—China, India. But Europe did have one element which enabled it to break away—and to enter an extraordinary process which allowed Europe to go on to shape the modern world. That extraordinary element was the Roman Catholic Church (RCC). The Catholics have had a bad press, owing to Protestant propaganda, so the role of the Church has to be seen afresh.

RCC was a vast, multifaceted institution in the Middle Ages, drawing the Judeo-Christian religious tradition, the Greek intellectual tradition, and the Roman political tradition all together into a single, overlapping institutional space. Its archives gave it an institutional memory unrivalled for its time. Literacy was concentrated in the Church and its monasteries; and to study, to keep the tradition alive, was commonly taken as a religious duty for clergy and monks. This pedigree was reflected in the kind of things that RCC could try to do in medieval Europe. I shall mention three aspects here: the strong political sense of the church; its nurturing of literacy and learning; and the ability to intervene down to the levels of family structure and the individual throughout Christendom.

First, following the decline of Rome, the Church had functioned as a fallback political institution too, able to exercise better political judgement than other institutions of the time; it was thus able to contribute significantly to stabilizing kingships in the Middle Ages (Saberwal 1995, ch. 3). Furthermore, when, in the late 11th century, the old Roman secular legal tradition began to be revived, the Church, far from opposing this development, proceeded to put its own Canon Law through legal systematization.

Second, the Church fostered a largely open tradition of literacy and learning. In the early Middle Ages, scholars in the monasteries debated complex issues for long centuries. I give two sets of examples —which allow me also to cite two classics on the history of the period.

One set of issues concerned the Church directly: Should clergymen marry? How to make sense of the Eucharist, the belief that the wafer and wine imbibed in the rite are really the body and blood of Jesus? Is it permissible to receive an office—Bishop of the Church, Abbot of a monastery—as a favour from a secular ruler? Who should control a clergyman, his secular ruler or his superiors within the Church? Churchmen debated such issues concerning their own social practices, the doctrinal bases of their rites, and the terms of their relationships with the loci of secular power; and they sought repeatedly to reform the prevailing social arrangements in the light of such reflection.[1]

European scholarship in the Middle Ages was much concerned with questions of government, including the nature of kingship. One issue here was the relationship between the king, the particular person, and kingship, an abstract concept invoking also a territory and its inhabitants. Later, with the revival of the legal tradition, legal scholars turned their thoughts towards the relationship between the king and the law. Is the king under the law—having to defer to laws established by tradition, or emerging from consultative assemblies—or is the king above the law—given his undoubted power and his own role in initiating law-making (Kantorowicz 1957, chaps. 3 and 4). Here were scholars, in and out of monasteries, who sustained an interest in issues central to the evolution of Europe's political institutions through the centuries.

In the 10th and the 11th centuries, scholars in the Church began to reach out to Arab philosophy in southern Spain. Thanks to this channel, the vast resources of classical Greek learning began to flow into medieval Europe. Partly to cope with the intellectual challenges so generated, what had been cathedral schools until the 12th century began to grow into universities in the 13th.

Third, the Church disposed of an entrenched hierarchy, with its representatives down in the localities, able to influence events there. For example, the Church promoted the idea of the monogamous 'Christian family'. It banned levirate and similar practices, and insisted, in principle, that any Christian may marry any other.

Then, in 1215, a great council of the Church instituted an obligation on every Christian to make an annual confession. This came close to putting a psychiatrist in every village, requiring every adult to unburden himself or herself to one's pastor or vicar once a year. It turned out, however, that the clergymen were not equipped to deal with the flood of anxieties that came their way in the course of the confessions. In response to this need, 13th century Europe generated a major new genre of writing: the Confessors' Manuals, which sought to advise the confessors how to respond to the confessions (Boyle 1981 has several studies on the theme).

Clearly Europe was learning to do a variety of things on a large scale. These capacities were being built around varied institutional forms.

By the end of the thirteenth century, Europeans were already working with a great variety of institutions. Illustratively:

- the Church itself had its religious hierarchy, of course, and the monasteries; and new orders of monks with their own distinctive charters were rising too;
- in the great cathedrals of Europe, cathedral schools began with training manpower for the church itself. By the twelfth century, these schools had to meet a burgeoning demand for trained men from kingships too. By the following century, these schools had transformed themselves into universities, which were clearly becoming academic institutions, with a strong sense of their own autonomy, intent on setting their own courses.
- Some universities drew into themselves the study of law, a field whose study had been revived since the twelfth century, initially at Bologna in northern Italy. The idea of systematic law gained ground. Kings needed men trained in law, as they sought to shift the bases of their own legitimacy and support, *from* the Church *to* the authority of law and of legal courts, to be maintained by the kingships. King's justice came to be administered in the localities through mobile judges who travelled from place to place.
- This was a time also for the growth of administrative hierarchies, with extensive use of written documents, say, in support of claims to ownership of land.

In sum, by the end of the thirteenth century, Europeans were working with so varied a lot of institutions that we may say that they had mastered the art of building them. Given a problem, say, organizing the Crusades, they would generate institutional forms addressing the tasks at hand. Over time these institutions would be reorganized, taking on different tasks suited to the changing circumstances.[2] Such, then, were the institutional skills and capabilities that helped launch Europe in its course of expansion at the end of the 15th century, bringing it to Asia too.

Modes of Knowing

Let us turn now to the cultural encounter between Europe and the Asian civilizations.

We can thank Europe for showing us the power of working with the empirical attitude stringently. Mankind has known other epistemologies, other modes of knowing: the trance for communicating with the gods; the ordeal to ascertain truth; consulting a sacred book— or a holy man or woman; seeking the implications of stellar configurations for human fortunes. Europe has demonstrated, and validated historically, the value of detached scholarship which goes wherever the track of enquiry takes it. To choose to be an academic is to stake one's life on this mode of knowing, yet the outcomes of what we do can be acutely troublesome. The empirical attitude spawned the whole new universe of science and technology, and we shall return shortly to the consequences, especially the socially disruptive consequences, of the new technologies.

Here I wish to comment briefly on the rise of this empirical attitude in the social domain. To be sure, any functioning society carries a sense of the empirical, and a complex civilization can scarcely rest on otherworldliness alone. It is a matter of degree, and there has been great variation between societies and civilizations. The Indian tradition did not much foster the habits of observing social phenomena systematically, and of reflecting on social experiences. Take the matter of encountering 'other' peoples. Cultural differences were handled rather through social insulation, as in the caste order. Indian merchants ranged far and wide over Central Asia, West Asia, East Africa, Southeast Asia and beyond, but none of them did ever write an account of the way of life of the people among whom they lived and traded.

The Chinese did better. Indeed, we owe a major part of the evidence for first millennium India to Chinese pilgrims looking for Buddhist texts in India; the impulse here was religious. The Chinese generated voluminous historical records for themselves too, and produced dynastic histories painstakingly; but their attention was centred on activity around the imperial court (see, for example, Wright 1963). The interest in observation did not take in much of the wider social domain.

In science and technology, too, the Chinese scored notable advances. Sivin (1977) has produced the biography of a distinguished eleventh century scholar active in these fields. Effort in this direction was hobbled in various ways. For instance, being a scholar, i.e. being a Confucian literatus, had close links with being a state official. As men who were primarily part of a great administrative service, these scholar-officials were liable to transfer from one job to another—running an astronomical observatory this year, organizing defence activity along the Great Wall of China the next year, and coping with a draught or a flood the year after. There was no question of their concentrating on one field for long (Sivin 1977).

Nor could they form scholarly associations—say of everyone interested in astronomy. The Chinese state was highly suspicious of all voluntary associations of this kind. In pre-modern China, for anyone to think of forming an autonomous, peer-group community of scholars was to ask for trouble—they would be suspected of conspiring against the rival faction, wielding more power at the moment, if not against the emperor himself (Sivin 1977; 1982).

How did the encounter with Europe influence the realm of knowledge in Asia? I concentrate on India, where the processes have been complex enough. In the caste order in the pre-colonial period, the patterns of learning and literacy had been specific to particular *jati*s: the Brahmin, the merchant, the cobbler, and so forth would not be expected to learn anything from, or to have much to teach, each other (Saberwal 1995, ch. 7 explores the historic location of literacy in Indian society). In the social flux of the colonial milieu, men and women began, slowly, to reach out of their *jati*s. In the process, they began to absorb various kinds of knowledge: Western learning, especially in the new educational institutions; and elements of other traditions in India's present and past: Islamic, Buddhist, and a multitude of traditions within the 'Hindu' space. I give you an example. Dances like Bharat Natyam and Odissi had been the province of *devadasis*, a virtual *jati* centred on temples. Formerly confined to the temples, the dance forms came to be secularized, available to ordinary citizens (Marglin 1985, pp. 27ff).

The 19th and 20th centuries witnessed this quite extraordinary flux and diffusion of ideas. The prevailing assumptions about the nature of knowing and of knowledge, and of its proper distribution in society, came to be recast. The older social arrangements and hierarchies, and their underlying ideas, had been anchored firmly within their relatively small-scale social universes. As some members of the hitherto repressed groups participated in the new flux of knowledge, their sense of social power grew. An array of anti-Brahmin movements, especially in southern and western India, questioned the established order—presaging later tendencies.

The realm of knowledge was changing in colonial India in other ways too, at two levels. At one level, the ascendant mode of knowing appealed to observation and verifiable experience. At another level, the understanding of the nature of the world, i.e. 'science', came to be organized in general rules, in general scientific principles. A similar recourse to general rules informed the legal codes, employed in law courts. And these general rules, whether in science or in legal codes, were held to be valid regardless of their context. That is to say, at least in principle, their validity did not depend on the status of their proponent.

The encounter between Europe and Asia did something to Europe too. I wish to comment on only one theme in that large story. Reliance on observation, on verifiable experience, and on a search for generalizations—all this was part of the epistemologies then rising in Europe, even for social and cultural phenomena. It was in Asia, in 'the Orient', that Europe encountered other major civilizations which had a strong sense of history, as in China, which had complex systems of speculative thought, as in India, and which had strong impulses for religious expansion, as in Islam; and there had been large empires everywhere. Europe came to see these civilizations, 'the Orient', as the Other.

Exposure to these civilizations, and to all the other societies, added enormously to Europe's experiential base concerning social phenomena. Other societies and polities were commonly organized in radically different keys, and the shock of this recognition was a crucial stimulus in the evolution of the social sciences, especially political science, sociology, and anthropology. For all our complaints about *Orientalism* (Said 1978), this recognition of difference between societies has been a major point of departure in the making of the social sciences.

Jack Goody maintained recently that the major differences between Europe and the Asian civilizations have been merely contingent differences, a matter of phasing (1996). One civilization is ahead today, another tomorrow. To be sure, no civilizational differences can be attributed to genetic or racial elements; in an extreme sense, the differences *are* contingent. The island of Singapore today illustrates this principle brilliantly. Yet, what has been a major engine for the growth of our understanding of the nature of social existence, over the past century and more, is at stake here: namely, the effort at figuring out what led the civilizations to take to their divergent courses. If we shove all differences under the carpet of contingency, we forego vital heuristic space.

Having said that, I wish to take note of the kind of intellectual power that the social sciences have attained during this period. Or, rather, about the kind of trouble that can erupt because of the evidence, and the insights, which our disciplines help us generate. We do not always recognise how seismic this evidence and these insights can be for many of our prevailing worldviews. I shall refer to two situations which, again, bear on South Asia.

The Vedas were composed some three thousand or more years ago. In the course of intricate processes over the past century and a half, which need not detain us, many Hindus in India have come to accept these as sacred texts, foundational for their faith. Several distinguished historians, writing history textbooks for the National Council for Educational Research and Training (NCERT) for use in schools throughout India during the 1960s and 1970s, chose to spell out how important the sacrifice of cattle, and the consumption of beef, were in the social practices of these Vedic people.[3] This presented difficulties for the faithful. They have been locating the origins of their faith in the sacred texts of Vedic people; and their children were studying textbooks which depicted these people as given to beef-eating—uncomfortable thought if you take the cow to be sacred. The profound dissonance that this would generate among the faithful is clear enough. The result has been a first class political row in India between those who claim that Hindus' religious sensibilities have been hurt, and those who insist on the scholarly obligation to stand by truth, and the intellectual authority of the professional historian.[4]

My other example is rather more serious. In the social sciences, we can take it as axiomatic that, whatever the origins of the physical universe, the social universes are wholly human constructs: this understanding is as entrenched in the social sciences today as the heliocentric view is in astronomy. I scarcely need tell you the implications, for religious traditions, of the proposition that everything social, including the religious traditions themselves, are human, not divine, constructs. For those who have not had access to alternate, secularly grounded understandings of the nature of human existence, the unhinging of faith and belief, of identities and lifestyles, can have cataclysmic consequences—for themselves and for others. I know of modern nations today where, for questioning the creation of the universe in the terms indicated in certain scriptures, I could be charged with blasphemy and put to death—with or without a court verdict.

Mercifully, most social science findings have only rather benign implications. On the larger scale, however, we have to count on support from the wider society and polity, and therefore we have to nurture these wider links. Yet the tradition of independent, critical scholarship is not well entrenched in our societies. The most innocuous finding may arouse passions in one or another quarter. While we have to stand by our insights, and take due risks in publishing them, it would be in order for us to try to anticipate and assess the likely consequences of what we do.

Technologies and Societies

My second domain rolls the argument back in time. One element in modern Europe's ability to dominate most of Asia was its more versatile technology, arising ultimately in the slow triumph of the empirical attitude. When the Europeans began to arrive in the sixteenth century, Asian technologies were not doing very well. In India, technology had come, by and large, to be fitted into the caste grid, with each trade to a particular *jati*, or caste group. Given high transport costs, inter-regional overland trade was limited to relatively high value items.

Chinese technology had bloomed under the T'ang (618–906) and the Sung (960–1275); witness the enormous body of recent work, spurred by Joseph Needham. Yet, by the late Sung, this technology had plateaued out, constrained by China's wider difficulties with the foundations of legitimate political and intellectual authority.[5]

Europe's edge in technology allowed it to impose, throughout much of Asia, vastly enlarged scales of activities, initially in commerce, but moving on to production, communications, and so forth. It employed inanimate energy, in biofuels, alongside organized human labour, for myriad purposes. Railways slashed transportation costs. These also brought in a complex technology which had evolved through a different mode of knowing, a new, empirical epsitemology. Tin and rubber drew millions of Chinese and Indians into Malaya—and the growth of commerce into Singapore.

Asia and its population were being incorporated into a social and economic order which was increasingly global but the controls of that order were in European, not Asian, hands. Technological changes of this order have been disruptive everywhere. The ideas, the skills, and the relationships that an Asian moving, say, from a village to a city or a factory carried with him might enable him to survive in a small enclave; but these did not equip him for moving in these settings confidently. His older identities in terms of lineage or caste, as in his village, proved to be too small and inadequate. Trying urgently to cope with unfamiliar settings, sometimes incomprehendingly, he would seek social anchors which would give his world some stability.

As people sought to reorient themselves to the larger social universes to which they were waking up, they responded to such ideologies and identities as happened to be canvassed in their regions. Nationalism swept through the continent, unevenly, but also other political ideologies, especially Marxism, and religious ones, arising in the great religious traditions.

In some ways it was the religious traditions, and the associated identities that were presented most energetically and had the greatest appeal. Some of their symbols, rituals, festivals, specialists, and so forth had long been familiar; and the traditions had long carried the impulses for self-propagation. The 19th century access to print culture—the printing press, and the several forms of communicating the printed word—gave this impulse fresh impetus.

It was a time marked, on one side, by extensive political, economic, and social dislocations and, on the other, by the disempowerment of indigenous peoples in colonial societies. In this milieu it became possible to carry into local communities, inexpensively, calls to exclusive, sharply defined, religious identities—projected around trans-local, 'Great', written religious traditions. What had long been familiar as the local, customary order of things, often came to be riven with growingly exclusive identities (eg. Oberoi 1994).

Those who left their familiar local communities for towns and factories could be just as responsive to the new calls. Barbara Metcalf cites Mattison Mines on the experience of south Indian Muslim villagers in recent generations. In their villages, earlier, they had been "indistinguishable as Muslims" from their non-Muslim neighbours; but as they migrated they found it advantageous to "dress, eat, and identify as Muslims when they go to the city, thus securing a basis for community in a context of physical dislocation (Metcalf 1999, p. 139)." They entered frameworks of identities, differences, and oppositions whose scales were much larger than what had prevailed before; and identities of larger scales often got strengthened in ways that set them in opposition to other identities of large scales, laying the ground for conflict between them (Saberwal 2004 explores this larger theme for India at some length).

Colonial regimes could apply power and force to control these conflicts; their successor regimes have needed to learn more complex skills for containing these conflicts and for reordering and for steering their societies. The availability of these skills, and of the institutions requisite, cannot always be taken for granted.

Institutional Forms

Asian societies had old institutional forms—say the mosque, the caste order, or the empire served by Confucian scholar-officials—available for a range of purposes. Contact with Europe brought in new institutional forms, and also a new range of purposes to pursue. In the evolving society, old and new institutional forms were arrayed across old and new purposes. What purpose would be pursued through which kind of institutional form became largely a matter of local convenience. You end up with cultural hybrids with every turn of the wheel.

Among the most consequential institutional forms in the colonial package was that of the state itself. The colonial state maintained an effective monopoly over the use of force, at least in public arenas. Its 'law and order' complex, with its law courts and general legal codes, released processes which had vast, unforeseeable consequences. For example:

- The more resourceful trading and moneylending castes—Marwaris, Gujarati *banias*, Nattukottai Chettiars, Syrian Christians, Punjabi Khatris—could spread out speedily, counting on the colonial courts' support for their operations in the new localities. The trading *jati* networks facilitated, too, the kind of aggregation of capital that was needed for industrialization, often in the new form of the joint stock company;
- A growing range of voluntary organizations, pursuing a variety of novel purposes, came into being. These included new religious associations like the Brahmo Samaj and the Arya Samaj, whose networks served, in turn, to underpin varied initiatives: in the case of Arya Samaj, these included schools, colleges, a bank, and a newspaper.
- The purposes pursued by these voluntary organizations included challenges to established caste hierarchies and to established

authorities within a caste organization. While the colonial state did not have a positive egalitarian agenda, nor was it committed to defending the ideology and practice of the caste order. By and large, colonial power stood aloof from challenges to the prevailing order; it was not available for suppressing the social rebels. Consequently, subaltern groups found for themselves rather more room for public manoeuver than had been available in earlier regimes. SNDP in Kerala, the Nadar movement in Tamilnadu, the Satya Shodhak Samaj—and later Ambedkar—in Maharashtra illustrate the range of these stirrings (Jones 1998 surveyed the literature; on Maharashtra, see Omvedt 1976).

Monographic accounts of these associations and movements suggest local, or at best regional, happenings. Seemingly innocuous initiatives, however, spreading over large tracts, sustained over generations, have had snowballing consequences—shaping history, and sometimes re-shaping social and political geographies. Let me give you two illustrations from Indian history since the 19th century.

The British had established a college in Delhi, Delhi College, even before they absorbed the city into the empire in 1857. The experience of teaching and studying in this College became a model for organizing an institution for a rather different kind of learning. I refer to the founding of an Islamic seminary in Deoband, northeast of Delhi, in 1867: an institution with its own large building, an apparatus for administrative control, set syllabus, annual admissions, examinations, and so forth.

To be sure Islam has had a long and distinguished tradition of learning and scholarship, organized in substantial institutions; yet nineteenth century India had not inherited anything like an Islamic university. The prevailing pattern was that of a few pupils gathered informally around the *maulvi* in a mosque. Departing from that pattern, the Deobandi style allowed both a systematization of religious learning and a vast expansion in the numbers of trained religious scholars. Over the decades, the institution has sent out thousands of Islamic scholars all over South Asia—and beyond; and many of these graduates went on to establish new seminaries themselves. The ideology prevailing at Deoband strove to promote a subcontinental sense of community among Muslims who would stand apart from their neighbours—by virtue of their adherence to distinctive beliefs, practices, clothing, and personal bearing: a classic case of a 'community' being imagined—and fostered actively, from about the middle of the 19th century (Metcalf 1982; see also Shaikh 1989).

Other agencies with analogous agendas were active, simultaneously, from the 'Hindu' side, e.g. the Arya Samaj (Jones 1976). Between Muslims and Hindus, a bar of separation began to harden by late 19th century— which was later put to purposes over which the mid-19th century social and religious visionaries had no control. The social ground they had helped shape was used by political actors to force the Partition of the subcontinent in 1947. Clearly, complex forces had been at work. Access to new institutional forms, modes of communication, and new ways of imagining futures were central to the new dynamic.

My other example concerns the colonial institution of law,[6] itself a domain of Western learning, that drew members of the old Indian literati in the 19th century. Learning and practising Western law turned out to be a multiple-use resource:

- Given the colonial laws of property and contract, backed by the courts and their enforceable decrees, legal skills opened the doors to a profession which, at the higher levels, could be very lucrative.
- The (Western) language of law turned out also to be an effective medium in which to engage the colonial rulers; and therefore men trained at law were lifted into salient roles in public life—and then into whatever elective bodies came to be established. Through the 1920s and the 1930s they were also involved in devising Constitutional schemes, anticipating the moment when the real thing would have to be done. New in India's long historical experience, they prepared for a democratic polity, taking a civil society space for granted.
- Consequently, influential men, grounded in, and committed, to the principles underlying the European legal tradition, happened to be members of the Central Legislature when it doubled up as the Constituent Assembly in 1946, and of the Parliament during the decade following. Of the twenty "most influential members of the Constituent Assembly" identified by Austin (1966, p. 19), twelve "were lawyers or had taken law degrees". A group of votaries of Western law, elected democratically (though indirectly, on a limited franchise), came thus to dominate the process of Constitution-making in India. The social assumptions, and the legal techniques, that shaped the Constitution were drawn from the West, almost

entirely from outside India—even though the underlying purposes were emphatically Indian. The Constitution wrote the assumptions of the civil society into the foundations of the law of the land even though contrary principles continued to hold sway in the society overall.

Values and Institutions

Modes of learning, technologies, institutional forms. My fourth domain is less tangible, but not less consequential. I refer to values: deeply embedded ideas which serve to canalize a society's ongoing processes in particular ways, giving them direction, and defining the society's characteristics. Challenges by alternative values, from within the society or outside, can lead to profound social reordering, which may add up to a change in the structure of society.

Long-term exposure to Europe, under variable equations of power, has presented every Asian society with powerful challenges to a wide range of values. We have already referred to the values of detached scholarship and of empirical enquiry. Insofar as the world of modern scholarship is, or ought to be, egalitarian, anti-hierarchical, 'equality' as a value is already implicit there; but it came to infect numerous other arenas also. In the organizing of complex Asian societies—China, India, Iran—the principle of hierarchy had probably been the most pervasive ordering device. Correspondingly, within a few generations, the idea of equality has induced a vast churning in at least some of these societies. This has been the most spectacular in China and in the other countries which harnessed the Marxist vision for their social revolutions. Somewhat similar visions were active in India on lesser scales, as we have noted. More generally, the idea of equality underpins the gender revolution too, affecting nearly all societies in the region which had been constituted patriarchically: the heat is felt more or less in every home, generating in some regions widespread anxieties—and reactions which may make women's lives more difficult than ever before.

The value of equality underlies, too, the notion of general, universalistic social norms and laws, and the notion of equality before law, a notion wich is necessarily anathema to societies which have been shaped around the value of hierarchy. Going beyond universalistic laws, some Asians have been learning to design and use higher order laws, namely the Constitutions. These texts are designed:

on one side, to secure governments which rest on novel ideas of
sovereignty and political legitimacy, governments whose legitimacy would
rest not on conquest—or on descent (or usurping) from a conqueror—
but on the recorded preferences of citizens; and, on the other, to secure
the citizens' rights against the power and the force commanded by
governments (Baxi 2002).

The organization of Asian societies had rested on a wide range of
corporate groups—lineage and clan in China, the joint family and *jati* in
India, the *millat* in West Asia. Agrarian societies tend to endow one with
dense bonds of kinship and the like, arising in one's social location at
the moment of birth. In the course of processes spread over some two
millennia, the ideological stress in Europe tended to shift from the
importance of the collectivity to that of the individual. As the burden of
kinship was lightened, individuals found it easier to enter relationships
more open-endedly, and to give their loyalties to all manner of other
groups or institutions: monastery, university, business firm, occupational
guild, and so forth.

The encounter with Europe showed Asian societies something of
the flexibility and resilience associated with the stress on the mobile
individual; but there were countervailing considerations too. A
collectivity has its social network, its shared traditions and symbolism,
and sometimes its shared occupational knowledge, skills, and
understanding. These are resources which can function as a kind of
social capital and are important resources for coping with the
uncertainties of a changing world. In the colonial world, the trading
castes in India used this social capital tellingly; and similar resources
came handy in the lower castes' challenges to caste hierarchies and, for
that matter, in mobilizing clusters of support in the national movement.
One effective strategy has been to learn to walk on both sides of the
road—to preserve something of one's collectivities even as one learned
to deal with the relatively impersonal worlds of the bureaucracy,
modern education, the professions, and so forth: what Andre Beteille
noticed long ago as the ambidexterity of "progressive" farmers in India
(1974, pp. 104–8).

Insofar as persons reached out of their collectivities to enter
relationships of a more open-ended kind, they laid the basis for voluntary
associations whose scale could grow. China had a long tradition of
vast numbers of a dispossessed peasantry rallying to a Taoist religious
figure, which sometimes employed Buddhist myths and symbolism. This

tradition of peasant rebellions was part of the backdrop for the great Chinese revolution.

It is voluntary associations resting on open-ended relationships that underpin the latter-day idea of the civil society and the social space for a democratic polity. Already by late 19th century, urban politics in Bombay city was learning the value of open-ended associations between men of diverse social and religious backgrounds. On one side, these associations witnessed public debates over alternate visions for the future, moving in the direction that led to the Indian National Congress. On the other side, some of these men recognized that, potentially, the most consequential arenas for their efforts at changing their society lay within their *jati*s, and we find there some remarkably tenacious efforts at social reform within the *jati*s (Dobbin 1972, ch. 5).

Conclusion

To conclude these ruminations on Asia's encounter with Europe: in this encounter, alien technologies and some of the associated organizational forms (State, schools, railways, printing, even elected governments) were close to colonial designs for government and were imposed relatively speedily. Alternate modes of knowing and values were slower in striking roots, at times becoming available as incidental to the new technologies, organizational forms, and the like—in the course of coping with new career paths in the wider colonial ambience.

In the course of this encounter, Asians had run into an alien civilization of an exceptional cast, one that had taken to the habit of seeking conceptions of maximal generality for anchoring its social, as well as its technical, arrangements. This habit had had momentous consequences in Europe: it had pushed a wide gamut of scientific activity and of technological skills; and the application of these skills had set off social processes so varied and pervasive that established patterns of society were being recast many times over.

Much of Europe's power and resilience have arisen in its appreciation, and systematic use, of general rules and laws—in two different directions: in social ordering, as in generally applicable laws and legal and administrative codes; and in cognition, in organizing its understanding of nature, in both the physical and the social realms, in terms of principles of maximal range. This historic process moves a step forward as these empirically validated understandings of the human condition begin to enter the ways in which we organize our societies.[7]

The civilizational encounter has challenged and tested every assumption of our existence, even when some of these have survived this ordeal-by-fire. The encounter has marked a break for most of us in Asia much more than it has for Europeans. For apprehending something of the depths, and the significance, of this experience, I commend to you a perspective that draws on the resources of both sociology and history, a perspective at work in several chapters in this volume.

Notes

[1] Stock, *The Implications of Literacy*, 1983; chapter 3 reviews the Eucharist debate at length.
[2] Saberwal 1995, chaps. 3 and 4, have a fuller argument.
[3] Sharma (1983, pp. 119–21) discusses the evidence on these practices.
[4] The question of beef-eating in history textbooks is only one strand in a wide-ranging assault on the autonomy of professional scholarship, at least in the social sciences, by a government led by men of the Hindu Right. I thank Supriya Varma for raising this theme with me and providing me with a copy of Professor Sharma's discussion.
[5] Why China fell behind in technology, after its astonishing early leads, was a major puzzle for the second half of the 20th century. See, for example, Bodde 1991; Sivin 1982.
[6] The discussion here follows Saberwal 2002 closely.
[7] See Saberwal and Sievers 1998.

References

Austin, Granville. 1972. *The Indian Constitution: Cornerstone of a Nation*. Bombay: Oxford University Press.

Baxi, Upendra. 2002. "The (im)possibility of Constitutional Justice: Seismographic Notes on the Indian Constitutionalism". In *India's Living Constitution*, edited by Z. Hasan, E. Sridharan and R. Sudarshan. New Delhi: Permanent Black.

Beteille, Andre. 1974. *Studies in Agrarian Social Structure*. Delhi: Oxford University Press.

Bodde, Derk. 1991. *Chinese Thought, Society, and Science: The Intellectual and Social Background of Science and Technology in Pre-modern China*. Honolulu: University of Hawaii Press.

Boyle, Leonard E. 1981. *Pastoral Care, Clerical Education and Canon Law, 1200–1400*. London: Variorum reprints.

Goody, Jack. *The East in the West*. Cambridge: Cambridge University Press, 1996.

Jones, Kenneth W. 1976. *Arya Dharm*. New Delhi: Manohar.

———. 1989. *Socio-religious Reform Movements in British India*. Cambridge: Cambridge University Press.

Kantorowicz, Ernst H. 1957. *The King's Two Bodies: A Study in Medieval Political Theology*. Princeton: Princeton University Press.

Marglin, F.A. 1985. *Wives of the God-King: The Rituals of the Devadasis of Puri*. Delhi: Oxford University Press.

Mines, Mattison. 1975. "Islamisation and Muslim Ethnicity in South India". In *Islam in Southern Asia: A Survey of Current Research*, edited by Dietmar Rothermund. Wiesbaden: Steiner.

Metcalf, Barbara Daly. 1982. *Islamic Revival in British India: Deoband, 1860–1900*. Princeton: Princeton University Press.

———. 1999. "Nationalism, Modernity, and Muslim Identity in India before 1947". In *Nation and Religion: Perspectives on Europe and Asia*, edited by Peter van der Veer and Harmut Lehmann. Princeton: Princeton University Press, pp. 129–43.

Oberoi, Harjot. 1994. *The Construction of Religious Boundaries: Culture, Identity and Diversity in the Sikh Tradition*. Delhi: Oxford University Press.

Omvedt, Gail. 1976. *Cultural Revolt in a Colonial Society: The Non-Brahman Movement in Western India, 1873–1930*. Bombay: Scientific Socialist Education Trust.

Saberwal, Satish. 1995. *Wages of Segmentation: Comparative Historical Studies on Europe and India*. New Delhi: Orient Longman.

———. 2002. "Introduction: Civilisation, Constitution, Democracy". In *India's Living Constitution*, edited by Z. Hasan, E. Sridharan, and R. Sudarshan. New Delhi: Permanent Black.

———. 2004. "Integration and Separation of Traditions: Muslims and Hindus in Colonial India". In *Traditions in Motion: Essays for Shereen Ratnagar*, edited by Supriya Verma and Satish Saberwal.

Saberwal, Satish and Heiko Sievers, eds. 1998. *Rules, Laws, Constitutions*. New Delhi: Sage.

Said, Edward W. 1978. *Orientalism*. Rev. ed. Harmondsworth: Penguin.

Shaikh, Farzana. 1989. *Community and Consensus in Islam: Muslim Representation in Colonial India, 1860–1947*. Cambridge: Cambridge University Press.

Sivin, Nathan. 1977. "Shen Kua: a Preliminary Assessment of his Scientific Thought and Achievements". *Sung Studies Newsletter* 13: 31–56 [biography reprinted from *The Dictionary of Scientific Biography*, Vol. 12, 1975].

————. 1995. "Why the Scientific Revolution Did Not Take Place in China—or Didn't it?" In *Science in Ancient China: Researches and Reflections*. Aldershot, UK: Variorum.

Stock, Brian. 1983. *The Implications of Literacy: Written Language and Models of Interpretation in the Eleventh and Twelfth Centuries*. Princeton: Princeton University Press.

Wright, Arthur F. 1963. "On the Uses of Generalization in the Study of Chinese History". In *Generalization in the Writing of History*, edited by Louis Gottschalk, pp. 36–58. Chicago: University of Chicago Press.

3

Locating Southeast Asia: Postcolonial Paradigms and Predicaments

Henk Schulte Nordholt

Geography and identity

Social scientists have cut up the world into convenient regions: Africa, Latin America, Western Europe, East Asia and so on. A core argument for the regionalization of socio-scientific inquiry has always been that geographic proximity implies long-term cultural, economic, and social exchange. Hence, societies within a certain region share important characteristics which makes it relevant to study them together. Moreover, these regional studies are both rooted in intimate local knowledge and devoted to productive comparison, and this combination should lead to conceptual innovation and theoretical sophistication. However, this argument needs to be questioned.

First, it is important to re-examine the ways in which particular regions are constructed, how seemingly 'natural' borders of these regions are defined by academic specialists working within particular political contexts, how a particular process of regionalization affects the questions these scholars address, and how within certain areas an hierarchy of core societies and marginalized peripheries is established.

Second, the formation of institutionalized communities of area specialists and the reproduction of the paradigms which explain and underpin both the identities of the area they study and the academic community they are part of create the danger of an inward-looking habitus. Such a community of area specialists is characterized by a highly specialized language and an idiosyncratic research agenda, favouring particular topics and excluding discussions which are, for instance, considered to be highly relevant in other 'areas' or academic disciplines.

Criticizing area studies, the historian Sanjay Subrahmanyam wrote:

> It is as if these conventional geographical units of analysis, fortuitously defined as givens for the intellectually slothful, and the result of complex (even murky) processes of academic and non-academic engagement, somehow become real and overwhelming. Having helped create these Frankenstein's monsters, we are obliged to praise them for their beauty, rather than grudgingly acknowledge their limited functional utility (Subrahmanyam 1999, p. 296).

By focusing almost exclusively on the production of 'local knowledge', the area studies approach tended to ignore larger comparative themes which were discussed within the academic disciplines which constitute the social sciences. As a result the study of societies within certain areas was often not informed by explicitly formulated theoretical questions. Cultures were seen in terms of isolated entities because area studies disregarded the historical connections between various regions in the world and the unequal power relationships between them (Wolf 1982). Instead geographical frameworks determined the explanation of regional phenomena. Just like the way landscapes could be imagined after they had been conceptualized and represented by paintings, it was geography that created regions by the very act of mapping. Geographies are in this respect powerful political discourses about space (Winichakul 1994). Politics make spatial orders and territoriality is considered to be a strategy that affects people's actions by controlling space and demarcating their room to manoeuvre. Area studies were politically informed geographies of identity which seemingly operated in a disconnected world. There were, however, important connections in the sense that the booming years of the area studies coincided with the Cold War. Area studies formed a convenient context in which a Western, anti-communist model of modernization cum nation building was propagated.

Genealogies of an area study

Southeast Asia has also been conceptualized as a meaningful region and Southeast Asian studies institutionalized in academia as well.[1] The geographic concept 'Southeast Asia' originated modestly in the first half of the 20th century and was in academic terms coined by Robert Heine Geldern who, in the 1920s, emphasized the ethnic, linguistic and cultural coherence of the region (Dahm and Ptak 1999).

The forerunners of the area study specialists were colonial language officers and administrators who were assigned to solve practical problems. They were mainly active in the fields of language studies, compiling authoritative grammars and dictionaries of local languages, and applied anthropology and rural sociology in order to control and manage local society. But there were also impressive efforts made in the fields of archaeology and what was to be defined as 'classical' literature in order to preserve and appropriate the cultural history of the colony. Except for some archaeologists these colonial scholars lived and worked within the boundaries of their colony without engaging in comparative research or abstract theoretical exercises (Anderson 1992; Nordholt 1994). What was set in motion was a segmented accumulation of colonial knowledge by a core of experts who often devoted a lifetime in digging up archaeological remains, translating and editing texts, collecting, mapping, and categorizing ethnological data, in short explaining the nature of local cultures and social structures within their colonial domains. Excluded were complex topics like colonial modernity, while sensitive political issues were mainly covered by colonial intelligence.

It was not scholarship but warfare that put Southeast Asia on the map (Emmerson 1984, p. 7). During the Pacific War the whole region was for the first time occupied by a single force. The Japanese occupation resulted in the establishment in 1943 of the allied Southeast Asia Command under Lord Mountbatten. Although this strategic region included for instance Ceylon and Hongkong and excluded eastern Indonesia and the Philippines (which fell under the authority of General MacArthur), the idea of Southeast Asia was born, and from 1944 onwards, when the first map of the area was produced, the region could also be visualized as a geographic reality.

Meanwhile in the United States the newly established Institute of Pacific Relations witnessed the first institutionalized effort to develop the Southeast Asian war theatre into a meaningful academic area, and scholars like John Furnivall, Rupert Emerson, Bruno Lasker and K.M. Panikkar started to publish books which mentioned 'Southeast Asia' in the title (Furnivall 1941; Anderson 1998).

The following period of decolonization seemed to put an end to the segmentary approach which had been typical of the colonial period. The area was now moving from a political strategic concept towards a region in search of an identity. However, from the outset, the specialists had trouble in demarcating their area. The 1955 edition of D.G.E. Hall's *A History of Southeast Asia* includes, for instance Ceylon, Taiwan and South China, but excludes the Philippines and New Guinea.

Two tendencies were in this respect at work. The first was a political bureaucratic one, taking colonial states and then nation-states as basic categories; the second was a search for content in terms of coherence and shared cultural traits and historical experiences in the region.

Eventually national borders determined what belonged to Southeast Asia and what not: Assam in the northwest, Yunnan in the northeast were excluded, whereas New Guinea (now Papua) was included. Despite the criticisms of Edmund Leach, flexible fields of dynamic cultural relationships were frozen within fixed political boundaries (Leach 1961).

The prospects of a decolonized region between the great political blocks of India and China and the Western colony of Australia fostered the need for and legitimized the emergence of 'Southeast Asia' as a viable geographical-analytical concept. Moulded by the Cold War, it has achieved a conceptual reality in the academic field. Especially in the United States and Australia, Southeast Asian studies initially became firmly rooted. As a result, Southeast Asian studies offered career opportunities and during the second half of the 20th century a new academic hierarchy was established consisting of various intellectual *mandala*, which were characterized by wide networks of patron-client relationships cemented by personal loyalties and intellectual indebtness.

The most powerful among the new centres that emerged after the Second World War in the United States were at Yale and Cornell, while Australia witnessed the emergence of centres at Monash University, which was modelled after Cornell, and the Australian National University, that followed the orientalist example of the School of Oriental and African Studies (SOAS) in London and Leiden in the Netherlands.

Despite the rapid growth of Southeast Asian studies in the United States, it remained a small and marginal field of study compared to the real academic powerhouses which covered China and Japan. Moreover, due to the great variety of languages in the region, the field of Southeast Asian studies turned out to be rather fragmented, because, just like their colonial predecessors, most scholars specialized in one particular country. Instead of publishing a US-based journal of Southeast Asian Studies, Cornell, for instance issued its famous journal *Indonesia*, which was in a sense a modern version of the Dutch colonial journal *Djawa*.

As Anderson remarked, it was actually in the classrooms where courses on Southeast Asian studies were given that students, and especially those from Southeast Asian countries, started to realize that they were Southeast Asianists. But, as it turned out, they would remain a minority (Anderson 1998, pp. 10–11).

Despite its relative weakness vis à vis Sinology and Japanology, Southeast Asian studies produced outstanding scholars whose work and reputation went far beyond the borders of the area. Clifford Geertz, Jim Scott and Benedict Anderson in particular, influenced large groups of anthropologists, historians and political scientists through their writings on interpretive anthropology, peasant society and resistance, and nationalism.

In contrast to the dynamic developments in the United States and Australia, the situation in Europe showed more institutional and intellectual continuity. The established centres like SOAS in England, various institutes in Paris and Aix-en-Provence in France and institutes in Leiden in the Netherlands still tended to focus exclusively on their former colonies and to stick to their traditional fields of study: philology, ethnology and colonial history.[2]

The history of the Koninklijk Instituut voor Taal-, Land- en Volkenkade (KITLV, or the Royal Institute of Linguistics and Anthropology) in Leiden illustrates in this respect the *longue durée* of colonial structures (Kuitenbrouwer 2001). Established in 1851 with the aim of supporting a conservative colonial policy, the institute gradually shifted in a more liberal direction around the turn of the 20th century. Whereas ethnological and linguistic explorations dominated the early years of the institute, which coincided with a period of colonial expansion, the rise of the late colonial state after 1910 coincided with studies on local law, applied anthropology, and, in increasing numbers, history. The independence of Indonesia in 1945 was not paralleled by a decolonization of Indonesian studies in the Netherlands. Despite isolated efforts by scholars like Andries Teeuw, Bob Uhlenbeck and Wim Wertheim to catch up with new developments in Indonesia and within the wider academic field, the KITLV remained well into the 1970s an old-fashioned bastion of Dutch orientalism. When in the late 1970s academic relationships between Indonesia and the Netherlands were re-established, the KITLV increased its activities as well. It should be emphasized however that most research was still conducted on historical topics dealing with the colonial past while there was a taboo on studies analysing the politics of the New Order. Till the end of the Suharto period, the KITLV was still trapped in this postcolonial predicament.

In Amsterdam Wim Wertheim made serious efforts to broaden the horizon towards a comparative study of South and Southeast Asia from a historical-sociological perspective. Despite the fact that in the 1970s this perspective was gradually overshadowed by ideological debates about the right course of the Chinese Cultural Revolution, comparative and historical-sociological approaches are still central research issues in Amsterdam.[3]

If ever an intellectual genealogy of Southeast Asian studies is constructed, the number of 'ancestors' would be limited to a handful of influential teachers. They include Wim Wertheim in Amsterdam, who for instance inspired Harry Benda, who went to Yale where he became the supervisor of, among others, Heather Sutherland, who went to Amsterdam where she supervised many Dutch and Indonesian students, including me. Harry Benda also became the first director of the Institute of Southeast Asian Studies (ISEAS) in Singapore. Another descendant of Wertheim is Prof Sartono Kartodirdjo in Yogyakarta who became the doyen of Indonesian historians. Moreover, students of Wertheim dominate(d) much of the field of South and Southeast Asian studies in the Netherlands.

Similar genealogies can be made with regard to the influence of pioneering scholars like George Kahin and Lucien Hanks in the United States, and George Coedès and George Condominas in France.

From yet a different perspective, China and Japan produced their own intellectual paradigms and lineages with regard to the 'lands below the winds' (*nanyang* or *nanpo*) which were primarily seen either in terms of overseas Chinese or investment opportunities.

History and identity: 'Fluid pluralism'

Despite its in-built diversity due to language differences, on the face of it, Southeast Asia became a convenient and rather successful marker for scholarly research, and there were several good reasons for adopting a regional perspective surpassing the colonial and national boundaries. Waves of 'Indianization' and its various forms of localization, the dynamics of small-scale polities, colonialism and the formation of modern states, the Japanese occupation, revolution and processes of nation-building, the penetration of development politics, these were all phenomena which were collectively experienced in most parts of the region.

Initially Southeast Asian studies were, like other area studies, dominated by political sciences and an a-historical structural functionalist approach of societies which was focused on political stability and economic development framed within an anti-communist ideology of modernization and nation-building. At a later stage, when the structural functionalist paradigm declined and the vulgar evolutionionism of modernization theory did not keep its promises, historians and anthropologists took the lead. It should be emphasized that the area studies specialists were not always loyal to the interests of the state who financed their positions.

Both Harry Benda and George Kahin, for example, voiced at an early stage their deep concern about the US involvement in Vietnam.

Historians and anthropologists especially succeeded in making Southeast Asia into a meaningful concept. According to Ruth McVey, history became the key discipline of Southeast Asian studies, because it was especially in the pre-modern history that an interconnected and more coherent Southeast Asia was located (McVey 1995, p. 5).

For a long time Southeast Asia was primarily seen from a Western perspective, i.e. in terms of processes of Indianization, Islamization and Western colonialism, whereas—with the exception of Vietnam—connections with China were considered to be less relevant. Today however, Southeast Asia is primarily seen in terms of its economic relationships with East Asia, and the wider framework of the Pacific Rim, while South and Southeast Asia are drifting apart. It took a long time before scholars were able to conceptualize Southeast Asia 'on its own terms', that is to say: not as a set of secondary cultures which were derived from the two superior neighbouring civilizations, India and China.

Harry Benda and John Smail wrote in this respect paradigmatic articles, which not only outlined the direction of research but also legitimated the study of Southeast Asia in institutional terms. Benda sketched a history of the region which was structured by big long-term processes like Indianization, Chinese and Hispanic influences (which included the Philippines) (Benda 1962). Inspired by the work of sociological historians like B.J.O. Schrieke and J.C. van Leur, John Smail criticized the Eurocentric approach of conventional historical studies and emphasized the autonomous nature of Southeast Asian history (Smail 1961).

Standard textbook wisdom implied that Indianization was a process of cultural transfer from civilized India to tribal Southeast Asia, from big to small, from pure to distorted. It was O.W. Wolters who modified this picture considerably by pointing at the active role of people in Southeast Asia in processes of localization through which foreign elements took root (Wolters 1982). Hermann Kulke pushed this argument much further when he proposed a convergence model in which small-scale religious polities in South Asia and Southeast Asia influenced *each other*, and South Asia was surpassed in terms of scale by development in the field of Southeast Asian architecture (Angkor Wat and Borobudur) (Kulke 1990).

Smail's plea for an autonomous history of Southeast Asia corresponded closely with the quest for national independence and a new national identity in the region itself. Craig Reynolds has argued that the quest for an authentic past was closely connected with the interests of the new nation-states in Southeast Asia (Reynolds 1995). Using the body of colonial knowledge in the field of archaeology and classical literature, a distinct and authentic national character was located in the pre-colonial past. A second attribute that was ascribed to old Southeast Asia was agency in order to affirm the capacity of people to localize external influences and turn them into authentic properties of Southeast Asian culture.

Writing about the ancient history of the region, Oliver Wolters emphasized the coherent character of the old Southeast Asian world long before the arrival of Western powers. It was a modern world which favoured up-to-dateness and spiritual success, where people were primarily interested in the here and now, in personal achievement, and displayed a relaxed attitude towards institutions. It was a world characterized by multi-ethnic polities and present-mindedness. Anthony

Reid sketched a similar picture of the cosmopolitan attitude of Southeast Asians in the 15th–17th centuries (Wolters 1994; Reid 1988). Kulke, Wolters and Reid made a considerable contribution to the quest for an authentic, and, for that matter, sympathetic, identity of Southeast Asia which was to be found in its past.

From an anthropological point of view the bilateral or cognatic kinship system has been mentioned as a unifying feature of social organization in the region. Others have attempted to locate underlying structural similarities in social organization which are rooted in ancient Austronesian ancestry (Hüsken and F. and J. Kemp 1991; de Jong 1977).

However, most research is not determined by the field because the field is not an autonomous phenomenon. What the field is about is to a large extent framed by external conditions and defined by theoretical notions. In this respect Southeast Asia has been the breeding place of concepts like 'plural society', 'loose structure', economic dualism and 'cultural involution', which have made a modest career in social science discourse outside the region (Evers 1980).

But it was eventually American anthropology that created a more or less coherent approach to Southeast Asia. Due to the Cold War a strong Marxist oriented political economy never developed with regard to Southeast Asia. Instead, we can trace the legacy of Max Weber looming large in the work of Clifford Geertz (as well as in the writings of both Wim Wertheim and Benedict Anderson). It was this Weberian/Geertzian anthropology which was practiced in various places in Southeast Asia as a result of which similar themes were elaborated (Ortner 1984; Bowen 1995). However, despite the similarity in conceptualizations, there never developed an anthropology of Southeast Asia, nor for that matter a Southeast Asian anthropology.

Despite the proliferation of area studies, there appeared to be a fair amount of discomfort about the 'Southeast Asianness' of Southeast Asia. Consequently, efforts to formulate essentializing conceptions of Southeast Asia which aim to define the region as a meaningful area seemed to fade away. Moreover, the dynamics, complexity and composite character of the societies in Southeast Asia defy any attempt at essentializing them. Like the rest of the world, they are forever becoming.

More often than not, the region's qualities were defined in terms of variety, fragmentation and openness to external influences. Hence, Southeast Asia is commonly characterized by its diverging rather than its unifying qualities. Attempts to define the region often emphasize its flow of people, commodities and ideas. This lack of specificity has, paradoxically, become one of the main building bricks of the edifice of Southeast Asian studies. In contrast to the giant neighbouring civilizations of China and India, Southeast Asia's cultural identity was defined in negative terms: it was not monolithic.

More positively phrased, Southeast Asia was characterized by its adaptive and creative openness to outside influences, the flexibility of its small-scale polities, or, following Anthony Reid, its 'fluid pluralism' (Reid 2000, p. 10). Fragmentation and hybridity became the keywords to understand Southeast Asia. The image of Southeast Asia which was produced by O.W. Wolters and Anthony Reid fitted, moreover, the needs of the late 20th century. It was an identity which emphasized openness, tolerance and the ability to adjust to new situations, on the basis of which modern Southeast Asia could face the challenges of globalization which require an open mind towards innovative transnational developments, a present-mindedness, and a multi-ethnic profile.

Alternative frameworks and postcolonial constraints

Since the ending of the Cold War, political support for area studies dwindled while at the same time globalization and the study of transnational flows became the new money-making enterprises in the academic world. Area studies had lost their relevance and were seen as old-fashioned remnants of a world that no longer exists. In 1996 the Social Science Research Council changed, for instance, its funding policy from area-based programmes towards the support of projects framed by broad themes. The consequences of this shift in focus in terms of academic infrastructure—appointments, language training and library facilities—are tremendous. The paradigm of the slow accumulation of local knowledge is now seen as something inferior compared to the fast flow of fancy theories about the global.

Current debates also address the question of whether 'Southeast Asia' was basically a 20th century Western construct which had more geopolitical reality than scholarly relevance and which is now losing its significance. Is it possible to conceptualize this region outside the protective realm of area studies? Is 'Southeast Asia' still a useful tool or category for analysis, or should we look for a radical reorientation?

Even if we take diversity, flexibility, and openness as guiding principles in the study of the region, the question remains what useful approaches can be derived from a Southeast Asian perspective, and whether other perspectives might be equally or perhaps even more productive. Looking beyond the conventional boundaries of Southeast Asia, it might be asked to what extent it makes more sense to employ entirely different comparative perspectives for specific areas or particular topics. It would be interesting to compare, for instance, the Philippines with Latin America because of their shared Spanish legacies; or India and Indonesia to gain a better understanding of colonial policies; to look for meaningful comparisons with Africa for such divergent issues as urbanization, ethnic conflict and genocide; to compare peasants in Mexico and Java; or religious issues in Thailand with those in Sri Lanka; or Brunei with Qatar. Moreover, political scientists and economists prefer to resort to larger geographies, such as East *and* Southeast Asia or the Pacific Rim.

Other topics of research acquire a meaning irrespective of the wider regional or more restricted national contexts. They are much more framed in the rhythmn of monsoons, the distinction between lowland and mountains or downstream and upstream relationships, contrasts between mainland and maritime Southeast Asia, the Chinese diaspora, and Islamic or Theravada Buddhist allegiances.

Also with respect to themes like political violence and the phenomenon of the post-colony it seems that comparisons with areas outside Southeast Asia, and especially Africa, offer more analytical insight.

Recent approaches to the region disclose the continuing mobility of people and goods, and the permeability of internal and external borders. If we agree on the arbitrariness of national boundaries, so should we with regard to regional boundaries. If an area derives part of its geographical-analytical value from long-term exchanges and influences, there is a strong case for looking more closely at the fringes and concentrating on the dynamics of border areas. How do people in the Andaman Islands or in Yunnan view adjacent regions? Or, in a broader context, how does Southeast Asia look like, when not the land but the sea is our vantage point, such as the Bay of Bengal or the South China Sea?

In a review of recent debates among historians about the pre-modern world of Southeast Asia, Heather Sutherland also emphasizes that we should be more aware of the flexible and shifting nature of boundaries. Using the example of Makassar she argues that, instead of a process of de-urbanization and decline, the port city became after the 1660s part of new networks which reached well beyond the conventional borders of Southeast Asia (Sutherland, forthcoming).

When around the turn of the 20th century, colonial expansion and state formation, signalling the era of high imperialism, resulted in increased territorial control and clearly demarcated borders, there was still ample room for various flows of trade, capital and labour which crossed the recently drawn lines on the map. From the west a British sphere of influence connected India, Ceylon, Burma, Malaya, Singapore, Northern Borneo, and parts of Sumatra, while from the east a giant network originating in China covered most parts of Southeast Asia. Since the 1950s major changes took place in the human and economic geography of Southeast Asia. Howard Dick argues that these changes in urbanization, industrialization and transport require a new kind of mapping in order to measure the main transnational flows of people, goods, money and information. Dick suggests a model of Southeast Asia as an open system, which is characterized by urban corridors, inhabited and dominated by urban middle classes, and predominantly oriented towards East Asia. In this conception, which resembles to some extent the old pre-modern world of Southeast Asia, national states no longer seem to be extremely relevant (Dick, forthcoming).

Like time, space is not a given because it is socially constructed, historically reproduced, and always contested (van Schendel and Nordholt 2001). Area studies produced their own geographies which tended to emphasize the importance of centres and core regions, while they marginalized the relevance of peripheries. Van Schendel uses in this respect the term 'geographies of ignorance' to indicate how large parts of these peripheries are pushed to the margins of the map. As an example he points at the borderlands in the north of Southeast Asia, the northwest of South Asia, the southwest of East Asia and the southeast of Central Asia which are not part of any of these areas. Here the notion of borderlands—conceptualized in between the national and the international levels—becomes relevant in order to investigate topics like illegal flows of drugs, arms and labour, organized by informal networks, which manage to escape state control (van Schendel, forthcoming). This field of research, which is easily overlooked if one maintains the standard

state perspective, does, however, not erase the importance of the nation-
state, because smuggling presupposes borderlines.

There are, in other words, a myriad of alternative perspectives possible
from within and outside the region. But, to what extent is the nation-
state really undermined by, for instance, the emergence of transnational
flows of capital and the interregional flow of identity politics?

To a large extent 'Southeast Asia' has been a thing of the West, and
it might be rightful to question how people in Southeast Asia have
perceived their own region. It should not be forgotten that during the
1950s one could hardly speak of a Southeast Asian consciousness. Instead
of an inward looking attitude, there was a very strong international
orientation among the political elites in Southeast Asia. This tendency
was illustrated by the efforts to establish bonds of solidarity among the
so-called non-aligned countries which materialized at the Bandung
conference in 1955.

The American efforts to establish a Southeast Asian counterpart of
NATO resulted in SEATO, an odd collection of countries like Pakistan,
New Zealand, Australia and England, with Thailand and the Philippines
as the only Southeast Asian members. The Cold War reinforced the
existing differences between (pen)insular and mainland Southeast Asia
and resulted among others in the US inspired establishment of the anti-
communist Association of Southeast Asian Nations (ASEAN) in 1967,
i.e. briefly after the anti-communist massacres in Indonesia and in the
middle of the Vietnam War. Members were Thailand, the Philippines,
Indonesia, Malaysia and Singapore, followed by Brunei. After the fall of
the Berlin Wall, Vietnam, Cambodia, Burma and Laos, completed
ASEAN's membership. For the first time in history, a formal association
of all the nation-states in the region had been established, but it turned
out to be a rather loosely structured organisation. It showed very little
solidarity during the monetary crisis of 1997–98, nor does it seem to take
innovative initiatives which enhance further regional integration.
Moreover in terms of economic cooperation, ASEAN has already been
overtaken by larger international configurations like APEC.

Being the 'natural' focus of most internal interaction within ASEAN,
Singapore witnessed in 1968 the establishment of the Institute of Southeast
Asian Studies, which is till today the most important regional institute
with regard to the study of the area. It is not without significance that
ISEAS was established with the help of outside expertise, notably its

first director, Harry Benda. Despite the networking capacity of ISEAS and an impressive number of edited volumes about Southeast Asia which are published by this institute, it seems however, that 'Southeast Asia' is primarily seen as the politically relevant environment of Singapore, and one may wonder in what respect and to what extent Singapore is really the centre of Southeast Asia.[4]

By and large ASEAN failed to foster a Southeast Asian academic community which is able to formulate its own agenda. Southeast Asian scholars were hardly persuaded to look across their national boundaries and to engage in comparative research projects. Instead, scholars from the region consider contacts with prestigious academic centres in the United States or Australia more profitable, while academic activities in Southeast Asian countries seem to be geared predominantly towards their own separate national projects. This tendency towards a segmentation of Southeast Asia is reinforced by the emphasis among the majority of Western scholars to concentrate on specific Southeast Asian countries instead of the region as a whole. Consequently the old colonial boundaries have by and large been maintained as a result of which the majority of Vietnamists, Indonesianists and Philippinists are still strangers to each other.

This is to be regretted because Southeast Asia has been the battle ground of major political conflicts which affected large parts of the region: Pacific War and national revolutions, while the Cold War generated not only the war in Vietnam, but also two major genocides in Indonesia and Cambodia, and mass killings in East Timor. Despite the fact that these conflicts should be studied in relationship to each other, it was ironically a non-area specialist who made a comparative analysis of the genocides in Indonesia and Cambodia (Fein 1993).

Southeast Asia is in many respects a region by default, while Southeast Asian studies have been framed by a postcolonial predicament. In the first place the area has been dominated by foreign institutions and scholars. Consequently, outside forces have to a large extent determined the research agenda of Southeast Asian studies and its major paradigms. A situation like this would be unthinkable in South Asian studies where very vocal groups of critical South Asian scholars—like for instance the subaltern studies group—dominate debates and theoretical developments. Also in comparison with the field of African studies, which is in the United States to some extent dominated by Afro-American scholars who push their own academic agenda, we notice the absence of a strong Southeast Asian intellectual diaspora in the Western world.

In the second place Southeast Asian academia was characterized by a strong postcolonial agenda, in the sense that research was often closely connected to the interests of the state (Nordholt and Visser 1995). James Scott has in this respect shown how state institutions have attempted to reduce and simplify complex realities into clearly arranged ideas and categories in order to control society (Scott 1998). Such simplifications cause a great deal of local and particular knowledge to be lost. Although Scott does not deal with this directly, national historiography is pre-eminently an activity which streamlines the complex and multi-dimensional narratives about the past by erasing large parts of these stories. Also in Southeast Asia national historiography has become the officially approved simplification of the past. The birthplace of this tradition was the European nation-state, which took shape in the course of the nineteenth century. Based on data from its own archives, the account of the birth, growth and flourishing of the 'motherland' was told. In this context, colonial history formed a sort of overseas appendix to this national epic which told in the case of the Indonesian archipelago the story of the establishment of 'Tropical Holland'. Following decolonization, nationalist historians in the former colonies adhered primarily to the patterns founded by their colonial predecessors, but embraced a different moral approach: colonial 'development' became 'exploitation', while 'bandits' and 'religious fanatics' became 'nationalist freedom fighters'.

The new national history books consecutively outlined the story of the nation in terms of a great precolonial civilization which contained already the essence of national identity, the heroic struggle against Western imperialism, the suffering and martyrdom under colonial exploitation, the subsequent national awakening and struggle for freedom, and the heavily fought battles for independence during the national revolution. In Indonesia a closing chapter was added during the New Order regime which tells how the nation fell prey to internal discord, and how it was saved just in time by Soeharto, who then led his country to lasting development and permanent stability and opened the door to 'the end of history'.

Colonial as well as nationalist historians emphasize the primacy of the state and are by and large silent about the thousands of victims who were part of that very same history. They show, moreover, little interest in comparisons with other regions or in themes which do not serve the interests of the state. Indonesia is no exception in this regard, as the silence about its own violent past is a common phenomenon in many postcolonial, as well as ex-colonial societies and is best understood in a comparative way (Nordholt 2002).

In a similar way a continuity of colonial conservatism can be identified in many anthropological studies. By emphasizing the static character of local societies, which are often defined as isolated categories, the role of the state is phrased in terms of conserving traditional values and a careful monitoring of changes towards development which are seen as inevitable.

Hence, a reorientation in the field of Southeast Asian studies necessarily implies also processes of intellectual decolonization. There have been efforts in this direction in recent books on modernity and the state in Southeast Asia (Kahn 1998; Yao 2001). One of the arguments put forward is that, despite the attention paid to processes of globalization, the role and power of the state in Southeast Asia should not be underestimated (Ang 2001).

In many Asian countries modernity refers to a desire for economic development, Western consumption goods and a greater profile on the international scene. At the same time, however, it implies an anti-Western or, more precise, an anti-democratic ideology, which emphasizes a cultural sovereignty based on authentic and collective values. These Asian—and not Southeast Asian!—values serve both to localize and naturalize capitalism in new Asian contexts as well as to counteract Western accusations of violations of human rights.

Broad comparisons, connections and local knowledge

In 1984 Donald Emmerson argued that Southeast Asia is a neutral name, a convenient residual category referring to anything south of China and east of India. It also offered possibilities for cross-cultural research within the area (Emmerson 1984, p. 21). This never materialized on a substantial scale, and the relevance of Southeast Asian studies was increasingly questioned. Even the authors of the handbook of Southeast Asian history carefully phrased their efforts as *a search* for Southeast Asia (Steinberg 1987).

Reviewing the decline of area studies, Ruth McVey proposes that instead of studying a fixed geographic area we should focus on Southeast Asians, and instead of nation-states as 'natural' categories in which we think, we should concentrate on networks. It is, moreover, no longer sufficient to rely exclusively on Western paradigms—which are often wrongly seen as having universal qualities. Instead we must acknowledge the existence of alternative local systems of knowledge (McVey 1998).

A similar approach is voiced by Arjun Appadurai when he makes the point that we should turn away from thinking in terms of fixed and immobile geographies, towards 'process geographies' which are characterized by interaction, motion, trade, travel, pilgrimage, warfare, proselytization, and colonization. In this respect he argues that '[r]egions are best viewed as initial contexts to themes that generate variable geographies, rather than as fixed geographies marked by pre-given themes.'[5] In a similar vein, Subrahmanyam emphasized the importance of looking at connections instead of comparing artificially separated entities. For, connected phenomena do not erase differences but put these in a proper context (Subrahamanyam 1999, p. 316).

It seems as if distances are disappearing in an age of globalization, but paradoxically the notion of locality seems to evaporate at the same time. The emphasis on transnational flows, which is accompanied by a collapse of the academic infrastructures of the good old area studies including library facilities and the essential basic knowledge of regional languages, block our access to local knowledge. In contrast to the colonial period, knowledge of languages (and archaeology) is rapidly decreasing, because the modern academic market prefers the production of new theories instead of the maintenance of local knowledge which implies an in-depth knowledge of languages. In this respect Benedict Anderson warned already a decade ago for a serious 'ecological disaster' due to the decline of area studies and language teaching (Anderson 1992). It can be argued that eventually the emphasis on the global does exclude us from a better understanding of the local contexts within which processes of globalization should be studied.

Ruth McVey emphasizes in this respect that the need for what she calls 'context sensitivity' 'can't be acquired on the cheap' (McVey 1998, p. 50). A similar concern is expressed by Arif Dirlik when he criticizes the new globalism, which is connected with new transnational capital and the idea of global governance. As such it constitutes also a new regime of knowledge which should, however, not erase a sense of place, because the study of concrete places as products of everyday human interactions, in their historical contexts and local particularities—and through their respective languages—remains crucial (Dirlik 1995). This is not only true for the conventional places of anthropological research, but also for the new Internet spaces where, for instance, young Indonesians surf and chat in a new dynamic Indonesian cyber dialect.

In academic terms, Southeast Asia does not constitute a coherent and meaningful area, and it will only survive as a residual geographic category. This does not mean that people, places and processes in Southeast Asia have lost their relevance. Ideally, topics of studies should be formulated on the basis of general and theoretically informed themes which opens the possibility of wider comparisons with people, places, and processes elsewhere, but not necessarily within the same region.

So, a broadening of perspectives beyond the old Southeast Asian area is necessary, but this makes sense only if it is combined with a thorough local knowledge, including a fluency in local languages. Only when recent developments in the social sciences are combined with the old crafts of language training and in-depth fieldwork can our efforts to understand what people in Southeast Asia are up to succeed. Otherwise, we get lost either in the theoretical poverty and misconceptions of the old area studies or in the dark woods of 'afterology' land where postmodernism, poststructuralism, and postcolonialism foster an anti-empirical attitude which threatens to cut off our access to an understanding of human interaction.

Notes

[1]   For a review of the development of Southeast Asian studies as an area study, see Donald Emmerson, "'Southeast Asia': What's in a Name?", *Journal of Southeast Asian Studies* 15 (1984): 1–21; Charles Hirschman, Charles Keyes, and Karl Hutterer (eds), *Southeast Asian Studies in the Balance: Reflections from America* (Ann Arbor: AAS, 1992); Anthony Reid, "Recent Trends and Future Directions in Southeast Asian Studies (outside SE Asia)", in *Toward the Promotion of Southeast Asian studies in Southeast Asia*, edited by Taufik Abdullah and Yekti Maunati, pp. 215–31 (Jakarta: LIPI, 1994); Ruth T. McVey, "Change and Continuity in Southeast Asian Studies", *Journal of Southeast Asian Studies* 26 (1995): 1–9; Ruth T. McVey, "Globalization, Marginalization, and the Study

of Southeast Asia", in Craig Reynolds and R. McVey, *Southeast Asian Studies: Reorientations* (Ithaca: SEAP, 1998), pp. 37–64; Benedict Anderson, *The Spectre of Comparisons: Nationalism, Southeast Asia and the World* (London/New York: Verso, 1998).

[2]   Despite the establishment of the European Association of Southeast Asian Studies (EUROSEAS) in the early 1990s which had the ambition to create a more comparative platform, most scholars who attend the EUROSEAS conferences are still primarily interested in 'their own country' within Southeast Asia.

[3]   W.F. Wertheim, *Indonesian Society in Transition* (The Hague: Van Hoeve, 1956); *East-West Parallels* (The Hague: Van Hoeve, 1964). It is interesting to note that in 2003 the Universities of Leiden and Amsterdam started preparations to launch a common MA programme in Comparative Asian Studies.

[4]   An ironic case in point is the fact that the Singapore-based journal *Southeast Asian Journal of Social Sciences* was re-named the *Asian Journal of Social Sciences* in 2001.

[5]   Arjun Appadurai, *Globalisation and Area Studies: The Future of a False Opposition* (Amsterdam: CASA Wertheim lecture series, 2000). Appadurai points at processes which include people who are engaged in new encompassing geographies, but it should be emphasized that processes of exclusion and marginalization are here at work as well.

References

Anderson, B. 1992. "The Changing Ecology of Southeast Asian Studies in the United States 1950–1990". In *Southeast Asian Studies in the Balance*, edited by Hirschman et al. 25–40.

————. 1998. *The Spectre of Comparisons: Nationalism, Southeast Asia and the World*. London/New York: Verso.

Ang, I. 2001. "Desperately Guarding Borders: Media Globalisation, 'Cultural Imperialism' and the Rise of 'Asia'". In *House of Glass*, edited by Yao Souchou, pp. 27–45. Singapore: ISEAS.

Benda, H.J. 1962. "The Structure of Southeast Asian History: Some Preliminary Observations". *Journal of Southeast Asian History* 3: 103–38.

Bowen, J. 1995. "The Forms Culture Takes: A State of the Field Essay on the Anthropology of Southeast Asia". *Journal of Asian Studies* 54: 1047–78.

Dahm, B. and R. Ptak, eds. 1999. *Südostasien Handbuch: Geschichte, Gesellschaft, Politik, Wirtschaft, Kultur*. München: H. Beck.

Dick, H. Forthcoming. "Southeast Asia as an Open System: Geo-politics and Economic Geography". In *Localising Southeast Asia*, edited by Kratoska et al.

Dirlik, A. 1995. "No Longer Far Away: The Reconfiguration of Global Relations and its Challenges to Asian Studies". In *Unsettled Frontiers and Transnational Linkages: New Tasks for the Historian of Modern Asia*, edited by L. Douw. Amsterdam: VU University Press/CASA [Comparative Asian Studies 17], pp. 19–32.

Emmerson, D. 1984. "'Southeast Asia': What's in a Name?". *Journal of Southeast Asian Studies* 15: 1–21.

Evers, H.D., ed. 1980. *Sociology of South-East Asia: Readings on Social Change and Development*. Kuala Lumpur: Oxford University Press.

Fein, H. 1993. "Revolutionary and Anti-revolutionary Genocides: A Comparison of State Murders in Democratic Kampuchea, 1975 to 1979, and Indonesia, 1965 to 1966". *Comparative Studies in Society and History* 35: 796–823.

Furnivall, J.S. 1941. Progress and Welfare in Southeast Asia. New York: Secretariat, Institute of Pacific Relations.

Hall, D.G.E. 1955. *A History of Southeast Asia*. London: MacMillan.

Hüsken F., F. and J. Kemp, eds. 1991. *Cognation and Social Organization in Southeast Asia*. Leiden: KITLV Press.

Josselin de Jong, J.P.B. de, ed. 1977. *Structural Anthropology in the Netherlands: A Reader*. The Hague: Nijhoff.

Kahn, J., ed. 1998. *Southeast Asian Identities: Culture and the Politics of Representation in Indonesia, Malaysia, Singapore and Thailand*. Singapore: ISEAS.

Kulke, H. 1990. "Indian Colonies, Indianisation or Cultural Convergence? Reflections on the Changing Image of India's Role in Southeast Asia". In *Onderzoek in Zuidoost Azië: Agenda's voor de jaren negentig*, edited by H. Schulte Nordholt. Leiden: Vakgroep TCZO&O [Semaian 3]: 8–32.

Kuitenbrouwer, M. 2001. *Tussen Oriëntalisme en Wetenschap: Het Koninklijk Instituut voor Taal-, Land- en Volkenkunde in Historisch Verband, 1851–2000*. Leiden: KITLV Press.

Leach, E. 1961. "The Frontiers of 'Burma'". *Comparative Studies in Society and History* 3: 49–68.

McVey, Ruth T. "Globalization, Marginalization, and the Study of Southeast Asia". In *Southeast Asia Studies: Reorientations*. Ithaca: SEAP, pp. 37–44.

———. 1995. "Change and Continuity in Southeast Asian Studies". *Journal of Southeast Asian Studies* 26: 1–9.

Nordholt, H. Schulte. 1994. "The Making of Traditional Bali. Colonial Ethnography and Bureaucratic Reproduction". *History and Anthropology* 8: 89–127.

———. 2002. "A Genealogy of Violence". In *Roots of Violence in Indonesia*, edited by F. Colombijn and Th. Lindblad, pp. 33–61. Leiden: KITLV Press.

Nordholt, N. Schulte and Visser L., eds. 1995. *Social Science in Southeast Asia. From Particularism to Universalism*. Amsterdam: VU University Press/CASA [Comparative Asian Studies 17].

Ortner, S. 1984. "Theory in Anthropology since the Sixties". *Comparative Studies in Society and History* 26: 126–66.

Reid, Anthony. 1988. *Southeast Asia in the Age of Commerce. Vol. 1. The Lands below the Winds, 1540–1680.* New Haven: Yale University Press.

———. 2000. *Charting the Shape of Early Modern Southeast Asia.* Singapore: ISEAS.

Reynolds, Craig. 1995. "A New Look at Old Southeast Asia". *Journal of Asian Studies* 54: 419–46.

Scott, J. 1998. *Seeing like a State: How Certain Schemes to Improve the Human Condition have Failed.* New Haven: Yale University Press.

Smail, J. 1961. "On the Possibility of an Autonomous History of Modern Southeast Asia". *Journal Southeast Asian History* 2: 72–102.

Subrahmanyam, S. 1999. "Connected Histories: Early Modern Eurasia". In *Beyond Binary Histories: Re-imagining Eurasia to c. 1830,* 289–316, edited by V. Lieberman. Ann Arbor: University of Michigan Press.

Steinberg, J., ed. 1987. *In Search of Southeast Asia. A Modern History.* Sydney/Wellington: Allen and Unwin.

Sutherland, H. Forthcoming. "Contingent Devices". In *Localising Southeast Asia: Geographies of Knowledge and the Politics of Space,* edited by P. Kratoska, R. Raben and H. Schulte Nordholt. Singapore: National University of Singapore Press.

Yao Souchou, ed. 2001. *House of Glass: Culture, Modernity, and the State in Southeast Asia.* Singapore: Institute of Southeast Asian Studies.

van Schendel, W. Forthcoming. "Geographies of Knowing, Geographies of Ignorance". In *Localising Southeast Asia.*

van Schendel, W. and H. Schulte Nordholt, eds. 2001. *Time Matters: Global and Local Time in Asian Societies.* Amsterdam: VU University Press/CASA [Comparative Asian Studies 21].

Winichakul, Thongchai. 1994. *Siam Mapped: A History of the Geo-body of a Nation.* Honolulu: University of Hawaii Press.

Wolf, E. 1982. *Europe and the People without History.* Berkeley: University of California Press.

Wolters, O.W. 1982. *History, Culture and Region in Southeast Asian Perspectives.* Singapore: ISEAS.

———. 1994. "Southeast Asia as a Southeast Asian Field of Study'. *Indonesia* 38: 1–17.

4

The Meaning of Alternative Discourses: Illustrations from Southeast Asia

Syed Farid Alatas

The term 'alternative discourses' refers to works that attempt to both critically assess mainstream ideas in the social sciences that are generally regarded as unproblematic, as well as generate alternative concepts and theories. To the extent that mainstream social science is Eurocentric, the practioners of alternative discourses often see themselves as contributing to counter-Eurocentric social science. This chapter introduces the notion of alternative discourses by way of providing illustrations from Southeast Asia.

Introduction

That the social sciences in much of the Third World lack creativity and originality is something that has long been recognized by social scientists everywhere and has even become the topic of many research papers and books. To be sure, part of the problem has to do with the fact that the social sciences in much of Asia, Africa and Latin America were introduced by colonial powers and failed to be sufficiently indigenized, domesticated, or nationalized in order that they could be more relevant.[1] This is due in part to the lack of continuity between the European tradition of knowledge and indigenous systems of ideas (Watanuki 1984, p. 283) and the non-existence of an organic relationship with the cultural history of the colony (Kyi 1984, p. 94).

While it is not true that there was nothing approximating social scientific theory in Asian and other non-Western societies prior to the introduction of the social sciences from Europe and America from the eighteenth century onwards, it is certainly worth noting that no indigenous schools or traditions in sociology or any other social science discipline ever came into being autochthonously in non-European societies.[2] What I am referring to here is a general problem of knowledge even in countries like India, Egypt, Turkey, Korea and the Philippines where the social sciences are relatively more developed. In Korea in the 1970s, for example, scholars were 'awakened' to the need to establish a more creative Korean sociology (Shin 1994).[3] For all the justifiable attacks against the Eurocentrism of Western scholarship, we cannot speak of a modern Khaldunian, Gandhian or Confucian school in, say, sociological theory. It is not surprising, therefore, that many scholars since the nineteenth century have questioned the relevance and validity of truth claims of the social sciences for the countries of Asia and Africa.

We may itemize the problems that beset the social sciences outside of their regions of origin as follows:

1. There is a Eurocentric bias in that ideas, models, problem selection, methodologies, techniques and even research priorities tend to originate exclusively from American, British, and to some extent, French and German works.[4]

2. There is little generation of original ideas in terms of the generation of novel concepts, new theoretical perspectives or schools of thought, or innovations in research methods.

3. There is a general neglect of local literary and philosophical traditions. While there are studies on local literature or philosophy, these traditions remain as objects of study and are not considered as sources of concepts in the social sciences.

4. The above problems can be seen to exist within the context of academic or intellectual imperialism, that is, the intellectual

domination of the Third World by the social science powers (United States, Britain, France and Germany).[5]

Southeast Asian diagnoses of the problem

Southeast Asian and other scholars have been addressing the state of the social sciences in Southeast Asia since the nineteenth century. Their assessments often involved the critique of Eurocentrism and the wholesale adoption of American and European social sciences in Southeast Asia. Many of these works have come out of Singapore, including those by Syed Hussein Alatas (1956, 1969, 1972, 1974), Blake (1991), Syed Farid Alatas (1993b, 1995a, 1995b, 1998a, 1998b), and Sinha (1997, 1998). Also important is the growing interest in feminist alternatives to mainstream discourses in Singapore sociology (see, for example, Chung 1989; PuruShotam 1992, 1993, forthcoming; Sinha 1999; Wee 1988; and Wee, Heyzer and Kwa 1995).

Among the first critics of the state of knowledge in Southeast Asia was the Filipino thinker and reformer, Jose Rizal (1861–96). An example of an alternative discourse can be found in Rizal's annotated revised edition of Antonio de Morga's *Sucesos de las Islas Filipinas* which first appeared in 1609. Prior to producing this work Morga served eight years in the Philippines as Lieutenant Governor General and Captain General as well as a justice of the Supreme Court of Manila (Audiencia Real de Manila) (Morga 1991[1890], p. xxxv). Rizal believed that Spanish colonization had virtually wiped out the precolonial past from the memory of Filipinos and presented his annotated edition in order to correct false reports and slanderous statements to be found in most Spanish works on the Philippines (Rizal 1962[1890], p. vii). This included the destruction of pre-Spanish records such as artefacts that would have thrown light on the nature of precolonial society (Zaide 1993, p. 5). Rizal found Morga's work an apt choice as it was, according to Ocampo, the only civil history of the Philippines written during the Spanish colonial period, other works being mainly ecclesiastical histories (Ocampo 1998, p. 192). The problem with ecclesiastical histories, apart from the falsifications and slander, was that they "abound in stories of devils, miracles, apparitions, etc., these forming the bulk of the voluminous histories of the Philippines (de Morga 1962[1890], p. 291 n. 4). For Rizal, therefore, existing histories of the Philippines were both false and biased as well as unscientific and irrational.

Similar problems were raised in Indonesia at first, not by Indonesians themselves, but by Dutch scholars. One of the first among the Dutch in particular, and Europeans in general, to challenge Eurocentrism in the social sciences was Jacob Cornelis van Leur, a scholar who tragically died at a young age in the Battle of the Java Sea against the Japanese (1937, 1940a, 1940b). Van Leur was critical of Eurocentric tendencies in Dutch scholarhip on the Netherlands Indies. He wrote in Dutch but several of his essays were translated into English (van Leur 1955). Van Leur is well-known for having written against a perspective arrived at from "the deck of the ship, the ramparts of the fortress, the high gallery of the trading house" (1955, p. 261), although he himself had not achieved such a level of objectivity in his assessment of, for example, the Islamization of Indonesia (S.H. Alatas 1962, pp. 225–26). For example, he questioned the appropriateness of the eighteenth century as a category in the history of the Netherlands Indies, as it was a category borrowed from Western history (1940a).

Gradually, Indonesians themselves began to write on the problem of Eurocentrism and other biases in the writing of Indonesian history (for example, Pané 1951). Soedjatmoko was critical, among other things, of the one-sided India-centric view of the history of the Hinduization of Java as it failed to yield any understanding of the nature of the Indonesian society which absorbed Hindu elements (Soedjatmoko 1960, p. 13).

Some scholars also highlighted the question of intellectual imperialism and related ideas. In the 1950s, Syed Hussein Alatas from Malaysia referred to the "wholesale importation of ideas from the Western world to eastern societies" without due consideration of their socio-historical context, as a fundamental problem of colonialism (S.H. Alatas 1956). It was further suggested that the mode of thinking of colonized peoples paralleled political and economic imperialism—hence, the expression academic imperialism (S.H. Alatas 1969). In the Philippines about the same time, Catapusan lamented that while sociology as a discipline existed and empirical studies were being undertaken, a distinctive Filipino cultural perspective had yet to emerge (Catapusan 1957). Tham Seong Chee, writing from Singapore, described such colonial thinking or the colonial mentality as being informed by "a false consciousness about values, person and goals. It is a mode of seeing one's society—its workings and the direction of its movement—by super-imposing on it another reality, that is to say, the reality of a foreign society" (Tham 1971, p. 39).

The idea of the colonial mentality was developed by Syed Hussein Alatas in the form of the concept of the captive mind (1972, 1974). The captive mind merely extends the application of the American and European social sciences to its own setting without the appropriate adaptation of the imported ideas and techniques to the Asian setting, an indication of continuing intellectual domination. There was a high demand for knowledge from the West among Asian scholars due to the need to maintain self-esteem independent of the objective utility of such knowledge (S.H. Alatas 1972, pp. 9–10). The global spread of the social sciences, because it "takes the form of an uncritical demonstration effect, introduces many defects and shortcomings" (S.H. Alatas 1972, p. 11). The uncritical imitation of Western social science pervades all the levels of the scientific enterprise including problem-setting, analysis, abstraction, generalization, conceptualization, description, explanation, and interpretation (S.H. Alatas 1972, pp. 11–12). Such defects in the social sciences include the prevalence of redundant propositions, highly abstract and general statements, inadequate familiarity with local facts, and the neglect of pertinent problems (S.H. Alatas 1972).

The captive mind lacks creativity and the ability to raise original problems, is characterized by a fragmented outlook, is alienated both from major societal issues as well as its own national tradition, and is a consequence of Western dominance over the rest of the world (S.H. Alatas 1974, p. 691). One dimension of this Western dominance is academic imperialism which was first discussed by Syed Hussein Alatas some thirty years ago as well as more recently (S.H. Alatas 1969, p. 2000).

Academic imperialism can be said to exist within the context of the structure of academic dependency, a notion I developed, writing out of Singapore. The idea of academic dependency links Western and Third World social scientists in ties that bind unevenly and unequally. Third World social scientists are dependent on their counterparts in the West for concepts and theories, research funds, technologies of teaching and research, and the prestige value attached to publishing in Western journals (S.F. Alatas 1995a, 1995b). Nevertheless, not all the woes of the social sciences can be blamed on academic dependency. There is a transnational flow of social science in the global marketplace of ideas. Within the structures of academic dependency lies a market of theories and concepts that have gained currency in Asia partly due to their marketability, which in turn is determined by successful rhetorical programmes that permeate the social sciences. For example, the proliferation of a new set of vocabulary and terminology accompanying the rise of a new perspective in sociology may be complicit in successfully peddling 'novel' ideas (S.F. Alatas 1995b, 1998b).[6]

The result of the mental captivity and academic dependency is the perpetuation of what Shamsul Amri Baharuddin refers to as 'colonial knowledge'. Using the example of Malay ethnicity, Shamsul demonstrates how colonial knowledge continues to be the most powerful form of knowledge in postcolonial societies, having been responsible for inventing the ethnic category 'Malay' which has since become internalized by Malaysians themselves (Shamsul 1999).

Shamsul focuses on yet another dimension of the problem of the social sciences in Malaysia (and Indonesia), that is, the 'kratonization' of the social sciences. By this he means the fragmentation of the social sciences into "government versus academic versus private sector types of social science" (Shamsul 1995, p. 108). When priorities are dictated by extra-academic considerations, then research agenda and writing tend to be dominated by "policy-oriented matters or profit-motivated business issues" (Shamsul 1995, p. 101).[7] This is an important issue that poses a challenge to the social sciences from within a nation's borders while the problems of academic dependency and academic imperialism originates from without.

The call for alternative discourses in Southeast Asia

In the preceeding section various diagnoses of the state of the social sciences were described. In addition to such works that carried out assessments of the state of knowledge, there have also been prescriptions of one variety or another of alternative discourses to serve as correctives to the type of social sciences that had been introduced during colonial times.

The call for alternative modes of thinking in the past had generally fallen on deaf years. Therefore, it is in the interests of historical accuracy and out of the moral responsibility to acknowledge the contributions of our predecessors that mention must be made of a few early pioneers of alternative discourses.

An early proponent of alternatives, although in a non-academic mode, was probably Abdullah bin Abdul Kadir Munshi (1796–1854). Among his several works is the *Kesah Pelayaran Abdullah* of 1838. Abdullah was a keen observer of the problem of Malay backwardness in his time, which he attributed to the prevailing feudal order. Abdullah was in favour of utilizing the Malay language as a means of developing the consciousness of the Malays. While he was certainly not against the art of Qur'anic recitation, he regarded as irrational the study of the Qur'an without understanding its contents (1965 [1838], p. 15). He lamented that the Malay elite did not play a leading role in patronizing learning among the Malays in order that the Malays would be able to produce works in the various branches of knowledge (1965 [1838], pp. 15–16). Abdullah goes on to assess the impact of feudalism on the Malay mind which he saw as opposing Islamic values. His is the first critical account of feudalism to emerge in Malaya and offered a perspective that broke with both the prevailing feudal and colonial viewpoints.[8]

Far more profound than Abdullah and a thinker in his own right was José Rizal. Rizal pioneered the notion of an International Association of Philippinists, the object of which was to study the Philippines from the "historic and scientific point of view" (Rizal-Blumentritt 1992, p. 229). Ocampo has noted that while Rizal is often referred to as rewriting Philippine history, he was in fact the first to write that history from the viewpoint of the colonized (Ocampo 1998, p. 106). The task of such a history was to correct the biases of the Spanish historical works on the Philippines, to establish which sources were reliable and, thereby, present an "Indio" point of view of Philippine history. Such an attempt was made by Rizal in his annotation of Morga's history, which was referred to above.

For this, a more than casual acquaintance with the conditions of the inhabitants of the Philippines was necessary. Rizal was critical of a work on the Philippines by the friar Casal. He regarded Casal as not being knowledgeable about the Philippines as he "is a happy man and he has only mingled with the happy and powerful" (Rizal-Blumentritt 1992, p. 234). This suggests that the point of view of the oppressed was also a feature of the new Indio history as Rizal saw it.

Both the Dutch as well as Indonesian scholars discussed the question of alternatives in the study of Indonesian history. While the notion of Indocentric history remains vague as a concept and appears to be "more successful in conception than in execution" (Kartodirdjo 1982, p. 30), it is possible to make some remarks on these early discussions.

In the preceding section, mention was made of van Leur's questioning of the appropriateness of the eighteenth century as a category in the history of Indonesia.[9] The eighteenth century is itself a category borrowed from Western history, signifying aspects specific to the West. Furthermore, it was not legitimate to consider the history of Indonesia as the history of the Dutch East India Company. Moreover, historians had made the error of assuming that 'Oriental' states were in decay in the eighteenth century as was the case in Europe prior to the early days of the Industrial Revolution. Therefore, what was needed was a new system of categories which could only be generated as a result of familiarity with Indonesian history as a history in its own right and not as a history of the Dutch overseas.

The Indonesian scholar Armijn Pané published an essay containing an outline for an Indocentric history of Indonesia (Pané 1951). This does not involve setting aside foreign works or sources but rather recasting them in the light of Asian and Southeast Asian rather than European history (Pané 1951). Indocentrism can be understood as correcting the history of Indonesia as a mere extension of the history of the Dutch overseas, by focusing on Indonesians as playing a role in history. The implications of this include attention to regional and local histories. Such microhistories in turn would call for a more multidimensional approach not found in the more conventional approaches to history (Kartodirdjo 1982, pp. 38–39). While the need for this would seem obvious, much of Southeast Asian history has yet to be rewritten in this spirit.

The 1960s saw several discussions for and against the possibility of a Southeast Asian point of view in the writing of history. The discussions were characterized by the two extremes of subjectivism and objectivism. John Bastin regarded the possibility of a new type of Southeast Asian history written from a Southeast Asian point of view as bleak. He noted that the type of Asian and Southeast Asian history that was written by Asians themselves was history in the Western tradition and that much of what was presented as history from an Asian point of view turned out to be propagandistic history (Bastin 1959, p. 12). Bastin was suggesting that neither the Western nor Asian historian could write history from an Asian point of view as neither could escape the conditioning of Western thought patterns and cultural influences (1959, pp. 10, 11). Adding to the problem is the fact that the bulk of source materials for Asian history are to be found in Western languages, which can only be comprehended within a Western historical framework (1959, pp. 10–11). As noted by Syed Hussein Alatas, the possibility of what Collingwood calls "emphatic understanding" or what Windelband, Dilthey, Rickert and Weber call *verstehen* as a means by which history could be understood from a Southeast Asian point of view was not entertained by Bastin (S.H. Alatas 1964, pp. 250–51).

Smail, in criticizing Bastin, goes to the other extreme to say that there is only one thought-world and, as a result, "whatever the modern Asian historian can achieve in the way of an Asia-centric perspective can equally be achieved by the Western historian" (Smail 1961, pp. 75–76).[10] Southeast Asia has come within the fold of a single world civilization with a single universal history and all that is meant by Asian-centric history is a history in which the "Asian, as a host in his house, should stand in the foreground..." (Smail 1961, pp. 76, 78). For Smail, the notion of an Asian-centric history is not a philosophical problem but rather a practical one (Smail 1961, p. 76). Little significance is attached to Western cultural hegemony over the "single world culture" that he posits.

Nevertheless, the more dominant view in these debates was in favour of a Southeast Asian point of view in the writing of history and called for the reconstruction of history. An example is the work of Syed Hussein Alatas, which aims to establish proposals for the reconstruction of the history of the Malay-Indonesian Archipelago that pertain to methodology and the philosophy of history (S.H. Alatas 1962, p. 221; 1964). He raised the problem of the 13th to 16th centuries in Malay-Indonesian history, noting that this was a neglected period in the study of Southeast Asian history in that it was not treated as a subject in its own right (S.H. Alatas 1962, p. 219). Alatas suggests that this period should be treated as an Islamic period with an individuality of its own as it was a period of intensive proselytization, and raises a number of historiographical problems such as periodization, unit of analysis, and historical viewpoint (S.H. Alatas 1962, p. 224).

Another early work on reconstruction is that of Syed Naguib Al-Attas, *Preliminary Statement on a General Theory of the Islamization of the Malay-Indonesian Archipelago* (1969), followed by another work along similar lines, *Islam dalam Sejarah dan Kebudayaan Melayu* [Islam in Malay

History and Culture] (1972). This work provides a general theory of the
Islamization of the Malay-Indonesian Archipelago grounded on the
history of ideas. Al-Attas accomplishes this by examining the "changing
concepts of key terms in the Malay language" in the 16th and 17th
centuries. The evidence that forms the basis for this general theory was
derived from literary primary sources in Malay, Arabic and Persian, and
the methods employed are those of "critical, commentative,
interpretation" of texts as well as the methodological concepts and
approach of modern semantic analysis" (Al-Attas 1969, pp. 1–2). Also of
importance with regard to the study of Islam in the Malay world of
Southeast Asia is Al-Attas' *The Correct Date of the Trengganu Inscription*
(Al-Attas 1970), which was the first serious attempt to settle the
controversy surrounding the authenticity of the famous Trengganu stone
inscription of the eighth Muslim century.

Other critical works of Al-Attas that assess and correct Orientalist
constructions include his writings on the origin of the Malay *syair* [poems]
and on Sufism in the Malay World (Al-Attas 1968, 1971, 1975).

Here, it may be interesting to note that Singapore has had a tradition
of producing alternative discourses since the 1970s. Examples include
the historical sociological research on colonial ideology that has been
carried out by Syed Hussein Alatas with a focus on the political
philosophy of Raffles (S.H. Alatas 1971) and (ii) the myth of Malay,
Javanese and Filipino laziness (S.H. Alatas 1977), as well as his call for
an autonomous social science tradition in Asia (1979, 1981), as well as
other works by Shaharuddin Maaruf (1984, 1989, 1992) and Sharifah
Maznah Syed Omar (1993). A further example includes the call by Wang
Gungwu for Asian perspectives in the social sciences (Wang 2001). Also
along these lines is an essay by Vineeta Sinha which critically assesses
the project *Open the Social Sciences* which is itself aimed at rethinking
and restructuring the social sciences (Sinha 2001).

It is not only in the field of history that prescriptions for alternative
discourses in Southeast Asia emerged. There have also been calls for the
indigenization of the social sciences, most notably in the Philippines.
The problems of such calls are well illustrated in the Philippine case. As
noted by Pertierra, the attempt to separate the various social science
disciplines from their imperial foundations often ends up in their being
reattached to the interests of the postcolonial nation-state at the expense
of civil society or local/regional interests (Pertierra 1994).

Although the call for indigenization has often been heard in Southeast Asia,[11] attempts to conceptualize this term are rare. One exception is Sinha who suggests a research agenda for those wishing to begin the process of indigenizing the social sciences rather than simply talk about it (Sinha 1997, pp. 176–78). This is as follows:

1. To question the epistemological status of social science concepts, including those of 'indigenous', 'native', 'West', and 'non-West';
2. To ground social theory in sociocultural and political conditions of a locality, without necessarily rejecting Western social science;
3. To theorize the global politics of academia with a view to uncovering its role in the perpetuation of a world division of labour in the social sciences, whereby non-Western scholars are the collectors of empirical data and Western scholars the theorists; and
4. To recognize multiple centres and sources of social theory, that is, to regard all civilizations as potential sources of social science theorizing.

The various works referred to above all provide alternative readings of Southeast Asian history and society, and call for revision and reconstruction which in turn necessitates reconceptualization and the innovative use of social science methods. The earlier works of Dutch, British, Indonesian and Malaysian scholars cited above, as well as many others not cited here, were pioneering attempts at alternative discourses and it is unfortunate that little attention is paid to them today. While they come under different names, what they have in common is the concerted effort to counter the Eurocentrism and Orientalism that inform the social and historical sciences. The label 'alternative discourses', therefore, is appropriate because they set themselves in opposition to what they understand as constituting the mainstream, which are largely Euroamerican-oriented discourses that continue to dominate the arts and social sciences of Southeast Asia.

Towards a definition of alternative discourses

The discussions on the state of the social sciences in Southeast Asia do not arise from an intellectual movement but rather from a diverse group of scholars, largely Southeast Asian and Western, from the various disciplines of the social sciences. Prescriptions range from calls for endogenous intellectual creativity and an autonomous social science tradition (S.H. Alatas 1979; 1981), to decolonization (Zawiah 1994), and the indigenization of the social sciences (Enriquez 1994; Sinha 1997). The general concern has been with the problems of the Eurocentrism and irrelevance of mainstream discourses and the need for alternative traditions.

The term 'alternative discourses', therefore, is one that we are introducing and should be taken to refer to that set of discourses that has emerged in opposition to what is understood to be mainstream, American and European social science. Alternative discourses constitute a revolt against 'intellectual imperialism'.

Pertierra recognizes the role of indigenized social sciences as a weapon in neocolonial struggles as long as the social sciences "act as the counter-point between the state and society" as opposed to becoming an "instrument of the state's colonization of civil life" (Pertierra 1997, pp. 10, 20). Sinha views the call for indigenization as arising out of the need to "'purge' the social sciences of Eurocentrism and thus register a crucial break from the hegemony of a colonial past..." (Sinha 1998, p. 16).

As a preliminary statement on the nature of alternative discourses, we may itemize some of their features as follows:

1. Their starting point is the critique of Eurocentrism and Orientalism in the social sciences.
2. They raise methodological and epistemological problems relating to the study of society, historiography or the philosophy of history.
3. They are implicitly or explicitly concerned with the analysis of the problems presented by the world division of labour in the social sciences in which Southeast Asian social science finds itself to be in a state of conformity, imitation and unoriginality.
4. They are committed to the reconstruction of social and historical discourses which involve the development of concepts, categories and research agenda that are relevant to local/regional conditions.
5. They are committed to raising original problems in social and historical studies.
6. They recognize all civilizations and cultural practices as sources of ideas for the social sciences.

7.   They are not in favour of the rejection of Western social science *in toto*.

We could then formulate a definition of alternative discourses as those which are informed by local/regional historical experiences and cultural practices in the same way that the Western social sciences are. Being alternative requires the turn to philosophies, epistemologies, histories, and the arts other than those of the Western tradition. These are all to be considered as potential sources of social science theories and concepts, and reliance on them would decrease academic dependence on the world social science powers. It then becomes clear, therefore, that the emergence and augmentation of alternative discourses is identical to the process of universalizing and internationalizing the social sciences. It should also be clear that alternative discourses refer to good social science because they are more conscious of the need for relevance to the surroundings, of the problem of the discursive wielding of power by the social sciences, and for the need for the development of new ideas. What is being defined as alternative is that which is relevant to its surroundings, creative, non-imitative and original, non-essentialist, counter-Eurocentric, autonomous from the state, and autonomous from other national or transnational groupings. As such, alternative discourses could be advocated for Western social science itself.

The search for alternative discourses is a contribution to the universalization of the social sciences to the extent that alternative civilizational voices are added to the ensemble of ideas and works. But there are varying degrees of alternativeness (and all the things this entails such as creativity, originality, non-essentialism, autonomy, and relevance to the surroundings) and, therefore, universality. At the lowest level, good social science in the Third World would insist on a cautious application of Western theory to the local situation. Here we cannot yet speak of alternative discourse. At a higher level of alternateness and, therefore, universality, both local and Western theories are applied to the local context. At yet another level of alternateness and universality, local, Western and other indigenous theories and concepts (that is, indigenous to other non-Western societies) are applied to the local setting. I have in mind as an example, the application of the Khaldunian theory of state formation to the Mongol conquest of China. The highest level of alternateness and universality refers to the application of locally-derived theories from within and without one's own society to areas outside of one's own area. Whatever the level of universality, there is in principle a commitment to the universal source of theories, concepts and ideas in general, although the extent to which ideas from without the locality are brought in and domesticated varies from one level to another.

It is difficult, therefore, to understand why some are not for the project of alternative discourses. What is being advocated here is not a school of thought nor a particular theoretical or metatheoretical perspective, but simply good social science.

Orientalism in reverse and nativism

Reactions to the problems of academic dependency and mental captivity have taken the form of a high degree of intolerance towards the Western social sciences. This attitude can be captured under the notion of Orientalism in reverse or nativism. The idea of Orientalism in reverse was developed by the Syrian philosopher, Sadiq Jalal al-'Azm. He quotes from the work of a fellow Syrian, Georges Saddikni, on the notion of man (Ar. *insan*) which runs thus: The philosophy of Hobbes is based on his famous saying that "every man is a wolf unto other men", while, on the contrary, the inner philosophy implicit in the word *insan* preaches that "every man is a brother unto other men" (Saddikni, cited in al-'Azm 1984, p. 368).

Al-'Azm then assesses the above statement as follows:

> I submit that this piece of so-called analysis and comparison contains, in a highly condensed form, the entire apparatus of metaphysical abstractions and ideological mystifications so characteristic of Ontological Orientalism and so deftly and justly denounced in Said's book. The only new element is the fact that the Orientalist essentialist ontology has been reversed to favour one specific people of the Orient (al-'Azm 1984, p. 368).

Orientalism in reverse is founded on an essentialist approach to both 'Oriental' and 'Occidental' civilizations and is, therefore, a form of auto-Orientalism. An illustration of Orientalism in reverse comes from the Japanese case. The *nihonjinron* (theories of Japanese people) tradition in Japanese sociology is grounded in essentialized views on Japanese society, with the stress on cultural homogeneity and historical continuity. This remains in the tradition of Western Orientalist scholarship on Japan with the difference that the knowing subjects this time are the Japanese themselves. Hence the term auto-Orientalism as discussed by Lie (1996, p. 5).

The logical consequence of Orientalism in reverse and auto-Orientalism is nativism. This refers to the trend of going native among Western and local scholars alike, in which the native's point of view is elevated to the status of the criterion by which descriptions and analyses are to be judged. This entails a near-total rejection of Western knowledge. It cannot be stressed more that the various prescriptions for alternative discourses discussed above are decidedly opposed to such nativistic approaches to knowledge.

The future of alternative discourses in Southeast Asia

There are a few obstacles to the further development of alternative discourses in the social sciences in Southeast Asia.

One has to do with the problem of academic dependency. Academic dependency is perpetuated by the relative abundance of American and European funding for research and training, the high levels of prestige attached to publishing in American and British scholarly journals, the greater value attached to a Western university education, as well as other factors. The intellectual dependency on ideas exists within this context. Such a context, therefore, is not conducive to the cultivation of alternative discourses.

On the other hand, is there a serious possibility of the reversal of academic dependency? One practice that would augur well for the emergence of alternative discourses is to lessen reliance on European or American standards that may not be appropriate and at the same time work towards the upgrading of local publication capabilities. Emphasis on the development of local publications such as journals, and working paper and monograph series must have high priority. This would also free academics from being tied to themes and research agenda that are determined by the contents of American and European publications. But this can only work if as much credit is given for locally published works by evaluators and promotion and tenure committees as it is for international publications. It is not a problem to produce local journals and other publication series. What is more difficult is to attach sufficient value and rewards to these publications such that they would attract higher quality works, tasks that requires a great deal of will.

Another obstacle is connected with the cultural environment of intellectual discourse. Even if some headway can be made towards lessening intellectual dependency, ultimately what must change is the intellectual culture in Asian societies. This can only be brought about through a process of conscientizing. This in turn can only take place through the various media of intellectual socialization, including the schools, universities and other institutions of higher learning. It is necessary that there be an active minority of social scientists in each of the major universities in Southeast Asia who are concerned with some of the problems that have been raised above, who are interested in revisiting the diagnostic and prescriptive literature of the past, and who have the interest and will to generate new concepts, categories, methods and techniques, and research agenda.

Notes

[1] On the concept of relevance, see Syed Farid (S.F.) Alatas (2001).
[2] Non-European precursors of the social sciences have frequently been identified, a notable example being that of the Arab historical sociologist 'Abd al-Rahman ibn Khaldun (733–808/1332–1406) (Ibn Khaldun 1981/1377). Nevertheless, neither the Arabs nor others have reinterpreted or reworked the theories of Marx, Weber or Durkheim against the backdrop of Arab historical experiences and cultural practices, or attempted to integrate modern Western theories with those of Ibn Khaldun. For exceptions see Cheddadi (1980), Gellner (1981) and my paper (S.F. Alatas 1993a).
[3] I am grateful to Kwon Eun-Young for translating some passages from Shin (1994) for me.
[4] For a discussion on various dimensions of Eurocentrism in the social sciences see Wallerstein (1996).
[5] Intellectual imperialism is discussed in detail in S.F. Alatas (2000).
[6] See also Altbach and Selvaratnam (1989).
[7] For other assessments of the social sciences in Malaysia and Indonesia see Rais et al. (1984), Malo (1989), Garna and Rustam (1990), and Rustam and Norani (1991).
[8] For an excellent discussion of Abdullah's thought, see Shaharuddin (1988, chap 2). I have relied on this work for the above account.
[9] This account on van Leur is taken from Hall (1959, pp. 7–8) who discusses van Leur's review (1940a) of Stapel (1938–40).

¹⁰ For another critical comment on Bastin, see Singhal (1960). This is a comment on Bastin's "The Western Element in Modern Southeast Asian History", an abbreviated version of his inaugural lecture cited above.

¹¹ For other examples see Bennagen (1980), Kleden (1986), Siti Hawa (1991), and Enriquez (1994).

References

Abdullah bin Abdul Kadir Munshi. 1965 [1838]. *Kesah Pelayaran Abdullah*. Singapore: Malaysian Publications, 1965 [1838].

Alatas, Syed Farid. 1993a. "A Khaldunian Perspective on the Dynamics of Asiatic Societies". *Comparative Civilizations Review* 29: 29–51.

———. 1993b. "On the Indigenization of Academic Discourse". *Alternatives* 18, no. 3: 307–38.

———. 1995a. "The Theme of 'Relevance' in Third World Human Sciences". *Singapore Journal of Tropical Geography* 16, no. 2: 123–40.

———. (1995b) "Dependency, Rhetorics and the Transnational Flow of Ideas in the Social Sciences". Paper presented at the Goethe-Institute International Seminar on Cultural and Social Dimensions of Market Expansion, Labuan, 16–17 October.

———. 1998a. "Western Theories, East Asian Realities and the Social Sciences". In *Sociology in East Asia and Its Struggle for Creativity*, edited by Su-Hoon Lee, International Sociological Association Pre-Congress Volumes, Social Knowledge: Heritage, Challenges, Perspectives. Maria-Luz Moran (general editor), pp. 73–82.

———. 1998b. "The Rhetorics of Social Science in Developing Societies". CAS Research Papers Series no. 1. Singapore: Centre for Advanced Studies, National University of Singapore.

———. 2001. "The Study of the Social Sciences in Developing Societies: Towards an Adequate Conceptualization of Relevance". *Current Sociology* 49, no. 2: 1–19.

Alatas, Syed Hussein. 1956. "Some Fundamental Problems of Colonialism". *Eastern World* (November): 9–10.

———. 1962. "Reconstruction of Malaysian History". *Revue du Sud-est Asiatique* no. 3: 219–45.

———. 1964. "Theoretical Aspects of Southeast Asian History". *Asian Studies* 11, no. 2: 247–60.

———. 1969. "Academic Imperialism". Lecture delivered to the History Society, University of Singapore, 26 September.

———. 1971. *Thomas Stamford Raffles 1781–1826: Schemer or Reformer*. Sydney: Angus & Robertson.

————. 1972. "The Captive Mind in Development Studies". *International Social Science Journal* 34, no. 1: 9–25.

————. 1974. "The Captive Mind and Creative Development". *International Social Science Journal* 36, no. 4: 691–99.

————. 1977. *The Myth of the Lazy Native: A Study of the Image of the Malays, Filipinos, and Javanese from the Sixteenth to the Twentieth Century and its Functions in the Ideology of Colonial Capitalism.* London: Frank Cass.

————. 1979. "Towards an Asian Social Science Tradition". *New Quest* 17: 265–69.

————. 1981. "Social Aspects of Endogenous Intellectual Creativity: The Problem of Obstacles—Guidelines for Research". In *Intellectual Creativity in Endogenous Culture*, edited by A. Abdel-Malek and A.N. Pandeya. Tokyo: United Nations University.

————. 2000. "Intellectual Imperialism: Definition, Traits and Problems". *Southeast Asian Journal of Social Science* 28, no. 1: 23–45.

Altbach, Philip G. and Selvaratnam, Viswanathan, eds. 1989. *From Dependence to Autonomy: The Development of Asian Universities.* Dordrecht: Kluwer Academic Publishers.

Al-Attas, Syed Naguib. 1968. *The Origin of the Malay Sha'ir.* Kuala Lumpur: Dewan Bahasa & Pustaka.

————. 1969. *Preliminary Statement on a General Theory of the Islamization of the Malay-Indonesian Archipelago.* Kuala Lumpur: Dewan Bahasa dan Pustaka.

Al-Attas, Syed Muhammad Naguib. 1970. *The Correct Date of the Trengganu Inscription.* Kuala Lumpur: Museums Department, States of Malaya, 1970.

Al-Attas, Syed Naguib. 1971. *Concluding Postscript to the Origin of the Malay Sha'ir.* Kuala Lumpur: Dewan Bahasa & Pustaka.

Al-Attas, Syed Muhammad Naguib. 1972. *Islam dalam Sejarah dan Kebudayaan Melayu.* Kuala Lumpur: Penerbit Universiti Kebangsaan Malaysia.

Al-Attas, Syed Muhammad Naquib. 1975. *Comments on The Re-examination of Al-Rānīrī's Hujjatu'l-Siddīq: A Refutation.* Kuala Lumpur: Museum Negara.

al-Azm, Sadiq Jalal. 1984. "Orientalism and Orientalism in Reverse", in *Forbidden Agendas: Intolerance and Defiance in the Middle East*, edited by John Rothschild, London: Al Saqi Books, pp. 349–76.

Bastin, John. 1959. "The Study of Modern Southeast Asian History". An Inaugural Lecture delivered in the University of Malaya in Kuala Lumpur on 14 December 1959, Kuala Lumpur: The University of Malaya in Kuala Lumpur.

Bennagen, P.L. 1980. "The Asianization of Anthropology". *Asian Studies* 18: 1–26.

Blake, Myrna L. 1991. "The Portability of Family Therapy to Different Cultural and Socio-Economic Contexts". *Asia-Pacific Journal of Social Work* 1, no. 2: 32–60.

Catapusan, B. 1957. "Development of Sociology in the Philippines". *Philippine Sociological Review* 4: 53–57.

Cheddadi, Abdesselam. 1980. "Le Systeme du Pouvoir en Islam d'Apres Ibn Khaldun". *Annales Economiès, Sociétés, Civilisations* 3–4: 534–50.

Chung Yuen Kay. 1989. *Gender, Work and Ethinicity: an Ethnography of Female Factory Workers in Singapore.* Ph.D thesis, Department of Sociology, National University of Singapore.

Enriquez, Virgilio G. 1994. "Towards Cross-Cultural Knowledge through Cross-Indigenous Methods and Perspective". In *Pamamaraan: Indigenous Knowledge and Evolving Research Paradigms*, edited by Teresita B. Obusan, Angelina R. Enriquez, Quezon City: Asian Center, University of the Philippines, pp. 19–31.

Garna, Judistira K and Rustam A. Sani, eds. 1990. *Antropologi Sosiologi di Indonesia dan Malaysia: Teori Pengembangan dan Penerapan.* Bangi: Penerbit Universiti Kebangsaan Malaysia.

Gellner, Ernest. 1981. *Muslim Society.* Cambridge: Cambridge University Press.

Hall, D.G.E. 1959. *East Asian History Today.* Hong Kong University Press, Oxford University Press.

Kartodirdjo. 1982. *Sartono Pemikiran dan Perkembangan Historiografi Indonesia: Suatu Alternatif.* Jakarta: Gramedia.

Ibn Khaldun, 'Abd al-Rahman. 1981 [1377]. *Muqaddimat Ibn Khaldun.* Beirut: Dar al-Qalam.

Kyi, Khin Maung. "Burma". In *Social Sciences in Asia and the Pacific.* Paris: UNESCO. pp. 93–141.

van Leur, J.C. 1937. "Enkele aanteekeningen met betrekking tot de beoefening der Indische geschiedenis" [Some Notes Concerning the Study of the History of the Indies], *Koloniale Studiën* 21: 651–66.

————. 1940a "Eenige aanteekeningen betreffende de mogelijkheid der 18ᵉ eeuw als categorie in de Indische geschiedschrijving" [Some Notes on the Possibility of the 18th Century as a Category in the Writing of the History of the Indies]. *Tijdschrift voor Indische Taal-, Land- en Volkenkunde uitgegeven door het (Koninklijk) Bataviaasch Genootschap van Kunsten en Wetenschappen* 80: 544–67.

————. 1940b. "De Wereld van Zuidoost-Azië" [The World of Southeast Asia]. In *Nederlanders over de Zeeën: 350 jaar Nederlandsche koloniale geschiedenis* [Dutchmen over the Seas: 350 Years of Dutch Colonial History, edited by J.C. de Haan and P.J. van Winter. Utrecht: De Hann, pp. 101–44.

————. 1955. *Indonesian Trade and Society: Essays in Asian Social and Economic History.* The Hague: W. van Hoeve.

Lie, John. 1966. "Sociology of Contemporary Japan". *Current Sociology* 44, no. 1: 1–95.

Malo, Manasse, ed. 1989. *Pengembangan Ilmu-Ilmu Sosial di Indonesia sampai decade '80-an*. Jakarta: CV Rajawali.

de Morga, Antonio. 1962 [1890]. *Historical Events of the Philippine Islands by Dr Antonio de Morga, Published in Mexico in 1609, recently brought to light and annotated by Jose Rizal, preceded by a prologue by Dr Ferdinand Blumentritt*. Writings of Jose Rizal Volume VI, Manila: National Historical Institute.

———. 1991 [1890]. *Sucesos de las Islas Filipinas por el Doctor Antonio de Morga, obra publicada en Méjico el año de 1609, nuevamente sacada a luz y anotada por José Rizal y precedida de un prólogo del Prof. Fernando Blumentritt*, Edición del Centenario, impression al *offset* de la Edición Anotada por Rizal, Paris 1890, Escritos de José Rizal Tomo VI. Manila: Comision Nacional del Centenario de José Rizal, Instituto Histórico Nacional.

Ocampo, Ambeth R. 1998. "Rizal's Morga and Views of Philippine History". *Philippine Studies* 46: 184–14.

Pané, Armijn. 1951. "Indonesia di Asia Selatan: Sedjarah Indonesia Sampai ± 1600" [Indonesia in Southern Asia: Indonesian History till ± 1600]. *Indonesia* 2: 1–36.

Pertierra, Raul. 1994. "A National Imagination and the Social Sciences: Indigenization and the Discovery of the Filipino". *Jurnal Antropologi dan Sosiologi* 21: 35–53.

———. 1997. "Culture, Social Science and the Conceptualization of the Philippine Nation-State". Paper presented at the International Workshop on Indigenous and Indigenized Anthropology in Asia, Leiden, 1–3 May.

PuruShotam, Nirmala. 1992 "Women and Knowledge/Power. Notes on the Singaporean Dilemma." In *Imagining Singapore*, edited by K.C. Ban, A. Pakir and C.K. Tong. Singapore: Times Academic Press.

———. 1993. "Caste: Woman. Occupation: Domestic Maid. Exploring the Realm of Foreign Full-time Workers in Singapore". In the *Proceedings of the International Colloquim on Migration, Development and Gender in the Asean Region*, edited by J. Ariffin. Kuala Lumpur: Population Studies Unit, University of Malaya.

———. n.d. "Gender and the Middle Class Way of Life". In *Sex and Power in Affluent Asia*, edited by K. Sen and M. Stivens. London: Routledge, forthcoming.

Rais, M. Amien, et al. 1984. *Krisis Ilmu-Ilmu Sosial dalam Pembangunan di Dunia Ketiga*. Yogyakarta: PLP2M.

Rizal, José. 1962 [1890]. "To the Filipinos". In de Morga, *Historical Events of the Philippine Islands*, p. vii.

Rizal-Blumentritt, Rizal, José Ferdinand. 1992. *The Rizal-Blumentritt Correspondence*, Vol. 1. Manila: National Historical Institute.

Rustam A. Sani and Norani Othman. 1991. "The Social Sciences in Malaysia: A Critical Scenario". *Ilmu Masyarakat* 19: 1–20.

Shaharuddin Maaruf. 1984. *The Concept of the Hero in Malay Society*. Singapore: Eastern Universities Press.

———. 1989. *Malay Ideas on Development: From Feudal Lord to Capitalist*. Singapore: Times Book International.

———. 1992. "Some Theoretical Problems Concerning Tradition and Modernization Among the Malays of Southeast Asia". In *Asian Tradition and Modernization: Perspectives from Singapore*, edited by Yong Mun Cheong, pp. 241–65. Singapore: Times Academic Press.

Shamsul Amri Baharuddin. 1995. "Malaysia: The Kratonization of Social Science". In *Social Science in Southeast Asia: From Particularism to Universalism*, edited by Nico Schulte Nordholt and Leontine Visser, Amsterdam: VU University Press, pp. 87–109.

———. 1999. "Colonial Knowledge and the Construction of Malay and Malayness: Exploring the Literary Component". *SARI: Journal of the Malay World and Civilization* 17: 3–17.

Sharifah Maznah Syed Omar. 1993. *Myths and the Malay Ruling Class*. Singapore: Times Academic Press.

Shin Yong-Ha. 1994. "Suggestions for the Development of a Creative Korean Sociology". In Korean Sociological Association, *Korean Sociology in the 21st Century*, pp. 15–30. Seoul: Moon-Hak-Kwa Ji-Seong-Sa.

Singhal, D. 1960. "Some Comments on 'The Western Element in Modern Southeast Asian History'". *Journal of Southeast Asian History* 1, no. 2: 118–23.

Sinha, Vineeta. 1997. "Reconceptualizing the Social Sciences in Non-Western Settings: Challenges and Dilemmas". *Southeast Asian Journal of Social Science* 25, no. 1: 167–81.

———. 1998. "Socio-Cultural Theory and Colonial Encounters: The Discourse on Indigenizing Anthropology in India". Manuscript, Department of Sociology, National University of Singapore.

———. 1999. "Making Harriet Martineau Visible in Androcentric Sociological Theory". Paper presented at the 3rd Asia Pacific Regional Conference of Sociology, Cheju City, Korea, 4–6 February.

———. 2001. "Re-building Institutional Structures in the Social Sciences through Critique". In *Reflections on Alternative Discourses from Southeast Asia*, edited by Syed Farid Alatas, Singapore: Pagesetters.

———. 1991. "Western Theory and Local Practice: Implications for Social Work Education in Malaysia". *Asia-Pacific Journal of Social Work* 1, no. 1: 26–47.

Smail, John R.W. 1961. "On the Possibility of an Autonomous History of Modern Southeast Asia". *Journal of Southeast Asian History* 2, no. 2: 73–105.

Soedjatmoko. 1960. "An Approach to Indonesian History: Towards an Open Future". An address before the Seminar on Indonesian History, Gadjah Mada

University, Jogjakarta, 14 December 1957. Ithaca: Translation Series, Modern Indonesia Project, Cornell University.

Stapel, F.W. ed., 1938–1940. *De Geschiedenis van Nederlandsch-Indië*. 6 Vols. Amsterdam: Joost van den Vondel.

Tham Seong Chee. 1971. "Intellectual Colonization". *Suara Universiti* 2, no. 2: 39–40.

Wallerstein, Immanuel. 1996. "Eurocentrism and Its Avatars: The Dilemmas of Social Science". Paper presented to Korean Sociological Association-International Sociological Association East Asian Regional Colloquium on "The Future of Sociology in East Asia". Seoul, 22–23 November.

Wang Gungwu. 2001. "Shifting Paradigms and Asian Perspectives: Implications for Research and Teaching". In *Reflections on Alternative Discourses from Southeast Asia*, edited by Syed Farid Alatas. Singapore: Pagesetters.

Watanuki, Joji. 1984. "Japan". In *Social Sciences in Asia and the Pacific*. Paris: UNESCO, pp. 281–95.

Wee, Vivienne. 1988. *Men, Women and Violence: A Handbook for Survival*. Singapore: AWARE And SAWL for the Task Force for the Prevention of Violence against Women, Singapore Council of Women's Organisations (SCWO).

Wee, Vivienne, Noeleen Heyzer, assisted by Aileen Kwa et al. 1995. *Gender, Poverty and Sustainable Development: Towards a Holistic Framework of Understanding and Action*. Singapore: Centre for Environment, Gender and Development.

Zaide, S. 1993. "Historiography in the Spanish Period". In *Philippine Encyclopedia of the Social Sciences*, pp. 4–19. Quezon City: Philippine Social Science Council.

Zawiah Yahya. 1994. *Resisting Colonialist Discourse*. Bangi: Penerbit Universiti Kebangsaan Malaysia.

5

Redrawing Centre-Periphery Relations: Theoretical Challenges in the Study of Southeast Asian Modernity

Beng-Lan Goh

The term modernity refers to a socio-historical transformative process which has its roots in the Western European experience from at least the 16th Century, marking a contrast to the medieval period. Implicit in this definition of modernity is the notion of historical progress that is based on a unilinear unfolding of time and experience whereby the Western mode of time and being is the norm against which all other experiences are judged. In recent years, this classical understanding of modernity has come under increasing critique with multiple formulations of the modern in the world that do not conform to the Western experience. The multiple formulations of modernity suggest that modernity is not necessarily only a Western phenomenon but that there are a variety of forms and meanings of the modern.

In parallel to these developments, the conceptualization of modernity has undergone radical changes. More recently, the idea that a rethinking of modernity can be positioned within or outside the West has increasingly given way to a conceptualization of modernity within the simultaneous processes of the global and the local and/or the East and the West. Traditional distinctions between the West and the non-West and the unfolding logic of modernity have been complicated. This paper explores displacements opened up by recent rethinking about both Western and non-Western experiences of the modern that provide ways out of the East-West binary and its associated unequal relations in the conceptualization of modernity.

I will take up two sets of debates on modernity to make my point. First, I identify recent studies that have reconceptualized modernity from the margins—both within as well as outside the West—in order to unsettle the centre-periphery hierarchy and locate equal force to knowledge and practices of non-Western contexts in constituting the modern condition. Second, I discuss how the recent reconceptualization of modernity poses a challenge to understanding the modern imaginaries and transformations in Southeast Asian societies in autonomous terms rather than resorting to invidious or derivative distinctions from that of the West. Here, I explore the theoretical grounds opened up for the recognition of new meanings and categories of the modern provided by the Southeast Asian models of modernity that defy Western narratives.

Unsettling the componential references of the 'West' and the 'non-West'

The interrogation of modernity appears to revolve around two inter-related questions, that is, first, how to dislodge the primacy of the category of the 'West', its history and culture, and second, how to understand the multiple formulations of modernity in their own terms and priorities without resorting to invidious comparisons. These questions have been tackled in differing ways across various disciplines. Historians, especially those studying economic and art history, are amongst those who have long taken up the critique of the authority of Western history. They have for a long time used empirical evidence of the longstanding interconnectedness of world history in terms of trade and material artefacts to point out the implicit errors in conventional thinking about history based on the idea of the superiority and priority of the West. A case in point is Donald Lach's *Asia in the Making of Europe*

(1965). In this four-volume book, Lach meticulously documents how non-European/Asian elements have a place in the making of artistic and technological developments during the European Renaissance. He presents a complex story of how Renaissance ideas in Europe came not solely from the territorial and cultural boundaries of the West, but were equally informed by knowledge accumulated from Western encounters with Asian civilizations, in particular the Greater Eastern Traditions of China, Japan and India. Other historical studies have also focused on empirical evidence of trade, economics and material origins and innovations outside the West that have been ignored by Eurocentric writing of history. For instance, attempts at revising Eurocentric history are found in the works of Chaudhuri's *Asia Before Europe* (1990) and Abu-Lughod's *Before European Hegemony* (1989). These studies show that there were various networks of trade and movement of people, material artefacts, and architecture operating in the non-Western regions of the world during the 13th and 14th centuries prior to the rise of the West. These, and subsequent studies, have highlighted the important roles played by various port cities during this period in regions that eventually came to be referred to as Middle-East, Central Asia, South Asia, East Asia, and Southeast Asia.[1] Other studies have contributed to dispelling the idea that Europe had a historical priority over the rest of the world in that the early world economy came about from a complex interaction of people, trade, material and technological innovations between the Western and non-Western worlds.[2]

Nevertheless, the critique of Western supremacy via historical empiricism remains inadequate on at least two fronts. First, these empiricist critiques of Western history are often only effective for conditions until at least the 13th century, when Europe was said to be peripheral to an 'Orient'-centred world economy. This is because the argument that Europe was not more progressive and not more advanced than other civilizations is only valid when referring to the period before 1492. After 1492, European dominance emerged with the discovery of America, which saw the extension of Europe to the Americas. European power further consolidated during the Enlightenment in the 17th and 18th centuries with industrial progress and colonialism in Western Europe. Second, a historical empirical approach is not enough to undo the authority of the West precisely because European hegemony is not merely associated with just territorial and economic conquests but also with its subject-constituting enterprise, that is, the formidable force of the West in defining knowledge about 'Others'. Here the problem is one over the canonization and discursive domination of Western knowledge whereby Eurocentric history and culture form the normative against which all others categories are derived and/or given meaning.

Arguably, the notion of the West as the custodian of reason and experience is influenced to a large extent by the critique of Orientalism— an influential theory expounded by Edward Said that frames world history in terms of geopolitics by arguing that the division between the East and the West, and the representations of each, were produced in the historical encounter of imperialism (Said 1991). Said's critique is in part spurred by poststructuralist concerns to uncover the power/knowledge processes under which the world/culture presents itself as real within an active deconstruction of the premises and knowledge claims of the West.[3] Inevitably, the quest to overcome the power of Eurocentric imaginations is accompanied by endeavours to recuperate subaltern or indigenous knowledge.

At the forefront of the efforts to recover subaltern knowledge is a genre of scholarship, labelled postcolonial criticism, that examines the exclusionary and ambivalent practices of Western or colonial discourses. Pioneered by the works of Said, Bhabha and Spivak, postcolonial studies have contributed immensely to our understanding of the danger of the return of originally colonial regimes of knowledge, albeit in renewed forms, in the bid to create non-Western knowledge in the critique of the West (Said 1991; Bhabha 1994; Spivak 1995). They have shed important light on the connections between indigenous/national and colonial/western imaginations and practices, highlighting the political and theoretical difficulties in the recovery of subaltern knowledge and experience in this process. Through their contributions, we have learnt of the need to be constantly vigilant with respect to the hidden ways in which efforts to recover indigenous knowledge can often unknowingly, or even knowingly, perpetuate the structures and presuppositions of the regimes of colonial knowledge and its modes of representation.[4] Nevertheless in this very strength also lies the weakness of postcolonial criticism. Despite its aims of recovering the 'non-West', the particular brand of deconstruction subscribed by postcolonial theorists has also seen it plagued by the conundrum of the irretrievability of indigenous experience and the paradoxical restoration of Western agency/power that it so seeks to eliminate. In their preoccupation to delimit the power of Western discourse, postcolonial theorists, in particular in the early works of Said, Bhabha and Spivak, often locate the West as the sole reference and original site of power and knowledge. By assuming that authority and knowledge come only from the West, their endeavours to undo the power of the West only lead to an ironic reaffirmation of its power as they become caught in a fixation upon the dominance of the West, the resistant non-West, and the binary relations produced.[5]

Subsequently, to avoid the inescapable authority of the West, other studies have instead turned to unsettle the componential references of the West and the non-West by showing that the presumptions underlying this divide are not as tenable as they appear to be. While a growing body of literature across various disciplines has taken up this challenge, the studies that I have in mind are not those that require an abandonment of Western history and theory, or those that take on essentialist explanations of local meanings. Such approaches are problematic not only in that differences become particularized but that they ignore the reality of the entwinement or world histories in which local contexts are not only shaped by their own historical forces within but also by histories outside their territories. Rather, I turn to studies that are characterized by a scrutiny of the exclusionary and hierarchical discourses of the West in order to reveal the complex genealogies of the modern that have been obliterated.[6] Let me begin by discussing studies that have complicated the traditional distinctions between the West and the non-West and posed new understanding towards the relations between the centre and the periphery that underpin modernity.

Paul Gilroy's *Black Atlantic* (1993) is an important study that is concerned with formulating a theory of Euro-American modernity from the perspectives of a minority group—the black diaspora—to unsettle the definition of Euro-American modernity along with its territorial and cultural presuppositions. In his study of the history of migration and cultural expression within the African diaspora of nineteenth and early twentieth-century Europe and the Americas, Gilroy challenges the idea that Euro-American modernity is solely the achievement of white Euro-American bourgeois society. Pointing out that Euro-American modernity was wrought about by slavery and imperial conquest, Gilroy argues that blacks in the West are integral to the unfolding of Euro-American modernity and as such are equally conventional bearers of modernity

(Gilroy 1993, p. 221). By focusing on the movements of the black diaspora across the Atlantic and their contributions to Euro-American modernity via the varied formations of culture and consciousness that arose from their interstitial position as people lodged between the forces of the local, the national, and the global/universal, Gilroy shows how Euro-American modernity is inevitably a transcultural, international, diasporic and hybrid formation (Gilroy 1993, p. 127).

In line with this move to disrupt conventions held about the West, the anthropologist Ann Stoler has shown that modern forms and practices did not necessarily originate within the boundaries of the West (Stoler 1992). Working on colonial practices in the Dutch East Indies, Stoler shows how the emergence of a bourgeois identity in the Netherlands came about as a result of racial practices of Dutch colonialists in their bid to separate themselves from marginal groups such as the mixed-blood population and the 'poor whites' in the colonies. In highlighting that the emergence of bourgeois identity occurred in the colonies instead of Europe, Stoler's study demonstrates the importance of the colonial project in constituting the modern experience. This makes possible a thinking that ideas can originate outside the boundary and cultural realm of the West, suggesting the complex origins of 'Western' ideas. Along this line of thought, several other scholars such as Paul Rabinow (1989), Anthony King (1990), Timothy Mitchell (1988), and Gwendolyn Wright (1991) have shown how practices and the institutions of urban planning and architecture associated with the West were first developed or experimented with in the colonies.

Indeed, the idea that modern consciousness did not originate in the West alone might also be inferred from Benedict Anderson's seminal work, *Imagined Communities*, as several scholars have pointed out.[7] In this book, Anderson suggests that the first truly modern nationalisms developed in the various creole-led independence movements throughout the Americas in the latter half of the eighteenth and the first half of the nineteenth centuries rather than in Europe (Anderson 1991, pp. 47–65). For Anderson, while the nationalisms of Western Europe may have, in some instances, prefigured the development of nationalisms in the new world, their allegiances were to the *ancien regime*. It was in the Americas that a new populist version of imagined communities of nation-states, common citizenship, and popular sovereignty emerged, later developed in Western Europe, and then spread to Eastern Europe and elsewhere in the world. More recently, Perry Anderson makes a somewhat similar argument in his critique of postmodernism by suggesting that the idea of modernism and postmodernism were first conceptualized in the distant periphery of Latin America and not in Europe against common assumptions (P. Anderson 1998). According to Perry Anderson, "modernismo" was a term coined in 1890 by a Nicaraguan poet in proclaiming Latin American writers' cultural independence from Spanish literature (P. Anderson 1998, p. 3). What is more, he argues that the idea of postmodernism appeared in the interstitial world of Latin America around the 1930s before its appearance in England or America (P. Anderson, pp. 1–6).

Another study that unsettles the West as the producer of modernity is found in Fernando Coronil's critique of capitalism as a Western process in a study on Venezuelan modernity, *The Magical State*. Drawing on Venezuela's location as an 'oil nation' and the intricate nexus between its history, political economy and the global capitalist system, Coronil argues that capitalism is necessarily a global process involving multiple social agents in complex interactions that integrate the periphery and the centre. Thus, when seen from a non-Western vantage point, the common definition of capitalism as originating in, and spreading outwards from, the West does not hold: people, structures and histories outside the West are equally complicit in the capitalist expansion.

These disclosures of the complex genealogies of modernity suggest that the currents that determine modernity do not flow only in one direction. If the origins of the modern can no longer be associated solely with the West, then it makes no sense to take the Western narrative of modernity as the normative standard against which to understand all other non-Western modernities, despite their intertwined histories. Neither would it be meaningful to speak of modernity in terms of the language of original and copy or first and late-comer. A privileging of the western narrative of modernity not only renders the efforts of non-Western people along with their new categories and meanings of the modern as insignificant, or worse, as simply derivative. Instead, there should be attempts at developing theories of modernity that recognize the non-West as a producer of knowledge which take the multiple histories and cultures at work in the world as parallel rather than as mere responses to the Western normative. Some studies have suggested that tropes such as "translation, hybridization, and even dislocation" might be more useful for comprehending non-Western modernity than the existing notions of "imitation, assimilation (forced or attempted), or rejection".[8] It is within this context that some studies have established important theoretical positions not just on multiple but also the coeval force and forms of rationalities and experiences in Western and non-Western contexts in defining modernity.

A contribution to the search for autonomous knowledge structures beyond prevailing conceptual constructs is Achille Mbembe's work on contemporary Africa. In trying to offer an intelligible reading of contemporary forms of social and political imaginations in postcolonial Africa beyond Western conceptualizations and representations, Mbembe (2001) calls for a need for a "different writing"[9] in order to recognize the different modes of time and rationalities that do not conform to prevailing concepts that are found in local societies. Central to "different writing" is the understanding of the close relationship between subjectivity and temporality. According to Mbembe, the experience of time in Africa "is not a series but an interlocking of presents, pasts, and futures that retain their depths of other presents, pasts, and future, each age bearing, altering, and maintaining the previous ones". (Mbembe 2001, p. 16). This time is not irreversible and is made up of disturbances, of unforeseen circumstances, oscillations that do not necessarily always lead to chaos or erratic public behaviour. As such African modern formations harbour a variety of trajectories that are neither convergent nor divergent but are instead better characterized as interlocked and paradoxical, with several public spaces each with their own logic that are yet entangled with other logics when operating in particular contexts. Given this condition, Mbembe argues that in order to grasp the effective reality of what it means to be an African subject in the context of such complexities, instability and crises, it is vital to integrate this non-linear sense of time into the analyses of modern subjectivities. Mbembe's arguments suggest that new imaginaries and practices can only be grasped if we expand dominant conceptual constructs to include alternative narratives of real historical processes. Thus, to Mbembe, a re-articulation of social theory so as "to account for time as lived, not synchronically or diachronically, but in its multiplicity and simultaneities, beyond the lazy categories of permanence and change..." is in order (Mbembe 2001, p. 8).

In step with this theoretical challenge is the work of Walter Mignolo, a literary and cultural studies scholar, which offers new grounds for recognizing the autonomy of non-Western knowledge and experiences in his critique of Eurocentric conceptions of history, society and modernity (Mignolo 2000, pp. 91–126). The novelty of Mignolo's approach is that he recognizes the discursive power of the West but also establishes a coeval standing for imaginations and experiences of non-Western societies in shaping the modern world by locating the encounter between the East and West as inevitable and creative sites for the release of new forms of knowledge. Tracing the coexistence and intersections of Europe and the Americas from the 15th Century, Mignolo argues for the simultaneity of modernity/coloniality and global design/local history in shaping the modern world. By positing the modern/colonial and the imperial/local as simultaneous processes, he shows that universal reason and history are not solely shaped by a transcendent West but are established by historical subjects in diverse cultural centres. This epistemological space for the force of the local in shaping universal knowledge is wrought about by "border thinking"—a locus for the release of "subalternized knowledge" in the encounter between outside and local forces. Drawn from the concept of "double critique/consciousness" in which a position of marginality enables one to become not only critical of the hegemonic but also reflexive of one's own traditions, Mignolo's "border thinking" is a site of enunciation for the release of *new* forms of thinking that while arising from both Eurocentric and local discourses has also broken away from them. It is essentially "another thinking" that is irreducibly different from the traditions from which it arose. For Mignolo, it is the everyday encounter with "Occidentalism" where material and cultural differences remain judged against categories and meanings of the "West" that makes possible the re-articulation of imperial discourses from the perspectives of local history. As such, "border thinking" is never neutral but imbued by polemic and emotional sensibilities of location, ethnicity, nationality, gender, class and so on. Drawing on a diverse set of Latin American discourses, Mignolo traces how fractured enunciations of border thinking had emerged at various intersections of Euro/American history as people living under colonial domination had to enact a "thinking process" in order to negotiate their life and subaltern reason (Mignolo 2000, pp. x, 100). Mignolo's "border thinking" thus provides for a coeval standing of local and imperial knowledge in that both are always simultaneous and have equal force and creativity in shaping the modern imaginary of the world in their inevitable intersection with each other across time and space.

These theoretical innovations that recognize the continued power of Western imaginations in the contemporary world but also provide a fresh way of looking at the East and the West as coeval forces by locating their encounter as inevitable and as productive sites for the birth of new knowledge are useful to the interrogation of Southeast Asian modernity from local perspectives. Indeed, in line with larger theoretical developments in the social sciences and the humanities, recent studies of Southeast Asian modernity have distanced themselves from universalistic approaches to more context-bound interpretations of modernity. A variety of locally distinctive modernities with their own temporal and historical specificities in the Southeast Asian region has been highlighted. While this epistemological shift to a particularistic analysis of modernity frees one to study the subjective constitution of modern meanings and the specific articulations between the local and the universal, a problem remains in that many of these debates stop short of using the varying local expressions of the modern to unsettle dominant definitions and categories of modernity. A danger in failing to push for the full autonomy of local meanings is the surreptitious return of Eurocentric definitions as dominant references when giving significance to the different narratives of modernity. Attempts at defining the different modern experiences in non-Western contexts in terms of alternative, abberant, deviant forms of modernity exemplify this trap as these terms presume an underlying notion of a dominant narrative against which their alterities become marked. It is here that the recent rethinking of modernity not only in terms of multiple but coeval forms of rationality, expression, and experience via direct engagements with Western knowledge and practices provides important epistemological grounds for a complete breakaway from Eurocentric conceptions yet without resorting to essentialist defence of difference. Thus, informed by the prioritization of equality and creative encounter in the interpretation of modern difference, I will next explore the theoretical grounds opened up in recent efforts to render autonomy and novelty to the modern imaginaries and practices found in Southeast Asian societies and the extent to which the local forms and meanings of the modern call into question the limits of Western definitions and categories of modernity.

Rethinking Southeast Asian modernity

Contemporary Southeast Asian societies have unquestionably presented us with new models of modernity. The Southeast Asian quest for modernity, characterized by the greater role of the state in adopting technical rationality from the West while recovering 'traditional' elements of culture, provides grounds for a theorization of non-Western modernity from local perspectives.[10] Like most post-colonies, the imperative to modernize in many of the Southeast Asian countries came directly from anti-colonial nationalism as political elites saw a course of modernization as vital for national survival. Nevertheless, the idea of modernization has colonial roots and is dependent on a set of hierarchy and meanings that set the West as the producer and forerunner of a rational, future-oriented, advanced capitalist modernity. Hence, for many Southeast Asian countries, modernization often means taking up Western forms and practices. Thus, as much as modernization is part and parcel of a nationalist ideology, it is also inevitably experienced as a set of given values imposed by and associated with the West. Not surprisingly, the Southeast Asian pursuit of modernization is marked by a perpetual indeterminacy over whether to embrace or reject Western forms and practices. For instance, let's just take the examples of Malaysia and Singapore. On the one hand, while there is an escalating anti-West rhetoric as politicians and intellectuals in these societies negotiate their social positions in the contemporary world, a desire for things and values Western has not vanished. In Malaysia, while it may be clear that former Prime Minister Mahathir was anti-West, nonetheless he had no qualms about promoting 'Western' architecture, technology, infrastructure, and urban development in the country. In fact, the mixing of Eastern and Western cultural forms is common in the search for an 'indigenous' Malaysian modernity: the Petronas Tower and its Islamic symbolism is one such example. In Singapore, despite endeavours to imagine an Asian modernity distinct from the West, achievements often only become meaningful when verified by, or benchmarked against, norms predetermined by the West, denoting a desire to be accepted into the developmental hierarchies of the West.

Given the prevalent and complex workings of the 'East-West' rhetoric in characterizing local expressions of the modern, it is inevitable that the 'East-West' question remains compelling to the inquiry into Southeast Asian modernity. Indeed, the exploration of Southeast Asian modernity has occurred largely against the backdrop of anti-colonial nationalism, nation-state formation, and globalization. I will single out three debates from recent studies that have highlighted the unfolding of different modern imaginaries and practices in Southeast Asia to explore the grounds for a recognition of new meanings and categories of modernity.

First, in seeking to define Southeast Asian modernity, some scholars have challenged dominant notions about the power of capitalism and the spread of Western ideas and forms of the modern. They assert that a conception of modern transformations in terms of the workings of capitalism cannot fully bring out what it means to be modern for Southeast Asians. While they do not refute that capitalism is a powerful transformative force responsible for aligning Southeast Asian modernity with Western forms of the modern, they insist that the social relations underlying capital are always cultural. The works of Adrian Vickers and Michel Picard on Balinese modernity form this genre of scholarship (Vickers 1996; Picard 1996; Picard 1997). Working on Balinese modernity, they are specifically concerned with recuperating the cultural agency and history of the Balinese people to show how local agents translate and find similarities with universal ideas of the "modern" rather than being "passive recipients of Western initiatives" (Vickers 1996, p. 6). Nevertheless, they are cautious to point out that the emergent modern forms are not to be understood in terms of the survival of cultural forms and practices relevant to former times. Rather, their studies emphasize the fundamental issues of power and cultural production operating under modern conditions within Balinese society. They show that there is no one single form of the modern for the Balinese, but that discourses of the modern are part of a set of power relations in which some are more authorized to act than others. Vickers, for instance, contends that Balinese cultures, like other Southeast Asian cultures, have a long history of translating and making outside forms anew and local. He suggests that the universal ideas of the 'modern' only came to be accepted and translated in Balinese society precisely because there were local precedents and experiences of the Balinese version of the 'moderen'.[11] Picard's study demonstrates that the Balinese notion of being modern involves a sense of holding on to tradition in which the category of religion/*agama* or the sacred is integral, as the Balinese endeavour to gain control of their lives amidst the rapid forces of tourism and change (Picard 1996). What these two studies show is that the Balinese expressions of the 'moderen' are products that came out of the encounter between the local and the foreign as people are active producers of meanings as they endeavour to take control of their circumstances. Recent volumes that attempt to develop a theory of the rise of the new middle class in modern Southeast Asia have also endeavoured to understand modern social differentiations through historical and cultural perspectives on class and power rather than via a narrow political-economic reading of the phenomenon.[12] Indeed scholars have highlighted how the category of the middle-class in contemporary Southeast Asia defies that of the bourgeois class, its equivalent in modern Europe, in that they both emerged under different circumstances and took on different social roles. Unlike the bourgeois class that was created by capitalist forces, the middle-class in Southeast Asia has been, to a large extent, created by state patronage and practices.[13] The entwinement of the state and the middle-class in Southeast Asia has led some scholars to see them as an 'encapsulated' class in which critique against the state is often weak, if non-existent, due to the inseparable interests of the middle-class and the state (Jesudason 1995). If ordinary people struggle to establish control over the intrusion of global modern forces on their lives, so do the nation-states of Southeast Asia. A volume on *Asian Forms of the Nation* examines how the development of the modern nation in the region was shaped by their individual pre-national histories (Tonneson and Atlov 1996). Others have pointed to the vital role played by the Malay language, the lingua franca for most of island Southeast Asia, in mediating other worldviews and events to the local populations of the region, thus shaping their distinct local modern identities (Siegel 1997, pp. 13–26). The arguments here are not about the recuperation of cultural essentialism or primordialism but rather to assert the historical experiences, cultural priorities, and linguistic particularities of societies that invariably influence the contemporary forms and narratives of the modern and their contestations.

This, in turn connects with a second type of study that explores the power of state hegemony and power in the making of modern subjects in the Southeast Asian pursuit of modernity. Shifting power away from Western/colonial imaginaries and practices to that of the national state yet not delegating it as another teleological force, these studies frame modern formations of the region within the situated locations of race, class, gender, religion, and so on. The allocation of power to national practices is defensible in that the larger role of the state in defining the projects of modernity in Southeast Asia has been well noted. In fact, these projects of modernity involve not only state attempts to transform the economy but also to construct new identities for their citizenry.[14] Some studies have pointed to the contested nature of these national projects of modernity. While recognizing the power of various Southeast Asian nation-states in shaping, representing and enforcing their economic and cultural formulations of modernity, these studies also seek to emphasize the historical complexity of social formations in these societies to show that state hegemony is always more fragile than it appears as there are always aspects of people's lives and practices that are never wholly subject to any regimes of control. Two volumes—*Modernity and Identity: Asian Illustrations* and *Southeast Asian Identities: Culture and the Politics of Representation in Indonesia, Malaysia, Singapore, and Thailand*—demonstrate just how state-sponsored programmes of modernity in Southeast Asia often involve the political and cultural domination of some groups over others within complex intersections of national and global forces of economic modernization. This has resulted in the resurgence and revivalism of ethnic and religious identities in the region as marginalized groups and classes construct different identities in order to create a constituency to further their own interests in their struggles against economic, political, and cultural domination.[15] Southeast Asian modernity, as the contributors show, is strongly characterized by national integrationist policies, but the drive to uniformity based on a dominant ethnic culture has resulted in disunity and a new resuscitation of traditional forms and the revival of ethnic and religious identities within a nexus of local, national and global tensions. Building on the complex modern formations of the region, others have also pointed to the non-secular nature of Southeast Asian modernity.[16] Given the important location of religious identity in many of these societies, in which the divide between state and religion is often ambiguous, if not perplexed, the character of Southeast Asian modernity is often one that is imbued with religious identifications: the significance of Buddhism in Thailand and several other mainland Southeast Asian states; Islam for Malaysia and Indonesia, as well as the Islamic insurgent areas of Mindanao in the Philippines and Southern Thailand; and Catholicism for the Philippines. In fact in a recent study, Robert Hefner coins the term "civil Islam", to explain religious transformations in contemporary Indonesia (Hefner 2000). Hefner's main emphasis is on what he sees as the "secularization" of Islam in Indonesia, or the Islamization of civil and public processes and structures—a phenomenon shared by Indonesia's neighbour, Malaysia. This inseparability of the religious and the secular in defining the public lives of Southeast Asian societies defy the dominant Eurocentric assumptions of a clear divide between the secular and the religious. Hence, while concepts such as "civil Islam" or "secularization" of religion may appear oxymoronic to dominant Eurocentric discourses, they represent a real public imaginary, practice, and category of the modern in Southeast Asian societies that do not conform and cannot be easily subsumed into any Western definition or category of the modern.

Finally, I turn to a group of studies that seek to denaturalize and historicize the contemporary formulations of the modern by showing how they are created from a complex intersection between colonial knowledge and their postcolonial effects. These studies are influenced by postcolonial criticism but seek to avoid the problem of an ultimate return of the power of Western imaginations and practices. Unsettling the debates on the coloniality of knowledge, these studies show that the renewed forms of colonial categories of race and culture in the postcolonial era need not only be understood in terms of their colonial but also postcolonial origins, especially in nationalist and local practices.[17] Abidin Kusno's study that seeks to highlight an active relationship between post-Independence architecture and colonial and postcolonial social effects in Indonesia is an example of this line of enquiry (Kusno 2000). Focusing on the histories and cultures of Indonesia, Kusno shows how the discourses of colonial architecture and urban planning continue to influence the politics of time and space in postcolonial Indonesia. In analysing the entwining of past and present, Kusno shows how the production of architecture and space is constituted by the cultural politics in erasing or reinserting colonial imaginaries among various groups of individuals and political and social reformers. Contrary to postcolonial assumptions that colonialism displaced local identities, Kusno's work demonstrates how colonial cultural frameworks become productive ground for the reworking and reproduction of new ideas of the modern in the postcolonial era. In addition, he observes that modern architectural discourses in Indonesia are not necessarily constructed vis-à-vis the West alone but are also produced in relation to other regional forces from the neighbouring countries of Southeast Asia. A volume edited by Aihwa Ong and Michael Peletz that explores the reworking of gender in Southeast Asian modernity has equally endorsed the need to uncover the webs of knowledge, power processes, and cultural politics created from the intersection between the ideologies of globalization, postcoloniality and nationalism (Ong and Peletz 1995). My recent study titled *Modern Dreams* exploring the particular conjecture of city, nation and modernity and the configurations of power and culture in contemporary Malaysia through an ethnographic study of a local conflict over urban redevelopment in the city of Georgetown, Penang, has also contributed to the debate on Southeast Asian modernity (Goh 2002). This study shows how the material and cultural dynamics in the local conflict are inseparable from the conditions under which the broader discourses of nation, ethnicity and class are generated, regimented and negotiated by institutional, spatial and everyday practices in contemporary Malaysia. The new cultural constructions of Malaysian modernity, as I show, incurred linkages with the colonial categories of nation and ethnicity but also generated new exclusionary and empowering practices that were played out from the highest bureaucratic levels to urban neighbourhoods and actively reconstituting urban culture and space. By locating agency and authority in new native and nationalist imaginations and their dialectical relationship with space, my study shows that binary relations can be shown to lose their distinctions as the colonial, global, local and national become entangled with one another constantly in new ways. Indeed, the coexistence and codependence of oppositions becomes the very grounds upon which differences are constructed within the modern Malaysian present.

Conclusion

From the above discussions we see that recent conceptualizations of modernity have redrawn a centre–periphery model so as to envision these relations as interconnected and dependent phenomena. This undermines a view of this relationship as hierarchical and unidirectional, making possible the conceptualization of the West and non-West, universal and particular as simultaneous and equal processes. The imperative to escape the teleological structures of the West in the interpretations of modernity lies in exposing the displacements found in both Western and non-Western experiences of the modern and locating autonomy to local meanings and practices across time and space. Recent studies of modernity, as we see, whether in the Western or non-Western contexts, have sought to uncover the specific cultural contexts and priorities and try to understand the ways in which modern forms and ideas are produced, imbued with local meanings, and contested in these societies. Implicated by these larger theoretical developments, recent studies have framed their inquiry into Southeast Asian modernity in terms of the contestations over the cultural and material orders of the West as well as about the constructions of difference within the modern present of local societies. In trying to understand Southeast Asian modernity in their own terms and with reference to their own priorities, these studies have revealed the interplay between specific historical and cultural contexts and the great range of modern forms and ideas thus generated and endowed with local, if not contested and different, meanings. By localizing struggles over power and meanings, the colonial, global, national and local can be shown to lose their distinct constituencies as they become entangled with one another in constantly new ways. Such local struggles within the intersection of the national, colonial, and global are precisely what makes contemporary Southeast Asian modernity fascinating, for they are the very spaces from which creative possibilities and meanings could emerge. The disruptions opened up by recent interrogations of Western and non-Western modernity and the ways in which these experiences are made to appear distinct under the aegis of various types of agency across time and space not only force a recognition of new modern imaginaries, practices and categories but also challenge us to think of how, now more than ever, the contemporary world offers occasions for a dialectical encounter between the West and non-West.

Notes

[1] See, for example, a recent volume edited by Leila Tarazi Fawaz and C.A. Bayly, *Modernity and Culture: From the Mediterranean to the Indian Ocean* (2002).

[2] Some examples are: James M. Blaut, 1999, *The Colonizer's Model of the World: Geographical Diffusionism and Eurocentric History*; Kenneth Pomeranz and Stevan Topik, eds., 1999, *The World that Trade Created: Culture, Society and the World Economy, 1400 to the Present*; Andre Gunder Frank, 1998, *Reorient: Global Economy in the Asian Age*.

³   For an elaborate discussion of the poststructuralist and postmodern critiques of the primacy of Western history and culture, see Robert Young, 1990, *White Mythologies: Writing History and the West*.

⁴   Some examples of postcolonial scholarship are: Ranajit Guha, 1997, *Dominance without Hegemony. History and Power in Colonial India*; Robert Young, 1995, *Colonial Desire: Hybridity in Theory, Culture and Race*; Gyan Prakash, 1992, "Writing Post-Orientalist Histories of the Third World: Indian Historiography Is Good to Think", in *Colonialism and Culture*, edited by Nicholas Dirks, pp. 66–104; Chandra Talpade Mohanty, 1995, "Under Western Eyes. Feminist Scholarship and Colonial Discourses", in *The Post-Colonial Reader*, edited by Bill Aschroft, Gareth Griffith and Helen Tiffin, pp. 259–63; Dipesh Chakrabarty, 1997, "Postcoloniality and the Artifice of History: Who Speaks for 'Indian' Pasts?", in *A Subaltern Studies Reader, 1986–1995*, edited by Ranajit Guha, pp. 263–94; Bart Moore-Gilbert, 1997, *Postcolonial Theory: Contexts, Practices, Politics*; and Anne McClintok, 1995, *Imperial Leather*.

⁵   Critiques of postcolonial theory are found in the following works: Ajiaz Ahmad, 1996, *Theory, Classes, Nations, Literature*; Sherry Ortner, 1996, "Resistance and the Problem of Ethnographic Refusal", in *The Historic Turn in the Human Sciences*, edited by Terrence J. McDonald, pp. 281–304; Nicholas Thomas, 1994, *Colonialism's Culture. Anthropology, Travel and Government*; Michael Hardt and Antonio Negri, 2000, *Empire*; and Anna Lowenhuapt Tsing, 1993, *In the Realm of the Diamond Queen: Marginality in an Out-of-the-Way Place*.

⁶   Classical conceptions posit modernity as a Western project or experience in which criticisms often come from either liberal or Marxist perspectives. Giddens, for instance, is one of the theorists of modernity who conceptualizes modernity as a 'Western' project and views capitalist modernity as a Western phenomenon before its expansion beyond the boundaries of the West (See Anthony Giddens, 1990, *Consequences of Modernity*). A neo-liberal critique of the Western experience of modernity is found in Marshall Berman's, 1983, *All that is Solid Melts into Air: The Experience of Modernity*. For a Marxist critique of Berman's analyses, see Perry Anderson, 1984, "Modernity and Revolution", in *New Left Review* 144 , pp. 16–113.

⁷   See Neil Lazarus, 1999, *Nationalism and Cultural Practice in the Postcolonial World*, p. 129.

⁸   Lila Abu-Lughod, 1998, *Remaking Women*, p. 18. Other studies that have taken on this approach are: Naoki Sakai, 1997, *Translation and Subjectivity: On 'Japan' and Cultural Nationalism*; Henrietta L. Moore, ed., 1996, *The Future of Anthropological Knowledge*; Aihwa Ong, 1996, "Anthropology, China and Modernities: The Geopolitics of Cultural Knowledge", in Moore, ibid., pp. 60–92; and Marilyn Ivy, 1995, *Discourses of the Vanishing: Modernity, Phantasm, Japan*.

[9]   Achille Mbembe, 2001, *On the Postcolony*, p. 14, his emphasis.

[10] For recent commentaries on state power in Southeast Asia, see Yao Souchou, ed., 2001, *House of Glass: Culture, Modernity, and the State in Southeast Asia*; C.J.W.-L Wee, 2002, *Local Cultures and "New Asia": The State, Culture, and Capitalism in Southeast Asia*; and Mary Margaret Steedly, 1999, "The State of Culture Theory in the Anthropology of Southeast Asia", in *Annual Review of Anthropology* 28, pp. 431–54.

[11] Adrian Vickers, 1996, p. 6, his emphasis.

[12] See Michael Pinches, ed., 1999, *Culture and Privilege in Capitalist Asia*; and Richard Robison and David Goodman, eds., 1996, *The New Rich in Asia: Mobile Phones, McDonalds and Middle-Class Revolution*; and Richard Tanter and Kenneth Young, eds., 1990, *The Politics of Middle Class Indonesia*.

[13] See volumes noted in the above footnote for debates on the rise and definitions of middle class.

[14] See Maila Stivens and Khrishna Sen, eds., 1998, *Gender and Power in Affluent Asia*; Alberto Gomes, ed., 1994, *Modernity and Identity: Asian Illustrations*; Joel S. Kahn and Loh Kok Wah, eds., 1992, *Fragmented Vision: Culture and Politics in Contemporary Malaysia*; and Joel S. Kahn, ed., 1998, *Southeast Asian Identities: Culture and the Politics of Representation in Indonesia, Malaysia, Singapore and Thailand*.

[15] For accounts of how gender and class have become important sites for the reworking of the modern in the Southeast Asian context, see Stivens and Sen, eds., 1998, *Gender and Power in Affluent Asia*; Aihwa Ong, 1990, "State versus Islam: Malay Families, Women's Bodies and the Body Politic in Malaysia", in *American Ethnologist* 17, no. 2, pp. 258–76; Laurie J. Sears, ed., 1996, *Fantasizing the Feminine in Indonesia*; and Saskia E. Wieringa, 1996, "Sexual Metaphors in the Change from Sukarno's Old Order to Suharto's New Order in Indonesia", Working Paper Series no. 23, The Hague Institute of Social Studies.

[16] The significant role of religion in the modernization process in Southeast Asia has long caught the attention of scholars. For an early volume, see Robert N. Bellah, 1965, *Religion and Progress in Modern Asia*.

[17] For an example, see Phyllis G.L. Chew and Anneliese Kramer-Dahl, eds., 1999, *Reading Culture: Textual Practices in Singapore*.

References

Abu-Lughod, Janet. 1989. *Before European Hegemony: The World System A.D. 1250–1350*, New York: Oxford University Press.

Abu-Lughod, Lila, ed. 1998. *Remaking Women: Feminism and Modernity in the Middle East*. Princeton, New Jersey: Princeton University Press.

Anderson, Benedict. 1991. *Imagined Communities: Reflections on the Origin and Spread of Nationalism*. Revised edition. New York: Verso.

Anderson, Perry. 1998. *The Origins of Postmodernity*. London and New York: Verso.

Ajiaz, Ahmad. 1992. *In Theory: Classes, Nations, Literatures*. London and New York: Verso.

Bellah, Robert N. 1965. *Religion and Progress in Modern Asia*. New York: The Free Press.

Bhabha, Homi. 1994. *The Location of Culture*. London and New York: Routledge.

Blaut, James M. 1993. *The Colonizer's Model of the World: Geographical Diffusionism and Eurocentric History*. New York: Guilford Press.

Chaudhuri, K.N. 1990. *Asia Before Europe: Economy and Civilisation of the Indian Ocean from the Rise of Islam to 1750*. New York: Cambridge University Press.

Chakrabarty, Dipesh. 1997. "Postcoloniality and the Artifice of History: Who Speaks for 'Indian' Pasts?" In *A Subaltern Studies Reader, 1986–1995*, edited by Ranajit Guha, pp. 263–94. Minneapolis and London: University of Minnesota Press.

Chew, Phyllis G.L. and Kramer-Dahl, Anneliese, eds. 1999. *Reading Culture: Textual Practices in Singapore*. Singapore: Times Academic Press.

Coronil, Fernando. 1997. *The Magical State: Nature, Money, and Modernity in Venezuela*. Chicago: University of Chicago Press.

Fawaz, Tarazi Leila and Bayly, C.A., eds. 2002. *Modernity and Culture: From the Mediterranean to the Indian Ocean*. New York: Columbia University Press, 2002.

Frank, Andre Gunder. 1998. *ReOrient: Global Economy in the Asian Age*. Berkeley: University of California Press.

Gilroy, Paul. 1993. *The Black Atlantic: Modernity and Double Consciousness*, Cambridge Massachusetts: Harvard University Press.

Goh Beng-Lan. 2002. *Modern Dreams: An Inquiry into Power, Cultural Production and the Cityscape in Contemporary Urban Penang*. Ithaca: Cornell Southeast Asia Program Publications.

Gomes, Alberto, ed. 1994. *Modernity and Identity: Asian Illustrations*. Bundoora, Victoria: La Trobe University Press.

Guha, Ranajit. 1997. *Dominance without Hegemony. History and Power in Colonial India*, Cambridge, Mass. and London: Harvard University Press.

Hardt, Michael and Negri, Antonio. 2000. *Empire*. Cambridge, Massachusetts: Harvard University Press, 2000.

Hefner, Robert W. 2000. *Civil Islam: Muslims and Democratization in Indonesia*. Princeton, New Jersey: Princeton University Press.

———. 1998. *Market Cultures: Society and Morality in the New Asian Capitalisms*. Boulder, Colorado: Westview Press.

Hefner, Robert W. and Horvatich, Patricia. 1997. *Islam in an Era of Nation-states: Politics and Religious Renewal in Muslim Southeast Asia*. Honolulu: University of Hawai'i Press.

Ivy, Marilyn. 1975. *Discourses of the Vanishing. Modernity, Phantasm, Japan*. Chicago: University of Chicago Press.

Jesudason, J. 1995. "Statist Democracy and the Limits to Civil Society in Malaysia". *Journal of Comparative and Commonwealth Politics* 33, no. 3: 333–56.

Kahn, Joel, ed. 1998. *Southeast Asian Identities: Culture and the Politics of Representation in Indonesia, Malaysia, Singapore and Thailand*. Singapore: Institute of Southeast Asian Studies.

Kahn, Joel S., and Loh Kok Wah, eds. 1992. *Fragmented Vision: Culture and Politics in Contemporary Malaysia*. Sydney: Allen & Unwin.

King, Anthony. 1990. *Global Cities: Post-Imperialism and the Internationalisation of London*. London and New York: Routledge.

Kusno, Abidin. 2000. *Behind the Postcolonial: Architecture, Urban Space and Political Cultures in Indonesia*. London: Routledge.

Lazarus, Neil. 1999. *Nationalism and Cultural Practice in the Postcolonial World*. Cambridge, Melbourne, and New York: Cambridge University Press.

Lach, Donald F. 1965. *Asia in the Making of Europe*. Chicago: University of Chicago Press.

McClintok, Anne. 1995. *Imperial Leather*. New York: Routledge.

Mignolo, Walter D. 2000. *Local Histories/Global Designs: Coloniality, Subaltern Knowledges, and Border Thinking*. Princeton, New Jersey: Princeton University Press.

Mitchell, Timothy. 1988. *Colonising Egypt*. Cambridge: Cambridge University Press.

Mohanty, Chandra Talpade. 1995. "Under Western Eyes. Feminist Scholarship and Colonial Discourses". In *The Post-Colonial Reader*, edited by Bill Aschroft, Gareth Griffiths and Helen Tiffin, pp. 259–63. London and New York: Routledge.

Moore-Gilbert, Bart. 1997. "Postcolonial Criticism or Postcolonial Theory?" In *Postcolonial Theory: Contexts, Practices, Politics*. London, New York: Verso.

Moore, Henrietta L. 1996. *The Future of Anthropological Knowledge*. London and New York: Routledge.

Ong, Aihwa. 1996. "Anthropology, China and Modernities: The Geopolitics of Cultural Knowledge." In *The Future of Anthropological Knowledge*, edited by Henrietta Moore, pp. 60–92. New York: Routledge.

———. 1990. "State versus Islam: Malay Families, Women's Bodies and the Body Politic in Malaysia". *American Ethnologist* 17, no. 2: 258–76.

Ong, Aihwa and Peletz, Michael G., eds. 1995. *Bewitching Women, Pious Men: Gender and Body Politics in Southeast Asia*. Berkeley: University of California Press.

Ortner, Sherry. 1996. "Resistance and the Problem of Ethnographic Refusal". In *The Historic Turn in the Human Sciences*, edited by Terrence J. McDonald. Ann Arbor: University of Michigan Press.

Picard, Michel. 1996. *Bali: Cultural Tourism and Touristic Culture*. Singapore: Archipelago Press.

————. 1997. "Cultural Tourism, Nation-Building, and Regional Culture: The Making of a Balinese Identity". In *Tourism, Ethnicity, and the State in Asian and Pacific Societies*, edited by Michel Picard and Robert E. Wood. Honolulu: University of Hawaii Press, pp. 181–214.

Pinches, Michael, ed. 1999. *Culture and Privilege in Capitalist Asia*. London: Routledge.

Pomeranz, Kenneth and Steven, Topik. 1999. *The World that Trade Created: Society, Culture, and the World Economy, 1400–the Present*. Armonk, N.Y.: M.E. Sharpe.

Prakash, Gyan. 1992. "Writing Post-Orientalist Histories of the Third World: Indian Historiography is Good to Think". In *Colonialism and Culture*, edited by Nicholas Dirks, pp. 389–90. Ann Arbor: University of Michigan Press.

Rabinow, Paul. 1989. *French Modern: Norms and Forms of the Social Environment*, Cambridge, Massachusetts and London: MIT Press.

Robison, Richard and David, Steven, eds. 1996. *The New Rich in Asia: Mobile Phones, McDonalds and Middle-Class Revolution*. London and New York: Routledge, 1996.

Said, Edward. 1991. *Orientalism*. London: Penguin Books.

Sakai, Naoki. 1997. *Translation and Subjectivity: On 'Japan' and Cultural Nationalism*. Minneapolis and London: University of Minnesota Press.

Sears, Laurie J., ed. 1996. *Fantasizing the Feminine in Indonesia*. Durham, NC: Duke University Press.

Siegel, James T. 1997. *Fetish, Recognition, Revolution*. Princeton, New Jersey: Princeton University Press.

Spivak, Gayatri. 1995. "Can the Subaltern Speak?" In *The Post-Colonial Studies Reader*, edited by Bill Aschroft, Gareth Griffiths, and Helen Tiffin. London and New York: Routledge, pp. 24–28.

Steedly, Mary Margaret. 1999. "The State of Culture Theory in the Anthropology of Southeast Asia". *Annual Review of Anthropology* 28: 431–54.

Stivens, Maila and Khrishna Sen, eds. 1998. *Gender and Power in Affluent Asia*. London: Routledge.

Stoler, Ann. 1992. *Race and the Education of Desire: Foucault's History of Sexuality and the Colonial Order of Things*. Durham and London: Duke University Press.

Tanter, Richard and Young, Kenneth, eds. 1990. *The Politics of Middle Class Indonesia*. Monash Papers on Southeast Asia no. 19, Clayton, Vic., Centre of Southeast Asian Studies.

Tonneson, Stein, and Hans Atlov, eds. 1996. *Asian Forms of the Nation*. Richmond, VA: Curzon Press.

Thomas, Nicholas. 1994. *Colonialism's Culture: Anthropology, Travel and Government*. Oxford: Polity Press.

Tsing, Anna Lowenhaupt. 1993. *In the Realm of the Diamond Queen: Marginality in an Out-of-the-way Place*. Princeton, New Jersey: Princeton University Press.

Vickers, Adrian, ed. 1996. *Being Modern in Bali: Image and Change*. Yale University Southeast Asian Studies Monograph 43. New Haven, CT: Yale University.

Wee, C.J.W.-L, ed. 2002. *Local Cultures and "New Asia": The State, Culture, and Capitalism in Southeast Asia*. Singapore: Institute of Southeast Asian Studies.

Wieringa, Saskia E. 1996. "Sexual Metaphors in the Change from Sukarno's Old Order to Suharto's New Order in Indonesia". Working Paper Series no. 23, The Hague Institute of Social Studies.

Wright, Gwendolyn. 1991. *The Politics of Design in French Colonial Urbanism*. Chicago: University of Chicago Press.

Yao Souchou, ed. 2001. *House of Glass: Culture, Modernity, and the State in Southeast Asia*. Singapore: Institute of Southeast Asian Studies.

Young, Robert. 1990. *White Mythologies: Writing History and the West*. London and New York: Routledge.

———. 1995. *Colonial Desire: Hybridity in Theory, Culture and Race*. London and New York: Routledge.

6

Rethinking Assumptions on Asia and Europe: The Study of Entrepreneurship

Mario Rutten

Characterizing Asian capitalists

For a long time, developments in South and Southeast Asia have inspired scholars to invent a terminology specific to the region because they believed that the processes studied did not seem to fit into the existing type of classification. Marx's 'Asiatic mode of production', Furnivall's 'plural society' and Boeke's 'dual economy' are perhaps the most well-known concepts that were conceived in colonial times to analyse South and Southeast Asian societies.[1] In the last few decades, several new concepts have been employed to analyse the present-day developments in South and Southeast Asia. The South Asian economy in general and that of India in particular has been characterized in terms of a 'semi-feudal mode of production' (Bhaduri 1973; Chandra 1974; Sau 1975), a 'semi-colonial semi-feudal mode of production' (Sen Gupta 1977), a 'dual mode of production' (Lin 1980), a 'constrained type of merchant capitalism' (Harriss 1981), an 'intermediate form of capitalist development' (Harriss 1982) and a socio-economic structure dominated by 'commercialism' (Van der Veen 1976; Streefkerk 1985).[2] The terms 'rent capitalism' (Fegan 1981), 'bureaucratic capitalism' (Robison 1986), 'statist capitalism' (Jomo 1988), 'dependent capitalism' and 'ersatz capitalism' (Yoshihara 1988) have been employed to analyse Southeast Asian economies, such as those of Indonesia, Malaysia and the Philippines.

What all these concepts have in common is the insistence that the characteristics of South and Southeast Asian developments are so specific that they merit a terminology specific to the region. The relations of production in these societies are held to be of a mixed nature. Capitalist and pre-capitalist relations of production are intertwined without any tendency of capitalist relations becoming more dominant. Merchant or financial capital is powerfully developed at the expense of productive capital; capital circulation instead of capital accumulation is the dominant tendency in South and Southeast Asia. Development of South and Southeast Asian capitalism has been largely confined to the tertiary sector: commerce, trade and services. The manufacturing sectors of the economy—agriculture and industry—have not been the driving force of economic growth in these countries. Development in South and Southeast Asia has not been the result of self-generating and self-sustaining autonomous economic growth, based on an open-market economy and fuelled by indigenous technology and serviced by indigenous skills. More than anything else, economic growth in South and Southeast Asia is considered to be a dependent type of development: dependent on foreign capital, foreign technology, distorted market mechanisms and a high level of government protection and state assistance.

One factor which is considered to be crucial in determining the nature of capitalist development in South and Southeast Asia has been the process by which the capitalist class emerges. Characterizations of the developments in South and Southeast Asia as a specific type of capitalism have therefore often been based on references to the characteristics of the capitalists operating in these countries. South and Southeast Asian capitalists are considered to be a specific type of capitalist because of the fact that they display a commercial orientation, follow a business strategy of economic diversification and do not directly apply capital to the production process in agriculture or industry itself but gain control of the claims on the product of others through the outlay of merchant or financial capital (Harriss 1981; Harriss 1982; Van der Veen 1976; Streefkerk 1985). Closely linked with these characteristics, South and Southeast Asian capitalists are termed a specific type of capitalists because of the fact that they are dependent on government finance and protection, and on foreign capital and technology. Their profits are not based on production but are in essence rent incomes that are the result of distorted market mechanisms following a high level of state intervention and regulations (Jomo 1988; Fegan 1981; Robison 1986; Yoshihara 1988).

At the core of these characterizations of the capitalist class in South and Southeast Asia often seems to lie a specific notion about the culture that underlies the economic behaviour of the Asian capitalists. The deformed nature of the capitalist class in Asia is sometimes thought to be the direct or indirect result of the existence of a specific Asian mentality. Beneath the terms used to characterize the specific nature of the Asian capitalists lies the implication of a specific business culture, one in which public and private interests mix effortlessly. Despite local variations, it is this business culture that runs through the region (Clad 1989, pp. 18 and 248). As part of this view, Asian capitalists are said to have a strong inclination to be consumption- rather than production-oriented. They are not inclined to reinvest their profits in productive activities but are notorious for squandering their profits on luxury consumer goods and demonstrative expenditure on social ceremonies, all of which enables them to maintain a lifestyle of leisure and consumption. In their economic behaviour they have a preference for skimming off quick profits made by others, instead of acquiring profits on the basis of productive investments. In their economic and social contacts, they cling to family relations and ethnic networks. To a large extent their economic decisions are not based solely on rational criteria, but are made with the purpose of enhancing their status within the community. In more general terms, it is usually

> thought that people in non-western societies are not prepared to make sacrifices now for the sake of future benefits. Behaviour directed toward the accumulation of goods or of capital is said to be lacking, the tendency being towards a way of life based on consumption. … (This) consumption orientation signifies little interest in saving, which is outweighed by the desire for present gratification.[3]

Following this line of reasoning with its emphasis on a business culture characterized by commercialism and dependency, it is often argued that the specific pseudo- or non-genuine nature of the South and Southeast Asian capitalists results from the fact that most of the capitalists operating in India, Indonesia, the Philippines and Malaysia today have a mercantile background and are often traders by origin. There have been doubts for a long time about the suitability of traders as industrialists. Many studies on Asia have emphasized that traders, given their stark profit motivation, cannot be considered a significant reservoir of industrial entrepreneurial recruits. They consider the production process as something fixed and static and are not prepared to invest more than the absolute minimum amount of capital in installations and machines. Ultimately, they remain committed to trade and quick turnover as the most important sources of profit. In all these respects, capitalists with a trading background are seen in contrast to true industrial entrepreneurs who are production-oriented, work within a long-term framework, are patient, tend to re-invest profits into industry, promote technological improvements, and are prepared to take risks.[4]

In sum, studies on South and Southeast Asia emphasize that socio-economic development in this part of Asia has been largely a constrained or deformed type of capitalist development. This conclusion is often based on references to the specific characteristics of the class of capitalists operating in these countries. More specifically, the existence of an autonomous, production-oriented class of industrial capitalists is mostly challenged by observers. The common view is that of a class of entrepreneurs who are commercially oriented and are heavily dependent on the government, foreign connections and biased regulations. Their behaviour and origin is generally thought to resemble that of the traditional dominant class of traders, who mobilize capital, organize labour and manage their enterprises along pre-capitalist lines of family and kinship. They are held to be notorious for dissipating their surpluses in conspicuous consumption and rarely make productive reinvestments of their profits but involve themselves, successively and simultaneously, in a wide range of disparate agricultural, commercial, and industrial activities.

Because of these characteristics, capitalist entrepreneurs in South and Southeast Asia are thought to be a specific type of capitalists, indicated by the use of a specific terminology, such as 'commercially oriented capitalists', 'merchant capitalists', 'dependent capitalists', 'bureaucratic capitalists', 'comprador capitalists', 'statist-capitalists' and 'rent capitalists'. What all these terms have in common is disapproval of the economic and social behaviour of the present-day rich farmers, traders and industrialists in South and Southeast Asia. More than a specific type of capitalist class, the class of capitalists in South and Southeast is generally assumed to be a deformed, a pseudo- or non-genuine type of capitalist class.

'Asian' assumptions about the early European industrialists
Underlying this common view of the capitalist class in South and Southeast Asia is the assumption that, either at present or in the past, either in Asia or in another part of the world, there once existed a class of pure, genuine and true capitalists. Without actually referring to the European path of industrial transition, it is this path and its generation of a class of industrial capitalists that is frequently invoked as a paradigm for the behaviour of South and Southeast Asian capitalists today. It is generally assumed that the early European industrialists, i.e. those entrepreneurs who operated in Europe at the time of the Industrial Revolution—mid-eighteenth to the mid/late-nineteenth century[5]—were true and genuine capitalists, unlike present-day South and Southeast Asian entrepreneurs.

I name these assumptions about the early European industrialists that underlie studies on Asian societies, 'Asian' assumptions. By 'Asian' assumptions I mean assumptions that underlie Asian Studies, more in particularly studies in which references are made to the class of Asian capitalists. 'Asian' therefore includes both the studies on Asia by Asian scholars and by non-Asian, mostly Western, scholars.

The 'Asian' assumptions about the early European industrialists are not invented, but often have their origin in notions that can be traced back in part to debates among European historians about the nature of the Industrial Revolution in general and the emergence of the early European industrialists in particular. Central to the 'Asian' notion of the Industrial Revolution is the idea that this period in European history has to be characterized, first and foremost, as a radical and sudden transformation of society. In this view, the changes that took place in Europe between the mid-eighteenth and the mid/late-nineteenth century were sweeping changes which signified a break with the past in many aspects of economic life. Two of the essential features of this radical and sudden transformation are generally thought to have been the emergence of a new production system, the factory, and the rise of a new producer, the industrialist.

The emergence of the factory-based production system arose from the demise of the putting-out and domestic system which had been the dominant forms of production before the Industrial Revolution. The characteristic feature of the putting-out and domestic system was that production took place in small household establishments and domestic workshops, basically a combination of domestic work and commercial capitalism. At the top were rich men who were given various names by contemporaries, but who are generally described by historians as "merchant-manufacturers". They either placed orders with master craftsmen in provincial towns, who then produced the desired goods in small-scale domestic workshops, or brought in the raw materials which they distributed to peasant-workers to process in their own cottages, often using simple machines (Wolf 1982, p. 270). Basically, the merchant-manufacturer was a merchant, a trader, not an industrialist; he was an organizer of production and its financing, not a producer (Crouzet 1985, pp. 5–6).

Commencing in the mid-eighteenth century, factory-based production is generally held to have become the dominant system of production in Britain. What was new about this factory-based system was the concentration of production in organizations under unified technical management and ownership, the employment of labourers, and the widespread introduction of technological inventions, especially of power-driven machinery (Wolf 1982, p. 274). A vital component was the increase in fixed capital at an unprecedented scale. From being commercial capital, a preponderant amount of capital became industrial, and from being floating and circulating capital, it increasingly became fixed capital, mainly as a result of the development of machinery, especially steam power (Crouzet 1972a, p. 39).

The introduction of this new way of organizing production was established by a new type of businessman, the industrialist, who at the end of the eighteenth century was beginning to emerge in his own right and in growing numbers. This new businessman is generally considered to have differed from the old type of merchant-manufacturer in many ways. Compared to the interests of the latter, production lay at the centre of the industrialist's work, and not at its periphery. Instead of dealing largely in liquid resources, as was typical for the merchant-manufacturers, the industrialists are thought to have created great deposits of fixed capital and re-embodied them in the product over time. They short-circuited and eventually eliminated the various intermediaries (Crouzet 1985, p. 9). They organized production, brought together capital and the labour force, selected the most appropriate site for operations, chose the particular technologies of production to be employed, devised new combinations of factors of production, were sometimes even innovators who initiated decisive economic change by breaking away from the constant trend towards equilibrium, bargained for raw materials, and found outlets for the finished product (Payne 1974, p. 14).

Who were these new and complete businessmen, these first industrialists? Where did they come from and where did they acquire their capital to start their industrial enterprises?

Central to the 'Asian' notion of the early European industrialists is that these industrialists did not belong to the category of merchants or merchant-manufacturers. There are some indications that, in the early eighteenth century, large traders who had earned money from the international trade had invested some capital in industry. Central to the 'Asian' notion, however, is that on the whole, rich merchants and merchant-manufacturers in Europe are thought to have rarely invested the profits of their mercantile or putting-out ventures in industry; it was still rarer for them to be active partners in industrial firms (Crouzet 1985, pp. 8, 100).

This 'Asian' notion that the early industrialists in Europe did not originate from the ranks of the merchants or merchant-manufacturers follows Marx's description of the second road to capitalism according to which a section of the existing merchant class began to 'take possession directly of production', thereby 'serving historically as a mode of transition', but becoming eventually 'an obstacle to a real capitalist mode of production and declin(ing) with the development of the latter.'[6] This view has been extended by Maurice Dobb who emphasizes that even though in the early days of the Industrial Revolution certain sections of merchant capital did turn towards industry and began to control production, at most they may have prepared the way for capitalist industrialization, and may in a few cases have reached it, but they did not bring about any thorough transformation (Dobb 1976, p. 161).

Following this line of thought, the instigators of the Industrial Revolution in Europe are thought to have originated from those social strata which had so far played a less prominent role in economic life: the class of independent, self-sustaining yeoman farmers and small and middle-scale craftsmen. This notion owes a great deal to Maurice Dobb's study in which he argued that it had been Marx's first road to capitalism which had been the dominant way in which the transition from feudalism to capitalism in Europe took place.[7] According to this 'really revolutionary way', a section of the rural and urban producers themselves had accumulated capital and had taken to trade, and in time had begun to organize production on a capitalist basis, free from the handicraft restrictions of the guilds. It is from the social stratum of independent, self-sustaining peasant-kulaks and small and middle-scale craftsmen that the early European industrialists are usually held to have originated. Being 'new' men, who did not originate from the classes that dominated the old social structure, these new producer-capitalists had every interest in dismantling the various barriers and guild privileges that were part and parcel of the traditional domestic and putting-out system of production (Dobb 1976, pp. 277–78).

This idea of the 'common' origin of the early European industrialists, as defended most prominently by Maurice Dobb, is closely connected to a more general belief that the chief agents of productivity in the early stage of European industrial development were mostly self-made men. It is this belief of the 'self-made man' who sprang from a 'humble origin' among peasant-kulaks and craftsmen which has strongly influenced 'Asian' notions about the early European industrialists, that is, that they were independent businessmen. Whatever profits they accrued were the fruits of their own hard work. There was no government assistance; all of them had to survive in an open, free market economy characterized by fierce competition (Crouzet 1985, p. 37).

Bearing in mind the putative humble origins of the first industrialists and the fact that the introduction of the factory system is thought to have required large concentrations of fixed capital, it is therefore generally assumed that "capital had been a serious problem during the industrial revolution, and that innovators and entrepreneurs had been hampered by its scarcity" (Crouzet 1972a, p. 4). However, "of serious shortage of capital we hear strangely little" (Wilson 1972, pp. 391–92). Presumably a business was launched with the savings of the industrialist himself and grew by the assiduous plough-back of profits (Campbell and Wilson 1975, p. 15). And indeed, "it has often been said that the early industrialists ploughed back their profits into their busines" (Heaton 1972, p. 419).

This way of financing industry through ploughing back profits was possible because of the unremitting thrift these industrialists are said to have widely practised as part of an overall sober lifestyle (Crouzet 1972b, p. 188). This practice of taking but a small part of the profits for their personal needs and leaving the remainder to accumulate in the business led to constant reinvestment and to a rapid growth of capital.[8] Establishing and expanding an industrial enterprise by saving out of income has frequently been regarded as the only form that accumulation can take, or at least the only form it took during the Industrial Revolution (Dobb 1976, p. 179).

This frugal living and saving behaviour of the first industrialists is considered to be the result of a pattern of deferred gratification, which may be defined as "…readiness to forgo present gratification in order to attain greater gratification of the same or another need at a later date" (Breman 1969, p. 15). This method of industrial expansion through saving and reinvestment, although in the first instance imposed by necessity, is said to have quickly acquired a virtue of its own in the minds of these early European industrial entrepreneurs (Kemp 1985, p. 20).

Fine virtues though they may be, frugality and saving did not automatically lead to increased production. The regular reproduction of capital by the early European industrialists, involving the continual investment and reinvestment of capital for economic efficiency, is therefore usually not associated with specific saving and frugal behaviour but with an overall attitude among the members of this class. Characteristic of this overall outlook, this very specific kind of ethic is the continual accumulation of wealth for its own sake, rather than for material rewards. Weber claims that it is this combination of a work drive and sober living that is the essence of the spirit of modern capitalism (Weber 1976, p. 172).

It is this capitalist spirit that is usually associated with the early European industrialists. Even though it was part of an overall ethic among the bourgeoisie of that time (Stearns 1975, p. 47), its exemplary protagonists are said to have been present among those who initiated the process of industrial growth in Europe.

It was Weber who considered that underlying this spirit of capitalism was religion: the Protestant ethic, that is the desire to acquire property not for enjoyment but for augmentation in the service of God and as a sign of His blessing (Weber 1976, p. 172). Although he emphasized that "...we have no intention whatever of maintaining such a foolish and doctrinaire thesis as that the spirit of capitalism...could only have arisen as the result of certain effects of the Reformation, or even that capitalism as an economic system is a creation of the Reformation" (Weber 1976, p. 91), religion is often considered to have been of importance in stimulating deferred gratification among the early European industrialists (Crouzet 1972b, pp. 188–89).

In a nutshell, 'Asian' assumptions about the early European industrialists consist of the following characterizations. Industrial growth in Europe was set in motion by a specific type of industrialist who had a peasant-kulak/yeoman or craftsman/artisan background and a single-minded devotion to his business. For him, it was not the process of circulation that was the decisive factor but it was the production process that lay at the centre of his activity and concern. Instead of following a policy of diversification like the merchant-manufacturers earlier, the early industrialist pursued a strategy of capitalization with resolute consistency by focusing all his energy on developing and expanding his business. He possessed a strong work ethos and practised a stringent personal economy and an austere lifestyle. He reinvested the results of his labour ethos and his sober way of life by expanding production and realizing continuous technological improvements. His behaviour was identical to the pursuit of profit, forever renewed profit, by means of continuous reinvestments of his surplus through expanding and improving production, all of this with no other purpose than to generate more surplus on an ever-expanding scale.

The early European industrialists

To what extent is this portrayal of the early European industrialists, on which the 'Asian' assumptions are based, a valid characterization? At the risk of stating the obvious, it is important to emphasize that such characterizations basically ignore the possibility of diversity. Findings gleaned from economic historical studies show, for example, that this characterization of the early European industrialists is not a true representation of the first industrialists in France, nor is it a true representation of all the categories of early industrialists in Britain. Several economic historical studies on France point out that the first French industrialists—i.e. those operating between ca. 1815 and 1870—have to be characterized as conservative and consumption-oriented industrialists who were more intent in enjoying their wealth, power, and prestige, than in pushing up the indices of production.[9] With rare exceptions, French enterprise was organized on a family of basis, mainly restricting its clientele to an intimate circle of friends and relatives. The French businessman was considered to have been insufficiently enterprising, preferring security behind tariff walls and seeking support from the state rather than investing in modern techniques and pushing into new markets (Landes 1972, pp. 400–406; Kemp 1985, pp. 60–69).

Similarly, economic histories of Britain point at the entrepreneurial failings of the second and third generation industrialists in Britain who operated at the end of the nineteenth century.[10] They emphasize the waning of the entrepreneurial energies of the founders' descendants for whom the industrial enterprise ceased to be an end itself and increasingly became a means for earning money to support a luxurious lifestyle. With the members of the family more actively pursuing their own interests outside industry, many of the industrial firms were gradually allowed to run down. This overall 'decline of the industrial spirit' in the later nineteenth century was caused, in part at least, by the fact that many of the industrial entrepreneurs were too busy becoming gentlemen, living and spending on a lavish scale (Coleman 1973, p. 97). They were often held to have been more focused on spending their wealth than on earning money through productive activities (Kemp 1985, p. 175).

These views on the first industrialists in France and the second/third generation industrialists in Britain do to a large extent give a stereotyped picture of their behaviour. Economic history with regard to the industrial revolution in France and with regard to the late nineteenth-century industrialization in Britain has gone through a process of renewal and reappraisal.[11] Here it is enough to emphasize that these views, despite their stereotyped nature, point to the possibility of diversity among the early European industrialists. They indicate that the 'Asian' assumptions about the early European industrialists have to be questioned for at least these two categories of early industrialists in Western Europe, one of them operating in Britain, the country that was the first in the world to industrialize. Following this, the test case of the 'Asian' assumptions about the early European industrialists seems to be the first industrialists in Britain, operating between the mid-eighteenth and mid-nineteenth centuries. These industrialists belonged to the very first industrialists in the world and are therefore considered to be the classic case of the emergence of a class of industrial capitalists.[12]

Before I discuss the findings of various historical studies on these first industrialists operating in Britain at the time of the Industrial Revolution, it is important to emphasize that this field of study is still blighted by a lack of detailed research at the factory level and of reliable quantitative data on the origin and nature of the industrial entrepreneurs.[13] On top of this problem of data scarcity and unreliability of the data used, many studies turn out to be based on biased samples.[14] This in itself should make us suspicious of the validity of the 'Asian' assumptions about the origins and behaviour of the early European industrialists, as presented in the previous section. This suspicion increases when we take a closer look at the findings of the economic historical studies on each of the various aspects of the origin and behaviour of the first British industrialists. In this overview, I do not pretend to give the subject an exhaustive treatment but focus only on those aspects of the emergence of the first industrialists in Britain that are important to understanding the discussion on the nature of the capitalist class in South and Southeast Asia today.

In contrast to the notion of the Industrial Revolution as a radical and sudden transformation of society, recent research and analysis support the view that industrialization in Britain was a gradual process during the classic industrial revolution period (Cameron 1985, pp. 2–9; and O'Brien 1986, p. 294). This being so the inescapable conclusion has to be that business organizations and procedures prevalent in the pre-industrial persisted into the industrial economy where they co-existed with other forms (Chapman 1973, pp. 123–24; Goodman and Honeyman 1988, p. 208).

Furthermore, recent insights into the history of technology of the eighteenth and nineteenth centuries challenge the view of rapid and universal technical change embodied in conventional notions of the Industrial Revolution. The substitution of machinery for labour, which is an essential feature of the Industrial Revolution concept, was an equally uneven and protracted process, as was the introduction of the factory organization (Goodman and Honeyman 1988, pp. 205–6, Coleman 1973, p. 103; Stearns 1975, p. 84; O'Brien 1986, p. 294). It is equally unlikely that the early stages of industrialization required such a hefty leap in investment as has sometimes been supposed. Capital requirements by the factory entrepreneurs were similar to those of the existing merchant-manufacturers; a relatively small proportion of their capital needed to be laid out in fixed plant and machinery (Kemp 1985, pp. 18–20; Crouzet 1972b, pp. 164–65). There is evidence too that many of the first industrialists used various capital economizing devices to escape large outlays of fixed capital (Heaton 1972, pp. 414–15; Crouzet 1972a, p. 38).

Payne argues that only a handful of the major pioneers of the Industrial Revolution would therefore apparently qualify as innovative and genuine entrepreneurs, while the vast majority of such businessmen appear to have been imitative (Payne 1974, pp. 13–16 and 34–45). The nature of the growth pattern was often conservative, being frequently characterized by sheer multiplication of existing plants and processes producing a fairly limited range of related products. Many small industrialists during the mid-nineteenth century did not even want to grow because they wanted to remain independent entrepreneurs who could run their enterprises all by themselves. They were able to make comfortable profits, which strengthened their resolve not to increase the scale of their operation beyond the size which would have involved partially entrusting their businesses to managers recruited from outside the family circle. All this made possible the continued existence of numerous small, often weakly financed family concerns, many of whom chose to specialize in the exploitation of only a limited portion of the full spectrum of demand for related products (Crouzet 1985).

Instability in production was a common phenomenon among the first industrialists in Britain. The mortality rates for these firms were high; getting started was relatively easy, but staying in business turned out to be much harder. Many bitter individual failures occurred, particularly during the early decades of the nineteenth century, when many new firms were established (Stearns 1975, p. 89). Instability was also common in the organization structure among these first industrialists. Many firms were partnerships, often small, family-linked partnerships. A characteristic feature of these partnerships was

> their rapid turnover, the frequent changes among their members; partnerships were unceasingly created, supplemented, terminated. Indeed, their death rate was high; many factories or works had a chequered history and changed hands at frequent intervals, while many industrialists

moved from mill to mill—several times in some cases—during their career (Crouzet 1985, p. 59).

All the evidence points to the fact that plurality of interests was common among the entrepreneurs of the Industrial Revolution. It has been pointed out that, especially in the eighteenth century, men of capital were frequently interested in several enterprises of different kinds. Many of the richer industrialists were as it were *brasseurs d'affairs*— rich people who had their fingers in several different pies, who were simultaneously involved in, say, trade, banking, landowning, mining, and industry (Crouzet 1972a, pp. 54–55; 1985, p. 63; and Jones 1974b, p. 161).

Following this brief description of the economic behaviour of these first industrialists in Britain, there is a common question which must be asked about these men: where did they come from and from where did they obtain their capital? Following Maurice Dobb's view, derived from Marx, the really revolutionary transformation of production and the breaking of the control of merchant capital over production was accomplished by men coming from the ranks of former craftsmen. Some of the first industrialists were indeed craftsmen who had assumed the role of manager and owner of the means of production by investing their capital in the employment of other smaller craftsmen (Crouzet 1985, p. 31). Undeniably the class of artisans was the breeding-ground for several famous machine-makers, including the greatest of them, James Watt, who was an instrument-maker before becoming interested in steam engines. On the whole, however, the rise among the craftsmen of a richer, capitalist element did not take place on a large scale.[15]

It now seems that the role of merchant-traders in the formation of the industrialist class is not as negligible as has often been maintained.[16] Their initiative in industrial investment did not come from foreign trading companies, but lay with humbler provincial middle bourgeoisie, who were less privileged and wealthy but more broadly based (Dobb 1976, p. 193; and Wolf 1982, pp. 271–72). Though important, this category of traders was clearly surpassed by businessmen who were already engaged in industry, i.e. by manufacturers or merchant-manufacturers in domestic production, and owners and managers of already centralized establishments.[17] Pertinently, many businessmen played the dual roles of merchant-trader and merchant-manufacturer simultaneously (Crouzet 1985, p. 54). By the end of the eighteenth century, many merchants gained absolute control over production by becoming manufacturers themselves. As a result, merchant and manufacturer were often one and the same person (Wilson 1972, p. 383).

A large amount of data has been collected about the financing of industrial enterprises, both at the time of their foundation and during their expansion. The idea that many, if not most, industrialists were self-made men—which was a popular view during the nineteenth century—was exposed as a myth by twentieth century economic and social historians. The number of industrialists even in the Industrial Revolution who began without capital or connections of any kind was a minute fraction of the whole (Crouzet 1985, pp. 50–51). In many enterprises, capital from diverse sources was used. Small partnerships were common, usually consisting of a group of relatives or friends, though sometimes a stranger was admitted as a sleeping partner (Payne 1974, pp. 18–19; Heaton 1972, pp. 416–17). Most firms were started with initial capital which had been accumulated through pre-factory system manufacturing or merchant-manufacturing activities, or through the trading of industrial raw materials or finished articles (Heaton 1972, pp. 416–17; Crouzet 1972b, p. 170).

There can no longer be any doubt that the founders of factory industries obtained capital from diverse sources, but that these sources were of unequal importance; industry itself supplied most of the capital for its own transformation, while commerce provided an important supplementary reservoir. The part played by bank capital seems to have been very small (Crouzet 1972b, pp. 182–3; and Heaton 1972, pp. 416–17).

Overall therefore, external supplies of capital were "less important than the personal or family funds which the industrialists scraped together and ventured in the new productive equipment. The power of heredity and the vitality of the family as an economic group stand out whenever we examine the history of the pioneer manufacturers" (Heaton 1972, pp. 416–17). In order to expand, the pioneer 'firms usually borrowed—on mortgage, bond or note of hand—from family and friends, solicitors and attorneys (or through their agency), or from other manufacturers or merchants with whom they had connexions" (Crouzet 1972b, p. 191). Payne shows that 'although the firms that were limited were by far the most important in their spheres of activity, judged by size of unit and amount of fixed capital, the vast majority of the manufacturing firms of the country continued to be family businesses in the mid-1880s' (Payne 1974, pp. 18–19). He even suggests that "...the over-representation of non-conformists among the *entrepreneurs who attained prominence* may be explicable not in terms of their religious precepts, their superior education or their need for achievement, but because they belonged to extended kinship families that gave them access to credit which permitted their firms, and their records, to survive, while others, less well connected, went to the wall" (ibid, p. 26).

Taken together, these economic historical studies reveal the variety of the sources of capital which had been used for establishment, the resorting by the first industrialists to the resources of their relatives and friends, on a personal basis, and the movement of capital between various branches of industry. In spite of all these financial sources, it is often emphasized that what permitted the Industrial Revolution to proceed at a relatively swift pace was the fact that enterprises increased their capital by ploughing back the greater part, or even the whole, of their profits immediately, regularly, and almost automatically. Entrepreneurs who operated at the inception of the Industrial Revolution are said to have immediately reinvested most of their profits (and even the interest on capital) in order to finance expansion.

It is probably true that this state of affairs enabled a number of enterprises—possibly most of them—to finance expansion entirely from their own sources (Crouzet 1972b, pp. 190–95). However, although there is every reason to believe that most of the additional capital required for expansion was indeed provided from the savings of the industrialists, this does not necessarily imply abstemious frugality and unremitting thrift as part of an overall sober lifestyle on the part of the industrialist's family. In the first industrial period, many industrialists did indeed live relatively simple: they resided close to their works, often in an adjacent house; the daily tour of the various departments was part of their way of life; they spent long hours at work, twelve or more a day, and closely supervised everything which went on in their factories. However, "once they had built up their businesses and secured their fortunes, they nearly always relaxed somewhat, withdrawing more money and adopting a more comfortable way of life. Some of them bought landed estates and built themselves large mansions" (Crouzet 1972b, p. 189). We must therefore not over-emphasize the frugality of these early industrialists. They were conscious of the need to save money, for this was the source of investment funds, but they also quickly espoused new pleasures in the guise of consumers (Heaton 1972, p. 421). They were eager to acquire a new standard of living and slowly began to separate themselves from the rest of the middle class. More and more successful business families sent their sons to public schools and many of them bought large mansions in which they employed servants and pursued a lifestyle of luxury and conspicuous consumption (see e.g. Jones 1974b, pp. 179–81).

During the first phase of European industrialization, the "status of many families which produced industrialists was rather low, and even when they had made fortunes, industrialists were heartily despised by the traditional ruling class for their low birth and bad manners, and for decades they remained beyond the pale of 'gentle' society" (Crouzet 1985, p 142). In England, social standing depended to a greater extent than elsewhere on the ownership of landed property (Habakkuk 1953, pp. 15–16). The purchase of landed estates by the first industrialists was therefore part of a widespread emulation of aristocratic lifestyles by the wealthier sections of the entrepreneurial class (Jones 1974b, pp. 160–62).

New aspirants to the landed gentry came from many industries, sometimes acquiring land by marrying into this class or even from time to time into the aristocracy, more often by straightforward purchase. It is evident from the terms of the marriage settlements between aristocrats and bourgeois heiresses that considerable material gains were necessary to induce the great families to contract them (Habakkuk 1953, pp. 18–9). Those industrialists who entered county society through the purchase of land wanted to seal their new status by reaching new heights of splendour in their residences, extensive landscaping of their park, and projects for improvements on their farms (Jones 1974b, pp. 162–78).

The ultimate industrial consequences of this draining of capital are hard to assess. The opportunity costs of land purchases were high and economic growth could surely have come faster without them. While part of the fortunes made in industry did leak into landownership and into a conspicuous lifestyle, from the commonsense point of view it appears that since manufacturing did expand, the counter-attractions of wealth and rural life may have retarded but could not block industrialization (Jones 1974a, pp. 105–6; and 1974b, pp. 179–81). Continuous investment and reinvestment in industry by these early industrialists therefore did coincide very well with an increase in wealth and conspicuous consumption.

There seems to be little doubt that social ambition provided an immensely powerful motor of business activity at the time of the industrial revolution. The pursuit of wealth was the pursuit of social status, not merely for oneself but for one's family, and this often meant the acquisition of a landed estate or the purchase or building of a great house. Coleman therefore argues that "no more then than today was the maximisation of profits an end; it neither was, nor is today, the only means employed. ...The ends are more intangible and varied: profits are a path to prestige, power, status, personal satisfaction, adventures made, purpose and achievements gained" (Coleman 1973, pp. 95–96).

The foregoing social and economic profile of the early industrial entrepreneurs clearly indicates that many of them were drawn from exactly the same class as before. The new industrial changes in late eighteenth-century Britain were linked organically and personally to an older economic world at every stage (Wilson 1972, p. 379). Only to some extent was the industrialist who emerged during the Industrial Revolution a new man. Continuity rather than discontinuity was the rule. Many of the first industrialists in Britain originated from the traditional dominant class of traders and merchant-manufacturers, who followed a strategy of diversification of their economic and social interests along with expanding their industrial affairs. Guided by a short-time horizon, these industrialists often did not reinvest their profits in the same enterprise but were notoriously quick to spread their risk by investing in different types of economic activities, either simultaneously or successively. Mobilization of capital and organization of the work was often done along the traditional, pre-capitalist lines of family and kinship. Although many of the first industrialists in Britain followed a lifestyle of frugality and sobriety, for many others investments of capital in their economic undertakings coincided with a lifestyle of luxury and consumption.

Asian Studies and European History

It is generally assumed that the emergence of the capitalist class in South and Southeast Asia is a historically unique phenomenon and the factors leading to it are so specific that they cannot be compared with the rise of the early industrialists in Europe. Any comparison of current industrialization in South and Southeast Asia with the European path to industrial transition is often regarded as historical determinism and therefore rejected.[18] To a large extent, this is of course correct. History does not repeat itself mechanically. A nineteenth-century pattern of development could hardly be repeated in detail today. All processes of change have their own prerequisites, which will differ from country to country and from one time to another. That the emergence of a capitalist class in South and Southeast Asia would be an exact duplicate of the rise of the class of industrial capitalists in eighteenth- and nineteenth-century Europe is of course ridiculous and should indeed be rejected out of hand.

Having accepted this, there is some danger in arguing that every comparison of the emergence of the capitalist class in South and Southeast Asia with the rise of the class of industrial capitalists in Europe is always to be regarded as historical determinism and therefore to be avoided under all circumstances. The rejection of general theoretical models for comparative study after the 1970s led to a concentration of research on Asia in its own right. The subsequent trend has been to emphasize the cultural uniqueness of business organization in different contexts, as seen for example in the literature on Indian business communities and Chinese business networks. Cogently, the terminology employed to characterize the class of present-day capitalists in South and Southeast Asia shows that this has not prevented comparisons with their European counterparts from taking place, but has 'forced' these comparisons to get below the surface and thereby to become unverifiable. As a result, most references to the pseudo- or non-genuine capitalist nature of the present-day South and Southeast Asian entrepreneurs are based on assumptions about the origins and nature of European industrialists of which the validity is seldom questioned. Viewing the persistence and value attached to these characterizations, it is important that these assumptions are made explicit and are tested on their tenability.

Economic historical studies on the early European industrialists, as discussed in this chapter, show that most of the 'Asian' assumptions about the European industrialists are not tenable, not even for the 'classic case' of the first industrialists in Britain. They point out that, because of lack of detailed factory-level research and reliable quantitative data, little can be said with certainty about their origins and nature. This in itself casts doubt about the validity of 'Asian' assumptions about the early European industrialists. The economic history of the first industrialists in Britain, as they were presented in the foregoing section, shows that these 'Asian' assumptions are based on a stereotyped model and present us with a distorted view of the emergence of the class of industrial capitalists in Europe.

These 'Asian' assumptions/myths about the emergence of the class of industrial capitalists in Europe have already often been challenged and invalidated by European economic historians for quite some time. In his study on *British Entrepreneurship in the Nineteenth Century*, published in 1974, P.L. Payne, for example, argues that the pioneer industrialists do not fully deserve the notion of high quality of entrepreneurial performance that is usually attached to them. Based on an overview of the studies available at that time, he questions the assumption that drive and dynamism were characteristic features of the British entrepreneurs of the Industrial Revolution (Payne 1974, pp. 30–31).

It is a curious fact that studies which have contributed so much to a revision of myths regarding the history of South and Southeast Asia have seldom made use of new insights by European economic historians to question their own view of the origins and nature of the class of European industrialists against which they have characterized the present-day capitalist class in Asia as being deformed, pseudo, or non-genuine. The fact that scholars studying Asian society do not question their assumptions about Western society, is not simply a matter of ignorance, but more an ideological choice, as argued by Heather Sutherland (1993). She emphasizes that the common view of Asian 'economic backwardness' as being rooted in the failure of Asian societies to maintain the 'proper' distinctions between political and economic spheres is based on ideological misreadings of European history. Her conclusion that "all too often, our ideas of the past are dominated by an idea of 'progress', derived from simplified myths about European industrialisation and growth" could equally well apply to our ideas of the present: "While recent research has modified our views of those sturdy entrepreneurs who set us happily upon the right path, the comforting folk-tales still lurk in our memories and influence our assumptions" (Sutherland 1993, p. 11).

It is this simplified image and lack of historical perspective regarding the roots of European capitalism that has enabled scholars studying Asian society to conclude that South and Southeast Asian industrialization seems to merit a terminology specific to the region. Based on an unchallenged, stereotyped impression of the behaviour of the early European industrialists, who are characterized as true and genuine capitalists, it is relatively easy, but highly questionable, to argue that the present-day South and Southeast Asian industrialists should be characterized as a class of pseudo-capitalists.

Moreover, our evaluation of the specific characteristics of Asian entrepreneurs has undergone several changes over time. In the 1960s and 1970s entrepreneurial characteristics of personalized management, economic diversification, collectivism, familism, close state–business relations, and an emphasis on social status, were soundly criticized by both Western and Asian scholars and policy-makers who considered them to be one of the main causes of Asia's backwardness. These critics argued that impersonal management practices, individualism, open competition, and frugality, were the only ways to compete successfully in the modern world economy. Following the rise of East and Southeast Asian economies, this notion was widely challenged in the 1980s and 1990s. It was then argued that the personalized management practices in diversified enteprises, collective forms of business organization along traditional lines, close state–business relations, and an emphasis on social status, have all been crucial factors in bringing about 'the Asian miracle'. More recently, this view has been challenged again. The Asian crisis of 1997 seemed to have set the stage for a return to the earlier notion that the specific characteristics of Asian businessmen are responsible for the lack of economic progress in the region. In these analyses, the origin of the Asian crisis lies in the inability of Asian businessmen to practise impersonal management styles, to confine themselves to one line of business, to operate independently of others and within a free market economy with minimum government intervention, and to delay consumption expenditures by making sacrifices now for the sake of future benefits.

These fluctuating views on the behaviour of Asian entrepreneurs again underline the need to develop a theoretical model for the comparative study of regional business classes that can help to explain similarities and differences in their practices and characteristics that is not arbitrarily based on a Western or Eastern model of economic behaviour. Now that a significant body of knowledge about economic development in Asia has been produced, the time has come to look again at European history and contemporary developments, employing insights gained from the Asian experience, and also for experts on Europe to look at the Asian examples. Such a comparative analysis needs to take into account the wide diversity in forms of business organization and entrepreneurship within and between Asia and Europe, and should look for the conditions that promote or inhibit the growth of industrial entrepreneurship and investment without relying on Eurocentric stereotypes of entrepreneurial behaviour. Therefore, one aim of comparative analysis should be to describe and account for various forms of entrepreneurship without resorting to stereotypes of what constitutes 'correct' capitalist behaviour or capitalism proper.[19]

Notes

This chapter is a revised and updated version of my earlier essay entitled "Asian Capitalists in the European Mirror" (1994).

[1] Over the past decades the debate over the originally Marxian concept of the Asiatic mode of production has grown considerably (see, for example, Thorner 1966; Krader 1975; and Sawer 1977). For an extensive discussion and a useful bibliography of the literature on the Asiatic mode of production, see Van der Wee (1985). For an overview of the debate on Boeke's characterization of the Indonesian economy as a 'dual economy', see Wertheim et al. (1966). See also Furnivall (1944) for his characterization of Indonesian society under Dutch rule as a 'plural society'.

[2] With regard to the colonial period, the terms 'colonial mode of production' (Banaji 1972; Alavi 1975) and 'peripheral capitalism' (Alavi 1981) have been employed, among others. For an extensive overview of the 'mode of production debate in India', see Thorner (1982).

[3] Breman 1969, pp. 16–17. In his study, Breman criticizes this notion.

[4] See, for an overview of this discussion with regard to the Indian situation, Streefkerk (1985, pp. 162–64) and Rutten (1992, pp. 171–75; and 1995).

[5] This period varies for the different countries in Europe. For Britain, the Industrial Revolution is usually said to have taken place between the mid-eighteenth and mid-nineteenth century. In other Western European countries, such as France and Germany, industrialization started later and the Industrial Revolution is usually thought to have taken place between the late-eighteenth/early-nineteenth and the late-nineteenth centuries.

[6] K. Marx, *Capital*, Vol. III, pp. 388–96.

[7] Dobb's study on the transition from feudalism to capitalism has provoked varied reactions, many of which have been assembled in one volume by Hilton (1976). I will return to this discussion in the next section.

[8] Crouzet (1972a, p. 3). Crouzet refers here to T.S. Ashton, *Iron and Steel in the Industrial Revolution* (Manchester, 1924), pp. 48, 156–61, 209–11.

[9] See, for example, the studies by Cameron (1958), Hoselitz (1968), Landes (1951 and 1972) and Kemp (1962).

[10] See, for example, the studies by Kindleberger (1964), Aldcroft (1964) and Wiener (1982).

[11] See, for alternative viewpoints on the French industrialists, e.g. Roehl (1976) and Cameron and Freedeman (1983). For alternative viewpoints on the British industrialists at the end of the nineteenth century, see, for example, McCloskey (1970) and McCloskey and Sandberg (1971).

[12] The Industrial Revolution in Britain was the first in a long line of similar processes in Europe and is therefore often taken as the classic case or model. Although today few economic historians are prepared to accept the idea of such a model and increasingly view "the First Industrial Revolution as something of a special and less of paradigm case for the economic history of Europe" (O'Brien 1986, p. 297), it is on this British model, and the notions attached to it, that most studies on South and Southeast Asia base their conclusions about the deformed, pseudo- or non-genuine nature of the behaviour of its capitalist class.

[13] There have been some attempts to solve the problem of availability of reliable and unbiased data on capital formation and origin of the first European industrialists. A pioneer and highly suggestive example of an attempt to build up a representative sample of entrepreneurs is the study by S.D. Chapman on fixed capital formation in the early cotton industry, published in two separate articles (1970 and 1973). Another example is Crouzet's project "of building up a 'national' sample, covering the main industries, *except mining*, including people from all parts of the country [Britain], and dealing with individuals who were active between the mid eighteenth and the mid nineteenth centuries" (1985, p. 54).

[14] In his overview of the literature on *British Entrepreneurship in the Nineteenth Century*, P.L. Payne emphasizes that many studies on the early industrialists in Britain are founded upon a biased sample, i.e. they do not provide details of a representative collection of businessmen, but only of those who are known to have been important or who were sufficiently successful to have created conditions favourable to untypical longevity; hence the survival of their archives (1974, p. 24).

[15] Crouzet (1985, p. 112). It might have been the equation of qualitative significance with quantitative importance that has led to the notion that the rise among the richer sections of the craftsmen was the critically important process in the early industrial development in Western Europe. See also Dobb (1976, p. 134) and Sweezy (1976, pp. 53–54).

[16] See, for example, Hagen (1962) and of course the study by Dobb (1976).

[17] See, for example, Crouzet (1985, tables 2 and 4); Coleman (1973); Chapman (1973); and Goodman and Honeyman (1988).

[18] Christer Gunnarson suggests that the outright rejection of the European experience as an object of comparison for developments in Third World countries can partly be explained by the Marxist and Rostovian connotation such a comparison involves. At a general level, both the Rostovian and the Marxist theory on economic development argued that what the newly industrializing countries are doing is following the road shown by the Western developed countries (Gunnarsson 1985, p. 189).

[19] For an excellent example of a detailed comparative analysis of our views on Asia and the West, see Jack Goody's *The East in the West* (1996).

References

Alavi, H. 1975. "India and the Colonial Mode of Production". *Economic and Political Weekly* 10, nos. 33, 34 and 35: 1235–62.

"Structure of Colonial Formations". 1981. *Economic and Political Weekly* 16, nos. 10, 11 and 12: 475–86.

Aldcroft, D.H. 1964. "The Entrepreneur and the British Economy, 1870–1914". *Economic History Review*, 2nd series, 17, no. 1.

Banaji, J. 1972. "For a Theory of Colonial Modes of Production". *Economic and Political Weekly* 7, no. 52: 2498–502.

Bhaduri, A. 1973. "A Study in Agricultural Backwardness under Semi-Feudalism". *Economic Journal* 83, no. 329: 120–37.

Bobek, H. 1962. "The Main Stages in Socio-Economic Evolution from a Geographical Point of View". In *Readings in Cultural Geography*, edited by Philip L. Wagner and Marvin W. Mikesell, pp. 218–47. Chicago: University of Chicago Press.

Braadbaart, O., and W. Wolters. 1992. *Rural Investment Patterns and Rural Nonfarm Employment in West Java*. Bandung: Akatiga Foundation, Centre for Social Analysis, West Java Rural Nonfarm Sector Research Project.

Breman, J. 1969. "Deferred Gratification, Entrepreneurial Behaviour and Economic Growth in Non-Western Societies". *Sociologia Neerlandica* 5, no. 1: 15–34.

Cameron, R.C. 1958. "Economic Growth and Stagnation in France". *Journal of Modern History* 30, no. 1.

———. 1985. "A New View of European Industrialization". *Economic History Review* 38, no. 1: 1–23.

Cameron, R. and C.E. Freedeman. 1983. "French Economic Growth: A Radical Revision". *Social Science History* 7, no. 1.

Campbell, R.H. and Wilson, R.G. 1975. *Entrepreneurship in Britain, 1750–1939*. London: A&C Black, Documents in Economic History.

Chandra, N.K. 1974. "Farm Efficiency under Semi-Feudalism: A Critique of Marginalist Theories and Some Marxist Formulations". *Economic and Political Weekly* 9, nos. 32, 33 and 34: 1309–31.

Chapman, S.D. 1970. Fixed Capital Formation in the British Cotton Manufacturing Industry, 1770–1815. *Economic History Review*, 2nd series, 23, no. 2: 235–56.

———. 1973. "Industrial Capital before the Industrial Revolution: An Analysis of the Assets of a Thousand Textile Entrepreneurs c. 1730–50". In *Textile History and Economic History: Essays in Honour of Miss Julia de Lacy Mann*, edited by N.B. Harte and K.G. Ponting, pp. 113–37. Manchester: Manchester University Press.

Clad, J. 1989. *Behind the Myth: Business, Money and Power in Southeast Asia*. London: Unwin Hyman.

Coleman, D.C. 1973. Gentlemen and Players. *Economic History Review*, 2nd series, 26, no. 1: 92–116.

Cunningham, H. 1980. *Leisure in the Industrial Revolution, c. 1780–1880*. London: Croom Helm.

Crouzet, F. 1972a. "Editor's Introduction: An Essay in Historiography". In *Capital Formation in the Industrial Revolution*, edited by F. Crouzet, pp. 1–69. London: Methuen.

———. 1972b. "Fixed Capital in the Industrial Revolution in Britain". In *Capital Formation in the Industrial Revolution*, edited by F. Crouzet, pp. 162–222. London: Methuen.

———. ed., 1972c. *Capital Formation in the Industrial Revolution*. London: Methuen.

———. 1985. *The First Industrialists: The Problem of Origins*. Cambridge: Cambridge University Press.

Dobb, M. 1963. *Studies in the Development of Capitalism*. Revised ed. New York: International Publishers.

Eerenbeemt, H.F.J.M. 1977. "Bedrijfskapitaal en Ondernemerschap in Nederland 1800–1850". In *Economische Ontwikkeling en Sociale Emancipatie, Deel II*, edited by P. Geurts and F. Messing, pp. 1–31. Den Haag: Nijhoff.

Evers, H.D. 1990. "Market Expansion and Political Pluralism; Southeast Asia and Europe Compared". Paper presented at the EIDOS-Winterschool, Trade, State and Ethnicity, University of Bielefeld.

Fegan, B. 1981. *Rent-Capitalism in the Philippines*. Manila: University of the Philippines, The Philippines in the Third World Papers no. 25.

Furnivall, J.S. 1944. *Netherlands India: A Study of Plural Economy*. Cambridge: Cambridge University Press.

Gerschenkron, A. 1970. *Europe in the Russian Mirror: Four Lectures in Economic History*. Cambridge: Cambridge University Press.

Goody, Jack. 1996. *The East in the West*. Cambridge: Cambridge University Press.

Goodman, J. and K. Honeyman. 1988. *Gainful Pursuits: The Making of Industrial Europe, 1600–1914*. London: Edward Arnold.

Granovetter, M., and C. Tilly. 1988. "Inequality and Labor Processes". In *Handbook of Sociology*, edited by Neil J. Smelser. Newbury Park, California: Sage.

Gunnarsson, C. 1985. "Development Theory and Third World Industrialisation: A Comparison of Patterns of Industrialisation in 19th Century Europe and the Third World". *Journal of Contemporary Asia* 15, no. 2: 183–206.

Habakkuk, H.J. 1953. "England". In *The European Nobility in the Eighteenth Century: Studies of the Nobilities of the Major European States in the Pre-Reform Era*, edited by A. Goodwin, pp. 1–21. London: Adam and Charles Black.

Hagen, E.E. 1962. *On the Theory of Social Change*. Illinois.

Hanagan, M. 1980. *The Logic of Solidarity: Artisans and Industrial Workers in Three French Towns, 1871–1914*. Urbana: University of Illinois Press.

Harriss, B. 1981. *Transitional Trade and Rural Development: The Nature and Role of Agricultural Trade in a South Indian District*. New Delhi: Vikas Publishing House.

Harriss, J. 1982. *Capitalism and Peasant Farming: Agrarian Structure and Ideology in Northern Tamil Nadu*. New Delhi: Oxford University Press.

Heaton, H. 1972. Financing the Industrial Revolution. In *Europe and the Industrial Revolution*, edited by S. Lieberman, pp. 413–24. Cambridge, Masachusetts: Schenkman.

Hilton, R., ed. 1976. *The Transition from Feudalism to Capitalism*. London: NLB, Foundations of History Library.

Holmström, M. 1985. *Industry and Inequality: The Social Anthropology of Indian Labour*. Cambridge: Cambridge University Press.

Hoselitz, B.F. 1968. "Unternehmertum und Kapitalbildung in Frankreich und England seit 1700". In *Wirtschafts- und Sozialgeschichtliche Probleme der Frühen Industrialisiering*, edited by W. Fischer, pp. 285–338. Berlin: Colloquium Verlag, Einzelveröffentlichungen der Historischen Kommission zu Berlin Beim Friedrich-Meinecke-Institut der Freien Universität Berlin, Band 1, Publikationen zur Geschichte der Industrialisierung.

Hudson, P. 1986. *The Genesis of Industrial Capital: A Study of the West Riding Wool Textile Industry c. 1750–1850*. Cambridge: Cambridge University Press.

Hüsken, F. 1989. "Cycles of Commercialisation and Accumulation in a Central Javanese Village". In *Agrarian Transformations: Local Processes and the State in Southeast Asia*, edited by Gillian Hart, Andrew Turton and Benjamin White, pp. 235–65. Berkeley: University of California Press.

Jomo, K.S. 1988. *A Question of Class: Capital, the State, and Uneven Development in Malaya*. New York: Monthly Review Press.

Jones, E.L. 1965. Agriculture and Economic Growth in England, 1650–1815: Economic Change. In E.L. Jones, *Agriculture and the Industrial Revolution*. Oxford: Basil Blackwell, pp. 85–127. [Originally published in *Journal of Economic History*, Vol. 25.]

―――. Industrial Capital and Landed Investment: The Arkwrights in Herefordshire, 1809–43. In E.L. Jones, *Agriculture and the Industrial Revolution*. Oxford: Basil Blackwell, pp. 160–83. [Originally published in E.L. Jones and G.E. Mingay, eds., 1967. *Land, Labour, and Population in the Industrial Revolution: Essays Presented to J.D. Chambers*. London: Edward Arnold]

Kemp, T. 1962. "Structural Factors in the Retardation of French Economic Growth". *Kylos* 15.

―――. 1985. *Industrialization in Nineteenth-Century Europe*. London and New York: Longman.

Kindleberger, C.P. 1967. *Economic Growth in France and Britain, 1851–1950*. Cambridge, Mass.: Harvard University Press.

Klein, P.W. 1977. "Kapitaal en Stagnatie tijdens het Hollandse Vroegkapitalisme". In P. Geurts and F. Messing. *Economische Ontwikkeling en Sociale Emancipatie, Deel I*. Den Haag, pp. 166–84.

Krader, L. 1975. *The Asiatic Mode of Production: Sources, Development and Critique in the Writings of Karl Marx*. Assen: Van Gorcum.

Kriedte, P., H. Medick and J. Schlumbohm. 1981. *Industrialisation before Industrialisation: Rural Industry in the Genesis of Capitalism*. Cambridge: Cambridge University Press. [Originally published in German in 1977.]

Landes, D.S. 1951. "French Business and the Businessman: A Social and Cultural Analysis". In *Modern France: Problems of the Third and Fourth Republics*, edited by E.M. Earle, pp. 334–53. Princeton: Princeton University Press.

―――. 1972. "French Entrepreneurship and Industrial Growth in the 19th Century". In *Europe and the Industrial Revolution*, edited by S. Lieberman, pp. 397–412. Cambridge, Massachusetts: Schenkman.

Lin, S.G. 1980. "Theory of a Dual Mode of Production in Post-Colonial India". *Economic and Political Weekly* 15, no. 10: 516–29; no. 11: 565–73.

McCloskey, D. 1970. "Did Victorian Britain Fail?". *Economic History Review* 23, no. 3.

McCloskey, D., and L. Sandberg. 1971. "From Damnation to Redemption: Judgements on the Late Victorian Entrepreneur". *Explorations in Economic History* 9.

McVey, R. 1992. "The Materialization of the Southeast Asian Entrepreneur". In *Southeast Asian Capitalists*, edited by R. McVey. Ithaca, NY: Cornell University, Southeast Asia Program, Studies on Southeast Asia.

O'Brien, P.K. 1986. "Do We Have a Typology for the Study of European Industrialization in the XIXth Century?" *Journal of European Economic History* 15: 291–333.

Payne, P.L. 1974. *British Entrepreneurship in the Nineteenth Century*. London: The Macmillan Press, Studies in Economic History.

Pollard, S. 1964. Fixed Capital in the Industrial Revolution in Britain. *Journal of Economic History* 24. [Reprinted in F. Crouzet (ed.), 1972, *Capital Formation in the Industrial Revolution*. London: Methuen, pp. 145–161.]

Richards, E. 1974. "The Industrial Face of a Great Estate: Trentham and Lillerhall, 1780–1860". *Economic History Review*, 2nd series, vol. 27, no. 3: 414–30.

Robison, R. 1986. *Indonesia: The Rise of Capital*. Sydney: Allen & Unwin, Asian Studies Association of Australia, Southeast Asia Publication Series no. 13.

Roehl, R. 1976. "French Industrialization: A Reconsideration". *Explorations in Economic History* 13, no. 3.

Rutten, M. 1992. "Artisan or Merchant Industrialists?: Small-Scale Entrepreneurs in the Countryside of West India". *The Journal of Entrepreneurship* 1, no. 2: 169–214.

―――. 1994. *Asian Capitalists in the European Mirror*. Amsterdam: Free University of Amsterdam. Comparative Asian Studies no. 14.

―――. 1995. *Farms and Factories: Social Profile of Large Farmers and Rural Industrialists in West India*. Delhi: Oxford University Press.

Sau, R. 1975. "Farm Efficiency under Semi-Feudalism: A Critique of Marginalist Theories and Some Marxist Formulations — A Comment". *Economic and Political Weekly* 10, no. 13: 18–21.

―――. 1984. "Development of Capitalism in India". *Economic and Political Weekly*, 19: 73–80.

―――. 1988. "The Green Revolution and Industrial Growth in India: A Tale of Two Paradoxes and a Half". *Economic and Political Weekly* 28, no. 16: 789–96.

Sawer, M. 1977. *Marxism and the Question of the Asiatic Mode of Production*. The Hague: Martinus Nijhoff.

Sen Gupta, N. 1977. "Further on the Mode of Production in Agriculture". *Economic and Political Weekly* 12, no. 26: 55–63.

Stearns, P.N. 1975. *European Society in Upheaval: Social History Since 1750*. New York: Macmillan. [First edition 1967.]

Streefkerk, H. 1985. *Industrial Transition in Rural India: Artisans, Traders and Tribals in South Gujarat*. Bombay: Sangam Books.

―――. 1993. *On the Production of Knowledge: Fieldwork in South Gujarat, 1971–1991*. Amsterdam: VU University Press, Comparative Asian Studies 11.

Sutherland, H. 1993. "Political Power and Economic Activity in the Malay World 1700–1940". Paper presented at the seminar 'Historical Dimension of Development, Change and Conflict in the South', 14 and 15 April, The Hague.

Sweezy, P. 1976. "A Critique". In *The Transition from Feudalism to Capitalism*, edited by R. Hilton, pp. 33–56. London: NLB. [Originally published in *Science and Society*, Spring 1950.]

Takahashi, K. 1976. "A Contribution to the Discussion". In *The Transition from Feudalism to Capitalism*, edited by R. Hilton, pp. 68–97. London: NLB. [Originally published in *Science and Society*, Fall 1952.]

Thorner, A. 1982. "Semi-Feudalism or Capitalism: Contemporary Debate on Classes and Modes of Production in India". *Economic and Political Weekly* 17, no. 49, pp. 1961–68; no. 50, pp. 1993–99; and no. 51, pp. 2061–66.

Thorner, D. 1966. "Marx on India and the Asiatic Mode of Production". *Contributions to Indian Sociology*, no. 9: 33–66.

Tilly, C. 1983. "Flows of Capital and Forms of Industry in Europe, 1500–1900". *Theory and Society* 12, no. 2: 123–42.

Upadhya, C.B. 1988. "The Farmer-Capitalists of Coastal Andhra Pradesh". *Economic and Political Weekly* 23, no. 27: 1376–82; no. 28: 1433–42.

Veblen, T. 1931. *The Theory of the Leisure Class: An Economic Study of Institutions*. New York. [First published in 1899.]

Veen, J.H. van der. 1973. "Small Industries in India: The Case of Gujarat State". Ph.D. thesis. Cornell University.

———. 1976. "Commercial Orientation of Industrial Entrepreneurs in India". *Economic and Political Weekly* 11, no. 35: M91–M94.

Weber, M. 1976. *The Protestant Ethic and the Spirit of Capitalism*. London: George Allen & Unwin [Originally published in Gesammelte Aufsätze zur Religionssoziologie, Tübingen, 1920–21.]

———. 1978. The Origins of Industrial Capitalism in Europe. In *Max Weber, Selections in Translation*, edited by W.G. Runciman, pp. 331–40. [Originally published in Gesammelte Aufsätze zur Religionssoziologie, Tübingen, 1920–21.]

Wee, M. van der. 1985. Aziatische Produktiewijze en Mughal India: Een Historische en Teoretische Kritiek. Ph.D. thesis, University of Nijmegen.

Wertheim, W.F. 1964. *East-West Parallels: Sociological Approaches to Modern Asia*. Den Haag: Uitgeverij Hoeve.

———. 1993. *Comparative Essays on Asia and the West*. Amsterdam: VU University Press, Comparative Asian Studies 12.

Wertheim, W.F. et al., eds. 1961. *Indonesian Economics: The Concept of Dualism in Theory and Policy*. The Hague: Van Hoeve.

Wiener, M.J. 1982 *English Culture and the Decline of the Industrial Spirit, 1850–1980*. Cambridge: Cambridge University Press.

Wilson, C. 1972. "The Entrepreneur in the Industrial Revolution in Britain". In *Europe and the Industrial Revolution*, edited by S. Lieberman, pp. 377–95. Cambridge, Massachusetts: Schenkman.

Wittfogel, K. 1957. *Oriental Despotism: A Comparative Study of Total Power*. New Haven: Yale University Press.

Part II

Linkages: Science, Society and Culture

7

Royal Antiquarianism, European Orientalism and the Production of Archaeological Knowledge in Modern Siam

Maurizio Peleggi

On the evening of 2 December 1907, before an audience of noblemen and state officials who had gathered in the ruined city of Ayutthaya for a three-day festive extravaganza, King Chulalongkorn (Rama V, r. 1868–1910) gave the inaugural speech to the Archaeological (or Antiquarian) Society (Borankhadi Samosom). Its objective, the sovereign explained, was the recovery of physical remains of the past as a means to compensate for the dearth of written documents and thus make possible the compilation of a history of Siam covering the last thousand years. The exhortation was put into practice the following day, which was devoted to a sightseeing tour of the local ruins.[1] As the culmination of several decades of royal antiquarian pursuits and a response to the establishment of the Siam Society by a group of expatriates in 1904, the founding of the Archaeological Society signalled the intention of systematically investigating the realm's historical landscape in the wake of its territorial and cartographic configuration as a modern state at the turn of the nineteenth and twentieth centuries.

It is hardly surprising to see Siam's status as the only formally independent country in Southeast Asia highlighted at the very beginning of a recent book on Thailand's prehistory in order to distinguish the history of archaeology there from that of the rest of the region: "The colonial powers introduced their traditional methods for archaeological research. ... Only Thailand stood firmly against the colonial tide, and in consequence, looked to its own resources. This came with royal inspiration."[2] Along with the three kings—Mongkut, Chulalongkorn and Vajiravudh—whose reigns spanned the period 1851 to 1925, much of this inspiration is credited to Prince Damrong Rachanubhab (1862–1943), the leading antiquarian of his time as well as the architect of the administrative centralization of the kingdom. Prince Damrong, who is memorialized in the national pantheon as the 'father of Thai history', wrote extensively on a variety of historical subjects, surveyed ancient sites, and played a pivotal role in the establishment of the cultural institutions (that is, the National Library and the National Museum) that were inherited by the constitutional government after the overthrow of the absolute monarchy in 1932. The narrative of the royal inception of Siamese archaeology obscures, however, the contiguity of this domestic endeavour alongside the colonial project of surveying and mapping out, along with the geographical landscape of subjected countries, their archaeological topography.[3]

Similar to the way the topographical mapping of Siam was carried out by British and French surveyors and cartographers, its archaeological mapping was pioneered by European Orientalists (French, but also Germans, Italians and Scandinavians). In both cases, Western disciplines whose authority derived from institutionalized academic fields were imported and eventually domesticated for the production of national knowledge—knowledge *about* as much as *in the service* of the Siamese nation. The argument has been convincingly made that the basic condition for the creation of Siam's 'geo-body' at the turn of the century lay in the epistemic shift whereby Western geography (*phumisat*) displaced Buddhist cosmography as a more authoritative mode of representing the earth's surface.[4] A parallel shift saw the modern, empirical concept of history (*prawatisat*) supersede indigenous modes of narrating past events such as folk and religious tales (*tamnan*) and court chronicles (*phongsawadan*).[5] By translating into Thai the names of the foreign 'sciences' (*-sat*, Sanskrit *sastra*) of the earth and the past, the neologisms *phumisat* and *prawatisat* made possible their localization in the domain of indigenous knowledge. Likewise, the neologism *borankhadi* (the lexical cast of archaeo[*boran*]-logy[*khadi*]) promoted a novel way of approaching, physically as well as conceptually, ancient artefacts: no longer as the foci of Hindu-Buddhist devotional practices, but as documentary evidence of the Siamese nation's historical unfolding.

Turn-of-the-century archaeology was intertwined both in the ideology of nationalism and racialist theory, which stressed biological factors as the reason for physical as well as cultural differences among peoples.[6] Accordingly, archaeologists developed a methodology in which "stylistic features constituted reliable clues to the historical and often ethnic origins of the artefact in question".[7] Such a methodology had a special bearing upon the study of Siamese antiquities. Early in the twentieth century, scholars tended to agree that the races autochthonous to the northern and central regions of the modern Siamese state were the Khmer and the Mon, who had imbibed the social, religious and artistic practices of the Indian colonists thought to have settled on the littoral since the beginning of the Christian era. The Thai, on the other hand, were viewed as latecomers to Siam, having supposedly migrated from southern China around the turn of the first millennium and thereafter displaced the earlier settlers.[8] The southward migration theory called for the identification, amidst the stylistic diversity of Siam's sculptural and architectural remains (investigation into the Palaeolithic began only in the 1960s), of a distinctive style that would testify to the political ascendancy of the Thai race. Yet, as Hungarian art historian Alfred Salmony noted at the start of the first monographic study of Siamese sculpture,

> In the case of the artefacts found in Siam it is often impossible to determine the racial stock of their makers, which makes the task of their ordering in a chronological sequence of styles especially difficult. European scholars are used to see in a work of art the expression of the spirit of a single people, a precise country. But as far as Siam is concerned, such a method is applicable only if one considers the creators of these artworks as belonging, in general terms, to the population of the Eastern Indies.[9]

The classification of Siamese antiquities that remains canonical to this day was established collaboratively by Prince Damrong and the French scholar George Coedès, who worked for the Bangkok library and museum from 1917 to 1929. Damrong's first-hand knowledge of the ancient monuments scattered in the kingdom's provinces complemented Coedès' expertise in the reading of Pali, Sanskrit, Khmer and Thai inscriptions as well as classical and Chinese sources. Siamese antiquities were classified into seven styles named after regional principalities (*muang*) that had ruled from the sixth to the fifteenth centuries over different regions of what, by the early 1900s, was bound into Siam's national territory. Due to the absence of documents, the historical evidence upon which Coedès and Damrong's stylistic classification rested was gathered largely from stone inscriptions. Indeed, the establishment of an art historical periodization coincided, to a large extent, with that of the chronology of Siam's early history. Coedès' fundamental contribution to the knowledge of the Siamese past has been, alas, largely erased from the Thai public consciousness, possibly because it did not accord well with France's late nineteenth-century role of villain in Thailand's national narrative.[10] Yet, far from being the autarchic endeavour purported by some, the production of archaeological knowledge in modern Siam was heavily dependent on Western scholarship and ideas, as this essay will demonstrate by investigating the material and discursive practices (surveying, collecting, classification and periodization) as well as the institutions and historical actors that participated in it between the 1860s and the 1920s.

Nineteenth-Century Royal Antiquarianism

Antiquarianism, a thirst for ancient objects as distinct from the study of their original setting, emerged in the Renaissance as by-product of the dominant elites' admiration of Greco-Roman civilization. The collecting and display of classical antiquities at the Italian urban courts, and later the court of France, spurred the earliest excavations in the sixteenth and seventeenth centuries and was further promoted in the eighteenth century by the vogue for the Grand Tour. In the latter half of the eighteenth century, and particularly in Britain and Germany, antiquarians turned to the search for remains of indigenous material cultures in line with the Romantic movement's reaction against Classicism and stress on the 'national' genius.[11]

More than a novel aesthetic sensibility, the rise of antiquarianism in Siam reflected the wider change in the elite's worldview, spurred by Western conceptions of time, space, and human action as well as history.[12] The Buddhist worldview, based on Hinduism's cyclical timeframe of birth, death and rebirth and compounded by the doctrine of impermanence (*anitchang*, Pali *anicca*), posits the decay of physical entities, animate as well as inanimate, to be inevitable. Material remains hold therefore no special significance except for holy relics. Emulating the exemplum of Indian king Asoka, who in the third century BC had hundreds of Buddhist shrines and stone inscriptions erected throughout his kingdom, the Siamese kings and nobility sponsored the casting of images and the construction of religious reliquaries (*chedi* and *stupa*) and monasteries (*wat*) as a means to accruing merit. While commonly designating an architectural type, the term *chedi* (from Pali *cetiya*, root *ci*, 'to heap up', 'to construct' and related root *cit*, 'to perceive', 'to remind') indicates also holy relics, the Bodhi tree and even the Pali Canon, as well as iconic and aniconic representations of the Buddha. The meaning of *chedi* may thus recall that of the word 'monument' (Latin *monumentum*, from *monere*, 'to remember') but only in the specific sense of a physical reminder of the Buddha and his teaching.[13] Given the unmatched importance of image-casting and monument-building as forms of merit-making, it was common practice to copy them from already existing 'reminders' that commanded special reverence within the transnational Buddhist ecumene.[14] By reproducing such a religious image or monument, the craftsman or builder extended its social life across time and space and made its iconic potency available to his patron (most often kings and members of the royalty).

Restoration of shrines and monasteries, while practiced, was not too common. As late as 1881, Norwegian naturalist Carl Bock observed that "... the Siamese, though ever building, seem seldom, if ever, to take steps to keep their edifices, sacred or secular, in repair. And more often than not, what they build they leave incomplete".[15] A mix of cultural beliefs and practical constraints can be adduced to explain this attitude. The moral obligation to sponsor the construction of new temples vis-à-vis the relative value of stone and bricks (up until the mid-nineteenth century domestic architecture for both commoners and nobility was built of wood) might have favoured the recycling of building materials to the detriment of restoration. A case in point is the demolition of the reportedly splendid temples of Ayutthaya. Blamed in the national mythology on the Burmese sack of 1767, it was at least partly the result of subsequent dismantlements to retrieve building materials for use in Bangkok.[16] Some of the reasons are also to be found in the prescriptions of the Brahmanic liturgy, which permeates the ritual practices of Siamese Buddhism, about damaged religious images as being unsuited to be the embodiment of the deity.[17] Not unlike Christian art in the Middle Ages, the social perception of images of the Buddha focused—and still does, to a large extent—on its 'cult value' rather than its 'exhibition' (or aesthetic) value, to paraphrase German critic Walter Benjamin, or its antiquity.[18]

The wide-ranging interests of King Mongkut (r. 1851–68), a reflection of his openness to the novel forms of knowledge spread by Catholic priests and Protestant missionaries since the 1830s, are well known. Even before ascending the throne, Mongkut spearheaded antiquarianism by identifying in 1833 the stone throne and the stela of the thirteenth-century King Ramkhamhaeng, both of which he had transferred to Wat Phra Keo, the monastery attached to the royal palace. The importance of Mongkut's discoveries can hardly be overstated. The Ramkhamhaeng Inscription, as the oldest extant specimen of the Thai script, has in particular been transformed into a veritable national icon. The recent questioning of its authenticity by a Thai art historian, who has proposed that the inscription is a forgery engineered by Mongkut himself, caused an intense scholarly debate, the ultimate result of which was to strengthen the inscription's pre-eminence among the relics of the national past.[19] Other notable achievements of Mongkut's antiquarian pursuits were the identification of the palace sites of Ayutthayan kings, two of which (in Ayutthaya and Lopburi) he renovated, and of the ancient Phra Pathom Chedi, in Nakhon Pathom province.

The Dynastic Chronicles of the Fourth Reign, which were actually composed at the beginning of the Fifth, relate in some detail Mongkut's appraisal of Phra Pathom Chedi as the realm's largest and oldest Buddhist monument, its restoration and the alleged supernatural events that accompanied it.[20] Mongkut took the large dimensions of the *chedi* to indicate that it enshrined an authentic relic and inferred from the stylistic contrast between its circular base (in the style of a Sinhalese *stupa*) and its Khmer-style tower (or *prang*) that the original monument had been reconstructed at some point in the past. One passage in the *Chronicles* highlights the emerging antiquarianism vis-à-vis the usual lack of interest

in ruins by describing how the historic and religious significance of Phra
Pathom Chedi, evident to Mongkut, was lost to his older brother, the
sovereign:

> Being such an ancient religious place, the pagoda ought not to be left
> surrounded by jungle, and the present King [Mongkut], prior to his
> ascension, had therefore made a suggestion to this effect, as a monk, to
> his royal elder brother, King Phra Nangklao. However, at the time, King
> Phra Nangklao, after listening to the prince-monk, said that the monument
> was inside the jungle; even if it could be restored, not much usefulness
> could come of it. Hearing that the then king did not favour restoring the
> pagoda, the present king had been determined ever since that time that
> if ever he became king, he would definitely restore and repair the
> pagoda.[21]

Still, King Mongkut's restoration of Phra Pathom Chedi concerned its
cult value, not its historic value. The iconic potency of the *chedi*—or
rather, the potency of the relic it supposedly enshrined—was 'restored'
by incorporation into a new, much larger structure, while the original
chedi was evoked by a model erected inside the temple's enclosure, which
was also endowed with a gallery of Buddha images.[22] The new *chedi*
collapsed in 1860 after a heavy storm; when its reconstruction was
completed in the Fifth Reign, Phra Pathom Chedi stood, at some 120
metres high, as the tallest Buddhist monument in the world. As for the
supernatural phenomena allegedly occurring at Phra Pathom Chedi
"many times each year, and every year", the author of the *Chronicles*
submitted two possible explanations, a magico-religious one and a
scientific one, making clear however which one he subscribed to:
"Whether such marvels were caused by the power of Buddha, or the
magic of Buddha's relics, or the power of the deities, or whether electricity
from the sky and from the earth clashed, was left to each individual to
decide, according to his own intelligence".[23]

In the Fifth Reign, antiquarianism was incorporated in the trope of
siwilai, the condition of being civilized, which informed the appropriation
of various forms of Western knowledge as well as changes in courtly
practices.[24] Indeed, not only was historical knowledge of major
importance in Europe's modern and wealthy nations, but the very
concept of progress (which, translated as *charoen*, provided a frequent
match to *siwilai* in royal discourse) implied the idea of a civilizational
lineage against which to measure a nation's present achievements, or
the lack thereof. One of the civilizational landmarks the young King

Chulalongkorn was shown during his visit to Batavia in 1871 was, along with the barracks, the custom house and the judiciary court, the museum.[25] King Mongkut had assembled a collection of scientific instruments and Chinese and European exotica which he eagerly showed to the British envoy John Bowring, who negotiated in 1855 the first commercial treaty between Siam and a Western state.[26] Mongkut's collection, whose denomination of *phiphitapan* ('varied things') was later used to translate 'museum', reminds one of the *Wunderkammern*, or curiosity cabinets, which European scholars and aristocrats assembled in the seventeenth and eighteenth centuries, an age of increasingly keen interest in natural phenomena. In 1884 Chulalongkorn relocated his father's collection in the Concordia Hall, a neoclassical edifice situated in the Grand Palace's outer court, and named it 'museum' (in English) with manifest modernizing flair. As with the Wachirayan Library, inaugurated that same year,[27] the palace museum was exclusively for the education of the court. In 1887 the collection was transferred to the nearby Wang Na, or Palace of the Front, following the death of his occupant, the *uparaja* or 'second king' (in fact, a sort of heir presumptive). Aware of the importance of museums as an index of a country's level of civilization, Rama V nominated curator Henri Alabaster, the ex-British consul in Bangkok. The permanent exhibition was housed in two edifices of the palace compound (one containing a zoological collection and some bronzes and ceramics, the other religious images), while a third building was used as a depot. However, hardly any funding was provided for the upkeep of the museum.[28]

In the Fifth Reign's final years, a collection of fifty images of the Buddha was assembled in the courtyard of Wat Benchamabophit, the newly built monastery in the residential Dusit district. Prince Damrong, who had assembled the statues at Rama V's request, wrote a brief account of his undertaking, explaining that the king requested that the statues be "selected from among numerous old and beautiful images made in various countries at different periods, and should be displayed in such a way that the public might acquire a knowledge of Buddhist iconography."[29] An aesthetic concern is also evident in the king's requirements that the images of the Buddha be of artistic value, of different style and about the same size. Damrong, who as minister of the Interior was in constant communication with provincial governors, started the search for suitable images both in the capital and the provinces:

Whenever a statue of the required size was found, it was brought down to the temple, and search extended into foreign countries. The second method was that whenever a statue was found of the required style, but too small to be placed in the gallery, an enlarged copy of this statue of the size required was made exclusively by private persons who offered them to the King, because the creation of images of the Buddha is considered an act of religious merit.[30]

Damrong's comment on the devotional dimension of the image-making practice highlights a tension between the aesthetic and the ritual regimes of perception of icons—a tension that persists in Thai contemporary society and underscores the elitism, even xenomania, of Chulalongkorn's project of displaying a collection of images of the Buddha for the aesthetic and artistic education of his subjects. Unlike the plaster casts of classical statuary on display in many a nineteenth-century Western museum, the images installed in Wat Benchamabophit, both the ancient ones and those cast for the occasion (including copies of Burmese, Japanese and Gandhara Buddhist statuary), were selected for their cult value, not their exhibition value.[31] And, indeed, no attempt was made at arranging the statues in a historically ordered display—the representational regime of the nineteenth-century museum.

Royal antiquarianism in the later Fifth Reign also pioneered the spectacular use of ruins for both domestic and international consumption. Ayutthaya's ruins, situated at a short distance from the royal summer residence of Bang Pa-in, were a regular destination of sightseeing tours by the court as well as foreign visitors. A British employee of the Royal Survey Department reported that in the early 1900s the provincial governor regularly cleared the vegetation and laid out paths for the visitors in the archaeological area.[32] The governor, whose title of Phraya Boran Ratchathani ('Lord of the ancient royal capital') was aptly changed to Phraya Boran Boranurak ('Lord preserver of antiquities'), was himself a keen antiquarian; he had conducted extensive reconnaissance of the old capital's area, identifying the sites of the palaces mentioned in the *Chronicles of Ayutthaya*, and established a museum in the Chantrakasem Palace, built in the Fourth Reign on the site of an Ayutthayan palace. Phraya Boran Boranurak was also the organizer of the celebrations for Rama V in December 1907, which had a distinctively antiquarian *mise en scène*, from the purpose-built royal pavilion, reportedly based on the descriptions of seventeenth-century European visitors to Ayutthaya, to the entertainments (*lakhon* performances, bullock races and traditional fireworks).

It was in this setting that the launch of the Archaeological Society took place. King Chulalongkorn's inaugural speech represents the most articulate formulation of historical thinking by a Siamese monarch. He started by pointing out that, while historical evidence in many countries dated as far back as one thousand years, and in some even thrice that length of time, Siam had suffered the misfortune of losing most of its historical record in wars. Extant evidence, continued Rama V, provided fragmentary documentation of the past four of five centuries only, not enough to make Siamese history notable. Moreover, even the existing royal chronicles were in need of verification. The king proposed that, in order to gain knowledge of the past thousand years of Siamese history, one should start by studying the several *muang* (Chiang Saen, Chiang Rai, Chiang Mai, Sawankhalok, Sukhothai, Ayutthaya, Lopburi, Nakhon Chaisi, Nakhon Si Thammarat) which had been powerful at one time or another in the past and were now united into the modern Siamese state. This was an extremely important passage, for it painted the historical landscape of Siam as multi-centric in obvious contrast to the picture of the supremacy of the Central Thai kingdoms which would become hegemonic in the 1930s. In concluding, the king stressed that documents and remains should be carefully examined; any findings, if proved authentic, would contribute to improving knowledge of Siam's past.[33]

Crown Prince Vajiravudh (later Rama VI, 1910–25), vice-president of the Archaeological Society, used his thespian talent to strike a pose à la Sherlock Holmes, the literary epitome of Victorian empiricism, carefully examining remains through a magnifying lens with a pipe hanging from his mouth, in a photographic portrait meant perhaps to publicize the new intiative. But Vajiravudh also turned antiquarianism into a tool to foster a collective historical imagination in the service of the political ideal of a national community (*chat*) unified around the institutions of the throne and the Buddhist religion.[34] Following a visit to Sukhothai in 1908, Vajiravudh wrote *Thiao muang phra ruang* (Journey to the realm of Phra Ruang), a travelogue in the Siamese literary tradition of the *nirat*, in which he lamented the ruinous state of monuments that symbolized the power and the artistic accomplishment of the ancient Thais. The antiquarian appreciation of ruins as evidence of a nation's civilizational lineage was invested by a polemical urgency typical of Vajiravudh's subsequent writings:

> It is my hope that, as a result of this book, the Thai people will understand that this Thai nation of ours (*chat thai rao*) is not a recent country and that it is not a country of savages (*khon pa*) or, to put it in English, 'uncivilised' people. Our Thai nation has been prosperous and thriving for a long time … Indeed, the manual skills and the industriousness of people in Phra Ruang's time were better than those of the people today … Ancient Thais were so inventive and capable that they built these imposing and beautiful monuments, which have lasted so long. The Thai of today, however, would rather demolish and discard these ruins because of their infatuation with modern things and their preference for what is imported from foreign countries…[35]

The objective of reviving traditional craftsmanship was also prompted by the need to display products of the 'national' manufacture at the international exhibitions Siam had been attending since the 1860s,[36] and led to the establishment in March 1912 of the Fine Arts Department (Krom Silpakorn). The contrast between past achievements and the alleged cultural decline of the present was to become, nevertheless, a key theme in King Vajiravudh's polemics against what he labelled the "cult of imitation"—the Westernization of the Bangkok middle-class lifestyle.[37] In later works (a *khon* or traditional drama, a modern play, and a western-style musical), Rama VI resorted to the legendary figure of Phra Ruang as a literary alter ego to urge his subjects, at a time of growing dissatisfaction with the absolute monarchy, "not [to] destroy our nation but combine your spirit and your strength to preserve the state".[38] But even as ancient history and historic monuments were increasingly regarded as an arena for the representation of the Thai national identity, institutional commitment to the study and conservation of antiquities would have to await the latter part of the Sixth Reign.

European Orientalists and Siamese Antiquities

The emergence of antiquarianism in Siam as an elite pursuit was paralleled by the upsurge of interest in the local monumental remains among European scholars. The posthumous publication in 1864 of the travel journal of Henri Mouhot (1826–61),[39] which revealed the existence of Angkor Wat to the European public, put mainland Southeast Asia on the map of explorers and archaeologists at the same time that the French were pushing colonial expansion in the region. Welcomed by the

Cambodian King Norodom, who had grown up as de facto hostage at the Bangkok court, the French had established a protectorate on Cambodia already in 1863. The province of Siemreap, where Angkor and other major Khmer archaeological sites lie, remained however under Bangkok's suzerainty until 1907, when it was returned to Phnom Penh's authority by virtue of the treaty that settled the border dispute with Siam. On that occasion the British *Daily Telegraph* approvingly wrote: "'It is well that its [Angkor's] future is to be cared for by so appreciative a people as our neighbours across the Channel'.[40] Prince Damrong himself, in a talk he gave some eighteen years later at the Siam Society, concurred that "we all owe a debt of gratitude to the French for trying their best to clear and to preserve those monuments for us, as a result of which, I am sure, we shall be able to study more of them as time goes on".[41]

The disputed status of Siemreap province throughout the early twentieth century did not prevent the French from carrying out extensive archaeological surveys in the area since 1866, when the Mekong River expedition led by Captain E. Doudart de Lagrèe surveyed the site of Angkor and made copies of the stone inscriptions found there. During the 1870s Louis Delaporte, a member of the de Lagrèe expedition, further explored the area and brought to light more Khmer sites. In 1881 another French navy officer, Etienne Aymonier, led an expedition into previously unexplored areas with the objective of compiling a comprehensive inventory of Khmer monuments.[42] The two volumes that document Aymonier's reconnaissance of archaeological sites significantly distinguished between Khmer ruins in Cambodia and those in the Cambodian provinces under Siamese authority.[43] This situation was viewed with both apprehension and disapproval since the Thai, once vassals of the Khmer, were now in control—however nominal—of the prime monumental remains of what the French regarded as a superior civilisation:

> For several centuries Cambodia let its yoke weigh on the Siamese and when its ancient power crumbled, it left indelible traces of this long domination in its language and political institutions. In her turn, Siam invaded and cut up the territory of its former masters on many occasions. It still holds a great deal of this territory, and it is in those provinces which are subject to her that one must look for the most important monuments: those that adorn the old Cambodian capital and her surroundings.[44]

The French colonial project of cataloguing Khmer remains as signposts of the territorial outreach of the Angkorean empire was given institutional endorsement by the establishment, in 1898, of the Mission Archéologique d'Indochine, whose name was changed three years later to École Française d'Extrême-Orient (EFEO) in concomitance with its transfer from Saigon to Hanoi. Publication of the *Bulletin de l'École Française d'Extrême-Orient* (*BEFEO*) also started in 1901. Contemporary initiatives by the British, who in 1899 founded the Archaeological Department of Burma, and the Dutch, who in 1901 established the Commission on Antiquities of the East Indies (upgraded to the Antiquity Service in 1913), heralded the professionalization of archaeological research in Southeast Asia. As noted by Anderson,[45] these agencies documented their conservation and restoration activities in voluminous printed reports in order to justify public funding but also published lavishly illustrated books for the metropolitan public, whose interest in the art and culture of overseas colonies was fuelled by the display of casts and replicas of monuments at international exhibitions and, increasingly since the end of the nineteenth century, of authentic remains in newly established museums (or museum departments), such as Paris' Indochinese Museum at the Trocadéro, where the artefacts removed from Cambodia and Siam's Cambodian provinces by Delaporte were put on display (they were later moved to the Musée Guimet).

The EFEO's brief included the systematic survey of archaeological sites in French Indochina as well as in other countries of East and Southeast Asia, monument conservation, gathering of artefacts and manuscripts as well as ethnographic research. The EFEO scope led French archaeologists to include Siamese historical sites in their surveys although Angkor Wat and Angkor Thom were taken as the benchmarks against which to assess the religious monuments of the Thai, who were said to have "built temples of colossal sizes, it is true, but ones deprived of any superior art, which can stand no comparison with the superb temples of the ancient Cambodians, so grand in conception and so elegant."[46] Already in the 1890s, architect Lucien Fournereau had surveyed a number of ancient monuments in Siam, drawing plans and elevations and recording them photographically, to complement his documentation of Khmer sites.[47] In 1908, Captain Lunet de Lajounquière, who had been sent to Cambodia to continue the inventory of Khmer monuments initiated by Aymonier, conducted a survey of Siamese antiquities that included the collections of the Bangkok and Ayutthaya museums.[48]

The state of Siamese archaeology at the beginning of the twentieth century is summed up in an essay written by Colonel G.E. Gerini, an Italian instructor at Bangkok's Royal Cadet Academy, for a volume published on the occasion of Siam's participation at the 1904 Louisiana Purchase Exposition.[49] After noting the scarcity of neolithic finds thus far ("chiefly, perhaps, on account of as yet insufficient and systematic exploration"), Gerini went on to outline a "Brahmano-Buddhist period" preceding the "phase of national Thai history" said to have started in the mid-thirteenth century with the kingdom of Sukhothai. According to Gerini, Brahmanism and then Buddhism, brought in by Indian traders, had penetrated in the second half of the first millennium AD the urban centres which he believed to be already established by the early sixth century: Sawankhalok and Sukhothai (whose origins Gerini dated as early as the first century AD), Kamphaeng Phet, Lamphun, Lopburi, Phra Pathom and Ligor (Nakhon Si Thammarat). Gerini did not touch on the issue of the ethnic identity of the builder of Siam's ancient monuments; however, he highlighted the influences of both northern and southern Indian architectural styles and the replacement, around the twelfth century, of laterite (the material of architectural remains in the Khmer-dominated northern and central regions of Siam) by brickwork, sometimes in conjunction with sandstone, which had been in use before that date in regions not subjected to the Khmer.

Colonel Gerini was one among thirty-seven expatriates and two Thais who resolved, at a meeting held at Bangkok's Oriental Hotel on 26 February 1904, to create a society for "the investigation and encouragement of art, sciences and literature in relation to Siam and neighbouring countries". The Siam Society drew its members, who at the end of 1904 numbered one hundred and thirty-four, mostly from the government service and the business community. Among those who made significant contributions to historical and archaeological research one must mention, besides Gerini, the German Dr Oscar Frankfurter, initially with the Siamese Foreign Office and later conservator of the Royal City Library, and the Siam Society president from 1906 to 1918; and the Swedish Major Erik Seidenfaden, of the Provincial Gendarmerie, who wrote a comprehensive English-language guidebook of Bangkok and central Siam (first published in 1927). On the invitation of the society's council, Crown Prince Vajiravudh and Prince Damrong accepted the honorary offices of patron and vice-patron, respectively. Patronage from members of the royal household did not, however, entail financial support. The initiatives of the Siam Society, most notably the publication of a journal which started in 1904 and continues to the present day, were founded entirely by members' subscriptions (20 baht a year, 240 baht for a life membership). The *Journal of the Siam Society*, whose first issue contained a detailed list of subjects about which contributions were invited,[50] was critical to the Orientalist project of situating the study of the kingdom's history, epigraphy, and archaeology (as well as geology, botany and zoology) within the domain of scientific disciplines. Far from making it marginal to the emerging field of Siamese studies,[51] it was precisely its use of English as a medium and its scholarly format (footnoted articles, book reviews, etc.) that made the *Journal of the Siam Society* the main source of authoritative knowledge on Siam and the acknowledged counterpart to publications such as *BEFEO*.

An Archaeology for the Siamese Nation

While the historic artefacts on display in the Bangkok temples and museum attested to past artistic achievements and a civilizational lineage that put Siam on par with European nations, no attempt was made in the first two decades of the twentieth century to either classify sculptural fragments and archaeological sites according to styles or order them in an art historical chronology coterminous with the unfolding of the Siamese nation. As for the Archaeological Society founded in 1907, its model would appear to have been more the Siam Society's dilettante spirit than colonial archaeological services. Thus, the claim made by the *BEFEO* pages in 1921 that "La connoisance scientifique du Siam est pour la plus grand part une oeuvre française", while exuding a typically Gallic self-aggrandisement, contained also more than an element of truth.[52]

Following his resignation as Minister of the Interior in 1915, Prince Damrong devoted all his energies to directing the Royal City Library, which had been created in 1905 by the amalgamation of the palace's Wachirayan Library and two collections of Buddhist texts.[53] Besides manuscripts and printed volumes, the Royal City Library housed also stone inscriptions (except for King Ramkhamhaeng's stela, which was on display in Wat Phra Keo) and hosted the Archaeological Society. In his new office, which he occupied for twenty years until going into self-imposed exile to Penang in 1933, Prince Damrong made the Library the prime institution for the study of the Siamese past by promoting the collection of manuscripts and their publication as commemorative volumes at the cremation of members of the court and the nobility. In 1917 Damrong invited thirty-one-year old George Coedès to replace the departing Oscar Frankfurter as the library's chief secretary. Born in Paris to a family of Hungarian Jewish émigrés, Coedès (1886–1969) had honed his philological skills on classical texts before developing an interest in Oriental languages which led him to spend a period at the EFEO in Hanoi before moving to Bangkok. He remained there until 1929, when he returned to Hanoi to direct the EFEO. In 1946 Coedès was appointed professor of Southeast Asian history at the École des Langues Orientales in Paris, where he taught until his retirement.[54] An extremely prolific scholar, Coedès had published by the end of his life eight volumes of translations of Pali, Sanskrit, Khmer, and Thai inscriptions; dozens of articles on the epigraphy, history and archaeology of Cambodia, Siam and Sumatra; and several books, the most famous of which, *L'États hindouisés d'Indochine et d'Indonésie*, was first published in Hanoi in 1944 (there were a second edition in 1948 and a third one in 1964).[55]

One of the last official acts of the Sixth Reign was the institution by royal decree, on 17 January 1924, of the Archaeological Service, "in consideration of the many vestiges of monuments and artefacts created by past kings and artists, and of the fact that such archaeological remains have an important historical value and can contribute to increase knowledge of the past for the country's benefit and glory". The royal decree specified the five objectives of the Archaeological Service as follows: to draw up an inventory of the archaeological finds and monuments worthy of study and conservation in the national interest; to prescribe methods for the conservation of such finds and monuments; to oversee and advise the officers assigned to conservation tasks; to liaise with the ministers, provincial governors and officers on all matters pertaining to the Archaeological Service's activity; and to submit an annual report on its activity to the sovereign.[56] The new agency was placed under the authority of the Royal City Library committee, presided over by Damrong and including Coedès. The latter's report on the Archaeological Service's first year of activity (April 1924 to March 1925) mentioned excavations at Wat Mahathat, Lopburi, and the creation of a museum there; excavations at Wat Phra Si Sanphet, Ayutthaya;

and the storage of recent finds in the Royal City Library in view of the reorganization of the museum's collection.[57] The renovation of the Royal City Museum, which was inaugurated by King Prajadhipok (Rama VII) on 14 November 1926, partook of the administrative restructuring of the kingdom's cultural institutions carried out at the beginning of the Seventh Reign (1925–35). The previous April the Royal Institute of Literature, Archaeology and the Fine Arts (Sinlapakon Sathan) had been created with Damrong as president and Coedès as secretary-general by the merger of the library, the museum, the Fine Arts Department and the Archaeological Service (these latter two formed the Institute's Archaeological Section with Phraya Boran Boranurak as vice-president).[58]

Coedès himself explained the intention behind the reorganization of the museum in the illustrated monograph he wrote on it: "faire un musée vraiment national consacré aux arts et à l'archéologie du Siam."[59] The objective of establishing a 'truly national museum' was pursued on two levels: one practical, the other conceptual. Practically, antiquities previously on display in the museums of Ayutthaya, Lopburi, Phra Pathom Chedi and in provincial administration halls were selectively transferred to the Bangkok museum, which incorporated also the archaeological collection assembled by Prince Damrong in the atrium of the Ministry of Interior and the Hindu images presented as gifts by colonial officials hitherto at Wat Phra Keo. Conceptually, Siamese antiquities were arranged into seven chronologically sequential, if partly overlapping, styles or 'schools': Dvaravati, Srivijaya, Lopburi, Chiangsaen, Sukhothai, Uthong and Ayutthaya. Except for the addition of the Uthong School, Coedès' classification of sculpture corresponded to that of religious monuments outlined by Damrong in *Tamnan phuttacedhi sayam* (published as a cremation volume in 1926).[60] Since the two had worked in close contact throughout the previous ten years, this classification of Siamese antiquities can be legitimately regarded as a collaborative result. By assimilating art styles to historical periods, Damrong and Coedès conflated, however, the history of art with political history, relying on the former to fill the lacunae of the latter and on the latter to provide a temporal framework for the former.

The earliest style in this art historical periodization illustrates aptly their 'circular' approach. Although 'Dvaravati' appears in Thai inscriptions only as the ceremonial denomination of the fourteenth-century Ayutthaya kingdom, Coedès linked it to the term 'Tolopoti/

Doholopoti', which designates in late sixth- and early seventh-century Chinese texts a kingdom situated between modern Burma and Cambodia. The label 'Dvaravati style' was applied to what at that time appeared to be the oldest finds unearthed in Siam: Buddhist images, bas-reliefs and votive tablets of stone and stucco, whose style resembled Indian art of the Gupta period (fourth to sixth century) and which had been excavated mostly in and around the town of Phra Pathom, in the lower Chaophraya basin. A connection was thus established between antiquities lacking a clear historical origin and a historical kingdom lacking a certain territorial location, and the Mon population, whom epigraphic evidence indicated as the basin's earliest settlers, identified as the makers of Dvaravati-style images.[61]

The existence of a Srivijaya School rested on equally speculative grounds. Coedès had earlier identified the term 'Srivijaya' found in inscriptions as the name of a kingdom centred in Palembang (southern Sumatra), which had supposedly exercised its suzerainty on the Malay peninsula from the eighth to thirteenth centuries. This periodization framed chronologically the eponymous style, which was used to classify the mostly bronze images of Hindu and Mahayana Buddhist deities originating from the towns of Chaiya and Ligor (Nakhon Si Thammarat), in Peninsular Siam. But while, on the one hand, there were enough stylistic similarities between the sculptures and architectural remains of the Chaiya-Ligor region and contemporary Javanese art (typified by the temple of Borobodur) to argue for a connection with the Sumatran kingdom, on the other hand, Coedès himself acknowledged that stylistic variability was so pronounced as to suggest that the Srivijaya School was the outcome of a process of Indianization that had long predated the establishment of Sumatran suzerainty over the Malay peninsula.[62]

Because of the inscriptions which indicated Lopburi (or Lavo) as an outpost of the Khmer empire, the classification under the label 'Lopburi School' of stone and bronze images unearthed in and around that town (in the middle of which stands Wat Phra Prang Sam Yot with its three laterite *prang*) was hardly controversial from a historical point of view. What makes this stylistic designation controversial is the fact that Coedès took the general characteristics of Lopburi Buddha images (elongated face, semi-round eyebrows, hooked nose) to show "une période de décadence ou plus exactement de transition" vis-à-vis the Angkor style, designated by the French as 'classical' Cambodian art. This appraisal raised, in turn, the question of whether the creators of the sculpture and architecture of Lopburi were 'provincial' Khmer artists or 'foreign' (that is, Thai) imitators of the metropolitan style.[63] This still debated question and the Mahayana Buddhist character of the Lopburi School's production, which contrasts with the Hindu imagery of Angkor, led Coedès to posit an individual evolution for the Khmer-style sculpture from central and northeastern Siam: the 'transitional' Uthong School, which combined Khmer stylistic elements with those of the Sukhothai School. At the same time, following the ingrained view of the Khmers' superior artistic genius, Coedès proclaimed Khmer-style sculpture originating from Siam to be stylistically inferior to Cambodia's.

Buddha images from the area corresponding to the modern northern district of Payap, which the Thai might have infiltrated in the earliest stage of their southward migration, were classified as belonging to the Chiangsaen School. The exclusive use of the bronze medium and the distinctive iconography of these images, seated cross-legged on lotus-blossom bases, pointed however to an external influence: the sculpture of the northern Indian kingdom of Magadha during the Pala period (eight to twelfth century), whose influence would have reached Chiangsaen via Pagan.[64] Prince Damrong had employed 'Chiangsaen' somewhat differently from Coedès as an 'umbrella' style for the art and architecture of the Chiang Mai-centred Lanna kingdom, from its foundation in the late thirteenth century to the Burmese conquest in the mid-sixteenth century.[65]

Framing chronologically the Sukhothai School was the town's rise as the fulcrum of an autonomous Thai kingdom following emancipation from Khmer suzerainty around the mid-thirteenth century. Coedès, who had previously established Sukhothai's dynastic sequence on the basis of epigraphic evidence (and in the process dated to 1292 the Ramkhamhaeng Inscription, thus authenticating it as the oldest evidence of the Thai script[66]), intimately linked political and cultural achievements and construed the Sukhothai kingdom—where self-rule was paralleled by unprecedented artistry inspired by the Theravada doctrine that would become Siam's national faith—as the first intimation of the Thai nation. The emplotment of the emergence of the 'Thai' artistic genius within the larger narrative of the political ascendancy of the Thai race was well served by the novel iconography of the Buddha images from Sukhothai, including those unearthed amongst the ruins of nearby Phitsanulok and Sawankhalok: supple bronze images in seated, standing and, characteristically, walking postures, with oval faces, hooked noses, arched eyebrows and half-closed eyes.

In spite of their obvious derivation from Sinhalese religious images, whose importation into Siam along with Theravada Buddhism had been even memorialized in popular lore,[67] the Sukhothai images were hailed as "the classic type of Siamese Buddha". In fact, as Prince Damrong espoused, "The Siamese do not reject the good and the beautiful just because it is of foreign origin. They borrowed the good and beautiful features of various different styles and merged them together. In this way, the characteristic style of Sukhodayan Buddhist art was formed, whose qualities are unsurpassed by any other period".[68] Coedès, on his part, censured art historians Alfred Salmony and A.K. Coomaraswamy for dating images in the 'classic' Siamese style as early as the turn of the first millennium AD (the latter had claimed that "quite definitely by the tenth and eleventh centuries the classic Siamese (Thai) type emerges and asserts itself"[69]). The French scholar was adamant that one could not speak of "Siamese" art in Siam before the thirteenth century, for the polished Buddha images praised by Salmony and Coomaraswamy could have hardly been created by "tribes" who were subjugated to the Khmer and were represented in the bas-reliefs of Angkor Wat as "véritables sauvages".[70]

Savagery, the semantic opposite of civilization par excellence, was invoked by Coedès to set the Indianized (i.e., civilized) Khmer apart from the twelfth-century Thai and thus defend his attribution of a pivotal historical role to Sukhothai where, as he put it in L'États Hindouisés, "between 1250 and 1350, the Siamese were able to develop their own characteristic civilisation, institutions and art".[71] Yet, linking artistic to political achievements meant limiting the Thai craftsmen's creativity to the century of duration of the Sukhothai kingdom. British consul turned government advisor turned art historian (and avid antiquities collector), Reginald Le May, employed a botanical metaphor to express this apparent irony in his 1938 book, in which he expanded Coedès' chronological framework of art styles into a fully fledged narrative of 'Buddhist art' in Siam:

> Once the Tai had established their dominion over the country from Sawankhalok in the north to Nakhon Si Thammarat in the south, the national art which was formed out of a coalescence of all the earlier

forces and currents quickly blossomed and as quickly faded, just as we see the brilliant, scarlet blooms of the Flamboyant tree suddenly burst upon us in April in all their glory and then, within one short month, fall to the ground and wither away.[72]

According to the 'law' of art history formulated in the eighteenth century by J.J. Winckelmann, canonization of the Sukhothai style as 'classical' entailed that a phase of stagnation and decline must follow. And, indeed, the sculptural output of the four-century-long Ayutthaya School was discounted as the sterile replication of a stylistic formula—an appraisal that, for once, saw Coedès in full agreement with Salmony and Coomaraswamy.[73]

Conclusion

Pursuing the cues of royal antiquarianism and seconding the nationalist quest for origins, the epigraphic and archaeological research of George Coedès from the late 1910s to the late 1920s validated the kingdom of Sukhothai as the *locus classicus* of Thai civilization, a golden age of paternalist rule, pristine faith and refined art. Nor was the myth of foundation of the Siamese nation born alone; its twin was the equally resilient myth of the Thai adroitness at appropriating and inventively adapting foreign knowledge, as the Burmese, Khmer and Sinhalese stylistic features evident in the older religious images were said to have been blended in the Sukhothai period to form a unique 'national' style. At the same time, Coedès was the first to acknowledge that his periodization and stylistic classification of Siamese antiquities should be considered provisional and subjected to future amendments and rectifications.[74] Yet, no substantial revision has thus far taken place.[75]

Thailand's major archaeological discovery in the intervening decades, as well as one of the most important internationally, that of the neolithic culture of Ban Chiang in the late 1960s, did not affect this framework, although it somewhat weakened the theory of Indianization by proving the indigenous origins of mainland Southeast Asia's material culture. When an exhibition held at the Bangkok National Museum in 1977 presented a classification of ancient sculptures into Mon, Khmer, Thai and Peninsular styles,[76] the curator's choice was met with scepticism and even open hostility.[77] By placing emphasis on the ethnic identity of craftsmen rather than on the antiquities' identification with historical political formations, the four-fold classification attempted, admittedly without success, to disentangle the history of art of ancient Siam from the nationalist framework, ultimately derived from Orientalist scholarship, within which it had been conceived.

Notes

I wish to thank Bruce M. Lockhart and Craig J. Reynolds for their insightful comments.

[1] National Archives, comp., *Chotmaihet phraratchaphiti ratchamangkhlaphisek ro.so. 126 127* [Documents on the the Royal Jubilee of 1907–1908], Bangkok, Fine Arts Department, 1984, pp. 23–25. The speech has been translated by Chris Baker as "The Antiquarian Society of Siam Speech of King Chulalongkorn", *Journal of the Siam Society* 89, nos. 1–2 (2001): 95–99.

[2] Charles Higham and Rachanie Thosarat, *Prehistoric Thailand: From Early Settlement to Sukhothai* (London: Thames and Hudson, 1998) p. 7. The terms 'Siam'/'Siamese' and 'Thailand'/'Thai' are value-laden. It is therefore useful to spell out the rationale of lexical usage in this essay: 'Siam' indicates the kingdom's name up to 1939; the adjective 'Siamese' refers to the kingdom as a geo-political entity and it is not a collective noun for its population; 'Thailand' is the name of the kingdom after 1939 according to international usage; finally, 'Thai' refers to that branch of the Tai-speaking *ethnie* that historically settled in northern and central Siam.

[3] See Dilip K. Chakrabarti, A *History of Indian Archaeology: From the Beginning to 1947* (New Delhi: Munshiram Manoharlal, 1988), pp. 115–16. Tapati Guha-Thakurta has discussed the practices of art history and archaeology in the context of emerging Indian nationalism in "Recovering the Nation's Art", in *Texts of Power: Emerging Disciplines in Colonial Bengal*, edited by Partha Chatterjee (Minneapolis: University of Minnesota Press, 1995), pp. 64–92; and "Tales of the Bharhut Stupa: Archaeology in the Colonial and Nationalist Imaginations", in *Paradigms of Indian Architecture: Space and Time in Representation and Design*, edited by G. H. R. Tillotson (Richmond: Curzon, 1998), pp. 26–58. On the construction of knowledge by colonial institutes of learning, see Tony Day and Craig J. Reynolds, "Cosmologies, Truth Regimes, and the State in Southeast Asia", *Modern Asian Studies* 34, no. 1 (2000), pp. 18–24.

[4] Thongchai Winichakul, *Siam Mapped: A History of the Geo-body of a Nation* (Honolulu, University of Hawaii Press, 1994), Ch. 3. Thongchai has also examined ethnographic practices in "The Others Within: Travel and Ethno-

Spatial Differentiation of Siamese Subjects 1885–1910", in *Civility and Savagery: Social Identity in Tai States*, edited by Andrew Turton (Richmond: Curzon, 2000), pp. 38–62.

[5] Charnvit Kasetsiri, "Thai Historiography from Ancient Times to the Modern Period", in *Perceptions of the Past in Southeast Asia*, edited by Anthony Reid and D.G. Marr (Singapore: Heinemann, 1979), pp. 156–70.

[6] Bruce G. Trigger, *A History of Archaeological Thought* (Cambridge: Cambridge University Press, 1989), p. 111.

[7] Suzanne Marchand, "The Quarrel of the Ancients and Moderns in German Museums", in *Museums and Memory*, edited by Susan A. Crane (Stanford: Stanford University Press, 2000), p. 196.

[8] The theory of the Thai settlers in Siam as a branch of an ancient Tai (or Ai-Lao) race that from the seventh to the thirteenth century would have dominated southern China's Nanchao kingdom (supposedly overthrown by Kublai Khan's southward advance) was successfully promoted, in Thailand even more than in the West, by the American Presbyterian missionary W.C. Dodd in his book *The Tai Race Elder Brother of the Chinese* (Cedar Rapids, IO: Torch Press, 1923). Although Dodd's ideas about the origins of the Tai people, who in his opinion had migrated in seven waves between the sixth century BC and the 1230s, later proved unfounded, he too saw the foundation of the Sukhothai kingdom in the mid-thirteenth century as marking their independence from Cambodian rule (ibid., pp. 10–17).

[9] Alfred Salmony, *La sculpture au Siam* (Paris: G. Van Oest, 1925), p. 1 (my translation). The book was also published in an English edition, *Sculpture in Siam* (London: E. Benn, 1925).

[10] The neglect of Coedès' contribution to the history of ancient Siam in contemporary Thailand might be slowly changing . A 'George Coedès Today Conference', organised by the Princess Maha Chakri Sirindhorn Anthropology Centre, Silpakorn University, and the Centre de Documentation et de Recherches d'Etudes Franco-Thaïes, was held in Bangkok on 9–10 September 1999.

[11] Trigger, *Archaeological Thought*, Ch. 2. On European antiquarianism, see *Producing the Past: Aspects of Antiquarian Culture and Practice 1700–1850*, edited by Martin Myrone and Lucy Peltz (Aldershot: Ashgate, 1999).

[12] The classic essay on this subject is Craig J. Reynolds, "Buddhist Cosmography in Thai History, with Special Reference to Nineteenth-Century Cultural Change", *Journal of Asian Studies* 35, no. 2 (1976): 203–20. See also Atthachak Sattayanurak, *Kanplianplaeng lokathat khong chonchan phunam thai tangtae ratchakan thi 4-pho.so. 2475* [Transformation of the Thai elite's worldview from the Fourth Reign to 1932], (Bangkok: Chulalongkorn University, 1995).

13 A.B. Griswold, "Introduction", in Prince Damrong Rajanubhap, *Monuments of the Buddha in Siam*, trans. Sulak Sivaraksa and A.B. Griswold, 2nd rev. ed., (Bangkok: Siam Society, 1973), v–vi. The term *phraboromrup*, indicating portraits and statues of kings (which first appeared in the second half of the nineteenth century), also has a sacral resonance that underscores the iconic status of visual representations of royalty. The Thai term for monuments of a secular nature, the first example of which was the Democracy Monument erected in 1942, is *anusaori*.

14 "The 'essence' of the original, corresponding approximately to its iconography, had to be reproduced; but the sculptural style—including things like facial expression, canons of proportion, and conventions for representing drapery—would depend much more on the artist's training than on the model." A.B. Griswold, "Imported Images and the Nature of Copying in the Art of Siam", in *Essays Offered to G. H. Luce*, vol. 2, edited by Ba Shin, Jean Boisselier and A.B. Griswold (Ascona, Switzerland: Artibus Asiae Publishers, 1966), p. 37.

15 Carl Bock, *Temples and Elephants* (London: Sampson, Law, Marston, Searle & Rivington, 1884), p. 82. Prince Damrong, in his essay, "Angkor from a Siamese Point of View" (*Journal of the Siam Society* 19, 1925, pp. 141–52), mentions a Siamese tradition whereby "whoever builds a monastery should leave something to his posterity to complete, otherwise he, too, completes his own life" (p. 149).

16 The recycling of construction materials from Ayutthaya at the beginning of the Bangkok era is mentioned by Prince Chula Chakrabongse in *Lords of Life: A History of the Kings of Thailand*, 2nd rev. ed. (London: A. Redman, 1967), p. 90. Such recycling continued throughout the Fifth Reign; see Craig Reynolds, "Monastery Lands and Labour Endowments in Thailand: Some Effects of Social and Economic Change, 1868–1910", *Journal of the Economic and Social History of the Orient* 22, no. 2 (1979), pp. 206–7.

17 R.H. Davis, *Life of Indian Images* (Princeton, N.J.: Princeton University Press, 1997), pp. 252–53.

18 Walter Benjamin, "The Work of Art in the Age of Mechanical Reproduction", in *Illuminations*, trans. Harry Zohn (New York: Schocken Books, 1969), pp. 224–25.

19 The essays dealing with the inscription are collected in *The Ramkhamhaeng Controversy*, edited by J.R. Chamberlain (Bangkok: Siam Society, 1991). For an appraisal of the controversy, see my *The Politics of Ruins and the Business of the Nostalgia* (Bangkok: White Lotus, 2002), pp. 42–43. The indifference towards the recent re-dating of an inscription found at Wat Bang Sanuk to 1219, which would make it some seventy years older than the Ramkhamhaeng Inscription, confirms the latter's iconic status. The historical hypotheses raised

by the re-dating are explored in David K. Wyatt, "Relics, Oaths and Politics in Thirteenth-Century Siam", *Journal of Southeast Asian Studies* 32, no. 1 (2001): 3–66.

[20] Chaophraya Thipakorawong, *The Dynastic Chronicles, Bangkok Era: The Fourth Reign*, vol. 2, trans. Chadin Flood (Tokyo: Centre for East Asian Cultural Studies, 1966), pp. 496–518.

[21] Ibid., p. 500.

[22] Ibid. Cf. Pierre Dupont, *L'archéologie mône de Dvaravati* (Paris: Publications de l'École Française d'Extrême-Orient, 1959), p. 136.

[23] Thipakorawong, *Dynastic Chronicles*, p. 515. Chaophraya Thipakorawong was also the author of the scientific treaty *Kitchanukit* (A book explaining various things), which was partly translated by Henri Alabaster in the 1870s as "The Modern Buddhist". Day and Reynolds, "Cosmologies, Truth Regimes, and the State", p. 9.

[24] See Thongchai Winichakul, "The Quest for '*Siwilai*': A Geographical Discourse of Civilizational Thinking in the Late 19th and Early 20th Century Siam", *Journal of Asian Studies* 59 (2000): 528–49; and my *Lords of Things: The Fashioning of the Siamese Monarchy's Modern Image* (Honolulu: University of Hawaii Press, 2002).

[25] National Archives, comp., *Chotmaihet sadet praphat tang prathet nai ratchan thi 5 sadet muang singkhapo lae muang betawia khrang ae lae sadet praphat prathet india* [Chronicles of the royal journey to the cities of Singapore, Batavia and to India in the Fifth Reign] (Bangkok: Fine Arts Department, 1966).

[26] John Bowring, *The Kingdom and People of Siam* (London: J.W. Parker, 1857), vol. 2, p. 279.

[27] Patrick Jory, "Books and the Nation: The Making of Thailand's National Library", *Journal of South-East Asian Studies* 31, no. 2 (2000): 354.

[28] A collection of Buddhist and Hindu images and sculptural fragments reputedly far more valuable than the museum's, including the gifts presented to Rama V by the Dutch colonial authorities on his 1896 visit to Java (bas-reliefs from the temples of Prambanan and Borobodur, a large Ganesha and three smaller sculptures), was housed inside Wat Phra Keo. George Coedès, "Les collections archéologiques du Musée national de Bangkok", *Ars Asiatica* 12, 1928 (monographic volume), pp. 8–9.

[29] Prince Damrong Rachanubhap, "Wat Benchamabophit and Its Collection of Images of the Buddha", *Journal of the Siam Society* 22 (1928): 19–28 (quote from pp. 20–21).

[30] Ibid., p. 21.

[31] Among the images cast for display in Wat Benchamabophit is the copy of the highly venerated Buddha Chinarat (dating to the fourteenth or fifteenth century) in Wat Phra Si Rattana Mahathat, Phitsanulok.

[32] P.A. Thompson, *Lotus Land* (London: Lippincott, 1906).

[33] King Chulalongkorn, "Samakhom subsuan khong buran nai prathet sayam" [The society for archaeological investigation in Siam] *Sinlapakorn* 12, no. 2 (1968): 42–46.

[34] Eiji Murashima, "The Origins of Modern Official State Ideology in Thailand", *Journal of South-East Asian Studies* 19, no. 1 (1988): 80–96.

[35] Quoted in Chawingam Macherin, "Kansongsaerim khwamru thangdan silpa wathanatham prawatisat lae borankhadi nai ratchakan thi 4–7" [Promotion of knowledge about art, culture, history and archaeology from the Fourth to the Seventh reigns], *Silpakorn* 18, no. 3 (1974): 70.

[36] See my *Lords of Things*, Ch. 6. In later nineteenth-century England the revival of craftsmanship had been advocated also by anti-modernist art critics such as John Ruskin and William Morris, with whose ideas Oxford-educated Vajiravudh was probably familiar.

[37] See Matthew P. Copeland, "Contested Nationalism and the 1932 Overthrow of the Absolute Monarchy" (Ph.D. dissertation, Australian National University, 1993), Ch. 3.

[38] Quoted in Walter Vella, *Chaiyo! King Vajiravudh and the Origins of Thai Nationalism* (Honolulu, University of Hawaii Press, 1978), p. 211.

[39] Henri Mouhot, *Travels in the Central Parts of Indo-China (Siam), Cambodia and Laos* (London: John Murray, 1864). A Frenchman, Mouhot lived in Britain after his marriage to the daughter of explorer Mungo Park and conducted his exploration of Southeast Asia under the aegis of the Royal Geographic Society. Mouhot's travel journal, edited by his brother, was first published in Britain.

[40] Quoted in the *Bangkok Times*, 1 May 1907.

[41] Prince Damrong Rachanubhab, "Angkor from a Siamese Point of View", p. 152.

[42] Charles Higham, *The Archaeology of Mainland Southeast Asia* (Cambridge: Cambridge University Press, 1989), pp. 19–20.

[43] Etienne Aymonier, *Le Cambodge I: Le Royaume actuel*, and *Le Cambodge II: Les provinces Siamoises* (Paris: E. Leroux, 1900; 1901). These volumes have been published in English translation as, respectively, *Khmer Heritage in the Old Siamese Provinces* and *Khmer Heritage in Thailand*, both trans. by W.E.J. Tips (Bangkok, White Lotus, 1999).

[44] Aymonier, *Khmer Heritage in Thailand*, p. 1.

[45] Benedict Anderson, *Imagined Communities: Considerations on the Origins and Spread of Nationalism*, rev. ed. (London: Verso, 1991), pp. 178–82. Anderson lists a third outcome of the activity of colonial archaeological services, the 'logo-isation' of monuments such as Angkor and Borobodur, which promoted their tourist consumption as well as their prominence in the postcolonial imagery.

46   Aymonier, *Khmer Heritage*, p. 53. The French bias towards Khmer architecture was such that it actually prevented appreciation of Khmer sculpture, the largest collections of which up to the 1920s were ironically in the Bangkok museum and in the hands of Thai private collectors, including Prince Damrong. George Coedès, "Bronze Khmers", *Ars Asiatica* 5, 1923 (monographic volume), pp. 9, 11.

47   Lucien Fournereau, *Le Siam ancien*, 2 vols (Paris: E. Leroux, 1895–1908).

48   E-E. Lunet de Lajonquière, "Le domain archéologique du Siam", *Bulletin de la Commission archéologique de l'Indochine* (*BCAI*), 1909; and "Essay d'inventaire archéologique du Siam", *BCAI*, 1912.

49   G.E. Gerini, "Siamese Archaeology", in *The Kingdom of Siam*, edited by A. Cecil Carter (New York: Knickerbockers Press, 1904), pp. 213–26.

50   *Journal of the Siam Society*, 1 (1904): 228–32.

51   Cf. Jory, "Books and the Nation", p. 353.

52   "Siam", *BEFEO* 21 (1921), p. 313.

53   Jory, "Books and the Nation", p. 359.

54   Ann Nugent, "Asia's French Connection: George Coedès and the Coedès Collection", *National Library of Australia News*, January 1996, pp. 6–8.

55   Coedès' work was published in English as *The Indianized States of Southeast Asia*, edited by Walter Vella and translated by Susan Brown Cowing (Honolulu: East-West Center Press, 1968).

56   The text of the decree is in *Prachum kotmai prachamsot* [Collected laws], vol. 36, B.E. 2466 (1923), pp. 222–24.

57   George Coedès, "Rapport sur les travaux du Service Archéologique pour l'anne 2467 (1924–25)", *Journal of the Siam Society* 19 (1925): 29–41. The museum's official denomination as *phiphithaphan sathan samrap phranakhon* (museum for the royal city) echoed the library's *hosamut samrap phranakhon*.

58   Coedès, "Musée national de Bangkok", pp. 8–13. A law instituted on 25 October 1926 made the export of ancient artworks conditional to the approval of the Royal Institute, while the administration of the museum was regulated by the subsequent law of 5 May 1927.

59   Ibid., p. 17.

60   The book was published in English translation as *Monuments of the Buddha in Siam*, cit. (The first edition was entitled *A History of Buddhist Monuments in Siam* [Bangkok: Siam Society, 1962]). Coedès did not submit a precise chronology for the various schools and Damrong gave only 'starting' dates, some of which have proven grossly mistaken. The standard periodization of the seven 'schools' is as follows: Dvaravati, 6th (7th)–11th century; Srivijaya, 8th–13th century; Lopburi, 7th–14th century; Chiangsaen, 11th–20th century; Sukhothai, 13th–15th century; U-thong, 13th–15th century; Ayutthaya, 1350–1767 (followed by the Rattanakosin, or Bangkok, School, beginning in 1782). See Theodore Bowie, M.C. Subhadradis Diskul,

A.B. Griswold, *The Sculpture of Thailand* (New York: Asia Society, 1972), p. 26.

61 Coedès, "Musée national de Bangkok", pp. 20–24 (cf. *Indianised States*, p. 292, n. 91).

62 Ibid., p. 25.

63 Ibid., pp. 26–29.

64 Ibid., pp. 30–31.

65 Damrong, *Monuments of the Buddha*, pp. 14–17.

66 Coedès, "Documents sur la dynastie de Sukhodaya", *BEFEO* 17, no. 2 (1917): 1–47; and "The Origins of the Sukhodayan Dynasty", *Journal of the Siam Society* 14, no. 1 (1921): 1–11.

67 Coedès, "Le Musée de Bangkok", p. 32–33.

68 Damrong, *Monuments of the Buddha*, p. 19. Damrong also writes (p. 4) that the early Thai "knew how to pick and choose. When they saw some good feature in the culture of other peoples, if it was not in conflict with their own interests, they did not hesitate to borrow it and adapt it to their own requirements."

69 A.K. Coomaraswamy, *A History of Indian and Indonesian Art* (London: E. Goldston, 1927), p. 176.

70 Coedès, "Le Museé de Bangkok", pp. 28–29. Cf. Salmony, *Sculpture au Siam*, plates 9–13; and Coomaraswamy, *Indian and Indonesian Art*, plates 321–322 and p. 177: "The Buddha heads referable to the classic Thai period, as well as the earliest of those from Phitsanulok, dating from about 1000 A.D. are the supreme achievement of the Thai genius."

71 Coedès, *Indianised States*, p. 222.

72 Reginald Le May, *A Concise History of Buddhist Art in Siam* (Cambridge: Cambridge University Press, 1938), p. 143.

73 Coedès, "Musée de Bangkok", p. 33. Cf. Salmony, *Sculpture au Siam*, p. 61; and Coomaraswamy, *Indian and Indonesian Art*, p. 178.

74 George Coedès, "Review of Reginald Le May's *History of Buddhist Art in Siam*", *Journal of the Siam Society* 30, no. 2 (1939).

75 For detailed studies that expand critically on Coedès and Damrong's classification, see Jean Boisselier and Jean-Michel Beurdeley, *La Sculpture en Thaïlande* (Fribourg: Office du Livre, 1974); and H.W. Woodward, *The Sacred Sculpture of Thailand* (London: Thames and Hudson, 1997).

76 Piriya Krairiksh, *Art Styles in Thailand: A Selection from National Museums and an Essay in Conceptualization* (Bangkok: Fine Arts Department, 1977).

77 "It is unfortunate for Thailand that some Thai scholars rely so much on Westerners in thinking and disregard themes that Westerners have not researched or documented ... the Fine Arts Department, which held a major arts exhibition at the National Museum, had done away with significant

art periods. This is a manifestation of disgrace to Thailand's history. While scholars throughout the world have not confirmed that Dvaravati art belongs to the Mon race, Thai scholars have simply jumped to that conclusion." No Na Paknam, *The Relationship Between the Art and History of the Thai People* (Bangkok: Office of the National Culture Commission, n.d.), pp. 2–3.

8

Foreign Knowledge: Cultures of Western Science-making in Meiji Japan

Gregory K. Clancey

The term 'transfer', most of us realize, is a misleading description of how scientific or technological knowledge travels. It reduces a partial, unpredictable, and culturally nuanced process to the simple action of sending a parcel through the mail. Historians of religion or art are not likely to write of the 'transfer' of their subject from one geographic location to another. Yet historians of science and technology, whose topic is in no sense less complex, still sometimes fall back on 'transmission' or 'replication', terms too casually borrowed from the mechanisms or laboratory procedures of the actors we study. Even when the perfect transfer of a technical or scientific regime from one place to another is the actor's intention—and one cannot invariably assume that it is— different circumstances at the 'receiving' end invariably produce different narratives, events, and forms. Certainly it is part of our job to notice these, even when historical actors invested in a story of transfer dismiss them as 'local anomalies'.

Meiji Japan is one of the most iconographic sites of scientific and technological 'transfer' in world history narratives. In the last decade or so, historians have begun to revisit and retell this story with cultural issues foregrounded, giving the narrative more depth and life than it was allowed as a prop to modernization theory.[1] This article is an attempt to further that scholarly trend. I intend to focus on an example of scientific knowledge-making in the Meiji academy at a time when it was still staffed largely by foreign professors—men whose official role was to perform as switches through which foreign knowledge flowed. My story is about how they were not perfect switches; how the 'Western knowledge' that was taught to the first generation of Japanese was in fact a local conversation, even when European teachers were speaking mainly to themselves. It is about how 'Western knowledge' in Meiji Japan inevitably mixed words, references, concepts, and evidence from far away with others invented or discovered close-at-hand. The story is relevant not only to Japan, but to anywhere in the colonially-ordered world where people believed they were replicating distant knowledge regimes but ended up creating peculiar new objects, sometimes in spite of themselves.

The government of Meiji Japan, as is well-known, established in the 1870s a College of Engineering (Kobudaigakko) and another for the humanities and sciences (Kaisei Gakko, later the Imperial University) staffed largely with foreign professors. Both institutions were cradles of Japanese science and engineering, if not 'Western learning' (yogaku) in general. They would merge in 1886. I will collectively refer to these and a handful of lesser institutions as 'The Meiji academy'. Despite its foreign staffing, this Meiji academy was not a tightly-marching phalanx of knowledge, practice, and opinion. Even more so than many universities in Europe, whose faculties were often inborn through generations of careful vetting, the foreign professors (yatoi) in the Meiji academy had migrated—often singly and suddenly—from various countries and disciplinary cultures, and had diverse institutional affiliations, work methods, interests, and ambitions. They naturally formed a small society among themselves in Tokyo, but they also, singly and in smaller groups, formed societies with Japanese patrons, colleagues, and students. Moreover, such social relations tended to be temporary, for most of the foreigners were destined to return home after one or two short-term contracts. For these and other reasons, expatriate constructions of 'Western learning' did not invariably mesh, and were sometimes in open conflict. Disagreement is of course normative in any academic setting. In the peculiar setting of the Meiji academy, however, with its official stress on intercultural transmission, serious epistemological rifts could call into question the very ceremony that expatriates were contracted to perform.[2]

It wasn't just a matter of differently interpreting 'Western' texts. Inevitably, *yatoi* were concerned not only with teaching but conducting their own research, which many tailored to the opportunities presented by being in Japan. Hired and credentialled as foreign experts, some nonetheless worked hard while in Tokyo to turn themselves into experts on Japan. Western fact-making about Japan constituted capital abroad, they knew, and was also marketable, some discovered, in Tokyo itself. The interest many developed in explaining 'Japan' using Western tools inevitably influenced the way that 'The West' (including its intellectual tools) was explained to Japanese. Thus did the already elusive object 'Western learning' further shift, fragment, attenuate—edit itself to fit local circumstances, if you will—as 'Japanese' research projects began to take shape among Tokyo's expatriate teaching staff.

To focus our gaze too insistently on the 'transmission' of this something called Western knowledge to Meiji Japan (or anywhere) is thus to lose sight of something else on which Western teachers were just as intently focused: organizing an unfamiliar landscape; contrasting that landscape with a normative (Western) one; and explaining their new location to themselves, each other, and their colleagues and patrons at home. The tool-boxes they had carried from Europe often proved inadequate, and were supplemented in many cases by locally-crafted instruments. Understanding 'Western knowledge' in Meiji Japan is thus to understand the expatriate community's particular fascinations, obsessions, and anxieties, and to follow their internal debates, many of which were of only tangential interest to colleagues in London or Berlin. It is also to follow their intimate relations with differing groups of Japanese, some above them (their governmental patrons) and some below them (their students). The 'local' or group dynamic of this knowledge-making is what I am after in the pages that follow. To trace it, one must abandon the sense that what happens locally is an epiphenomenon of a transcontinental 'process'. Science, like knowledge-making in general, turns out to tangle the local and cosmopolitan in intricate and unpredictable ways.

Earthquakes

Expatriate professors in Meiji Tokyo were interested in a variety of things individually, and a fewer number of things collectively. Among their stronger collective interests were earthquakes. For most *yatoi* from northern Europe (and those from Britain and Germany formed a critical mass) earthquakes were exotic and disturbing phenomena not necessarily encountered in previous Asian postings. Being in Japan for any length of time, however, foreigners experienced tremors, often at frequent intervals. In the reports of many expatriates, Japanese themselves appeared relatively unconcerned by mild earthquakes, even to the point of not noticing them. Thus was the unfamiliar movement of the earth experienced as simultaneously a personal, natural, and cultural problem. The questions: 'when will the earth shake, and how severely' (personal safety); 'why does the earth shake' (natural science); and 'why don't Japanese seem to care when the earth shakes' (social science) followed closely behind one another and became confounded in many expatriate accounts.

In the aftermath of the moderately severe Yokohama earthquake of 1880, Tokyo-area *yatoi* founded the Seismological Society of Japan (SSJ).[3] This club and its topic, which also attracted substantial numbers of Japanese, subsequently became one of the more focused outlets of *yatoi* research and energy. Unlike Tokyo's Asiatic and Elocutionary Societies, and most of others founded by expatriates, the Seismological Society was not modelled on a colonial or continental one. It was unique to Japan. The Society's core members—professors on the science and engineering faculties of the Meiji academy—were intent on using the Society to elevate 'seismology' from a geological sideline into a modern (instrumental) science. Over the course of the 1880s, they would successfully enlist members of the larger *yatoi* community, residents of Yokohama, their Japanese students, and elements of the Japanese government into the construction of two machines: a physical one called a 'seismograph' for inscribing earthquake shocks, and a human one of literally hundreds of people, some in remote parts of Japan, who would monitor earthquake-recording devices, send their inscriptions to Tokyo, and allow Tokyo's 'seismologists' to understand and report in their journal (published in both English and Japanese editions) what earthquakes were and how to mitigate their effects.[4]

When the Society was founded, its secretary John Milne would later write, "Tokyo was in reality a city of many [seismological] inventions... their name was legion."[5] At the first meeting of the SSJ in 1880, Milne remarked "we see around us a mighty forest of pendulums, springs, and delicately balanced columns." It was at the same meeting that James Ewing, Tokyo University professor of Mechanical Engineering and Physics, unveiled his 'seismograph'—the direct ancestor of the present device—essentially a seismometer attached to a disc of smoked glass (and later a continuous roll of smoked paper) on which various earthquake features could be recorded.[6] The seismograph became the instrumental kernel of the new Society's enthusiasm, yielding as it did product (a 'seismogram') that was not only highly readable, but, like a telegram, vendible (between Tokyo and Europe) and reproducible in scientific reports and papers.[7]

Seismology was a 'Western science' made largely in Meiji Japan. In Europe and America it remained a largely amateur pursuit or geological sideline—lacking its own journals, textbooks, or academic positions—as late as 1900. None of Tokyo's foreign 'seismologists' had even toyed with that self-description before they arrived in Japan. Yet Tokyo became, by the mid-1880s, the centre of a new 'international' seismology: the home of the discipline's one professional journal, best-equipped laboratories, most productive research programmes, and eventually, its first credentialled graduate students and professors. What began as an extracurricular *yatoi* interest moved inside the Meiji academy when Tokyo University established the world's first chair in seismology in 1886 and gave it to Sekiya Seikei, a student of James Ewing's. Milne's student Omori Fusakichi would go on to build an international reputation that equalled or surpassed that of his mentor. This first generation of Japanese seismologists would have few foreign colleagues who were equally well-credentialled.

What makes the rise of Japanese seismology all the more unusual is that it lay outside the Japanese government's planned absorption of 'Western learning'. The act of framing an 'earthquake problem' was done by foreigners hired to teach and research other topics, which is why they initially organized themselves in a private society. Either the Meiji government did not consider earthquakes a pressing problem, or it sensed in the course of scouting expeditions abroad that seismology—having yet to be institutionalized in the European academy—had little to offer. At a time when all parties were invested in a model of science and technology transfer, none had imagined that a branch of 'Western learning' could develop spontaneously in Japan and eventually be exported abroad as a Japanese specialty. Yet this was to be seismology's peculiar trajectory.

Seismology as ethnography

Japanese seismology was indeed a different animal from the practice which then went by that name in Europe, and not only because of its greater emphasis on instrumentality. In perusing the Society's journal one finds certain agendas operating under its guise which were quite alien to European geophysics. Only in Japan, for instance, did the study of earthquakes incorporate ethnography. It was the contention of the Society's co-founder and leading light John Milne that earthquakes were the key to understanding the Japanese "national character".[8] Subtextual to 'Japan's earthquake problem' was why the Japanese were as they were to European eyes, e.g. 'timid' and 'fatalistic'; a people who cultivated 'the temporary' and not 'the permanent'. A working hypothesis for Milne and certain other members of the Seismological Society was that the answer lay in earthquakes and volcanoes. The idea that much of what appeared odd and unusual about Japan could be explained by reference to its natural phenomena helps to account for the breadth and depth of *yatoi* interest in seismology, an interest that extended well beyond issues of how and why the earth moved. It equally helps account for the interest taken in seismology by a large and influential group of Japanese.

In a paper entitled "Earthquake Effects Emotional and Moral", which Milne delivered before Japan's Seismological Society in 1887, he wrote:

> ...nations which have been subjected to influences like these (earthquakes) may possibly acquire some slight peculiarities, characterizing them from nations which have been free from such influences...Certainly it may be said that the successful or serious nations of the present day, characterized by their enterprise and commerce, are not those whose misfortune it has been to fight against unintelligible terrorisms of nature.[9]

The modifier "unintelligible" allows the dike-building Dutch to remain with the "successful" nations, while "the present day" and "serious"— markers for The Scientific Revolution—isolate the obvious successes of

Greece, Rome, Byzantium, and Spain. Although these Mediterranean civilizations "have led nations", Milne admitted, they were also artistic and superstitious, with "a passion for games of chance" and "the cultivation of arts conducive to pleasure" (i.e. like the Japanese). Said Milne: "Is it not likely that a continuation of these conditions might result in a disregard for the serious affairs of life, and unfit a nation for competition with those living in more favored regions?" Where, he rhetorically asked, "can [we] find a light-hearted carelessness, pleasant geniality, and a happy disposition better developed than is met with in this country [Japan]?" His answer was Naples, another famous earthquake zone. Thus did Milne attempt to build a common ethnography of what he referred to in this and other writings as "earthquake countries".[10]

The mechanism in Milne's scheme by which earthquakes had made nations unfit for competition resembles Darwinian selection, which informs its language throughout:

> Not only may seismic forces have stimulated the imagination to the detriment of reason, but amongst the weaker members of a community, by the creation of feelings of timidity resulting perhaps in mental aberrations like madness and imbecility, the seeds have been sown for a process of selection, by which the weaker members in the ordinary course of racial competition must succumb.[11]

The "community" which Milne describes seems, at once, Japan itself and the 'community of nations' with which Japan is in "racial competition". He was simultaneously providing an explanation for 'Japan' to an audience of Europeans, and attempting to isolate for an audience of westernizing Japanese the most fundamental barrier to their identity as successful Darwinian competitors.

Darwinian schema and language was then rampant among the younger, intellectual species of the Japanese archipelago. Milne could have been confident of sharing basic assumptions with elements of his Japanese audience, who had grown used to examining their 'national character' through the eyes of foreign teachers and analysing their 'national condition' using a toolbox of foreign texts.[12] Among the original patrons of the Seismological Society was Tokyo University President Kato Hiroyuki, one of the most famous Japanese proponents of Spencerian (social) Darwinism.[13] Kato would soon be the first president of the Imperial Earthquake Investigation Committee.[14]

Milne's own mix of Darwinism and geological determinism was informed in particular by Henry Thomas Buckle, whose *History of Civilization in England* was "a great favorite" among Imperial University students (according to the memoir of then-Prime Minister Ito Hirobumi) and had already inspired the first Meiji-period Japanese cultural history, Taguchi Ukichi's *Short History of Civilization in Japan* (published serially 1877–83).[15] It was on reading Buckle that Imperial University President Kato had famously converted, in 1879, from the doctrine of 'natural rights' to that of 'natural laws'.[16] "Buckle" said Milne in the same address, "shows how the wonder of a people may be excited with all great natural phenomenon."[17] Buckle presented England as the normative (i.e. steady) state of both society and nature, realms which he explicitly linked. Britain owed its multiple successes, according to Buckle, to a lack of "destructive perturbations", which elsewhere had shaken societies off a natural evolutionary path toward liberal democracy.[18]

The most novel aspect of Milne's ethnography, which may have further convinced him of its palatability to a Japanese audience, was its vitiation of the binarism 'East and West'. As an "earthquake country", Japan was now to be classified with nations which were well-springs of European civilization. Thus could the widely-conceded Japanese artistic talent be explained as the 'positive' side of its experience with earthquakes, seismicity having "excited the Japanese imagination". Moreover, notions about inferiority and superiority which were so vaguely (and hence insidiously) contained in 'East and West' were by this means shifted in the direction of natural, mechanical causes, which might be overcome in equally mechanical ways.

It testifies to the strength of 'East and West' that at least one important member of Milne's audience attempted to preserve that mapping using Milne's own evidence. In the discussion following Milne's lecture, Basil Hall Chamberlain, Tokyo University professor of philology and Japanese, claimed to have surveyed Japanese literature and poetry for references to earthquakes, and found only a single one. Rather than concluding that Japanese culture had been relatively uninfluenced by the shaking of the earth, Chamberlain, seeking to bolster a part of Milne's case, cited the very absence of references as an indication of their profound effect; of their having produced a "lesser range of imaginative facility" in the Japanese mind. Certain as he and other *yatoi* were that earthquakes were the penultimate Japanese natural phenomena, their absence from the national literature could only be explained by a gradual dulling of the collective imagination brought on by the phenomenon itself. Ignoring entirely Milne's category of "earthquake countries", Chamberlain concluded that this lack of "imaginative facility" was what "distinguishes the Japanese, and Eastern Asiatics in general, from the nations of the European race". In Greece and Rome, he was suggesting, the same natural phenomenon had had the opposite cultural effect.[19]

Chamberlain's response was too much for Sekiya Seikei, appointed the year before to the first chair of seismology at Tokyo University. Sekiya pointed out that after the Ansei earthquake of 1855, eighty works on earthquakes had been produced by Japanese authors, ranging from the scientific to the literary. In answer to Chamberlain's suggestion of Japanese passivity, Sekiya noted that the disaster generated great excitement and even spontaneous acts of charity. As for Milne's paper, Sekiya was more circumspect, saying only that Milne "threatens to exhaust all that there is for workers in seismology to investigate", a statement that could be read in a number of ways. Sekiya and Milne's own student Omori Fusakichi would subsequently collect excerpts from nearly 500 books, diaries, and other written materials relating to over 2,000 earthquakes between 416 A.D. and 1867. These were published in 1904 as "The Materials for the Earthquake History of Japan from the Earliest Times Down to 1866".[20]

In replying to both Chamberlain and Sekiya, Milne sided with Chamberlain, despite the latter's mangling of Milne's own argument. "All great calamities produce mental effects", he stated, "and with savage nations these were more permanent than with civilized nations." Chamberlain's evidence described for Milne a permanent effect from the period of Japan's primitiveness, while Sekiya's was drawn from the late Tokugawa period, when Japan was more civilized. How the intense interest in the Ansei earthquake could have arisen in spite of a 'permanent' dulling effect on the Japanese imagination was a question that went unasked.[21]

It also escaped comment that much of Milne's evidence of "timid" feelings and mental strain was drawn not from the community of Japanese, but the community of foreigners in Japan. His paper actually begins with the effects of an earthquake on "a visitor in an earthquake country". The foreigner develops a "feeling of timidity" over time through repeated seismic events, one advanced rather than mitigated by his contact with the local (foreign) community.

> The reason that the mental condition of the new-comer becomes changed
> is possibly the influence of those with whom he is associated, who have
> gradually impressed him with what might be the result of the gentle
> motion he feels, or perhaps it is an increasing nervousness and fear as he
> gradually recognizes his utter inability to avert these disturbances or
> predict their consequence. In this way a whole community by repetitions
> of small earthquakes may be gradually worked into a state of mental
> nervousness.[22]

Milne gives the concrete example, obviously from a personal experience,
of a dinner party interrupted by an earthquake, where "the chandeliers
commenced to oscillate". Some (guests) rise from their seats, others
perhaps for example's sake, perhaps from stupefaction, keep their places,
but each fixes his gaze upon his neighbour.[23]

Thus was "gradually develop[ed] an increasing terrorism", which
according to Milne had even been responsible, "in the case of persons
of delicate health", for death.[24]

Milne was not alone in depicting Japan's foreign residents as suffering
from permanent feelings of anxiety. Engineer Henry Dyer wrote of "the
numerous nervous disorders so common among the foreign residents in
Japan"[25] and another engineer, George Cawley, of "the shock to the
nervous system induced by an ordinary earthquake". Cawley credited
his own nervousness "more to the creaking and rocking motion of a
flexible house than the vibrations of the ground". It was partly "to palliate
this nervous shock" he wrote, that he "prefer[red] rigid to flexible
buildings".[26] Tokyo architect Josiah Conder had spoken in London of
how Japanese houses "sway about in the most alarming manner".[27] It
was the seismograph of the foreign body that, in the accounts of foreigners
themselves, was most consistently recording shock and alarm. Japanese
were generally described, in the same accounts, as being relatively
impervious to the same effects. Hence the importance of the foreign
body (specifically the foreign nervous system) as an earthquake witness
in Milne's account. Foreign feelings—terror and dread—became in these
accounts normative reactions. Their absence among Japanese was at the
root of the phenomenon to be scientifically explained, yet through
evidence provided, in large part, by the foreign body itself.

Milne's paper and the follow-up discussion demonstrate that
seismology was not just subterranean science. Like so many nineteenth
century science projects, it was also bedrock for new constructions of
race, even if the category "earthquake countries" (and its less visible

twin, 'non-earthquake countries') threatened to disrupt the controlling binarism 'East and West'; even if "earthquake countries" and other bio-geologic mappings suggested that Japan's 'problems' might be not simply 'racial' but environmental, and even mechanical. It also reveals a pre-occupation with explaining not only 'Japan' (and a confounding of the physical and social) but explaining the foreign community to itself—in this case the divergence between its own reactions to earth tremors and the reactions of Japanese.

Biology as architectural history

Japanese seismicity not only singled out the nervous systems of expatriates. It seemed to single out for damage or destruction the foreign community's own buildings. The reason that the seismic event of 1880 was referred to as the "Yokohama earthquake" was because its destructive effects were confined to the foreign residences and shops of that treaty port, even though the epicentre was nearer Tokyo. Most of Yokohama's brick chimneys had toppled, and a few of its western-style houses had completely collapsed. The Japanese buildings in Yokohama, by all accounts, had remained largely undamaged despite their having swayed about with the motion of the waves. Moreover, the only part of Tokyo itself which sustained recordable damage was the Ginza, the district of Western-style masonry buildings designed by a foreign architect. Here was an even more immediate reason for the intensity of *yatoi* interest in seismology.[28]

We are used to the claim that 'Western knowledge' swept non-Western knowledge systems before it because of its demonstrable effectiveness. This was also assumed to be the normal order of things in the Meiji academy. But it was an order thrown into crisis by the poor performance of Western-style structures in Japanese earthquakes. The Yokohama earthquake, and even more so the Great Nobi Earthquake of 1891, which brought down British-designed railway bridges and government buildings while leaving Edo-period castles and pagoda intact, raised fundamental questions about the Western engineering curriculum.[29] The survivability of certain Japanese building-types suggested that they might incorporate principles of construction, or even physics, which Europeans had not yet encountered.[30] In Europe's Mediterranean earthquake zone, buildings and whole cities tended to collapse in serious shocks, often with catastrophic loss of life. British engineers in Japan had coaxed themselves into believing, however, that Southern European methods were simply inferior to their own; that British methods in Japan might still constitute an act of rescue. When Western-style structures began to crack or fall down, however, and nearby Japanese wooden ones escape damage, the phenomenon proved riveting—and deeply controversial—to Western teachers and their Japanese students and patrons alike.[31] The spectacle eventually engaged even the Japanese public. Following the Great Nobi earthquake, numerous newspaper illustrations, book covers, and multi-panel paintings appeared showing shattered Western railroad bridges juxtaposed with a triumphantly intact Nagoya Castle. This suggested not just a limit to foreign knowledge, but a demonstrable Japanese insight.[32]

There were conflicting *yatoi* reactions to this earthquake crisis. The major fault line lay between scientists on the one hand, and engineers and architects on the other. For most of the scientists in the Seismological Society, evolutionary theory not only informed their ethno-geologic geography, but it undergirded a belief that Japanese buildings must have 'adapted' over time to earthquakes and destructive nature. To Europeans trained in the natural sciences, it would have seemed 'natural' by the 1870s that there was a close fit between indigenous buildings and nature, that native building systems would have 'evolved' survival mechanisms suited to their local environments, just as Japanese minds had 'evolved' their own mechanisms to overcome the fear of a shifting earth. These scientists, including Milne, thus extended their ethnographic investigations to the Japanese built landscape—the temples, pagoda, shrines, and even castles—looking for "aseismic adaptations" that would demonstrate this process of cultural evolution, one closely linked to a natural phenomenon. They were predisposed, in other words, to believe that traditional Japanese architecture was inherently earthquake-resistant, and were eager to explain the principles that made it so. The key, many believed, lay in its flexibility—the complicated joint structures of Japanese carpentry. This investigative program continued into at least the Taisho era, when Milne's student and successor Omori Fusakichi hooked up seismographs to Japan's major pagoda, demonstrating their ability to synchronize their swaying to seismic waves.[33]

To *yatoi* engineers and architects, however (and to many of the Japanese they trained), Newtonian mechanics was much closer and more relevant than Darwinian or Lamarckian biology. They rejected not only the scientists' evolutionary theories, but even their evidence that Japanese buildings performed better than their own. They argued in particular instances that Western principles had not been given a 'fair trial' because of poor workmanship by Japanese contractors, or that only exceptional or lucky Japanese buildings survived destructive quakes. When engineer R.H. Brunton wrote in 1873 that typical Japanese buildings were "of all structures, the worst adapted" to (earthquake prone) Japan, he was constructing a sentence that made little sense to expatriate biologists and geologists. Yet it was echoed for more than two decades by other engineers, who conceived 'nature' as a force to be adapted, rather than one which primarily adapts.[34]

The Japanese landscape (natural and cultural) hence became the site and subject of a sometimes intense polemic between *yatoi* biologists, geologists, physicists, architects, and engineers lasting at least into the 1890s, when the last of them returned home. Physicists theorized the movement of carpentry joints in Buddhist temples, and botanists explained the structure of the five-story pagoda as they might a species of willow, often with open hostility to the project being conducted by their engineer and architect colleagues, i.e. re-landscaping Japan in the image of modern Britain. The claim that the pagoda rode out seismic waves was often coupled with the observation, sometimes made approvingly, that factory chimneys did not. For some, it seemed, earthquakes were nature's own device for preserving the Japanese landscape in its pre-modern condition; for preventing 'an eruption of Birmingham into Arcadia'.[35] Thus did architecture professor Josiah Conder attack the "romantic and fallacious prejudices" of unnamed colleagues, "which sound like a mockery when coming from the lips of those who advocate advance in other kindred sciences."[36] Former Kobudaigaku principal Henry Dyer warned seismologist Milne to abandon his research into Japanese-style structures, because "the supposed necessity of making special designs for buildings in earthquake countries [has] a very bad effect on the development of architecture in those countries".[37] He meant, most likely, that it undermined Japanese faith in the European engineering curriculum that Dyer had himself established.

A bio-aesthetic reading of the Japanese landscape clearly informed the work of zoologist Edward S. Morse, who, though not a member of the Seismological Society, was the first to teach Darwinian theory in Japan. A scholar and collector of brachiopods, Morse's cataloguing of Japanese seashells soon expanded in the direction of human habitations. He eventually produced a 300-page treatise on ordinary Japanese houses, profusely illustrated with his own sketches, published in 1886 as *Japanese Homes and their Surroundings*. Recently re-published in paperback, the book is still the standard English language text on Meiji-period domestic architecture.[38]

Writing in a conversational style for a popular audience, Morse openly lampoons *yatoi* architects and engineers. The typical English architect, he writes,

> ...recognizes but little merit in the apparently frail and perishable nature of these structures [Japanese houses]. He naturally dislikes the anomaly of a house of the lightest description oftentimes sustaining a roof of the most ponderous character, and fairly loathes a structure that has no king-post, or at least a queen-post truss; while the glaring absurdity of a house that persists in remaining upright without a foundation, or at least without his kind of foundation, makes him furious.[39]

Zoologist Morse came to be the leading foreign expert not only on Japanese domestic architecture, but Japanese ceramics. Scientists so easily extended their inquiries from the 'natural' to the 'cultural' in Japan, because 'nature' and 'culture' there were not neatly demarcated. Disciplines which carefully maintained those borders in Europe continually violated their jurisdictions in this new place; architects, engineers, and scientists were all equally unclear about which side of The Great Divide to put many Japanese objects on.[40]

Morse was also among comparatively few Western writers to show Japanese proactively resisting fire, which alongside seismicity, was the destructive force of nature most prominently on *yatoi* minds. The American Morse may have been sensitive to conflagration as a shared trait of the United States and Japan, and one which differentiated both cultures from modern Europe.

> A fireproof building is certainly beyond the means of a majority of this people, as, indeed, it is with us [Americans] and not being able to build such a dwelling, they have from necessity gone to the other extreme, and built a house whose very structure enables it to be rapidly demolished

in the path of a conflagration. Mats, screen-partitions, and even the board ceilings can be quickly packed up and carried away. The roof is rapidly denuded of its tiles and boards, and the skeleton frame-work left makes but slow fuel for the flames. The efforts of the firemen in checking the progress of a conflagration consist mainly in tearing down these adjustable structures.[41]

Compare that passage to one by former British consul Sir Rutherford Alcock, in which Japanese are said to

...take the burning down of a whole quarter periodically, much as they do the advent of an earthquake or a typhoon—calamities beyond the power of man to avert. They build their houses accordingly with the least possible expense, as foredoomed sooner or later to be food for the flames.[42]

Alcock's account of Japanese passivity ignores not only carpenter-firemen, but a centuries-long history of fire safety laws, such as the 1661 regulation mandating the replacement of thatch with tile in urban areas.[43] Claims of fatalistic Japanese approaches to natural disaster were common in such writings, however, undergirded by the European construction of a passive Buddhism and, as Morse suggests, the perceived ephemerality of a Japanese material culture made largely of wood.

The case of Japanese seismology demonstrates that 'transmission' is not the only possible frame in which to study 'Western science' in non-Western cultures. If we still need a metaphor borrowed from science itself, my suggestion would be 'speciation'. Seismology was essentially a new species of Western science initially more relevant and vital in the Japanese archipelago than it was in the capitals of northern Europe. As it continued to develop in Japan after its foreign practitioners went home, however, it creatively made use of its anomalous status, and built sometimes surprising bridges back toward the Western metropole. I have written elsewhere of how Japanese practitioners successfully negotiated seismology's odd birthright, using it to make a Japanese reputation in Eurocentric 'international science' while methodically dismantling many of the racist assumptions and practices that had spurred its founding. I'll end the current discussion with a single example.[44]

Japanese Scientists in Western Ruins

After the turn of the twentieth century Japan would defeat a European nation (Russia) in war, and Japanese seismology would begin mounting overseas expeditions in the manner of the Western sciences. Omori Fusakichi led teams of Japanese scientists who gathered seismic data in India, Chile, and post-catastrophic San Francisco. This last site he visited at the invitation of American geologists made suddenly aware of seismology's importance, but having as yet no full-time seismologists of their own. According to Omori's biographer, American children stoned the Japanese scientists as they walked among the ruins of San Francisco, injuring Omori and drawing an official apology from California's governor. As the stoning incident makes graphic, Omori did not live in a world where 'Japanese scientist' was as yet an unproblematic identity. Nonetheless, Japan's Imperial Earthquake Investigation Committee, the successor to the Seismological Society of Japan, was already coming to consider the whole Asia-Pacific region as its natural research site. In 1908 Omori would even follow the "Earthquake Belt", a trans-Eurasian feature that he had helped chart, name, and publicize, into the "earthquake countries" of Europe itself.[45]

On December 28, 1908, the most destructive earthquake in modern European history occurred in Calabria and northern Sicily, centred near the city of Messina. Within 35 seconds, about 120,000 people died or were mortally wounded, 55,000 in Messina itself and 9–10,000 in nearby Reggio. Both cities were essentially laid flat, about 98 per cent of their houses collapsing, and killing over half of Messina's total population.[46] Omori, already acquainted with numbers of Italian scientists, immediately led a Japanese research team to the earthquake zone. Collaborating with Italian seismologists, he filed a "Preliminary Report" on Messina in Japan's English-language *Bulletin of the Imperial Earthquake Investigation Committee* a few months later in 1909.[47] His was the first scientific report on the disaster to be published in English.

"The enormity of the destruction in Messina", wrote Omori, "is really beyond one's imagination". It was not rare, he stated, "that 15 or more dead bodies were found buried one upon the other in the space of a single small room at the ground floor" of a typical house. Because the apartment houses in Messina were four to six stories tall and the streets narrow, "it was certainly impossible for the majority of the people to save themselves, even if they had succeeded in escaping out of doors".[48] Omori compared the horrors of Messina to the situation in the similarly-sized Japanese city of Nagoya following the Great Nobi Earthquake of

1891. The rates of ground acceleration (intensity) in Messina and Nagoya were roughly comparable, he wrote, the Nobi quake being, if anything, slightly stronger.

> The population of Nagoya in 1891 was 165,339, which was nearly equal to that of Messina and the vicinity, and of which only 190 were killed in the earthquake. Thus, even supposing the intensity of seismic motion in Messina (1908) to be equal to that in Nagoya (1891), the number of the persons killed in the former city was about 430 times greater than that in the latter. That is to say, about 998 out of 1000 of the number of the killed in Messina must be regarded, when spoken in comparison to a Japanese city, as having fallen victims to seismologically bad construction of houses.[49]

Omori had actually made this observation about lethality rates at least nine years earlier, and using data that had been available not only to him, but to every seismologist in the world, since 1891. Even in those areas most devastated by the Nobi earthquake, he noted in an article of 1900, only 4 to 5 per cent of the population had died. "The comparatively small number of the killed", he wrote in 1900, "was doubtless due to the fact that common Japanese houses are built of wood".[50] This meshed with the claim of his colleague Sekiya Seikei, made as early as 1887, that when Japan's wooden houses 'collapsed' they often did so only partially, sometimes allowing their inhabitants to walk from the ruins.[51]

Thus did Japanese seismology begin, in the early twentieth century, to create scientific knowledge about the West in post-catastrophic Western landscapes. It was Omori's science that first made comparative lethality rates a category of seismological interest and research. His arguments, made in perfect English prose and illustrated by superior multi-coloured maps and diagrams, would not go unheard. Italian seismologist Alfredo Montel, in his book *Building Structures in Earthquake Countries*, published the year after the Messina quake, discussed the devastation and sought to draw lessons from the ruins. Much of what he claimed to have learned about earthquakes and aseismic structures he credited to the published research of Omori. There is, one suspects on reading Montel, a felt solidarity with Japan, another "earthquake country", politically unified in the same decade as Italy, whose native seismologists had only recently taken control of their own landscape from the scientists of Britain.[52]

Notes

This chapter was previously published in *Historia Scientiarum* (Tokyo) Mar. 2002, 2nd Series, v. 11, no. 3, and is reproduced here with the kind permission of the journal's editor.

[1] A landmark article in this regard is Graeme Gooday and Morris Low, "Technology Transfer and Cultural Exchange: Western Scientists and Engineers Encounter Late Tokugawa and Meiji Japan", *Osiris* 13 (1998–99): 251–80. The authors use nuanced case studies to suggest that 'cultural exchange' is the more revealing frame. A broader-based work which breaks similar ground is Tessa Morris-Suzuki, *The Technological Transformation of Japan: From the Seventeenth to the Twenty-First Centuries* (Cambridge, U.K.: Cambridge U. Press, 1994).

[2] On science and technology in the Meiji academy see Gooday and Low, op. cit.; James Bartholomew, "Japanese Modernization and the Imperial Universities, 1876–1920", *Journal of Asian Studies* 37, no. 2 (Feb. 1978); W.H. Brock, "The Japanese Connexion: Engineering in Tokyo, London, and Glasgow at the End of the Nineteenth Century", *The British Journal for the History of Science* 14 (1981): 229–34; Takahashi Yuzo, "William Edward Ayrton at the Imperial College of Engineering in Tokyo ..." , *IEEE Transactions in Education*, 33, no. 2 (May 1990): 198–205.

[3] This section summarizes arguments made at greater length in my "Foreign Knowledge, or Art Nation/Earthquake Nation: Architecture, Seismology, Carpentry, The West, and Japan, 1877–1923" (Ph.D. Dissertation, Massachusetts Institute of Technology, 1998). For more on Tokyo's early seismologists, see Gooday and Low, op. cit., pp. 121–27; A.L. Herbert-Gustar and P.A. Nott, *John Milne: Father of Modern Seismology* (Tenterden, Kent: Paul Norbury, 1980); and Charles Davison, *The Founders of Seismology* (Cambridge, U.K.: Cambridge U. Press, 1927).

[4] The Seismological Society of Japan was racially mixed from the beginning, with 36 Japanese and 63 foreign members. Most of the foreign members were British. The Society always had a Japanese president, and became more accommodating to the Japanese membership over time, publishing its *Transactions* in both languages starting in 1883, and at the same time instituting parallel Japanese and foreign officer positions (for notes on its structure, see *Transactions of the Seismological Society of Japan* [hereafter *TSSJ*] 2 [July–Dec. 1880]; TssJ v. 5 [May–Dec. 1882]).

[5] Quoted in Herbert-Gustar and Nott, op. cit., p. 80.

[6] John Milne, "Notes on the Recent Earthquakes of Yedo Plain and their Effects on Certain Buildings", *TSSJ* 2 (July–Dec. 1880), p 35; A 'seismograph' invented by the Italian earthquake researcher Luigi Palmieri (who also invented the

word in 1859) was actually operating in Tokyo's meteorological observatory by 1876. The seismograph invented by Ewing (and further developed by Milne and Thomas Gray) operated on an entirely different principle, however, and represented a new level of sensitivity. The English actually downgraded Palmieri's device by re-classifying it as a 'seismoscope' and the Ewing-Grey-Milne machine became the standard for late nineteenth century seismographs.

[7]   Wrote the Swiss earthquake investigator F.A. Forel in 1887: "More had been learnt from the seismograph-tracer of the Anglo-Japanese observers in two years, than twenty centuries of European science had been able to show", Note by Prof. F.A. Forel, *TSSJ* 11 (1887): 165. "Seismometry", as the invention of seismic recording devices was called in Tokyo, was at least indirectly influenced by the Kobudaigakko interest in telegraphy. The new seismographs and telegraphs were in effect siblings, as Thomas Gray, one of the seismograph's 'fathers', and the one most responsible for the construction and actual workings of the final prototype, was Kobudaigakko professor of Telegraphic Engineering. Seismographs were mechanical rather than electrical devices although, like telegraphs, clocks were integral to their working. For more on technology in the Meiji academy see Graeme Gooday, "Teaching Telegraphy and Electrotechnics in the Physics Laboratory: William Ayrton and the Creation of an Academic Space for Electrical Engineering in Britain, 1873–1884", *History of Technology* 13 (1991): 73–111.

[8]   As early as the first meeting of the Seismological Society of Japan, in 1880, John Milne had said "Should we, for instance, wish to know the reasons why the people of Japan or England are as we see them now, we shall find ourselves driven back from history to geology." *TSSJ* v. 1 (Apr.–June, 1880).

[9]   Milne, "Earthquake Effects Emotional and Moral" *TSSJ* v. 11 (1887): 91–113; quotations from pp. 94, 109.

[10] Ibid., p. 109.

[11] Ibid.

[12] Kenneth Pyle's discussion of young intellectuals in this period excavates a language rich in Darwinian metaphors. Even the nativist Shiga Shigetaka's "Declaration of Principles Held by *Nihonjin*" (the newspaper of the Seikyosha movement), published in 1888, describes *kokusui* ('the national essence') as a force which "germinated, grew, and developed through adaptation to the influence of all environmental factors." The "future evolution" of *kokusui*, continued Shiga, "will be no more than the proper application of the fundamental principles of biology."(Kenneth Pyle, *The New Generation in Meiji Japan: Problems in Cultural Identity, 1885–1895* [Stanford: Stanford U. Press, 1969] p. 68). Also see Pyle, pp. 36–37, 61, 110–11, 150.

[13] For a discussion of the influence of social Darwinism in Meiji Japan, and on Kato in particular, see Watanabe Masao, *The Japanese and Western Science*

(Philadelphia: U. of Penn. Press, 1976), pp. 65–83. Pyle calls Kato "perhaps the best-known exponent of Darwinian theories in Japan" (Pyle, p. 111). See also Morris Low, "The Japanese Nation in Evolution: W.E. Griffis, Hybridity, and the Whiteness of the Japanese Race", *History and Anthropology* 11, 2–3 (1999).

14 Kato's long patronage of seismology was partly a function of his Imperial University presidency, but his name is met with so consistently in the writings of seismologists that it seems to have extended beyond that. In an 1883 monograph on seismometry, for example, James Ewing thanks Kato "for providing me with the means of establishing a Seismological Observatory".

15 Pyle, p. 23.

16 According to Watanabe, Kato learned from Buckle that, in Kato's own words "any statement is meaningless if it is not based on science". (Watanabe, op. cit.), p. 71.

17 Milne, p. 109.

18 Pyle, pp. 23, 89. There is a good but brief discussion of Buckle in Theodore Porter, *The Rise of Statistical Thinking, 1820–1900* (Princeton: Princeton U. Press, 1986), pp. 60–61.

19 Milne, p. 111. Historian Richard Minear classes Chamberlain among the three "most influential Japanese scholars of the last hundred years", and one of the best examples, in Japanese studies, of Edward Said's 'orientalist'. (Richard Minear, "Orientalism and the Study of Japan", *Journal of Asian Studies* 34, no. 3 (May 1980): 507–10. 'The Orient', as we have seen, could be mapped in various ways, but Chamberlain was particularly consistant (and insistent) in applying the geographic (East–West) dyad. Chamberlain, president and long-time member of Tokyo's 'Asiatic Society', was also one of few *yatoi* with a command of Japanese. Milne relied upon Chamberlain's linguistic skills in his later cataloguing of Japanese earthquake records.

20 Milne, p. 112; Kikuchi Dairoku, *Recent Seismological Investigations in Japan* (Tokyo, 1904), p. 9.

21 Milne, p. 113.

22 Ibid., p. 92.

23 Ibid., p. 93.

24 Ibid., pp. 93–94.

25 Henry Dyer, correspondence regarding Milne's "On Construction in Earthquake Countries" in *Minutes of the Proceedings of the Institution of Civil Engineers*, v. 83 (1886), p. 311.

26 George Cawley, "Some Remarks on Construction in Brick and Wood and their Relative Suitability in Japan", *Transactions, Asiatic Society of Japan* v. 6, Part II (1878), p. 316.

27 Josiah Conder, "Domestic Architecture in Japan", *Proceedings of the Royal Institute of British Architects*, v. 3, no. 10 (1887), p. 198.

[28] Milne, "The Earthquake in Japan of Feb. 22, 1880" TSSJ, Part II, 1880, pp. 1–
115; Ibid, "Notes on the Recent Earthquakes of the Yedo Plain..."

[29] See Milne and W.K. Burton, *The Great Earthquake in Japan, 1891* (London and
Yokohama: Standford, 1892).

[30] As early as the mid-1870s, *yatoi* physicists John Perry and W.H. Ayrton
conducted research into the joint structures of Japanese temples, which they
reported in a locally-circulated pamphlet entitled "On Structures in
Earthquake Countries". Ayrton describes and quotes from this now-lost
pamphlet in remarks following a paper by I. Hattori in *Transactions of the
Asiatic Society of Japan*, v. 6, part 2, 1978, p. 289.

[31] In the weeks following the Nobi earthquake, Japan's English-language
newspapers were full of articles by seismologists, architects, and others giving
often conflicting, and polemical, descriptions of the comparative damage to
'foreign' and 'Japanese' structures. See in particular *The Japan Weekly Mail*,
Oct. 31–Nov. 21, 1891.

[32] Some of these post-Nobi images are available in the digital image collection
of the library of Tokyo University's Earthquake Research Institute.

[33] See, for example, Milne, "On the Earthquake Phenomena of Japan", *Report
of the 54th Meeting of the British Association for the Advancement of Science*
(London, 1885) and "On Construction in Earthquake Countries", *Minutes of
the Proceedings of the Institution of Civil Engineers*, v. LXXXIII, Session 1885–86,
part 1, paper 2108. Omori's investigations of *gojunoto* are reported in
"Measurement of the Vibration of Gojunotos, or 5-story Buddhist Stupas
(Pagodas)", *Bulletin of the Imperial Earthquake Investigation Committee*, v. 9,
1918–19, pp. 110–152.

[34] R.H. Brunton, "Constructive Art in Japan, Part II", *Transactions, Asiatic Society
of Japan*, v. 3, part II (1875), p. 72. For nearly identical statements see Henry
Dyer, Correspondence Regarding Milne's "On Construction in Earthquake
Countries" in *Minutes of the Proceedings of the Institution of Civil Engineers*, v.
83, 1886, p. 310, and C.A.W. Pownall, "Notes on Recent Publications Relating
to the Effect of Earthquakes on Structures" *TSSJ*, v. 16, pp. 1–8.

[35] The physicists are Perry and Aryton (see note 30) and the botanist is
Christopher Dresser, who came to Japan as a designer and art collector, but
wrote of the structure of *gojunoto* (pagoda) in *Japan: Its Architecture, Art, and
Manufactures* (New York, 1882). His contention that the *shinbashira* or central
mast of pagoda were aseismic devices embroiled him in controversy with
Kobudaigakko professor of architecture Josiah Conder. The polemic they
conducted in the British press is described in Suzuki Hiroyuki, *Victorian
Gothic no Hokai* (Tokyo: Chuo Koron Bijutsu Shupan), pp. 72–78.

[36] Josiah Conder, "The Practice of Architecture in Japan" *Japan Weekly Mail*,
Aug. 28, 1886.

37 Dyer, Correspondence..., op. cit.

38 Edward Morse, *Japanese Homes and Their Surroundings* (Rutland, Vt.: Charles E. Tuttle Co., 1972).

39 Morse, p. 10.

40 Cherie Wendelken notes that "the [Japanese] house, particularly the common house, does not appear as a significant object of interest to the architect as historian, practitioner or restorationist until the Taisho Period (1912–26)." (Cherie Wendelken-Mortensen, "Living With the Past: Preservation and Development in Japanese Architecture and Town Planning", Ph.D. dissertation, Massachusetts Institute of Technology, 1994, p. 28).

41 Morse, pp. 12–13.

42 Rutherford Alcock, *The Capital of the Tycoon: A Narrative of Three Year's Residence in Japan* (NY: Greenwood Press, 1969), p. 124.

43 Wendelken, "Living with the Past", pp. 25–26. This was one of a number of such regulations enacted after the Meireki Fire, which destroyed the greater portion of Edo (Tokyo) in 1660. The Meireki Fire would not be matched in ferocity or extent of damage until the fire following the Great Kanto (Tokyo) Earthquake of 1923.

44 For a discussion of Japanese seismology under Omori Fusakichi see my "The Science of Eurasia: Meiji Seismology as Cultural Critique" in *Historical Perspectives on East Asian Science, Technology, and Medicine*, edited by Alan Chan, Gregory Clancey and Loy Hui Chieh (Singapore: Singapore University Press and World Scientific, 2002).

45 Asahi Shogakko PTA, *Watashitachi no daisenpai jishingaku no chichi Omori Fusakichi* (Tokyo, 1972).

46 Various casualty figures have been published for this earthquake. My figure of 120,000 comes from a table in Wakabayashi, *Design of Earthquake-Resistant Buildings* (NY: McGraw Hill, 1986). The percentage of collapsed houses, first reported by Omori [see citation below], was repeated by Davison in 1936 (Charles Davison, *Great Earthquakes* [London, 1936] p. 203).

47 Omori Fusakichi, "Preliminary Report on the Messina-Reggio Earthquake of Dec. 28, 1908; *Bulletin of the Imperial Earthquake Investigation Committee*, v. 3, no. 1, 1909.

48 Ibid, pp. 38–39.

49 Ibid, pp. 39–40.

50 Omori, "Notes on the Great Mino-Owari Earthquake of Oct. 28, 1891", *Publications of the Earthquake Investigation Committee in Foreign Languages, No. 4* (Tokyo: EIC, 1900), p. 13.

51 Sekiya Seikei, "The Severe Earthquake of the 15th of Jan., 1887", *TSSJ*, vol. XI, 1887, p. 83.

52 Alfredo Montel, *Building Structures in Earthquake Countries* (Rome, 1909).

9

British Colonial Rhetoric on 'Modern Medicine' and 'Health at Home': Realities of Health Conditions in 19th Century Britain

Vineeta Sinha

Introduction

The field of colonialism, health and medicine has been extensively and creatively theorized by scholars located in a range of disciplines and the emergent literature on the subject is voluminous, varied and valuable. Any analysis of the relationship between colonialism and health requires a recognition of the complexity and multi-dimensionality of this encounter. So far a variety of themes within this domain have engaged the theoretical and practical interests of scholars. Some examples include the impact of colonialism on indigenous systems of healing (Levine 1998, Marks 1997), on the use of 'modern medicine'[1] to dominate and thus govern colonized populations, i.e., with emergent issues of power and social control (Haynes 1999, Lorcin 1999), utilization of modern medicine by 'natives' (Leng 1982) and even the benefits of Western medicine for maintaining good health of 'natives' and lessons to be learnt from Eastern experiences (Given 1929).

Despite the variety of themes addressed, a common thread runs through these accounts and discussions: that is, a sustained and singular focus on the colonies and the colonized populations, and the subject matter so defined is the state of health and healing in non-Western, colonized contexts (Denoon 1989, Manderson 1987, Patterson 1981, Yeoh 1991). I propose that this mode of approaching the field of colonialism and health is limited in being one-sided, in bracketing off attention to actual health conditions and healing strategies current in colonizing societies at specific points in colonial history. This chapter attempts to redress this imbalance by explicitly focusing on *one* colonizing context, and detailing the health scene in nineteenth-century Britain and the nature and impact of modern medicine in managing day-to-day health issues at 'home'.

By now historical accounts of medicine and health care in Britain are plentiful (Lane 2001, Porter 1987, Wohl 1983). Much of the more insightful work has emerged under the banner of 'social history of medicine'[2] in currency for the last 3 decades (Berridge 1990). Proponents of this approach have rightly critiqued the earlier technical and narrow accounts of the history of medicine, divorced from their social, economic and political dimensions. These studies have thus provided the much-needed context for understanding the development of the practice of medicine. However, it is interesting that this material, which spans the period of British colonization, pays minimal or no attention to the role of colonial/imperial activities in shaping health directions, discourses, policies and practices in Britain itself.

As I see it, practitioners located within these two fields of 'colonialism and health' and the 'social history of medicine' do not engage each other either on empirical or theoretical platforms. In my assessment, it would indeed be instructive to connect the insights and theorizing from these two fields—a link that has so far not been made explicit. Such convergence I argue would produce a more rounded and comprehensive account of health, both at 'home' and in the colonies. The value of, and rationale for, making such a connection is detailed in the argument presented in the pages that follow.

I begin with brief discussions of the notion of 'difference' and its status under hegemonic conditions, followed by a consideration of the ways in which health has been theorized as an issue in colonialist projects. The third and largest portion of the paper carries the following discussion: The rhetoric[3] of British colonialism required and produced somewhat glowing images of 'home' that were defined in stark contrast to the inhospitable conditions in the colonies. In colonial health discussions, narratives of scientizing and civilizing 'native' populations were expressed through the assumed superior status of modern medicine rather than reflecting actual medical practices or sanitary conditions 'back home'. I use specific historical data to gauge the extent to which these 'differences' between home and the overseas dominions can be sustained. Further, the nineteenth century has been viewed as the age of medical innovation and hence of the resultant 'modern medicine' as a harbinger of progress. How does this image actually compare with the prevailing state of health conditions and healing strategies in nineteenth-century Britain?

Identifying and recognizing differences

The seventeenth and eighteenth centuries bear witness to increased contact between 'non-Western' societies and a rapidly expanding 'West',[4] manifested especially in the form of colonial encounters. However, 'Occidental' interaction with the 'Orient' did not begin with colonialism. A significant body of writings (Alvares 1991, Chaudhuri 1965, Glamann 1958, Kabbani 1988, Kaul 1989, Lach 1968, Raychaudhuri 1962, Schwaab 1984) suggests evidence of pre-colonial and non-hegemonic (Abu-Lughod 1989) interaction between the 'Occident' and the 'Orient'.[5] Historians view sixteenth century Europe as being marked by 'dramatic change' (Koenigsberger and Mossse 1968), and define it as an age of 'overseas discovery' (Mackenney 1993). At the confluence of rising mercantile capitalism, evangelical Christianity and the Renaissance spirit, Europe encountered the rest of 'humanity' (Todorov 1982). Much of the early interest in exploring otherwise 'uninhabitable' parts of the New World and the 'Orient' was motivated by the wish for profit and wealth—such as the silver mines of Peru and spices from the Indonesian archipelago.

In the resulting confrontation with 'other' communities 'differences'—economic, social, religious, political and physical—between the colonizers and the colonized were selectively emphasized. These divergences were highlighted and, more often than not, perceived to be too dramatic to be reconcilable. For example, the 'discovery' of Africa and its constructed 'European' image served to polarize 'Europe' and 'Africa'. According to Mudimbe (1988, p. 107):

> Nineteenth century writers, focusing on differences between Africa and Europe, tended to demonstrate the complete lack of similarity between the two continents and attempted to prove that in Africa the physical environment, the flora and fauna, as well as the people, represent relics of a remote age of antiquity.

Lyons (1975, pp. 86–87) further adds:

> though they did not disagree amongst themselves about which European "races" were inferior to others, Western racial commentators generally agreed that Blacks were inferior to whites in moral fibre, cultural attainment, and mental ability; the African was, to many eyes, the child in the family of man, modern man in the embryo.

According to Hammond and Jablow (1977, pp. 36–37):

> The basic attitudes which arbitrarily relate these essentially unrelated qualities—paganism, nakedness, cannibalism—are those which assign all cultural differences to the single category of savagery; and one trait as it distinguishes a savage from a European becomes an index to the existence of the other traits which are part of the syndrome.

The terms, 'India', 'Africa' and 'America' and the images they produced in the minds of Christian 'Europeans' were as much constructions as was Europe itself. Such imaginings rose out of lengthy colonial interactions between representations of European imperial power and local wielders of power, in pluralistic, plurinational regions. Significantly, a Europe that imagined 'Africa' or 'India' was not itself a preexisting entity but was constructed while inventing diverse groupings as 'others'. Further, the mould in which 'others' were cast reflected European preoccupations in the eighteenth and nineteenth centuries more than the empirical realities the labels 'West' or 'non-West' suggested.

Europeans who travelled to India, Southeast Asia, the Americas and Africa were not alone[6] either in their awe and aversion to the strange customs of 'barbaric' people or the physical and environmental peculiarities of newly discovered places. 'Other' lands were often described as 'unhealthy' and their geography and climate considered unsuitable for European temperament (Gordon 1928). In Eurocentric historiography, the Orient is imagined and presented in highly exotic terms but also defined in a stark contrast to the Occident (Said 1978).

European knowledge of health and medicine in distant lands increasingly became available from about the 16th century (Thornton 1983). Incidence of diseases in 'exotic' places and ways of dealing with them have been noted by the earliest travellers.[7] Apart from noticing unhealthy conditions and strange healing practices amongst 'savages', scholarly interest in the subject did sometimes prevail. Borri, a Portuguese traveller in Cochin-China between 1617 and 1622, documents the presence of native physicians. He says:

> From experience the local doctors are able to cure a number of diseases, which the European physicians "know not how to treat." When first meeting a patient, the native physicians feel the pulse for a long while. Then they make a specific diagnosis or say frankly that the patient has an incurable ailment. The physician prepares his own medicines to keep secret his prescriptions. As a consequence there are no apothecaries in this country. If the cure fails the physician receives nothing. Their medicines "do not alter the course of nature" but are palatable, nourishing, and assist nature "in its usual operations." Bleeding is used but not as often as in Europe (in Lach and Van Kley 1965, p. 262).

According to Alchon (1991, p. 131):

> But colonialism dictated that both rulers and subjects perceive differences rather than similarities, and so it was with medical conditions.

Theoretically, it is valuable to reflect on the question of whether it is possible to merely note differences without judgement or whether the recognition of differences in the context of emerging or pre-existing hegemonic relations necessarily produces an evaluation and hence ranking of the identified differences (Todorov 1982).

Health as an issue in colonialist projects

There is a substantial body of writing on the subject of health in the European colonies (Arnold 1986, Brown 1978, Fanon 1978, Gottschalk 1988, Hume 1986, Ityavyar 1992, Lasker 1977, Swaan 1989, Twumasi 1988). It is limiting to view 'colonialism' in monolithic, essential and totalizing terms. Clearly, there were as many interpretations and implementations of colonial policies as there were colonizers and colonized. However, some universal statements can be made without being over-general: European colonial offensives in various parts of Africa and Asia have led almost inevitably (although in differing ways) to domination by Western structures, in economic, socio-cultural and political arenas. This applies to the health domain as well. According to Gish (1979, p. 205):

> Western medicine, like virtually all other things European, received official support while traditional systems either received none or were consciously suppressed. In addition, the transfer of wealth from the colonies to Europe encouraged the further rapid development of scientific and other institutions so that Western medicine and other scientific systems could in fact come to outstrip those of other parts of the world.

The immediate aim of colonial administrators and medical missionaries was to offer 'European' medical services in the colonies to serve the medical needs of the expatriate European populations, both civilian and military. Initially, this entailed posting a few surgeons and providing a supply of medicines and medical paraphernalia for managing patients. The model of a medical system that was introduced was a "hospital-centred, curative system, using large quantities of manufactured goods such as pills, serums, powders, dressings, hospital equipment and medical vehicles" (Paul 1978, p. 279). Gish (1979, p. 205) suggests that:

> Typically the pattern of "modern" medical care during the colonial era had three major components: the urban hospital, the rural dispensary often Christian related and the hygiene or public health element. In essence this remains the pattern in the Third World right up to the present.

It has been noted that often, under the guise of performing benevolent service to the 'natives', modern medicine was sometimes placed at the service of colonialists to dominate, subjugate and control 'native' populations. Colonialist implementation of modern medicine often had ideological underpinnings, a fact colonial medical histories have only recently acknowledged. We now know of the political use that was made of medicine in the colonies. Paul (1978) describes the use that the colonial powers made of medicine in mass propaganda and espionage activities in the colonies. He further argues that doctors were used in France, Germany, Spain and Britain as diplomatic agents. Using the case of

Morocco, Paul characterizes British, French and German physicians as "secular missionaries" engaged in such activities:

> Like their religious counterparts, they used medical skills to gain access to remote and resistant elements of the Moroccan population. They sowed discontent among groups and tribes and conducted standard military intelligence; gathering strategic information on the military organization and defences, carrying out political and social research, and preparing maps for pending colonial invasion (Paul 1978, p. 277).

It is clear at the same time, however, that the introduction of 'modern medicine' did not categorically and inevitably lead to devastating and negative consequences (Patterson 1981; Paul 1978). Some very significant improvements have indeed been made possible by the introduction of 'modern medicine'.

Despite the accruing benefits, though, the introduction of 'modern' and 'scientific' (and superior) medical services was nonetheless seen to augment the lofty agenda of 'civilizing' the ignorant, backward, and superstitious indigenous populations. The conflation of science and medical practices was coterminous with providing such 'modernist' resources as hospitals, dispensaries, doctors, medical equipment and medicines. The underlying belief in the efficacy of modern medicine over traditional forms of healing was firmly entrenched in the rhetoric. Where active suppression of traditional medicine was absent indigenous healers met with neglect, not to mention competition, from government-sponsored medical services. For example, the British colonial policy of non-intervention in native customs often resulted in dismissal, contempt and indifference to traditional healing. In some ways, the knowledge of existing non-Western healing strategies and a 'hands off' policy was advantageous to the British. It absolved the Colonial Office of having to provide for adequate and comprehensive medical facilities especially in light of native resistance and opposition to modern health care facilities. Despite this *practice*, the existing climate led to the widely held belief and opinion that the triumph of modern medicine over native methods of healing was inevitable and indeed desirable.

Although execution of colonial health policies was influenced by a number of diverse and contextually specific factors, some common issues have emerged from these writings. I focus on only one of these themes here. The nature of the colonial economy and the forced movement of people for mining, plantation labour, and other goals, across continents and often under unhealthy living conditions, produced a debilitating state of health in the colonies. Natives and migrant labour who lacked the means and independence to care for their health suffered most. For the most part, colonial governments did not consider it their responsibility to institute wider sanitary and public health measures for the good of the masses. The link between colonialist health projects and public health schemes of health planning agencies is explicit. In fact, Brown (1978, p. 252) argues persuasively that "The professional public health field today owes much of its growth and development to the needs of colonialism and neo-colonialism."

Public health movements in parts of Europe emerged in the eighteenth century—a phenomenon that occurred later in North America. The lessons learnt at 'home' were implemented in the colonies of Africa and Asia by dominant European powers, sometimes in collaboration with their North American counterparts. The activities of the American-based Rockefeller Foundation at the turn of this century illustrate this association well.[8] In the early 1900s, the Rockefeller International Health Commission (RIHC) organized campaigns against diseases such as hookworm, yellow fever and malaria in parts of the British Empire,[9] Latin America and Asia in order to consolidate the American position in the global economy. Schools of tropical medicine were founded to apply the knowledge of medical sciences in combating tropical diseases (Hunter 1985). Such information was deemed necessary to preserve the workforce of the "mother country" in the colonies given that the "imperialist powers were severely hampered by disease" (Brown 1978, p. 252).

In this context, concerns with health were directly related to questions of worker productivity and output. As such, the RIHC "identified health as the capacity to work, and measured qualitative improvements in health by quantitative increases in productivity" (op. cit., p. 260)—empiricist and quantitative measurements of health. Health planners who set up schools of public health to improve general sanitary and health conditions were motivated by economic and political considerations, although humanitarian ideals were overtly invoked.

Modern medicine or rather its image as a science was a necessary component of colonial discourse vis-à-vis health. Another integral element was a particular construction of 'Europe' or the 'West' and its asserted and unique difference from the 'non-West'. These two elements were related and indeed supported each other. While I lack the space to narrate fully the second process, the story of modern medicine is relevant. An account of healing practices and sanitary conditions in 19th England also follows. This allows us to consider if and how the achievements of modern medicine impacted the day-to-day health conditions during this time, a link that is implicitly assumed in colonial health discussions.

Healing practices and health conditions in nineteenth-century England

The literature on the history of medicine and health care provision allows us to reconstruct the following scenario in nineteenth-century Britain. One recurring theme is the obvious and pervasive heterogeneity of healing traditions in Britain at the time. That medical pluralism was a defining feature of the health scene is an important historical fact, particularly in view of the subsequent dramatic rise of modern medicine. The parallel incidence of 'other' healing approaches and the prevalence of folk healers, with their knowledge of herbs, oils and healing techniques, are well documented by historians (Chamberlain 1981, Donnison 1977, Numbers 1985). The extensive availability and utilization of 'lay' healing knowledge, primarily a female province (Bourdillon 1988, Campbell 1938, Ehrenreich and English 1973, Jex-Blake 1886, Verluysen 1980), was also the norm of the day. Scholars agree that the medical scene in 19th-century England (Lane 1984, Woodward and Richards 1977) and North America (Gevitz 1977, Numbers 1985, Smith 1985) was typified by tremendous diversity in healing options and individuals who possessed healing knowledge and the 'right' to practice healing.

Attempts to theorize the dominant position of modern medicine have generated a vast body of literature on the subject. Most of these devote at least some space to a discussion of 'medical practitioners' antecedent to the rise of scientific medicine as an occupation in both in England and America (Gelfand 1981, Holloway 1964, Jewson 1974, Lane 1984, Peterson 1978, Shryock 1948, Waddington 1984, Youngson 1977). In *Medical Care and the General Practitioner 1750–1850* (1986), Irvine Loudon documents the establishment of the medical profession in England. More importantly, the author describes his work as "the study of rank-and-file (medical) practitioners" in his efforts to contextualize the rise of doctors of medicine. Loudon stresses that existing research on medical practitioners has focused on elites to the neglect of "ordinary" folk practitioners, about whom there is tremendous historical evidence. In England, prior to 1850, there was a tripartite division of medical practitioners into physicians, surgeons and apothecaries.[10] Loudon (1986, p. 13) further notes that one problem with categorizing diverse practitioners and their healing in eighteenth century England into "orthodox" and "unorthodox"[11] has to do with the following: "that when there was no system of formal education, registration and licensing, no sharp lines could exist between the qualified and the unqualified".

In describing medical practices in North America, Numbers (1985, p. 43) notes:

> Among the most ardent American champions of home health care were the medical sectarians who arose in the nineteenth century to challenge the heroic therapy of the regulars with their seemingly endless rounds of bleedings, blisterings and purgings. Over the years a multitude of sects appeared, each offering the long-suffering public a surer, safer, and often cheaper way to health. There were botanics, and Eclectics, homeopaths and hydropaths, movement-curists and mind-curists, and others too numerous to mention. Despite their many differences, they all shared one trait: *an enthusiasm for the practice of domestic medicine* (emphasis added).

Gender and working-class interests were explicit in the Popular Health Movements of nineteenth century America. Ehrenreich and English (1973, p. 23) argue that these movements were an "assault on medical elitism, and an affirmation of the traditional people's medicine". In this period there was obviously room for "sectarian", "irregular", and "do-it-yourself" healing practices (Numbers 1985). The agendas of organized feminist and health movements came together in ways that threatened the dominance of established medical practice of the time.[12]

The British medical profession was continually "dogged" by the presence of "quacks" and perturbed by the growing problem of "quackery" in the 19th century.[13] The British Medical Association (formed in 1832) called for the elimination of the "evils of quackery" from the community. It was an uphill battle; the Association was limited doubly by existing legislation and the clear public support for the services offered by medical "quacks". However these unqualified and unregistered practitioners were viewed by the medical profession, it is clear that they provided health care options that were considered cheaper and safer and popular with the masses. Writing of England in 1837, John Hogg, M.D. laments that:

> One cause prejudicial to health, partly of a moral and partly of a physical nature, is the credulity which prevails to a great extent among the English people, causing them to be led, by quacks of various kinds, to the injury of both mind and body; and on the physical side are the empirics who, by mountebank representations, prevail on the credulous to swallow large quantities of drugs (Hogg 1837, pp. 344–45).

The eighteenth century was popularly known as the age of 'heroic' medicine in Europe and North America. Heroic remedies (Porter 1987, p. 30) refer to "the drastic measures" employed by medical men to heal patients during the 18th century in England and other parts of Europe (Ehrenreich and English 1978, Winslow 1980). Medical doctors then did not enjoy either high prestige or a good reputation. Neither doctors nor hospitals were willingly patronized, the latter being viewed as "dying houses", although as Berridge (1990) notes, they were not utilized by large numbers of the public. There was ample justification for this reluctance. The medical practices of 'educated' and learned men of the profession included such procedures as bloodletting, 'cleansing' through purging laxatives and enemas, generous prescription of drugs and spirits, and surgery without knowledge of anaesthesia or antiseptics, performed under unsanitary conditions (Ehrenreich and English 1973, Porter 1987). Historians have called the 18th century the 'golden age of quackery' (Porter 1987, p. 40), when irregulars, quacks and patent-medicine vendors could be identified. Crucially, this occurred at a time when medical practice was largely unregulated in England.

Although a number of significant changes typify the health scene in 19th century England, the popularity of patent medicines (Berridge 1990) and self-medication were carried over from the preceding century. In Britain, the growing popularity of 'secret remedies' and 'patent medicines', labelled by the medical profession as 'quack medicines' was seen to be a problem in the early nineteenth century. By 1912, its popularity reached "formidable proportions" (Vaughan 1959, p. 91–92):

> The great newspaper empires of the twentieth century were in the process of construction, and a vital part of their foundations was the revenue from advertisements. There were few restrictions on what the advertiser could claim, which was generally less important than what he could pay for his space.

> The trade was an industry in its own right, embracing the activities of great companies with million-pound capitals…It was said that in 1908 the amount of money spent by the public on secret remedies was the then sum of 2,500,000/-.

The marketing of patent medicines was by no means confined to home grounds. The vendors found a lucrative market in the overseas dominions too. An example from British Malaya is illustrative. From the earliest years, European and Asian private doctors established medical practice in the Straits Settlements. Private opticians, nurses, midwives, surgeons, dentists and vaccinators advertised their services in the Singapore-based newspaper, the *Straits Times*. In addition to private consultations, many of these doctors also operated dispensaries (Brooke 1921, pp. 500–502), and doubled up as druggists and pharmacists.[14] The dispensaries filled physicians prescriptions and carried a variety of 'patent medicines', 'drugs and chemicals', 'medicinal waters', 'tonics' and 'nutritive stimulants' (*Straits Times*, 1884–1901). Some of these preparations were reported to cure specific medical ailments, but many of them professed to be 'cure alls'. According to Stanley (1904, p. 523), "the Chinaman is attracted by the merest scum only of so-called western civilization furnished by well-advertised patent medicines and itinerant quacks in the sacred name of trade". In *The Gardens of the Sun: A Naturalist's Journal* (1880), F.W. Burbidge writes about Singapore:

> In many Chinese and Kling[15] shops European tinned provisions and patent medicines may be obtained at a very slight advance on home prices, as these petty traders watch the sales of old ships' stores very closely, and are thus enabled to purchase very cheaply (1880, p. 22).

For example, "Holloways Pills" advertised in the local press made these claims:

> This Great Household medicine ranks amongst the leading necessaries of life. These most famous pills purify the blood, and act most powerfully, yet soothingly on the LIVER, STOMACH, KIDNEYS and BOWELS, giving tone, energy and vigor to these great main springs of life. They are confidently recommended as a never failing remedy in all cases. Where the constitution for whatever cause, has become impaired or weakened, they are wonderfully efficacious in all ailments incidental to females of all ages: and as a General Family Medicine are unsurpassed (*Straits Times*, June 8, 1885).

We do not have comparative figures for the Straits Settlements and the Malay States but business must have been lucrative, given that the same products continued to be advertised in the press over a number of years and often, new items were featured. The proprietors purchased space in the local newspapers, assuring themselves and their products of prominent advertisement, a phenomena that has also been documented in Britain (Vaughan 1959) and North America (Gevitz 1988, Pierce 1906, Young 1961).

It is crucial to note that this diversity of healing practices and tensions and professional rivalries between practitioners were present in England[16] *at about the time* attempts were being made to 'civilize' natives, through the imposition of modern medicine. It is clear that during the period under consideration, in England, modern medicine was but *one* of many healing traditions. Further, there is evidence that regular doctors were engaged in a long-drawn out struggle and assumed dominance and privilege after a period of sustained struggle (Blake 1990, Larkin 1983, Waddington 1984, Witz 1992). For example, Doyal records (1986, p. 28):

> It is important to stress, however, that western scientific medicine represents *only one particular medical tradition*. While this is now the dominant mode of mediation between individuals and ill health, *this has not always been the case* (emphasis added).

A multiplicity of healing practices and practitioners, circumscription of biomedicine, its institutionalization, the legitimate and the eventual dominance of 'scientific medicine' are developments explained variously by scholars.[17] The most persuasive arguments are those that view the hegemony of bio-medical models as a by-product of inter-occupational conflict (Doyal 1986, Numbers 1985, Waddington 1984, Witz 1992) and not those that proclaim the inevitable triumph of rational, scientific values in the health domain.

Furthermore, the 'battle' of bio-medical orthodoxy was not easily won. Much of the history of modern medicine glosses over the zealous opposition from those practitioners who were being edged out, i.e., 'irregulars' and 'women' (Fraser 1988). Although it is impossible to generalize as to their mode of resistance it is nonetheless important to recognize their protest. Modern medicine was then, and is now claimed, to be a product of the 'West'. Its defining features continue to be listed thus: its grounding in scientific research, its objectivity, neutrality, rationality and hence its efficacy. Such a formulation clearly serves to distinguish modern medicine from more 'traditional' and 'non-rational' approaches to healing, both in the 'West' and in the colonies. But it must be noted that the suppression and marginalization of other forms of healing occurred not just in the colonies but also at home, enabling the eventual dominance of modern medicine, self-defined as both 'Western' and scientific.

Louis Pasteur's and Robert Koch's researches into bacteriology, and Edward Jenner's contribution to the science of vaccination clearly marked a departure from earlier ways of viewing and treating diseases. But these radical ideas, and the kind of medical practices they might lead to were *both new* to Euro-American healing scenes.[18] For example, the 'germ theory of disease', today more or less unchallenged, was not received with open arms. Its proponents encountered scepticism, resistance, and ridicule. In late 19th-century America, even the ordinary medical doctor viewed this theory with suspicion. According to Ehrenreich and English (1978, p. 89):

> New York doctors used to walk out on medical papers dealing with the Germ Theory of Disease because "They wanted to express their contemptuous scorn for such theories and refused to listen to them".

Of American medicine in 1879, Rosenberg (1985, p. 28) says:

> The reductionist assumption that a specific organism might be responsible for the manifestation of a particular disease seemed difficult to comprehend; though there was much talk of a "germ theory" it was enveloped in obscurity and was received with incomprehension and hostility.

The most condemnatory pronouncement was perhaps delivered by George Shrady, editor of the journal *Medical Record* in 1879:

> Judging the future by the past, we are likely to be as much ridiculed in the next century for our blind belief in the power of unseen germs, as our forefathers were for their faith in the influence of spirits, of certain planets, and the like, in inducing certain maladies (in Rosenberg 1985, p. 33).

Shrady was not to know how wrong he would be proven. The battle for scientific medicine based on "physiological, microscopical, chemical" (in Ehrenreich and English 1978, p. 89) theories was eventually won, including the establishment of the 'germ theory'[19] as the basis of disease causation. This triumph of modern medicine, was accomplished by 'scientizing' healing, through elaborate systemic reforms of medical education and licensing, certification and registration of qualified medical practitioners. Berlant (1975), Numbers (1985) and Waddington (1984) discuss how apothecaries and surgeons in Britain, and homeopaths, osteopaths and herbalists in America, resisted the increasing monopoly and policing exercised by socioeconomically and politically powerful medical societies and corporations. The eventual suppression of 'unorthodox' healing practices and the dominance of 'regulars' was accomplished by securing institutional and structural support. The 'regulars' were able to promote their cause with legalistic reforms, licensing laws, limiting access to institutions of education and, vicariously, through the 'success' of the ideology of science and technology in Western society.

Nineteenth-century Europe witnessed intense scientific, including medical, activity. It is important to explore the extent to which the great 'discoveries' of science were actually put to the service of medicine and the degree to which they were translated into the *practice* of healing both at home and in the colonies. Historians note that despite these, advances were being made primarily in theory and research, located in the laboratories, and not *in practice* (Ehrenreich and English 1978, Flinn 1965). By the latter half of the nineteenth century, the health of populations in England had improved in comparison to earlier periods. However, this could not necessarily be attributed to scientific progress. Instead several alternative explanations were offered. For one, it has been theorized that 'common sense', 'application of elementary medical principles' (Flinn 1965, p. 19), and changes in diet, personal hygiene and living conditions, were more instrumental in curtailing disease and illness in the 19th century. As a second example, McKeown has argued that "long term improvement in living and dietary standards, presumably reflecting market mechanisms, was responsible for most of the mortality decline" (in Cherry 1996, p. 20)

Finally, Chadwick, a well-known public health and sanitary reformer was strongly opposed to theories of 'contagion' as explanations of disease causation. Instead, he was "...of the view that sickness sprang from pestiferous 'miasmas' or contaminated atmospheres" (in Porter 1987, p. 57).

This shifted the focus to sanitary reform and away from the theoretical and experimental work of medical doctors. Although many medical developments have been dated to the 19th century, several devastating health-related episodes in this same period in England mar the story of medical progress and benefit. As Porter (1987, pp. 52–53) so graphically describes:

> Throughout Victoria's reign, a succession of scandals, revelations and reports uncovered appalling health risks, failures in the public provision of such elementary utilities as water and waste disposal, and mismanagement of medical services: many of these were the consequences of the staggering increase of slum housing, industrial pollution and occupational disease caused by a rocketing population and ultra-rapid industrialisation.

The question thus emerges: in nineteenth-century England, what definitive role did modern medicine at the time play in the maintenance of day-to-day health of ordinary individuals and in handling epidemics, other diseases and wider public health concerns? Porter's commentary on the subject is quite decisive and corroborated by others (Berridge 1990, Cherry 1996, p. 18): For the organized medical profession played a surprisingly ambivalent and often secondary role in the vast expansion of Victorian state health provision (Porter 1987, p. 56).

He further cautions that it would be a mistake to think that:

> ...medicine was coming into its own, a knight in shining armour rescuing Britannia from the dragons of filth, cholera and other epidemics, environmental pollution, food adulteration and all the other health hazards produced by rampant population growth and unregulated market forces (op. cit., p. 56).

A related aspect of colonial health discourse was the portrayal of native systems of healing and health conditions in the colonies not only in disparaging terms, but also as different from those at 'home'. Writing in 1845, T.A. Wise, a doctor of medicine resident in India, declared the ancient Hindu system of medicine to have been neglected and supplanted now by "superstition and quackery", saying that "the native practice of medicine may now be said to be in this lamentable state of depression over all Hindustan" (Wise 1860, p. v).

British colonial authorities invested a great deal in naming the discipline of tropical medicine and subsequently schools too, to better understand, master and manipulate tropical conditions that produced such unique diseases, as cholera and the plague. In his account of *Medicine and the Raj, 1835–1911*, Anil Kumar finds the very formulation of such a discipline rather intriguing:

Though the name given to it was tropical medicine, there was hardly anything tropical about it apart from the fact that it operated in a tropical environment. Most of the so-called tropical diseases which the tropical doctors dealt with were to be found in Europe as well. Europe had known cholera, plague and smallpox for centuries. What distinguished them in a tropical climate was their intensity and ferocity (1998, p. 11).

However, specific diseases continued to be defined as illnesses peculiar to specific colonized spaces, e.g., India as the 'natural home' of cholera (Ramasubban 1988) if not particular to the colonized races i.e., as 'diseases of the natives' (Parkes 1878). The rhetoric of colonialism further presented the colonies as uninhabitable for the European races, given the incidence of lethal if not debilitating illnesses therein. Yet, the actual experiences in the colonies for the civilian and military personnel of the British colonial administration in India reveals a different story:

Together with the geological, botanical, zoological and meteorological surveys of India, the medical men aimed to understand the Indian environment and render it habitable and bountiful for the Europeans. Despite the much condemned tropical heat and miasmas, the British led a healthier and richer life with increased vitality and life expectancy even when compared to the European standards (Kumar 1998, p. 216).

Sanitary and health conditions in England during the 18th and 19th centuries were far from ideal. The impact of industrial capitalism had a deleterious effect on the English countryside and more so in the cities. Balfour and Scott (1924), describing London of 1833, provide a graphic image:

...the sanitary state of England at that time was totally different from that which obtains today. There was no Public Health organization, and though the type of dwelling had generally improved, towns were cleaner, a greater sense of decency prevailed, there was some effort at fighting small-pox, and a feeble attempt at quarantine measures was in existence, yet the state of things as viewed in the light of present-day experience was deplorable. Peculiarly sad and debasing, and often brutal were the conditions governing labor, more especially in factories and workshops ...The so-called good old days were in large measures dirty and dangerous old days (p. 13).

The same story of sordid, squalid, over-crowded, unventilated, sanitary conditions in urban centres throughout Britain in the eighteenth and nineteenth centuries, is told by every historian of British public health (Flinn 1965, Lane 2001, Porter 1987, Wohl 1983). The great revolution in sanitary reform was heralded by the Public Health Act of 1848 in which "for the first time the British Government charged itself with a measure of responsibility for safe-guarding the health of the population" (Flinn 1965, p. 1). The recognition of a link between poverty and disease came late but was hard to avoid and highlighted the need for extensive sanitary reforms in the country. Interestingly, there was a school of thought that located the spread of disease in 19th century Britain to a marginal and economically weak group: the Irish immigrants. The Irish Poor Inquiry of 1836 heard: The Irish in Birmingham are the very pests of Society, they generate contagion (in Flinn 1965, p. 15).

The Inquiry concluded thus:

> from the filthy conditions of the bedding, the want of commonest articles of furniture, the uncleanly habits of the inmates themselves, and the numbers which, without distinction of age or sex, are closely crowded together, they [the Irish] are *frequently the means of generating and communicating infectious disease"* (ibid. 15; emphasis added).

That the Irish were targeted as carriers of filth and disease is instructive in light of Britain's colonization of Ireland. Further parallels can be found in other British colonies, where the inability to contain the spread of infectious diseases and high mortality rates were also attributed to some 'ignorant' sectors of the community and their unclean habits. Compare Brodie's (1937, p. 306) portrayal of 'Eastern people' with the Irish image:

> The habits, customs and mode of living still prevailing among Eastern people can be put down as the *contributory cause of many of these deaths.* the people themselves are illiterate and superstitious, and indulge in many primitive practices which relate to almost every stage in life, birth, puberty, betrothal, marriage, pregnancy, childbirth, illness and death. There exists a considerable amount of poverty, much overcrowding, and the habit common to all, of sleeping in stuffy rooms, the windows of which are tightly shuttered in order to keep out ghosts and thieves (emphasis added).

Pre-Victorian England was no stranger to infectious diseases. Up to the nineteenth century, populations in parts of England were afflicted with smallpox, tuberculosis, cholera, and the plague.[20] Despite this history of epidemics, the state had clearly not undertaken any widespread sanitary and public health measures, as Chadwick's *Sanitary Report* of 1842 shows. It was only under tremendous pressure of public opinion that the British government assumed administrative responsibility and instituted relevant public health legislation, fairly late in the day at home and even later in the colonies. Evidently, these encounters with diseases did not prepare the British colonialists to deal with health in their 'overseas dominions'. As Balfour and Scott (1924, p. 5) record: "It was, however, long before the lessons learned at home were applied abroad."

A central consideration in the state's inaction towards public health reforms was the huge financial cost of this project. The following reasoning was as valid to public health in Britain as in the colonies:

> A Medical Officer is confronted with an almost insuperable difficulty when he sets out to request the expenditure of good money for the purpose of improving general health and thereby the earning capacity of a community, unless he can show that the measures he is putting forward will yield a profit for the individual, and that at no distant future (op. cit., p. 357).

> Yet in many of our colonies little or nothing is done to check the relatively enormous mortality amongst infants, although every child has for the State an economic value, and every healthy child a high potential value, which attains its maximum during the years of production (op. cit., p. 358).

An example from the Straits Settlements supports this observation. With the extension of British political control beyond the Straits Settlements and the Federated Malay States to the Unfederated Malay States, only in 1874 did state intervention in the health concerns of the general population became more of a reality. From this point onwards, with intense economic development and diversification in the region, the Colonial Government had to safeguard the interests of labour in the colonies, including the general welfare of the communities there. This heralded a period of greater state intervention in societal restructuring including in the health domain.

However, Parmer (1989, p. 51) is of the opinion that it was only in the 1920s that "major efforts to improve the health of the population get underway". He notes the role of Sir Laurence Guillemard, Governor of the Straits Settlements and High Commissioner of the Federated Malay States (FMS), and the Chief Secretary, George Maxwell in bringing about greater awareness of preventive public health measures in the colonies. They instituted programmes jointly to fight epidemics, particularly malaria and venereal diseases, and to protect infant and maternal welfare.

In later years a division between 'health' and 'medical' domains of the services led to increasing public health consciousness at the institutional levels in the colonies. A transition from hospital-based, curative medicine primarily for military and civil officers of the Crown in the late eighteenth century to state-sponsored public health policies was accomplished in Malaya, starting from the 1920s.

Some closing thoughts

Admittedly, the range of subjects raised by the arguments presented here is far too diverse to be addressed in a single chapter. This project is not just work in progress, but really barely just begun. With this caveat, I offer some thoughts in closing.

The preceding account of health and sanitary conditions as well as the state of modern medicine in nineteenth-century Britain has been revealing and illustrative on several fronts. The image of modern medicine presented and propagated in British colonial rhetoric was one of a scientific, rational, objective and more efficacious system of healing (Arnold 1988, p. 18). This image of modern medicine persisted from the 18th through to the early 20th centuries. Medicine, it has been argued, was one of the 'tools' (Headrick 1981) and resources amongst numerous to modernize and civilize colonized populations. Further, the transfer of modern medicine to the colonies and their subsequent adoption by the colonized peoples was seen as indicative of a progressive outlook. This also resulted in removing the veils of ignorance and superstition of native systems of healing—defined as irrational, non-scientific and backward. This rather grand and specific image of modern medicine was accompanied by a multitude of promises made on its behalf in improving the lot of humanity by solving the problems of disease and death universally.

This rhetoric is interesting in the face of two important historical facts: one, going by the evidence we now have of the experience, practice and functioning of modern medicine in 19th century in Britain, we may be better positioned to rethink both the image and the actual benefits of modern medicine. As has been demonstrated, the realities of health and sanitary conditions in 18th to 19th century Britain given the 'possession' and availability of modern medicine were clearly at odds with the benefits imagined; two, the desire to civilize colonized populations through the transferring of a science-based system of modern medicine remained just that in many cases. The story of health care provisions in the British colonies during the period of colonial administration is repeatedly one of neglect and inaction. It is clear that this lofty sentiment and intent as seen in colonial rhetoric was not acted upon till quite late in the day, for a variety of different and complex reasons.

In view of these disjunctures between images, realities and actual colonial health policies and practices, the articulated colonial rhetoric can and does sound hollow. Neither were these gaps *unknown* to participants whose utterances constituted this rhetoric, nor should it come as a surprise to students of politics today. Yet, at the time these statements about the moral imperative of modern medicine were being made, together with its capacity for civilizing, they were meant to and did carry a definite political and moral load.

Why should this have been so? This question assumes even greater significance in view of this knowledge: that the image of modern medicine was fashioned from a set of theoretical advances in medical science and not from tested applications and workability in practice. Riley demonstrates that "the nineteenth-century colonial spread of western [sic] medicine preceded the 20th century achievement of relative scientific orthodoxy" (1977, p. 549). The conjoining of medicine and science was crucial here, especially given the prominence accorded to scientism from the 18th century onwards. In this context Richard Brown's notice of the relationship between scientific knowledge and political and economic power (1993, p. 153) is relevant. He further notes: "The rhetorically constructed character of scientific knowledge and hence its openness to social and political influence" (ibid., p. 153).

This analysis certainly applies to the case at hand. We also see here the ideological success of science as a paradigm and hence of modern medicine, which was not rooted in the actual demonstration of its efficacy but merely in the *assertion* that it was by definition (as a science) both desirable and inevitable. Scholars have further noted that the invocation of scientism and objectivity, as well as the rooting of colonial projects in this paradigm, provided legitimation and justification for imperialist expansions.

Through a discussion of the health and sanitary conditions in nineteenth-century England and an investigation of systems of healing prevalent at the time, I have demonstrated the following: that medical pluralism characterized British society; that the selection of modern medicine as the representative of 'Western', 'European' medicine, as evident in colonial rhetoric, was in the first instance ideological more than anything else and the dominance of scientific medicine was only secured after tremendous opposition, both from religious and secular quarters; that the presentation of the colonies as breeding grounds for infectious diseases and, by contrast Britain as haven of healthy living is not supported by the historical record, and that there are disjunctures between the claims made on behalf of modern medicine and the realities of its achievements in managing day-to-day health conditions in the 19th century. In sum, I argue that the constructed images of health and healing practices prevalent at 'home' in colonial health descriptions were at odds with actual conditions. The larger implication is that the health and sanitary scenarios at 'home' and in the colonies in the 19th century might have been more similar than different.

Notes

[1]　The terms 'modern' medicine, 'Western' medicine, 'European' medicine, etc., are clearly not self-evident. This is even more so when discussing the practice of healing and medicine in different parts of the world during the 18th and 19th centuries coinciding with periods of rapid European expansion the world over.

[2]　The label itself incorporates a variety of approaches but one of the early proponents of the field sums up the basic sentiment here: "medicine is an activity whose developments can be most fully understood only when considered in relation to the network of social interaction within which it occurs" (1951, in Berridge 1990).

[3]　I would like to clarify my use of the term 'rhetoric' in this instance. This rhetoric can be abstracted from the statements, utterances and pronouncements of various parties: European travellers, missionaries, and personnel of the British Colonial Office, etc. This must be distinguished from the actual opinions held and acted upon by colonial officers and administrators who were based in the colonies and who were having to translate colonial policies into practice. The latter's position often varied from the rather generalized and abstracted rhetoric produced for public consumption.

[4]　The meanings of the terms 'non-West' and 'West' are neither self-evident nor references to territorial or geographical locales. Similarly, other references to

these places in the names of 'Europe', 'Asia' or 'America' are equally problematic. All of these are constructed categories shaped by dictates of specific times, places and political agendas. The contemporary meanings attributed to them and recognized so effortlessly and 'naturally' have been consciously produced and transformed over the years.

5   Much of this interaction is traceable to travellers' accounts of overland voyages, maritime contact and European missionary activities (Kaul 1989). The movement was not just from the 'Occident' to the 'Orient'. We have overwhelming evidence of Arab, Chinese and Indian travellers and traders to different parts of the world (Alvares 1991; Kabbani 1986). Clearly, the 'West' took an aggressive lead in exploring 'other' lands starting in the 15th century. The chronicles of Arab, Chinese, Javanese and Indian merchants and travellers to lands in Asia and further afield, are testimonies of contact between these peoples prior to European 'discovery' of the Orient.

6   Tome Pires describes the island of Timor as "not very healthy" and the voyage, although "renumerative…is also unhealthy" (in Smith 1968, p. 113). Similarly, Wang Ta-Yuan says of Timor:

> The climate is unhealthy:
> Formerly Wu Chai of Ch'uan (-chou?) sent a junk to trade with over an hundred men on board. At the end (of their sojourn there) eight or nine-tenths of them were dead, and the others, who took the junk back, were weak and emaciated. They were like wandering ghosts and filled with fear. What a terrible thing! Though the profits of trading in these lands were a thousand fold, what advantage is there? *Tao i chih lio or "Description of the Barbarians of the Isles"* (ibid.).

7   European interest in 'other' healing approaches is evident in the careers of Garcia d' Orta and Dr Nicolas Bautista Monardes. Garcia d' Orta, a Portuguese who served as a personal physician to Maritm Affonso de Sousa and accompanied him to Goa, "was the first European to describe the vegetable drugs and diseases of India in one of the first books by a European to be published in the East in Goa on 10 April 1563" (Boxer 1963, p. 3). Dr d'Orta justified his decision to leave Portugal for Asia:

> I have a great desire to know about the medicinal drug (such as are called drugs of pharmacy in Portugal) and these other remedies and simples which there are here, as well as fruits and pepper [spices]. I would like to learn their names in all the different languages, as also the countries where they grow, and the tress or plants which bear them, and likewise how the Indian physicians use them (p. 8).

Garcia d'Orta's investigations culminated in the publication of *Coloquios* (1563), a detailed account of Asian and Indian material medica, its botany (Boxer 1963) and a discussion of medicine in general. Dr Nicolas Bautista Monardes, a contemporary of d'Orta who hailed from Seville, was an armchair theorist and never visited the New World, but compiled a most comprehensive account of the materia medica of American plants and their therapeutic value in the Americas. According to Boxer:

> Both of them compiled what were virtually complete monographs on many important items of our actual material medica, which were then unknown or only inaccurately known to the Western world (op. cit., pp. 23–24).

[8] The dates of the Rockefeller Sanitary Commission (1890–1914) and the Rockefeller Foundation Campaigns (1914–22) are critical. Interestingly, the first target populations of the Rockefeller public health programmes were not non-Western countries but the southern states in the United States of America. The Southern states were perceived as being 'backward' and in need of industrialization and modernization. Improving the health of the southern populations, by way of eliminating diseases such as hookworm, carried an overt economic agenda. Brown (1978, p. 253) suggests that:

> Despite their humanitarian outward appearances, the major Rockefeller public health programs in the southern United States were intended to promote the economic development of the South as a regional economic, political, and economic cultural dependency of the northern capital. Rockefeller Foundation public health programs in foreign countries were intended to help the United States develop and control the markets and resources of those nations.

[9] The International Health Division of the Rockefeller Foundation played an important role in combating hookworm in the Straits Settlements and indeed in introducing other health measures and services in the 1920s. An arrangement was made between the Foundation and the Straits Settlements Government for a three-year Rural Sanitation Campaign" (Parmer 1989, p. 58).

[10] According to Waddington (1984, p. 1):

> In eighteenth and early nineteenth century England there were three quite separate medical corporations—the Royal College of Physicians, the Company of Surgeons (from 1800 the Royal College of Surgeons) and the Worshipful Society of Apothecaries—each of which had its own charter and its own bye-laws, and each of which granted licences to practise in the particular branch of medicine or surgery for which it was responsible.

Waddington notes "that these professional divisions were also clearly recognized in English law" (op. cit., p. 5) until the passing of the Medical Act in 1858. He further makes the point that the formal structure of the medical profession, as legally defined probably gives a misleading picture of the actual day-to-day practice of medicine (op. cit., p. 9), where the strict division of medical labour was not maintained, leading to overlapping roles.

[11] Still, in the literature, there is a reference to the 'regular' and the 'irregular' practitioners, the latter described as the itinerant and the 'quacks'. Clearly the definition of some practitioners as 'quacks', and their subsequent suppression reflects the power imbalance amongst the diverse groups of practitioners.

[12] However, as Ehrenreich and English (1973, pp. 27–30) stress, it was precisely the rifts between the two groups that to a large extent facilitated the reassertion of medical monopoly in American medicine.

[13] The problem of 'irregulars' also dogged regular doctors in North America. The American Medical Association founded in 1847 surveyed the range of medical practitioners and found "40,000 regulars" as well as a "long list of irregular practitioners who swarm like locusts in every part of the country" (in Ehrenreich and English 1989, p. 60).

[14] Some examples of prominent dispensaries in Singapore at the close of the century were, the "Singapore Dispensary", "Maynard & Co. Ltd", "The Dispensary" and "Medical Hall".

[15] According to Siddique and PuruShotam (1982, p. 176), Kling was:

> The local term used to refer to South Indians. A popular legend has it that it is the onomatopoeic sound made by the ankle chains of the early Indian convicts. However, most likely it is a corruption of the ancient Indian kingdom of Kalinga for people who came from these regions.

[16] Parallels could also be found in the colonies, where native healing practices were defined as 'non-scientific,' 'irrational' and 'barbaric' practices.

[17] For instance, some scholars have theorized this as the progress and triumph of modern medicine over superstitious and primitive healing practices (Burrow 1977; Youngson 1979).

[18] One theme I would like to further pursue is the nature of 'modern medicine' that was in fact transferred to the colonies and the forms it adopted there. Did it for example incorporate the latest discoveries and innovations in medical knowledge at a therapeutic level? A related theme would be the actual 'science' that was imported.

[19] Echoing European sentiments of the time, A.L. Hoops writing a history of medicine between 1830 and 1929 says this: Pasteur and Koch are the most typical representatives of the trend of modern medicine (Hoops 1930, p. 57).

[20] In England, the smallpox epidemic of 1837–40 claimed 42,000 lives and thirty years later 44,000 people died of the same disease in 1870–73 (Wohl 1983, p. 133). Cholera first struck England in 1831–32 (32,000 died), and again in 1848–49 (62,000 died), 1853–54 (20,000 died) and 1866–67 (14,000 died) (op. cit., p. 118). According to Wohl:

> Of all the killers, respiratory or intestinal, tuberculosis was the greatest, perhaps accounting for one-third of all deaths from disease in the Victorian period (op. cit., p. 130).

References

Abu-Lughod, Janet. 1989. *Before European Hegemony: The World System in A.D. 1250–1350*. New York: Oxford University Press.

Alchon, Austin Suzzane. 1991. *Native Society and Disease in Colonial Ecuador.* Cambridge: Cambridge University Press.

Alvares, Claude. 1991. *Decolonizing History.* New York: The Apex Press.

Arnold, David. 1986. "Cholera and Colonialism in British India". *Past and Present* 113: 118–51.

Arnold, David, ed. 1993. *Imperial Medicine and Indigenous Societies.* Manchester: Manchester University Press.

Balfour, A. and H.H. Scott. 1924. *Health Problems of the Empire: Past, Present and Future.* London: W. Collins, Sons and Co.

Berlant, Jeffrey Lionel. 1975. *Profession and Monopoly.* Berkeley: University of California Press.

Berridge, Virginia. 1990. "Health and Medicine". In *The Cambridge Social History of Britain 1750–1950,* edited by F.M.L. Thompson, pp. 171–242. Cambridge: Cambridge University Press.

Blake, Catriona. 1990. *The Charge of the Parasols.* London: The Women's Press.

Bourdillon, Hilary. 1988. *Women as Healers: A History of Women and Medicine.* Cambridge: Cambridge University Press.

Boxer, C.R. 1963. *Two Pioneers of Tropical Medicine: Garcia d'Orta and Nicolas Monardes.* London: Hispanic and Luso-Brazilian Councils.

Braudel, Fernand. 1973. *Capitalism and Material Life 1400–1800.* New York: Harper and Sons.

Brooke, Gilbert. 1921. "Medical Work and Institutions". In *One Hundred Years of Singapore,* Vol. 1, edited by Walter Makepeace, Gilbert Brooke and Roland Braddell, pp. 487–519. Singapore: Oxford University Press.

Brown, Richard E. 1978. "Public Health and Imperialism: Early Rockefeller Programs at Home and Abroad". In *The Cultural Crisis of Modern Medicine,* edited by J. Ehrenreich, pp. 252–70. New York: Monthly Press.

Brown, Richard Harvey. 1993. "Modern Science: Institutionalisation of Knowledge and Rationalisation of Power". *The Sociological Quarterly* 34, no. 1: 153–68.

Burbidge, F.W. 1880. *The Gardens of the Sun: A Naturalist's Journal on the Mountains and in the Forests and Swamps of Borneo and the Sulu Archipelago.* London: John Murray.

Burrow, James G. 1977. *Organized Medicine in the Progressive Era: The Move Toward Monopoly.* Baltimore: Johns Hopkins University Press.

Campbell, Kate. 1938. *The History of Women in Medicine.* Hodder Press.

Chadwick, Edwin. 1842/1965. *Report on The Sanitary Condition of the Laboring Population of Great Britain.* Edinburgh: Edinburgh University Press.

Chamberlain, M. 1981. *Old Wives' Tales: Their History, Remedies and Spells.* London: Virago.

Chaudhuri, K.N. 1965. *The English East India Company; the Study of an Early Joint-Stock Company.* New York: A.M.K.

Cherry, Steven. 1996. *Medical Services and the Hospitals in Britain, 1860–1939.* Cambridge: Cambridge University Press.

Curtin, Philip. 1964. *The Image of Africa: British Ideas and Action, 1780–1850.* Madison: University of Wisconsin Press.

Denoon, Donald. 1989. *Public Health in Papua New Guinea: Medical Possibility and Social Constraint, 1884–1984.* Cambridge: Cambridge University Press.

Donnison, J. 1976. Medical Women and Lady Midwives: A Case Study in Medical and Feminist Politics. *Women's Studies* 3: 229–350.

————. 1977. *Midwives and Medical Men.* London: Heinemann.

Doyal, Leslie with Imogen Pennell. 1979. *The Political Economy of Health.* Boston: South End Press.

Ehrenreich, Barbara and Deirdre English. 1973. *Witches, Midwives and Nurses: A History of Women Healers London*: Writers and Readers Publishing Co-operative.

————. 1978. *For Her Own Good: 150 Years of the Expert's Advice to Women.* London: Pluto Press.

Ehrenreich, J. 1978. *The Cultural Crisis of Modern Medicine.* New York: Monthly Review Press.

Fanon, Frantz. 1978. "Medicine and Colonialism". In *The Cultural Crisis of Modern Medicine*, edited by J. Ehrenreich, pp. 229–51. New York: Monthly Review Press.

Flinn, M.W. 1965. "Introduction". In *Report on The Sanitary Condition of the Laboring Population of Great Britain*, pp. 1–73. Edinburgh: Edinburgh University Press.

Fraser, Gertrude Jacintha. 1988. Afro-American Midwives, Bio-medicine and the State: An Ethnohistorical Account of Birth and its Transformation in Rural Virginia. Ph.D Dissertation. Department of Anthropology, Johns Hopkins University.

Gelfand, T. 1981. "The Decline of the Ordinary Practitioner and the Rise of the Modern Medical Profession". In *In Doctors, Patients and Society: Power and Authority in Medical Care*, edited by S. Statum and D.E. Larsen. Waterloo, Ontario: Wilfrid Laurier University Press.

Gevitz, Norman. 1988. *Other Healers: Unorthodox Medicine in America.* Baltimore: Johns Hopkins University Press.

Gish, Oscar. 1979. "The Political Economy of Primary Care and 'Health by the People'". *Social Science and Medicine* 13C: 203–11.

Given, D.H.C. 1929. "Lessons from the East Applied to the Medicine Prevention in the West". *The Malayan Medical Journal* 4: 55–62.

Glamann, Kristoff. 1958. *Dutch-Asiatic Trade 1620–1740.* The Hague: Martinus Nijhoff.

Gordon, G.A.C. 1928. 'The Health of the European Child in Singapore and Malaya.' *The Malayan Medical Journal* 3: 32–40.

Hammond, D. and A. Jablow. 1977. *The Myth of Africa.* New York: The Library of Social Sciences.

Haynes, Douglas Melvin. 1999. "The Social Production of Metropolitan Expertise in Tropical Diseases: The Imperial State, Colonial Service and the Tropical

Diseases Research Fund". *Science, Technology and Society* 4, no. 2 (July–Dec): 205–38.

Headrick, Daniel. 1981. *The Tools of Empire*. New York: Oxford University Press.

Hogg, John. 1837. *London As It Is*. New York: Garland Publishing Inc.

Holloway, S.W.F. 1964. "Medical Education in England, 1830–1858: A Sociological Analysis". *History* 49: 299–324.

Hume, John Chandler Jr. 1986. "Colonialism and Sanitary Medicine: The Development of Preventive Health Policy in the Punjab, 1860–1900". *Modern Asian Studies* 20: 703–24.

Ityavyar, Dennis A. 1987. "Background to the Development of Health Services in Nigeria (Pre-colonial and British colonial rule)". *Social Science and Medicine* 24, no. 6: 487–99.

Jewson, N. 1974. "Medical Knowledge and the Patronage System in 18th-century England". *Sociology*: 369–85.

Jex-Blake, S. 1886. *Medical Women: A Thesis and a History*. Edinburgh: Oliphant, Anderson and Ferrier.

Kabbani, Rana. 1986. *Europe's Myths of Orient*. Bloomington: Indiana University Press.

Kaul, H.K., ed. 1979. *Travellers' India: An Anthology*. Delhi: Oxford University Press.

Koenigsberger, H.G. and George L. Mosse. 1968. *Europe in the Sixteenth Century*. London: Longmans.

Kumar, Anil. 1998. *Medicine and the Raj; British Medical Policy in India 1835–1911*. New Delhi: Sage Publications.

Lach, Donald F. and Edwin J. Van Kley, eds. 1965. *Asia in the Making of Europe; A Century of Advance: Southeast Asia*. Chicago: The University of Chicago Press.

Lander, K. 1922. *The Study of Anatomy by Women before the Nineteenth Century*. Proceedings of the 3rd International Congress of the History of Medicine, London, pp. 125–34.

Lane, J. 1984. "The Medical Practitioners of Provincial England". *Medical History* 28: 353–71.

Larkin, J. 1983. *Occupational Monopoly and Modern Medicine*. London: Tavistock.

Leng Chee Heng. 1982. "Health Status and the Development of Health Services in a Colonial State: The Case of British Malaya". *International Journal of Health* 12, no. 3: 397–417.

Levine, Philippa. 1998. 'Modernity, Medicine and Colonialism: The Contagious Diseases Ordinance in Hong Kong and the Straits Settlements". *Positions* 6, no. 3: 675–705.

Lewin, Evans. 1924. *The Resources of the Empire and their Developments*. London: W. Collins Sons & Co. Ltd.

Lorcin, Patricia M.E. 1999. "Imperialism, Colonial Identity and Race in Algeria, 1830–1870: The Role of French Medical Corps". *Isis* 90, no. 4: 653–79.

Loudon, Irvine. 1986. *Medical Care and the General Practitioner, 1750–1850*. Oxford: Clarendon Press.

Lyons, R.H. 1975. *To Wash an Aethop White*. New York: Teachers College Press.

Mackenney, Richard. 1993. *Sixteenth Century Europe: Expansion and Conflict*. London: Macmillan.

Macleod, Roy and Milton Lewis, eds. 1988. *Disease, Medicine and Empire: Perspectives on Western Medicine and the Experience of European Expansion*. London: New York: Routledge.

Manderson, Lenore. 1987. "Health Services and the Legitimation of the Colonial State: British Malaya 1786–1941". *International Journal of Health Services* 17, no. 1: 91–112.

Marks, Shula. 1997. "What is Colonial about Colonial Medicine? And What has Happened to Imperialism and Health?" *Social History of Medicine* 10, no. 2 (August): 205–19.

Mudimbe, V.Y. 1988. *The Invention of Africa: Gnosis, Philosophy and the Order of Knowledge*. Bloomington: Indiana University Press.

Numbers, Ronald. 1985. "Do-it-Yourself the Sectarian Way". In *Send Us a Lady Physician*, edited by Ruth J. Abram, pp. 43–54. New York: W.W. Norton & Company.

Parkes, Edmund. 1878. *A Manual of Practical Hygiene* (5th ed.). London: J. & A. Churchill, New Burlington Street.

Parmer, Norman J. 1989. "Health and Health Services in British Malaya in the 1920s". *Modern Asian Studies* 23, no. 1: 49–71.

Patterson, K.D. 1981. *Health in Colonial Ghana: Disease, Medicine and Socio-Economic Change, 1900–1955*. Waltham: Crossroads Press.

Paul, James. 1978. "Medicine and Imperialism". In *The Cultural Crisis of Modern Medicine*, edited by J. Ehrenreich, pp. 273–86. New York: Monthly Review Press.

Peterson, M.J. 1978. *The Medical Profession in Mid-Victorian London*. Berkeley: University of California Press.

Pierce, R.V. 1906. *The People's Common Sense Medical Adviser in Plain English or Medicine Simplified*. Buffalo: World's Dispensary Printing Office and Bindery.

Porter, Roy. 1987. *Disease, Medicine and Society in England, 1550–1860*. Cambridge: Cambridge University Press.

Raychaudhuri, Tapan. 1962. *Jan Company in Coromandel, 1605–1690: A Study in the Interrelations of European Commerce and Traditional economies*. S-Gravenhage: M. Nijhoff.

Riley, James Nelson. 1977. "Western Medicine's Attempt to Become More Scientific: Examples from the United States and Thailand". *Social Science and Medicine* 11, no. 10 (July): 540–60.

Ramasubban, Radhika. 1988. "Imperial Health in British India, 1857–1900". In *Disease, Medicine and Empire*, edited by Roy Macleod and Milton Lewis. London: Routledge, pp. 38–60.

Rosenberg, Charles. 1985. "American Medicine in 1879". In *Send Us a Lady Physician*, edited by Ruth J. Abram, pp. 21–34. New York: W.W. Norton & Company.

Said, Edward W. 1979. *Orientalism*. New York: Random House, Vintage Books.

Schwaab, Raymond. 1984. *The Oriental Renaissance*. New York: Columbia University Press.

Shryock, Richard H. 1948. *The Development of Modern Medicine: An Interpretation of the Social and Scientific Factors Involved*. (2nd ed.) London: V. Gollancz.

Siddique, Sharon and Nirmala PuruShotam. 1982. *Singapore's Little India*. Singapore: Institute of Southeast Asian Studies.

Smith, Ronald Bishop. 1968. *The First Age; Of the Portuguese Embassies, Navigations and Peregrinations to the Kingdoms and Islands of Southeast Asia 1509–1521*. Bethesda, MD: Decatur Press.

Thompson, F.M.L., ed. 1990. *The Cambridge Social History of Britain 1750–1950*. Cambridge: Cambridge University Press.

Todorov, T. 1982. *The Conquest of America: The Question of the Other*. New York: Harper Torchbooks.

Twumasi, Patrick A. 1988. "Colonialism and International Health: A Study in Social Change in Ghana". *Social Science and Medicine* 15B: 147–51.

Vaughan, Megan. 1991. *Curing Ills: Colonial Power and African Illness*. Stanford: Stanford University Press.

Verluysen, M. 1980. "Old Wives' Tales? Women Healers in English History". In *Rewriting Nursing History*, edited by C. Davies. London: Croom Helm.

Waddington, Ivan. 1984. *The Medical Profession in the Industrial Revolution*. Dublin: Gill and Macmillan Humanities Press.

Wise, T.A. 1860. *Commentary on the Hindu System of Medicine*. London: Trubner & Co.

Witz, Anne. 1992. *Professions and Patriarchy*. London: Routledge.

Wohl, Anthony S. 1983. *Endangered Lives: Public Health in Victorian Britain*. Cambridge, Mass: Harvard University Press.

Woodward, John and David Richards. 1977. *Health Care and Popular Medicine in 19th Century England: Essays in the Social History of Medicine*. New York: Holmes and Meier Publishers.

Yeoh, Brenda. 1991. "Municipal Sanitary Surveillance, Asian Resistance and the Control of the Urban Environment in Colonial Singapore". Research paper. Oxford: School of Geography, University of Oxford.

Young, James Harvey. 1961. *The Toadstool Millionaires: A Social History of Patent Medicines in America before Federal Regulation*. Princeton: Princeton University Press.

Youngson, A.J. 1979. *The Scientific Revolution in Victorian Medicine*. New York: Holmes & Meier Publishers, Inc.

10

Poverty, Gender and Nation in Modern Vietnamese Literature During the French Colonial Period (1930s–40s)

Van Nguyen-Marshall

Modern Vietnamese journalism and prose fiction owe a debt to French colonialism. The conditions and opportunities created in the early twentieth century by colonial rule allowed for the emergence of new types of literature—modern novels and short stories—which in turn posed a serious challenge to colonialism itself. This chapter will examine two prominent groups of Northern Vietnamese writers of the 1930s and 1940s, whose novels and short stories on poverty reflected Vietnamese intellectuals' preoccupation with social and moral problems associated with colonialism and global capitalism.[1]

The first group is the Tu luc van doan (Self-Reliance Literary group), an organization of Westernized liberal intellectuals. The second group is composed of left-leaning social realist writers. Although the fiction examined here provided contemporary readers with descriptive and seemingly apolitical portrayals of poverty, they were not simply critiques of society in general. The works of the first generation of Vietnamese modern prose writers were strong indictments against French colonialism. The treatment of female characters and use of gendered imagery made these short stories and novels expressions of anti-colonial sentiment. In these works, the symbolic feminine nation and masculine Confucian moral order were used to express the authors' anguish over the moral degeneration of their society and the loss of their nation. By openly exhibiting scenes of absolute poverty and social deterioration after nearly half a century of colonization, these writers made a mockery of the French claim to a 'civilizing' mission.

Another underlying theme in this chapter is the issue of identity and representation. For the most part, the intellectuals of Northern Vietnam were men of middle to upper-middle class families, who had access to education and lived in an urbanized and Westernized environment. Many of the writers examined here lived a relatively comfortable life in comparison to the misery they described in their stories. Of interest is how these writers positioned themselves vis-à-vis the poor about whom they wrote. The Vietnamese intellectuals clearly saw themselves as beneficiaries of Western modernity in terms of scientific and technological advances as well as intellectual influences. It is also clear that they were painfully aware of the separation between them and the majority of the people of their country. One senses that it was precisely the desire to close the gap between the small group of urban intellectuals and the mass of rural poor that resulted in the copious amount of literature written about the lives of the poor. Notwithstanding their good intentions and genuine concerns for those living in poverty, the first generation of Northern Vietnamese prose writers were raised on Confucian elitism and schooled in Western science and arts. This bicultural heritage shaped the writers' understanding and portrayal of poverty. In this context the literature written about the lives of the poor is valuable for its symbolic as opposed to its realistic depiction of colonial poverty.

Prose fiction in twentieth-century Vietnam

Colonialism was the backdrop to the development in prose fiction and journalism in Vietnam. In addition to exposing the Vietnamese educated class to Western literature, French colonial policies on language and censorship played an important role in the development of modern prose fiction (novels and short stories).[2] The emergence of prose fiction in the early twentieth century, like the development of journalistic writing, was greatly encouraged by the development and proliferation of *quoc ngu* (the national script).[3] The boom in *quoc ngu* newspapers also contributed to the emergence of modern fiction, as newspapers were vehicles that introduced Western literature in translation to a wide Vietnamese audience. *Dong Duong tap chi* (Indochina Review), for example, carried translated installments of French classics, such Alexander Dumas' *The Three Musketeers*, Victor Hugo's *Les Misérables*, and La Fontaine's *Fables*.[4] Later, when Vietnamese writers began producing their own modern fiction, newspapers and periodicals provided a forum for their work. Social realist writer Nguyen Cong Hoan, for example, had his first short story published in *An Nam tap chi* (The Journal of Annam), and later became a regular contributor to *Tieu thuyet thu bay* (Saturday Novels).[5]

While French colonial censorship was strict, prohibiting any overt discussion of politics, it was more relaxed where literature was concerned.[6] This small measure of freedom made literature a more popular genre for writers. It was, therefore, in literature that one found the drama of individuals played out with important political and national implications. David Marr estimates that "a good proportion of the fiction, drama, and poetry was written with quite serious social, political and cultural objectives in mind."[7] In prose fiction and reportage/documentary writing Vietnamese intellectuals had an opportunity to explore and make sense of the modernizing and globalizing forces that were changing their society.

By the 1930s many of these intellectuals had been educated in French or Franco-Vietnamese schools, where they would have been immersed in Western thought and literature.[8] The Vietnamese writers examined in this chapter were strongly influenced by Western writers literary trends. The Self-Reliance writer Nhat Linh's favourite French author was André Gide, whose influence can be detected in his novel, *Nang thu* (Autumn Sun).[9] Pham The Ngu noted that Nhat Linh's novel *Doi Ban* (Two Friends) bore signs of the influence of both Gide and of Dostoevsky,[10] while realist writer Nguyen Hong credited Maxim Gorky and Charles Dickens as his literary influences.[11] The first generation of Vietnamese fiction writers, therefore, held the curious position in society, not unlike that of other Asian and African writers, of trying to formulate or construct a national perspective from a standpoint of cultural and intellectual hybridity. These writers, in their 'problemization' of colonial poverty, adapted the tools of the colonizers—the modern novel and short stories—to launch their attack on colonial rule and to suggest a vision of national unity and independence.

A remarkable feature of the literature and investigative journalism that emerged in the 1930s and particularly in the 1940s was the attention given to portrayals of the lives of the poor. Literary interest in the poor had a global precedent in the works of writers such as John Steinbeck and George Orwell.[12] The economic downturn resulting from the Great Depression provided material for Steinbeck's stories of rural poverty, just as it did for Vietnamese writers. Indochina was not spared the negative affects of the 1930s Great Depression, which brought about considerable unemployment, and a decline in the standard of living for many middle-class families. Taken as a whole, the literature of this period reflects an attempt by socially conscious Vietnamese intellectuals to grapple with social issues such as drug addiction, prostitution, and familial disintegration, all of which were related to poverty. In other words, the authors were articulating and 'problematizing' the poverty that surrounded them. Poverty was no longer a problem only for the individual, but one that affected both society and nation. Greg Lockhart suggests that the categories of society and nation as they were used in early twentieth-century Vietnam were new, reflecting the enormous socio-psychological transformation that accompanied colonization and the collapse of the Vietnamese monarchical and moral order.[13] Even while Northern Vietnamese intellectuals were presenting poverty as a new social problem, their critiques were based on traditional Confucian morality. In other words, the prose fiction writers were urging the elite to resume its Confucian duty vis-à-vis the poor, and were calling for a return to Confucian ethical and moral behaviour toward the poor.

For the sake of organization, I will discuss the writings on poverty as produced in Northern Vietnam in two general groups. The first group is the bourgeois liberal *Tu Luc Van Doan* (translated as the Self-Reliance Literary Group); the second is the social realist writers, which includes both fiction and *phong su* (reportage/documentary) writers. The boundaries for these groups are of course flexible and porous. Thach

Lam, a member of the Self-Reliance group, for example, also wrote an investigative report on the urban poor.[14] While the Self-Reliance Literary Group was an actual association which functioned openly with its own manifestos and activities, the other group of writers did not exist as a formal organization or even as a loose ad hoc association, but only as a construct of academic studies.[15]

Images of Poverty in the Writings of the Self-Reliance Literary Group

Nguyen Tuong Tam, better known by his pen name Nhat Linh, founded the Self-Reliance group in 1933. The group's manifesto declared its commitment to bringing new, progressive egalitarian ideas to Vietnamese society. The Self-Reliance group advocated individual freedom (for men *and* women), condemned Confucianism and superstition, and sought to simplify the Vietnamese writing style.[16] To this end, the Group published two journals *Phong Hoa* (Customs) and *Ngay Nay* (This Day), and ran a publishing house, Doi Nay (Life Today), which they used to disseminate the group's ideas for cultural and literary reform. *Phong Hoa* was controlled and published by Nhat Linh and the Self-Reliance group from 1932 until the French authorities shut it down in 1936.[17] Partly modelled on the French journal *Le Rire*, *Phong Hoa* was immensely popular, particularly for its satire.[18] Pham The Ngu wrote that when *Phong Hoa*, the first satirical periodical in Vietnam, was initially published, it "exploded like a bomb", bringing laughter to the society.[19] *Ngay Nay*, a much more "artistic and lavish" magazine than *Phong Hoa*, was produced in 1935 during the time when the Self-Reliance group's popularity and influence were on the wane.[20]

Much of the writing of the Western-educated, urban middle-class liberal intellectuals of the Self-Reliance Literary group attacked what they considered to be antiquated and stifling Confucian practices, such as arranged marriages and polygamy.[21] Their protagonists were usually middle-class, educated young men and women who were suffocating under the weight of traditional expectations and restrictions. Common problems facing the main characters included a lack of freedom to love, to create, or to develop one's potential. Greg Lockhart suggests that by focusing its attack on traditional customs (something seemingly apolitical) the Self-Reliance group was making an "oblique" attack on French colonial rule, which "sought to maintain traditional customs in the perceived interests of political and social stability".[22] Some short stories and novels of the Self-Reliance group, however, focused directly on the poverty and injustices that ordinary peasants and workers endured in their daily lives. These stories were even stronger statements against the destruction and the contradictions of colonialism.

Feelings of guilt pervade the Self-Reliance group's stories on poverty; guilt felt by children of the rich when confronted with the miseries of their compatriots.[23] Stories such as Nhat Linh's "Hai ve dep" (Two Aspects of Beauty), or Thach Lam's "Mot con gian" (A Fit of Anger) attested to the authors' anguish over their privileged lives in comparison to the lives of rural and urban labourers.[24] Without a doubt, members of the group were educated urbanites of the privileged class. Khai Hung (pen name of Tran Khanh Giu), whose romantic novels were highly popular among the youth, was the son of a mandarin province chief. Up to the age of twelve, Khai Hung studied the Confucian classics, and was later given a Western education at the Albert Sarraut *lycée*, a school reserved for children of French and mandarin families. In 1931 Khai Hung began teaching at the famous Thang Long private school.[25]

Nhat Linh, the main architect of the group, and his brothers, the writers Thach Lam (Nguyen Tuong Lan) and Hoang Dao (Nguyen Tuong Long), were born into a family of civil servants with mandarin roots. In his reminiscence of his childhood, Nhat Linh's youngest brother, Nguyen Tuong Bach, emphasizes their family's modest and rural background. Bach, who was trained as a medical doctor, writes that he and his brothers were born in a poor district town, surrounded by ricefields and mountains.[26] Bach relates that Nhat Linh lived simply, preferring to eat like a poor peasant, consuming such plain food as rice and salted sesame seed mixture.[27] This desire to be close to the common people and to emulate their lifestyle was probably carried out with greatest enthusiasm by Thach Lam. After his marriage, Thach Lam moved into a simple hut with a thatched roof in a village near Hanoi's West Lake.[28] He was reported to have told friends that although he could build a fancy brick house, he preferred to live simply, in his own chosen poverty. As a friend of Thach Lam recorded, Thach Lam often claimed:

> To be able live in a thatched hut, sleep on a bamboo bed, eat bean greens, and yet still find beauty in the thatched roof, softness in the bamboo bed, and tastiness in the bean greens, is to know how to live artistically.[29]

This romanticized perception of rural poverty can easily be detected in writings of the Self-Reliance members. While Nhat Linh and other Self-Reliance writers were no doubt sincere in their concerns for the plight of poor people, their romantic portrayal of poverty suggests a gap between their imagined poverty and reality.

The fact that the Self-Reliance writers tried to be 'like' the peasants, demonstrates how distant they actually were from Vietnam's rural culture. Alexander Woodside, commenting on the mass exodus of educated youths from the villages during the early twentieth century, notes that "[n]owhere was the problem of the separation of the intelligentsia, and of intellectual youths, from agricultural problems more acute than in Tonkin".[30] Being removed from the experience of poverty, the Self-Reliance writers were presenting their own imagined portrait of poverty, a sympathetic one-dimensional picture of the rural poor. A few stories written by Nhat Linh, Khai Hung, and Thach Lam will be discussed below. These stories, with their heavy reliance on the traditional trope of woman as nation, illustrate the authors' sense of guilt, compassion, and powerlessness when dealing with deprivation of their society. The authors' portrayal of women and use of feminine imagery also serve to reinforce the implicit message that poverty was a new social problem connected to colonialism.

Nhat Linh's story, "Dau duong xo cho" (In the Streets)[31] is about a society in a downward spiral. The narrator and his siblings had been living in wealth and comfort as children of a mandarin, but when their father died they had to leave their native village to seek a living elsewhere. They were now forced to live among the poor, among the "lowly" households (*gia dinh hen ha*), profiting from the latter's drug addiction. The frequent use of adjectives such as "lowly" (*hen ha*) in connection with the poor reinforces the theme of the story: poverty is not just about the lack of material things, but a cultural and spiritual deprivation. The narrator described the poverty surrounding him and stated: "It is truly a wicked society, but it is wicked because it is so poor."[32]

To demonstrate the connection between poverty and moral deterioration the narrator relates an incident concerning his neighbour, Mrs. Hien, whose husband pulled a rickshaw for a living. The narrator expressed sympathy for his young and beautiful neighbour who had the misfortune to be married to an opium-addicted, ugly man. Mrs. Hien, however, did not dwell on her poverty and bad luck; instead, she spent her days working on her weaving to earn extra money, which she spent on opium for her husband. The narrator stated: "She does not think about her own self. Her brown shirt is faded and has patches on the arms, shoulders and back, yet she would not save money for a new shirt."[33] Mrs. Hien was obedient and loyal to her husband, fulfilling her role in the Confucian order. Her husband, however, a slave to opium, was unable to do the same. He took from her and gave nothing back. Exploited and subservient, Mrs. Hien was like the country itself, caught in its own traditions and unable to free itself from its colonial master. Nhat Linh's "Nuoc chay doi dong"[34] (Water Runs in Parallel Streams) also features a poor and beautiful female character, who was seemingly unaware of the injustice of her life situation. Several years later when Sinh, the narrator, saw her again, he lamented:

> Oh life! This is how some people's lives are! And that's all they have! One thought that a beautiful girl would be unable to live in poverty and baseness (*ngheo hen*), and thus one feels pity and sympathy...but this beautiful girl whom one pities doesn't know that she is suffering, she never thinks to ask if she is suffering. Indifferent and unmoved, she lives according to her life situation...like the river water flowing in the riverbed.[35]

This passive image of the poor is again presented by Nhat Linh in "Hai ve dep" (Two Aspects of Beauty),[36] a short story about a young educated man, Doan, coming to terms with his new awareness that his comfortable life was gained through the exploitation of poor peasants. With his new consciousness, Doan had no choice but to act; Doan was committed to bringing enlightenment to the people, like a responsible Confucian gentleman. Doan concluded that the unending cycle of poverty that seemed unchanged since his childhood was the result of lack of knowledge:

> [T]hese people suffered and lived in dark night because they had no one to enlighten them, to teach them to live any other way and make them long for a finer life.[37]

What exactly Doan will or can do to make the peasants' lives "finer" is left vague.

In this story, both the rich and poor—the exploiter and exploited— were portrayed as being unaware of their situation. As a consequence, it fell upon the shoulders of enlightened people such as Doan to make them aware, so that the cycle of exploitation could be stopped. In a similar fashion, the ferry girl in "Nuoc chay doi dong" was presented as being unaware of and indifferent to her poverty. This portrayal perhaps reflects Nhat Linh's personal view on poverty relief—that it is the moral duty of the modern educated people, like Doan, to make people conscious of their own oppression. In 1937 Nhat Linh along with Hoang Dao, and Khai Hung organized a charity to help the poor with housing in the outskirts of Hanoi.[38] The name of the charity is noteworthy: Hoi Anh Sang (Beam of light), a name that invokes the image of enlightenment and improvement coming from the intellectual class. Like the journalists writing about charity in the conservative Northern newspapers, Nhat Linh was emphasizing the elite's duty to help the poor—a reinstatement of Confucian social responsibility.

In the Self-Reliance literature about rural and urban poverty, female characters feature prominently and heroically. The poor women in Nhat Linh's short stories were hardworking and self-sacrificial. These qualities continue even now to be idealized as desirable traits of a 'good' Vietnamese woman by the present Vietnamese government.[39] Although these female characters were admirable, they were also victims, and worse, they were passive, indifferent victims. In "Hai ve dep", Nhat Linh's polarized representation of Doan's two mothers, his deceased, poor, biological mother and his wealthy foster mother, could be seen as symbolic of a native mother country overtaken and exploited by an 'advanced' foreign nation. This symbolic use of woman/mother as nation was Nhat Linh's way of critiquing French colonial rule, which although it provided some benefits for the wealthy collaborating class, also created an environment in which exploitation and moral degradation flourished. It also dramatized Doan's (and by extension, Nhat Linh's) ambivalence and uneasiness with his bicultural heritage— his hybrid identity.

The homage to the self-sacrificing woman was again featured in "Anh phai song"[40] (Darling, You Must Live), a short story written by Khai Hung. This is a tragic story about a poor woman who chose death in order to save her family. It is a classic example of maternal sacrifice, a sacrifice that she had to face because of poverty. Khai Hung portrayed Mrs. Thuc as a 'simple peasant' whose mind did not know how to imagine, or how to think in an orderly way.[41] She was, nevertheless, a loving and hardworking mother and wife, whose tragic fate was effectively and movingly presented.

Rousing readers' sympathy and indignation was the goal of Thach Lam's collection of short stories, *Gio dau mua* (The first wind of the season).[42] Thach Lam was the most prolific of the Self-Reliance group in writing about the lives of the lower-middle class and those in absolute poverty. Pham The Ngu stated that Thach Lam was not especially concerned, as Nhat Linh and Khai Hung were, with propagandizing social revolution, but was more interested in telling life stories of the poor.[43] Although Thach Lam's stories are less moralizing than Nhat Linh's and Khai Hung's, his portrayal of the poor is similar in its gentle romanticizing of poverty, and particularly of rural poverty. There is a clear message in Thach Lam's writings: rural life with its simplicity and poverty is preferable because the rural poor are still morally upright, honest and kind, unlike the superficial, mean urban rich people. Like Nhat Linh and Khai Hung, Thach Lam drew attention to the hardship women suffered in shouldering the responsibility of meeting their families' needs.

Thach Lam's "Nha me Le" (Mrs. Le),[44] a moving short story about Mrs. Le and her eleven children living in abject squalor, typifies how the author represented rural poverty. This story was published in 1937, and what Thach Lam chronicles in the second part of the story perhaps reflects the economic hardship of the early 1930s connected with the Great Depression, and the deterioration of Vietnamese society under French colonialism. As casual farm work became scarce and as marketing activities began to shift to a more urbanized centre, Mrs. Le was having difficulty finding work. People's attitudes and values were changing. Her eldest son used to go fishing in neighbouring ricefields, but could no longer do so, as the increasing commercialization of the economy made private property a sacred thing. The story ends with Mrs. Le dying from a vicious dog attack. A rich landlord let loose his dog on her when she came begging for food. Significantly the dog that attacked and killed Mrs. Le was a French breed.

The hardship endured by poor rural women is again highlighted in the short story, "Co hang xen" (The Market Girl).[45] The story tells of the difficult life of a young woman Tam, whose life was completely devoted to supporting her own, and later her husband's, families. The fate of Tam was not uncommon. Tam comforted herself with the thought that all the other women she knew also worked hard all their lives to support their families. The unending hardship was all Tam expected of her life. The story ends with her returning in the evening to her husband's village:

> The black ring from the rows of bamboo of Bang village suddenly appeared in front of her, dark and thick. With sadness Tam saw clearly her entire life; a life of a market girl from young until old, completely filled with hardship and worries…She lowered her head and walked quickly into the dark alley.[46]

Like the female characters in the stories examined thus far, the female characters in Thach Lam's works played crucial roles in keeping the family together during times of poverty. Mrs. Le and Tam were the main breadwinners for their families. Thach Lam portrayed them as the ideal Vietnamese woman: hardworking, loving, good natured and, most of all, willing to sacrifice herself for others. Similarly, Khai Hung's Mrs. Thuc (in "Anh phai song") deliberately gave up her life for the sake of her children. Mrs. Hien of Nhat Linh's story, "Dau duong xo cho", also embodied some of the qualities that were idealized and associated with femininity in Vietnamese culture, such as loyalty to her opium-addicted husband, and resourcefulness in trying to come up with money to help him with his habit. Mrs. Hien was basically a good woman, tainted by the poverty and depravity around her. These female characters were portrayed with sympathy and with admiration for their strength and endurance. They were victims of poverty, and of a degenerating society in which there was a remarkable absence of men willing or able to shoulder some of the responsibilities. Death, opium addiction, or disinterest (on the husband's part) had made women the sole breadwinners.

One sees the use of woman as admirable victim not only in the Self-Reliance stories, but also in other Vietnamese literary and historical writings, from the legend of the warrior Trung sisters to Nguyen Du's famous *Tale of Kieu*.[47] These legendary women and the feminine characteristics of perseverance and self-sacrifice, have been mythologized in the Vietnamese national self-image.[48] With a long history of foreign invasions and occupations, one conventional and enduring national self-image features Vietnam as a physically weak and small country, but one strong in ethnic solidarity, loyalty and morality. Thus the literary use of woman as a metaphor for the nation was pervasive in traditional literature and poetry; depicting woman/nation as vulnerable, but pure and loyal, qualities which in the end would prevail over injustice. It is ironic that the Self-Reliance writers, who attacked the traditional ways, themselves invoked this conventional image of women in their writings about the poor.

The Self-Reliance writers, as the first generation of Vietnamese modern fiction writers, could not escape their bicultural heritage. With one foot in the Vietnamese and one in the Western cultural world, intellectuals like Khai Hung, whose own wife was described as "still maintaining the Confucian custom with a set of black-dyed teeth",[49] were cultural *métis*.[50] They were the progeny of an unequal and forced union of Vietnamese and French cultures. This transculturalism can be detected in their works, which had the outer appearance of being thoroughly Westernized. Hue-Tam Ho Tai states that despite "the self-proclaimed modern outlook of the Self-Reliance Literary Group...the novel [Khai Hung's] also showed clear evidence of the influence of late Ch'ing fiction."[51] Tai points out that the ending of Khai Hung's novel *Nua chung xuan* (In mid-spring) resembles that of Nguyen Du's Vietnamese classic, *Story of Kieu*. Moreover, Tai also saw influences from Qing (Ch'ing) fiction in Nhat Linh's *Nang thu* (Autumnal Sun), while others have commented on its similarity to André Gide's *La Symphonie Pastorale*.[52] In similar fashion, traces of Confucian elitism and values were embedded in the Self-Reliance short stories about the poor. In their writings on the plight of the poor the Self-Reliance members were using the traditional trope of woman as nation to reinforce Confucian values such as loyalty, perseverance, ethical conduct and social responsibility.

Therefore, by depicting the predicaments and hardship of the poor in a gendered manner, with poverty and vulnerability connected with femininity, these stories did more than attack the injustices of the society. These stories reminded educated urban readers of their nation in crisis. This was a subtle indictment of French colonial rule, which promised progress and modernization with its 'civilizing' mission while peddling alcohol and opium and, at the same time, impoverishing the Vietnamese with heavy taxes, increasing landlessness and unemployment. Moreover, by depicting the poor as passive, feminine victims, the Self-Reliance writers were perhaps positioning themselves—active and modern—as having moral authority over the poor peasants.

Class, poverty and social realism

The second group of writers that will be examined became popular in the mid-1930s and early 1940s. Social realist writers such as Nguyen Cong Hoan and Nguyen Hong wrote about social injustice, cruel treatment of the poor by the rich, and the lack of humanity among people in both urban and rural settings. Tam Lang's documentary work on rickshaw men will be included here, even though it is technically not of the fiction genre. Nevertheless, the attempts of the social realist writers to capture and relate the truths about their society render their fictitious stories close in theme and spirit to the investigative reporting of Tam Lang.

In contrast to the Self-Reliance group, the social realist writers were more class-conscious and less romantic, particularly when writing about poverty and village life. The social realist writers examined here were from the lower middle class. In their stories there is less moralizing, and more bitterness and outrage about the injustice and misery which they witnessed. Although there is a strong element of class-consciousness in the writings of these authors, the poor were not idealized. Both rich and poor were capable of utter cruelty and brutality toward their fellow human beings. Moreover, these are not works calling for social revolution or class warfare, but a call for more kindness and humanism in people's behaviour. On a larger scale, by portraying the misery of the poor, these writers, like the Self-Reliance writers, were also critiquing colonial society. However, in contrast to the Self-Reliance writers who tended to assign admirable feminine characteristics to the poor, the social-realist writers represented poverty as a dignity-destroying process in which the destitute person was stripped of self-respect and humanity. The implication was that colonization dehumanized Vietnam by destroying the traditional moral order while leaving nothing in its place.

This section will begin with the works of Nguyen Cong Hoan, who first began writing in 1920 at the age of seventeen.[53] Born in 1903 in Hung Yen province, Hoan was the son of a mandarin in charge of education for a district. As a boy, Hoan was taught Chinese by his paternal grandmother. Despite their mandarin background, his biographers assert that his family was poor. As a result, Hoan was sent to live with his uncle who was district chief.[54]

A prolific writer, Hoan had already written eighty short stories and nine novels by 1935.[55] Hoan's stories were hugely popular because they were often satirical and funny. His gift was his ability to present hypocrisies, contradictions, and absurdities of colonial life in a humorous manner which lightened the bleakness of his stories.[56] Vietnamese literary critics have often compared Hoan's work to those of internationally famous masters of short stories and satire, such as Anton Chekhov, Guy de Maupassant, and the Romanian dramatist, Ion Luca Caragiale.[57] Hoan, however, flatly denied benefiting from any foreign influences. Perhaps this was an attempt to appear 'authentically' Vietnamese, a 'common' man, like Thach Lam living in his 'peasant' hut. One literary critic defends his 'authenticity': "...he does not just mimic or follow one European writer, even though he wrote many short stories that are just as profound and outstanding as those of the three famous writers [Caragiale, de Maupassant, and Chekhov]".[58] A contemporary, Hoang Trung Thong, writes, "Nguyen Cong Hoan often told me that he does not read anybody's work. But I know he does. A person like him cannot not read Guy de Maupassant, or Anatole France..."[59] The Vietnamese communist theoretician Truong Chinh states that although Hoan could read French, he read very little French literature. Hoan apparently read only de Maupassant's "the Beggar", and portions of Hugo's *Les Misérables*, and Dumas' *Le Comte de Monte Cristo*.[60] According to Truong Chinh, it was almost as if he refused to be influenced by anyone. Another writer states that Hoan had access to left-wing material, such as *Viet Nam hon* (The Soul of Vietnam), *Le Paria* (of the French Communist Party), and the works of Sun Yat Sen, Phan Boi Chau and Lenin.[61] This same writer also relates that when Hoan was young he liked Molière's satirical plays and that he and his brothers would stage them for their parents. As these various writers attest, foreign literary influences on Hoan (or the lack of them) were of great interest to his contemporaries. They also demonstrate Hoan's awareness and fear of the overwhelming Western influences among Vietnamese intellectuals, and the gap that might exist between Vietnamese intellectuals and rest of 'the people'.

Whatever the case might have been during his intellectual and creative development, Hoan certainly had ample access to works of Western literature both in their original languages and in translation. As Nguyen Minh Chau notes, Hoan was writing in an age of cultural borrowing, when there were strong foreign influences on literature.[62] In other words, Hoan, like others of the first generation of Vietnamese writers, grew up in a period in which educated intellectuals were just as familiar with

Molière's plays as they were with *The Story of Kieu*. Acknowledging the transcultural nature of literary influences, however, does not in any way make Hoan less "the writer of the miserable" (*nha van cua nhung hang nguoi khon nan*), a title given to him by a contemporary literary critic.[63] His portrayal of poverty, however, like that of the Self-Reliance group, should be seen as an intellectual's imagined representation of a social problem with political and national symbolism.

Nguyen Cong Hoan's stories are often biting in their ridicule of social climbers and the bourgeois, as well as bold in their portrayals of human greed and cruelty. In his short story, "Rang con cho cua nha tu san"[64] (Teeth of a Capitalist's Dog) Hoan suggested that life for the poor was worse than the fate of dogs. Mocking rich Vietnamese people and their infatuation with Western things, Hoan had the dog's owner bragging about how well-mannered his dog was:

> Thus we know that even the French bred dogs are truly smarter than our Annamese [Vietnamese] dogs. Annamese dogs not only have an ugly coat, but also often eat filth…[65]

This story goes on to show the absence of any moral or ethical principles guiding human relationships. From the rich man's point of view, the beggar's life was worth less than his dog's two front teeth.

This same theme is again related in, "Hai thang khon nan"[66] (The Two Wretched Knaves), a story about Mr. Lan, a widower, who was impoverished by a major flood and had to resort to selling his son. With a heavy heart, Mr. Lan took his son to the rich household of Mr. Representative (the local member of the Native Chamber of People's Representative), where a negotiation ensued about the price for the boy. To the dismay of Mr. Lan, Mr. Representative first made a pitifully low offer of thirty cents, then, upon inspection of the boy, he lowered it to twenty-eight cents. Even though he was torn up about the sale, Mr. Lan, when given an opportunity to void the transaction, decided to not do so and chose instead to satisfy his own hunger. This story shows how everything, even one's own children, could become a commodity to be bought and sold. It also highlights the disintegration of one of the three sacred Confucian bonds—the bond between father and son.

Similar messages about the lack of humanity, filial piety, and ethical conduct can be found in Hoan's other fiction of the 1930s and 1940s. The stories "Bao hieu: tra nghia cha" and "Bao hieu: tra nghia me"[67] tell of a rich company owner and his wife who made an ostentatious public display of grief at the funeral for the rich man's father. At the same time, however, they mistreated the man's mother who lived in poverty. In "Thang an cap"[68] (The Thief) a young beggar was violently beaten after he ate a bowl of noodles without paying (because he did not have any money). The story ends with an absurd scene in which the noodle seller demanded that he "return" the stolen goods. In "Cai von de sinh nhai"[69] (An Investment to Make a Living) an epileptic man, who, though he could not hold down a job because of his frequent seizures, was also unable to make a living begging since he did not have any apparent physical disabilities. Having to choose between starving and maiming himself, he jumped from a tree and crippled himself in order to beg for a living. Hoan's novel, *Nhung canh khon nan*[70] (Scenes of Wretchedness) is about an immoral clerk and a corrupt society which allowed him not only to get away with his treachery, but to prosper. *Cai thu lon*[71] (The Pig's Head), a novel banned by the French authority, is about village political life, which was filled with corruption, bribery and costly, meaningless rituals and customs.

The difference between Nguyen Cong Hoan and the Self-Reliance writers in their respective portrayal of the poor is stark. Hoan's representation of poverty is less romantic than those found in the writings of the Self-Reliance group. Hoan relied heavily on sarcasm, irony and humour perhaps to make his story more entertaining, and perhaps to elude censorship. However entertaining these stories may be, they convey a clear message about the social deterioration of Vietnamese society, and particularly the deterioration of the Confucian moral order as a result of the impact of colonialism and capitalism. Therefore, like the Self-Reliance writers, Hoan was calling for a return to Confucian ethical and moral values and behaviour.

The social realism of Nguyen Hong's fiction also conveys a similar message of moral and spiritual degeneration. Despite a troubled past, Hong began his literary career at an early age.[72] At nineteen he produced his first novel, *Bi vo* (The Down and Out), which won the Self-Reliance award for the best "reportage novel" in 1937. In 1938 Hong's autobiographical work, *Nhung ngay tho au* (Days of Childhood), which was inspired by the autobiographical writings of Maxim Gorky and Charles Dickens,[73] was serialized in the Self-Reliance Group's journal *Ngay Nay*. In 1937 Hong became involved in left-wing politics, and in 1945 he joined the Viet Minh.[74]

In the introduction to *Bi vo*, Hong related that at sixteen, when he was released from prison, he and his mother moved to Hai Phong where they lived a life of utter deprivation.[75] His motive for writing was the desire to accomplish something worthwhile as a dedication to his gentle and loving mother, who had suffered so much in her life.[76]

This devotion to his mother is evident in his sympathetic portrayal of poor women in *Bi vo* and in his other works. His admirable female characters are similar to those in the Self-Reliance stories discussed earlier, women whose endurance, moral strength, and willingness to sacrifice themselves render them models of the idealized Vietnamese woman, and symbols of the Vietnamese nation. Hong's fiction, however, seems more realistic: his characters live a less romantic poverty than those of the Self-Reliance stories. Like Nguyen Cong Hoan, Hong spared his readers little of the seediness, brutality, and cruelty of the living conditions of the poor, both in the city and in the countryside. In his novel, *Bi vo* and short-story collection *Bay Huu*, his protagonists are mostly thieves, gang members, prostitutes, smugglers, and murderers. They use slang and are coarse, unlike the polite characters in the stories of the Self-Reliance writers. Despite being criminals, the characters in Hong's stories elicit sympathy and admiration because the reader is shown how society is responsible for making them what they are, and, in the face of all suffering, these characters still exhibit moral courage, perseverance, love, and loyalty. Like Nguyen Cong Hoan's depiction, Hong's colonial reality is bleak, with poverty and a collapsing moral order making it a world ruled by deceit and greed. In Hong's works, however, there is hope: hope found in love and loyalty that could be found in even Hong's hardened criminal characters.

Bi vo is a novel about Binh, a young, innocent peasant girl whose life unfolded tragically, in a similar fashion to that of Kieu, the heroine of the famous *The Story of Kieu*.[77] Binh's tragic story began when her lover, who had impregnated her, abandoned her. When Binh's son was born, her parents sold him against her wishes. Out of shame and wanting to spare her parents ridicule from the village, Binh left for the big city, Hai Phong, where she encountered more deceit and cruelty. Binh found herself working in a brothel, then becoming the wife of a notorious thief, Nam Sai Gon, who loved her deeply.[78] All the while Binh nursed a dream of being able to buy her son back and returning to her village to take care of her younger siblings and ageing parents. Like Kieu, the female protagonist in Nguyen Du's story, Binh, despite her life of prostitution and crime, still remained pure and good: she was steadfast in her loyalty to her criminal husband and filial to parents who showed her no love or kindness.

The portrayal of steadfast loyalty and enduring love in the face of absolute deprivation and hopelessness appears in Hong's other stories found in the short story collection, *Bay Huu*.[79] The leading story of this collection, "Bay Huu" (Seven Huu) is about a young female gang member, Bay Huu, who exhibited courage and loyalty even in mortal danger. In "Trong canh khon cung" (In a Scene of Utter Misery), a dissatisfied ferry owner, after witnessing the strong love between an impoverished couple, felt ashamed of her resentment for her paralyzed husband and of her desire to have an affair. The story "Chin Huyen" (Nine Huyen) is about a widow, Chin Huyen, who, despite failing health, risked her life in order to rescue an old friend and partner in crime. Chin Huyen had left the criminal world after her husband's death and was struggling to raise her children by herself in an honest way. Her decision to help free an old friend who had been captured by the local authority plunged her back into a life of crime. The reader, however, realizes that because of her illness, Chin Huyen and her children would have been doomed either way. In the criminal world, however, Chin Huyen at least had trusted allies. "Day, bong toi" (Here, Darkness) is a love story between Mun and Nhan. It is not a typical love story about passion, but a story of enduring love between two poor people and their five children. Mun and Nhan remained faithful and loving to each other even as they became more impoverished. At the end, with the blindness of Nhan (the husband) and death of his wife, the family was reduced to begging simply to survive.

As in the fiction of Nguyen Cong Hoan, the social realism of Nguyen Hong is bold in its portrayal of the harsh life of the poor. In Hong's depiction, ethical or moral principles no longer guided people's behaviour. In both the urban and rural areas corruption and injustices dominated, providing little opportunity for people to improve their lives, except through crime. In contrast to the fiction of Nguyen Cong Hoan, however, Nguyen Hong's stories exhibit a hope that is embodied by many of his female characters, who remained loyal and morally strong in their relationships and conduct.

Although Hong resembles the Self-Reliance writers in his gentle and compassionate portrayal of people (particularly women) living in poverty, the poor people in his stories were not passive and indifferent, as they were depicted in the Self-Reliance stories. In Hong's stories people made conscious choices. In *Bi vo*, Binh chose to break Nam Sai Gon out of jail, and thereby returned to their relationship even when she could have had a leisurely life as a police detective's mistress. She chose Nam because he was the only person who really loved her. The poor in Hong's stories were aware of their living conditions and strove to improve their lives. Unlike Thach Lam's market girl, Tam, who bowed her head and accepted her miserable fate, Hong's characters took action. Chin Huyen, for example, was poised to kill an authority figure to save her friend, while Mun's resourcefulness and energy enabled her to feed her blind husband and five children. These were not passive victims.

Thus, as readers find a sense of outrage in Nguyen Cong Hoan's work, they find a sense of compassion for the poor in Nguyen Hong's. Both authors conveyed a similar message: there was spiritual and moral degeneration in Vietnamese society under French colonialism. At the heart of this social corruption was material poverty, which pushed people into immorality and criminality. Their fiction highlights the hollowness of the French rhetoric of a 'civilizing' mission. This theme is also found in Tam Lang's documentary report about the lives of rickshaw men, *Toi keo xe* (I Pull a Rickshaw). In Tam Lang's work, however, the emphasis is on how inhumane treatment of the poor makes them into a class of *"cu li"* (coolie) with no morality.

Documentary or reportage writing became popular during the middle to late 1930s. Following European examples, such as that of French journalist Maryse Choisy who did investigative reporting in brothels, middle-class Vietnamese journalists disguised themselves as rickshaw men and servants to write about the poor.[80] Lockhart attributes the development of reportage writing which focuses on the 'underclass' of society to the "democratic transformation in the political, social, and literary consciousness during the colonial era"[81] and to the destruction of "the ancient sense of hierarchy and communal order".[82] Lockhart argues that Tam Lang's use of the active first person voice in *Toi keo xe* is subversive on two levels. It is subversive in a class sense, providing a perspective from the 'bottom' up; but it is also subversive in suggesting the emergence of a new sense of society and national identity.[83] When one examines Tam Lang's representation of the poor and his use of gendered imagery, however, it becomes clear that *Toi keo xe* is a denunciation not only of the exploitation of the urban poor, but also of the destruction of a moral order on a national scale. This destroyed moral order is a Confucian one in which ethical principles guided people's behaviour. Therefore, while Tam Lang might have been using a Western medium (first person documentary reporting) and challenging the social hierarchy, he was also mourning the loss of the 'old' Confucian morality.

Tam Lang (Whose real name is Vu Dinh Chi) was born in 1900 of a middle-class background.[84] He was educated in the Franco-Vietnamese school system, and began a career in journalism in the 1920s. By the 1930s Tam Lang began writing satirical pieces attacking social injustices. *Toi keo xe* was serialized in 1932, and published as book in 1935. Tam Lang also wrote *Dem Song Huong* (Night on the Perfume River), a reportage piece about prostitution in Hue, published in 1938.[85] In 1946 he joined the Viet Minh, but, disillusioned, he moved back into the French zone and in 1954 left with the mass anti-communist migration to South Vietnam.[86]

To write *Toi keo xe*,[87] Tam Lang supposedly disguised himself as a 'coolie' to work as a rickshaw man. According to Vu Ngoc Phan, this was the first documentary work of its kind in Vietnam, and Tam Lang's revelations caused a stir among contemporary readers, who thought the writer had made it all up.[88] Tam Lang's work presents a vivid example of how people from the middle class could become impoverished, and even farther, become 'coolies'—a term for unskilled labourers that, as elsewhere, carried derogatory connotations. His reporting makes clear that there were two kinds of poverty: the 'natural' kind that seemed tolerable, and the second kind of poverty in which the poor were stripped of dignity and humanity. In pre-modern and modern Europe similar distinctions had been made between 'deserving' and 'undeserving' poor; between the honest hardworking poor and the dangerous vagabond. But in Tam Lang's documentary, the reader can explore this difference from the point of view of the 'coolie' himself. From this perspective, one sees that the injustices and inhumanity that 'coolies' faced daily harden them, rendering them dangerous and 'undeserving'.

Tam Lang documented the life of Tu, a Confucian scholar, turned poor, turned rickshaw man, turned 'coolie', subsequently becoming an opium addict and pimp. When Tu and his family first lost their fortune, he began pulling his own rickshaw in his hometown, but at that time, although poor, he was not despised. However, due to an injustice, the

French authorities imprisoned Tu and confiscated his house and rickshaw. After being released from prison, Tu had to go Hanoi to become one of the 'horse people', a term commonly used at that time to refer to rickshaw men. Working for cruel and greedy employers and constantly having to deal with customers who try to cheat him, Tu became a 'coolie'. Tam Lang quoted Tu:

> Eating with dogs, one has to put one's head down with them. Although I'd pulled a rickshaw for seven years, it was only from the day I was beaten that I completely became a coolie.[89]

As a 'coolie', Tu shamelessly partook in immoral and criminal activities, declaring that he now worshipped only money. It is clear, however, that he was unable to accept this way of life, as he used all his money for opium which he used to escape his reality. Tu's life symbolizes the disintegration of the pre-colonial Confucian ethical order, which was not replaced by an equivalent order in the colonial capitalist society.

Tu, the former Confucian scholar, was demoralized by the meanness in his society, and by opium—which was known, according to Tam Lang, by its slang name: Miss *Phu Dung*, or the Opium Lady.[90] The dictionary meaning of *phu dung* is hibiscus. Two of the dictionaries contain the phrase: *a phu dung*, with *a* meaning gal or damsel, and the entire phrase defined as opium.[91] Another dictionary states that *phu dung* is an old literary term for a beautiful woman.[92] It is unclear when this term came about, and how extensively it was used. It is not a coincidence that the users of this drug, which was personified as a beautiful woman, were mostly men. Those impoverished addicts who did not have ten cents to buy real opium, went to see the "Black Queen". At the Black Queen's place, for five cents an addict could get a bowl of black water that was made from water boiled with old rags used to clean opium lamps and pipes, broken opium implements, and opium residue.[93] Gendered images abound: feminine opium, an agent of social corruption, destroys the masculine social–moral order, personified by Tu, the former Confucian scholar.

Like the writings of Nguyen Cong Hoan and Nguyen Hong, Tam Lang's *Toi keo xe* attempts to provide a realistic portrayal of the life of the poor. Focusing on telling the stories of beggars, rickshaw men, prostitutes, and thieves, these social-realist writers were articulating the contradictions in colonial society: the stark contrasts between rich and poor, humanity and cruelty, and between the promises of modernity and the 'backwardness' of reality. The social realist writers aimed to arouse awareness, sympathy and understanding for the poor. They also emphasized the destruction of the Confucian moral order (symbolized by masculine images), and the lack of any replacement to guide people's behaviour. Thus while these writers were borrowing Western literary genres of the short story and documentary writing and challenging the traditional social hierarchy in the use of the first person pronoun, they were in the end reinforcing the importance of Confucian social and moral values.

Conclusion

Vietnamese literature on poverty of the 1930s and 1940s was a vehicle for social criticism, and indirectly for anti-colonial expressions. The poverty that occupied both the Self-Reliance group and the social-realist writers was the kind associated with being a 'coolie', where one was not only lacking money, but dignity. The Vietnamese fiction writers did not make a distinction between 'deserving' and 'undeserving' poor, a distinction that was important in the dominant discourse on poverty in Early Modern Western Europe. Poor people portrayed in early twentieth-century Vietnamese fiction were hardworking and morally upright. It was their poverty that led to their moral, spiritual and cultural deprivation, and not the other way around. Drug and alcohol addiction, prostitution, and crime played a large part in this degeneration. Society at large also contributed to the poor's destitution by allowing greed and money to rule. This type of poverty was portrayed as new, as a recent development accompanying the collapse of the pre-colonial moral order and the rise of the capitalist system brought in by colonialism.

By using gendered imagery—a feminine nation and a masculine Confucian moral order—writers were able to connect the humiliation and misery of the poor to a larger problem: the loss of their nation. The contrast between the grim poverty portrayed by the fiction writers and the colonial promises of modernity and progress is jarring. The Self-Reliance and social-realist writers examined here, however, went only as far as arousing readers' awareness and indignation. With the exception of some of Nguyen Cong Hoan's later works, which were banned, the literature examined here did not call for rebellion. These were not works advocating class warfare or even anti-colonial uprising. This descriptive as opposed to prescriptive approach no doubt reflects the tight colonial censorship. It also reflects the development of the abilities of this first generation of Western-educated intellectuals to grapple with the global forces brought on by colonialism and capitalism. In their attempts to articulate and formulate poverty as a problem in the larger social and national realms, the prose writers were coming to terms with their hybrid cultural makeup, and their material and cultural privileges. Despite their Westernized backgrounds, the writers' critiques of colonial poverty was rooted in Confucian values and morality. Even the iconoclastic Self-Reliance writers, who openly denounced Confucianism as backward, were reinforcing the idealized feminine qualities of loyalty and perseverance, and were calling for the elite to take up their responsibility for poor relief.

By the late 1930s, more overtly anti-colonial writings appeared, including the works of such writers as Ngo Tat To, and of communist party leaders such as Truong Chinh and Vo Nguyen Giap on rural poverty,[94] clarify the subtle critiques in the earlier literature. Moreover, the writings of the late 1930s were more prescriptive, providing solutions to the problem of poverty. Thus, while French colonialism fostered the conditions for the emergence of modern Vietnamese literature, this new prose fiction and reportage writing became an important means for Vietnamese intellectuals to voice their concerns about the moral–social degeneration of their country. Poverty was the locus in which material, moral, and spiritual deprivation could be explored, and a subject that writers could use to articulate their anguish about the fate of their nation.

Notes

[1]   The French colonized Vietnam, Cambodia, and Laos from the late 1800s until 1954. Under French colonization, Vietnam was divided into three regions, Cochin China, Annam, and Tonkin, and each region was ruled separately. The region under consideration here is Tonkin, which the Vietnamese referred to as Bac Bo (Northern Region).

[2]   According to John Schafer and The Uyen, the first Vietnamese novels appeared in 1910. In that year Tran Chanh Chieu published *Hoang To Anh ham oan* [The Unjust Suffering of Hoang To Anh], and Truong Duy Toan, published *Phan Yen ngoai su* [an Unofficial History of Phan Yen]. Ho Bieu Chanh followed with *Ai lam duoc?* [Who can do it?] in 1912. Schafer and The Uyen, "The

Novel Emerges in Cochinchina", *The Journal of Asian Studies* 52, no. 4 (November 1993): 854–84.

3   Cao-Thi Nhu-Quynh and John Schafer, "Ho Bieu Chanh and the Early Development of the Vietnamese Novel", *Vietnam Forum* 12 (1988): 100.

4   Neil Jamieson, *Understanding Vietnam* (Berkeley: University of California Press, 1993), p. 79. These novels were translated by Nguyen Van Vinh.

5   Pham The Ngu, *Viet Nam van hoc su gian uoc tan bien. Van hoc hien dai, 1862–1945* [The new and concise history of Vietnam's Literature. Modern literature], vol. III (Saigon: Quoc hoc tung thu, 1965), p. 505.

6   Ngo Vinh Long, *Before the Revolution* (Cambridge: MIT press, 1973), xv.

7   David Marr, *Vietnamese Tradition on Trial* (Berkeley: University of California Press, 1981) p. 51.

8   Ibid., pp. 8–9.

9   Greg Lockhart, introduction to "Broken Journey: Nhat Linh's 'Going to France'", *East Asian History* 8 (December 1994), p. 82.

10 Pham The Ngu, *Viet Nam van hoc su gian uoc tan bien*, vol. III, p. 463.

11 Greg Lockhart, *The Light of the Capital: Three Modern Vietnamese Classics* (Kuala Lumpur: Oxford University Press, 1996), p. 21.

12 Ibid., p. 17.

13 Greg Lockhart, *Nation in Arms* (Sydney: Allen and Unwin, 1989), ch. 2.

14 Thach Lam co-wrote the reportage under the pen name, Viet Sinh, *"Ha noi ban dem"* [Hanoi by Night], serialized in *Phong Hoa*, 1933. This reference was taken from Lockhart, "Introduction", *The Light of the Capital*, p. 44.

15 As academic constructs, these categories have been defined in various ways by different scholars. Vu Ngoc Phan, for example, discussed Thach Lam's work in the section for social novels (*tieu thuyet xa hoi*), Khai Hung as a writer about customs, and Nguyen Cong Hoan as a realist writer (Vu Ngoc Phan, *Nha van hien dai: Phe binh van hoc* [Modern writers: Literary criticism], five volumes. Glendale: Dai Nam, n.d. First published by Tan Dan, Hanoi, 1942). Pham The Ngu divided the literature of the 1930s into two main groups according to their publishers: The Self-Reliance group's Ngay Nay publishing house and the Tan Dan press. Although Pham The Ngu discussed Nguyen Cong Hoan, Vu Trong Phung, Lan Khai, and Le Van Truong as writers of the Tan Dan group, he admitted that no such group ever existed (Pham The Ngu, *Viet Nam van hoc su gian uoc tan bien*, vol. III). Maurice Durand and Nguyen Tran Huan categorize the Self-Reliance writers along with Nguyen Cong Hoan, To Hoai, Vu Trong Phung, Ngo Tat To and others under one group, which they called the "Socialist-realist" (*An Introduction to Vietnamese Literature*, New York: Columbia University Press, 1985, p. 179). Hue-Tam Ho Tai, however, uses this term, "socialist realist" as a category for the literature that dominated North Vietnam after the

communist revolution. Tai, along with Vietnamese literature specialists, such as Nguyen Dang Manh, classify the literature that flourished in the 1930s focusing on social issues, such as poverty and inequity, as critical realist [*hien thuc phe phan*]. See Hue-Tam Ho Tai, "Duong Thu Huong and the Literature of Disenchantment", *Vietnam Forum* 14 (1993), pp. 89–90; Nguyen Dang Manh, "Ve tac pham 'Tac den' cua Ngo Tat To", in Ho Si Hiep, ed., *Ngo Tat To, Nguyen Huy Tuong, To Hoai* (Ho Chi Minh city: Van Nghe, 1997), p. 42.

[16] Alexander Woodside, *Community and Revolution in Modern Vietnam* (Boston: Houghton Mifflin Company, 1976), p. 88.

[17] Lockhart, Introduction to "Broken Journey: Nhat Linh's 'Going to France'", p. 93.

[18] Ibid.

[19] Pham The Ngu, *Viet Nam van hoc su gian uoc tan bien*, vol. III, p. 441.

[20] Durand and Nguyen Tran Huan, *An Introduction to Vietnamese Literature*, p. 161; see also Jamieson, *Understanding Vietnam*, p. 158.

[21] Ibid.

[22] Lockhart, introduction to "Broken Journey", p. 76.

[23] Tai, *Radicalism and the Origins of the Vietnamese Revolution*, p. 250.

[24] "Hai ve dep" will be discussed in more details below. "Mot con gian" (1937) is about a rich Vietnamese man, who, in a fit of anger, inadvertently caused the complete destitution of a rickshaw man and his family. *Thach Lam truyen ngan chon loc* [Selected short stories of Thach Lam], compiled by Tran Manh Thuong (Hanoi: Hoi Nha Van, 1996), pp. 27–35.

[25] Ho Si Hiep, *Khai Hung, Thach Lam*, Ho Chi Minh City: Van Nghe, 1996, pp. 9–10.

[26] Nguyen Tuong Bach, "Nhat Linh, nhung ngay Ha Noi va tai hoi nghi Hong Kong '47" [Nhat Linh, Hanoi days and at the Hong Kong conference '47], *Khoi Hanh* 5, no. 57 (July 2001): 20. The article was an address Bach made at the 31st anniversary of Nhat Linh's death in July 7, 1994, Westminster, California.

[27] Ibid.

[28] Ho Si Hiep, ed., *Khai Hung, Thach Lam*, p. 64.

[29] As recorded in Dinh Hung's memoir, quoted by Ho Si Hiep, ibid., p. 65.

[30] Woodside, *Community and Revolution*, pp. 126–27.

[31] Nhat Linh, "Dau duong xo cho", in Nhat Linh and Khai Hung, *Anh phai song*, reprint, Ho Chi Minh City: Van Nghe [n.d., circa 1999], pp. 121–29. The short story collection was first published in 1937 by Doi Nay, Hanoi.

[32] Ibid., p. 122

[33] Ibid., p. 123.

[34] Nhat Linh, "Nuoc chay doi dong", in Nhat Linh and Khai Hung, *Anh phai song*, pp. 130–40.

35 Ibid., p. 139.

36 "Hai ve dep" was first published in Nhat Linh, *Toi Tam* [Darkness]. Hanoi: Doi Nay, 1936. The version I used ("Two Beauties") is a translated one found in James Banerian, *Vietnamese Short Stories*. Phoenix: Sphinx Publishing, 1986, pp. 37–57.

37 Ibid., p. 55.

38 Jamieson, *Understanding Vietnam*, p. 158.

39 Lisa B.W. Drummond, *Mapping Modernity: Perspectives on Everyday Life in Vietnam's Urbanizing Society* (Ph.D. dissertation, The Australian National University, Canberra, 1999), ch. 3.

40 Khai Hung, "Anh phai song", in Nhat Linh and Khai Hung, *Anh phai song*. Hanoi: Doi Nay (n.d., circa the early 1930s), pp. 5–13.

41 Ibid., p. 9.

42 Thach Lam, *Gio dau mua* (Ha Noi: Doi Nay, 1937).

43 Pham The Ngu, *Vietnam van hoc su gian uoc tan bien*, vol. III, p. 490.

44 Thach Lam, "Nha Me Le", *Thach Lam truyen ngan chon loc*, pp. 85–93. The story was first published in *Gio dau mua* (Hanoi: Doi nay, 1937).

45 Thach Lam, "Co hang xen", *Thach Lam truyen ngan chon loc*, pp. 183–200. The story was first published in *Soi toc* (Hanoi: Doi Nay, 1942).

46 Ibid., p. 200.

47 By the 1930s Kieu, the main protagonist from Nguyen Du's famous story [*The Tale of Kieu*] had become a "symbol of the disintegration of the Vietnamese nation." See Tai, *Radicalism and the Origins of the Vietnamese Revolution*, p. 109.

48 Lisa B.W. Drummond, *Mapping Modernity: Perspectives on Everyday Life in Vietnam's Urbanizing Society*, ch. 3.

49 Si Ho Hiep, *Khai Hung, Thach Lam*, p. 9.

50 Françoise Lionnet, "'*Logiques métisses*': Cultural Appropriation and Postcolonial Representations", in Kostas Myrsiades and Jerry McGuire, eds., *Order and Partialities: Theory, Pedagogy and the "Postcolonial"* (New York: State University of New York Press, 1995), pp. 111–36.

51 Tai, *Radicalism and the Origins of the Vietnamese Revolution*, p. 252.

52 Lockhart, Introduction to "Broken Journey", p. 82.

53 Vu Thanh Viet, ed., *Nguyen Cong Hoan: Cay but hien thuc xuat sac*, pp. 435–37.

54 N.I. Niculin, "Nha van Nguyen Cong Hoan" (The writer Nguyen Cong Hoan), p. 82; Nguyen Hoanh Khung, "Nguyen Cong Hoan (1903–1977)" in Vu Thanh Viet, ed., *Nguyen Cong Hoan: cay but hien thuc xuat sac*, p. 281.

55 Pham The Ngu, *Viet Nam van hoc su gian uoc tan bien*, vol. III, p. 505.

56 Truong Chinh, "*Buoc duong cung* tieu thuyet cua Nguyen Cong Hoan", p. 380.

57 Phan Cu De, "Nguyen Cong Hoan", in Nguyen Cong Hoan: cay but hien thuc xuat sac, edited by Vu Thanh Viet, p. 39. Here De was quoting an article in *Tap chi van hoc* (Literature Review), no. 3, 1977.

58 Ibid.

59 Hoang Trung Thong, "Nguyen Cong Hoan nhu toi biet" (Nguyen Cong Hoan as I knew him), in *Nguyen Cong Hoan: cay but hien thuc xuat sac*, edited by Vu Thanh Viet, pp. 148–49.

60 Truong Chinh, "Doc 'tuyen tap Nguyen Cong Hoan'" (Reading "The collection of Nguyen Cong Hoan"), in Vu Thanh Viet, ed., ibid., pp. 330–31.

61 Nguyen Hoanh Khung, "Nguyen Cong Hoan", p. 281.

62 Nguyen Minh Chau, "Nha van Nguyen Cong Hoan" (The writer Nguyen Cong Hoan), in Vu Thanh Viet, ed., ibid., p. 116.

63 Thai Phi gave him this title when he reviewed Hoan's first short story. Pham The Ngu, *Viet Nam van hoc su gian uoc tan bien*, vol. III, p. 505.

64 Nguyen Cong Hoan, "Rang con cho cua nha tu san" (written in 1929), *Nguyen Cong Hoan truyen ngan tuyen chon*, compiled by Le Minh (Hanoi: Van Hoc, 1996), vol 1, pp. 62–68.

65 Ibid., p. 64.

66 Nguyen Cong Hoan, "Hai thang khon nan" (written in 1930), *Nguyen Cong Hoan truyen ngan tuyen chon*, pp. 79–83.

67 Translated as "Announcing one's Filial Piety: Repaying one's Father's Devotion", and "Announcing one's Filial Piety: Repaying one's Mother's Devotion", written in 1933, in *Nguyen Cong Hoan truyen ngan tuyen chon*, pp. 213–27.

68 Ibid., written in 1932, pp. 184–91.

69 Ibid., written in 1933, pp. 289–94.

70 *Nhung canh khon nan*, volume I (Hanoi: Hoi nha van, 1997). First published in 1932 by Duong Xuan thu quan.

71 *Cai thu lon* (Hai Phong: Hai Phong Publishing House, 1989). First published by Doi Moi, Hanoi, in 1939.

72 Lockhart and Lockhart, *The Light of the Capital*, pp. 157–8.

73 See Lockhart, Introduction to the *The Light of the Capital* for a discussion on the importance of Hong's autobiography in Vietnamese history and literature.

74 Ibid.

75 Nguyen Hong, "Toi viet 'Bi vo'" [I write 'Bi vo'], *Bi vo*, Hanoi: Van Hoc, 1996 (First published in 1937, by Doi Nay, Hanoi), pp. 7–11.

76 Ibid.

77 In this nineteenth-century verse narrative written by Nguyen Du, the victim/ heroine Kieu, a righteous and loyal woman, was thrown into an immoral world where she encountered deceit, betrayal and cruelty. She was first separated from her true love, sold to a brothel, made a concubine, and then

a wife of a bandit. Through it all, however, Kieu remained pure and loyal.

78   Nam Sai Gon literary means "Five Saigon", a nickname given to him since he came from Saigon. In Nguyen Hong's stories about gangs and thieves, everyone went by a nickname, usually led by a number. Binh, for instance, became Tam Binh (Binh Number Eight) since she was the eighth woman to start work at the brothel.

79   Nguyen Hong. *Bay Huu: Truyen hay tien chien* [Bay Huu: Prewar great stories] (Glendale: Dai Nam, n.d).

80   Lockhart, Introduction to *The Light of the Capital*, p. 17.

81   Ibid., p. 5.

82   Ibid., p. 8.

83   Ibid., pp. 10–13.

84   Ibid., pp. 51–52.

85   Vu Ngoc Phan, *Nha van hien dai*, vol. III, p. 564.

86   Lockhart, *The Light of the Capital*, p. 52.

87   Tam Lang, "I Pulled a Rickshaw", Greg Lockhart and Monique Lockhart, trans., *The Light of the Capital*, pp. 51–120.

88   Vu Ngoc Phan, *Nha van hien dai*, vol. III, pp. 561–64.

89   Tam Lang, "I Pulled a Rickshaw", Greg Lockhart and Monique Lockhart, trans., *The Light of the Capital*, p. 97.

90   Ibid., p. 70.

91   Nguyen Van Khon, *Viet-Anh tu dien*. Saigon: Khai Tri, 1966; Bui Phung, *Tu dien Viet-Anh* (Hanoi: The Gioi, 1997).

92   Van Tan, *Tu dien tieng Viet* (Hanoi: Khoa hoc xa hoi, 1994).

93   Tam Lang, "I Pulled a Rickshaw", Greg Lockhart and Monique Lockhart, trans., *The Light of the Capital*, pp. 108–12.

94   Van Nguyen-Marshall, *Issues of Poverty and Poor Relief in Colonial Northern Vietnam: The Interaction between Colonial Modernism and Elite Vietnamese Thinking* (Ph.D. Dissertation, University of British Columbia, 2002), ch. 7.

11

Family Linkages between India and Britain: Views from Gujarat and London

Mario Rutten and Pravin J. Patel

International migration, although certainly not a new phenomenon, has increased over the past few decades (Appleyard 1991, p. 5). People of South Asian origin, in particular from India, have always formed a significant part of this migration process. The Indian diaspora as it exists today gained momentum in modern times after the abolition of slavery in the British empire, and the subsequent introduction of the indenture system in 1834, followed in the 1920s by the *kangani* or *maistry* system. Together with the smaller-sized 'passage' or 'free' migration, these forms of migration resulted in the fact that between 1834 and 1938 about 30 million Indians left their country of origin. Most of them went to British colonies in Africa, Asia, and the Caribbean. Although many of these migrants did return to India in the end, a substantial number of them settled down in countries such as Kenya, Tanzania, Uganda, Mauritius, South Africa, Burma (Myanmar), Ceylon (Sri Lanka), British Malaya (Malaysia), British Guyana (Guyana), and Trinidad and Tobago. As a result, many of these countries still have today a sizeable population of Indian origin (Jain 1989, p. 165).

Migration from India to the West is a more recent phenomenon. At the end of the twentieth century, about 2 million persons of South Asian origin resided in Europe, the United States and Canada. The majority of them, about 1.26 million, live in Britain (Jain 1993, pp. 34–35). Over the past four decades, a substantial number of studies have been conducted on Indian migrants in Britain. Together, these studies provide us with insight into various historical and contemporary aspects of the migration patterns of different Indian communities. Geographically, Indian migrants in Britain are concentrated in the urban counties of England, from Kent in the Southeast to Lancashire in the Northwest. The largest number of them, about 36 per cent of the total Indian population, live in Greater London, while 22 per cent have settled in the Midlands area (Ram 1989, pp. 101–2). With regard to their region of origin in India, the Gujarati and Punjabi communities are by far the largest Indian communities in Britain (Jain 1993, p. 36).

Following this predominance of Gujarat and Punjab as the region of origin, many studies conducted on the Indian migrants in Britain over the past forty years have focused on these two communities.[1] These studies usually focus on the position of the migrants in Britain, discussing their socio-economic background and problems of adaptation, adjustment, assimilation, or integration into the host society. Although most of them also refer to the history of chain migration of the migrants and occasionally to their present-day relations with their home region, linkages between the Indian community in Britain and their relatives in India are seldom the focus of research. The same holds true for those studies that deal with various aspects of those communities in Gujarat or Punjab that have a history of migration abroad. Although these studies often point to the importance of emigration on the local society and economy, the actual linkages that may exist between those who left the region and those who stayed behind are usually not empirically studied.[2]

This paper discusses the social linkages between Indian migrants in Britain and their family members in India. It considers the home and the migrant community in the same unit of analysis rather than as separate communities. It is based on fieldwork conducted in 1998 among members of the Patidar community in rural central Gujarat and among their relatives in London in 1999. In order to study the linkages between the

Patidars of India and Britain we collected information through a survey of 313 households in six villages in central Gujarat who have relatives in Britain, out of which 157 were selected for in-depth case studies. This was followed by a survey among 159 Patidar households in Greater London, of which 80 were selected for in-depth case studies. Members of the Patidar households in Greater London originated from the six villages in central Gujarat and many of them were direct relatives of the families studied in India. Most of the quantitative information presented in this paper refers to the survey conducted in the villages in India on the 313 Patidar households with relatives in Britain.

Members of the Patidar community in London have a long history of national and international migration. Many of them migrated to East Africa in the early part of the twentieth century and from there to Britain in the 1960s and 1970s. The findings of our research indicate that the members of this community still maintain frequent long-distance family linkages with their home region in India. Marriage arrangements, kinship networks, frequent visits, property, remittances, and religious affiliations keep many of the Patidar migrants in London well-linked to the villages in Gujarat. This has resulted in a two-way flow of people, capital and ideas. These linkages between India and Britain, however, are not static or without problems. There are differences of opinion between the Indian migrants in London and their relatives in Gujarat on the nature of their relationship and on the type of help rendered.

Patterns of migration

Gujarat is one of the prosperous states of India. Being a coastal state it has a long tradition of overseas trade. Gujarati business houses have existed in Africa since the thirteenth century and Gujarati businessmen, particularly the Ismaili Muslims, have been bankers and moneylenders of high reputation (Dobbin 1996, pp. 109–30). Among the Hindus of Gujarat, the members of the Patidar caste from central Gujarat have emigrated to East Africa in large numbers since the late nineteenth and early twentieth centuries.

The Patidar community is an upwardly mobile, middle-ranking peasant caste which can be found in several regions of Gujarat, but has its main concentration in the Charotar tract of Kheda District in central

Gujarat (Pocock 1972). With about fifteen to twenty per cent of the district population, the Patidars form a substantial minority that have been able to acquire economic, social and political dominance since the early part of the twentieth century, at both regional and state levels (Hardiman 1981; and Rutten 1995).

Participation of the Patidars from central Gujarat in the process of migration abroad has a long history. From the late nineteenth and early twentieth centuries onwards, family members of Patidar businessmen had already started to migrate to Madhya Pradesh, Orissa, West Bengal, Andhra Pradesh and other states of India, to trade in the locally produced biddy-tobacco. This form of migration was mainly confined to the upper stratum of the business community in central Gujarat. A more spectacular form of migration, which was one of the first streams of migration among the Patidars of middle class origin in central Gujarat, was the migration to foreign countries, especially to East African countries such as Kenya, Uganda and Tanzania. This pattern of migration started during the period of economic deterioration around the turn of the century and accelerated during the 1920s and 1930s. Many Patidars who had never before been further than Ahmedabad or Baroda began to pick up the trade connection which had existed for two thousand years between Gujarat and Africa (Pocock 1972, p. 63; Desai 1948, pp. 18 and 141; and Tambs-Lyche 1980, pp. 35–40).

This early migration abroad from the Charotar tract was closely related to the job opportunities offered by British colonial rule in East Africa. During the first decades of the twentieth century especially, many Patidars from middle- and lower middle-class peasant backgrounds migrated as passage or free migrants to countries like Kenya, Tanzania and Uganda. Colonial rule and the completion of the East African railways offered these educated middle-class Patidars white collar clerical occupations, and initiated a new era of economic opportunities to be exploited by the members of this peasant caste who took up a variety of commercial and professional activities. Most of these Patidar migrants went to East Africa on the basis of a work permit provided by fellow villagers who had gone before, or on the basis of a marriage with a Patidar girl or boy living in an East African country. These marriages were known as *permitian lagn* (marriage arranged with a view to get a permit to go to Africa), because the main purpose for the Patidar family in the village was to provide one of their sons or daughters with an opportunity to migrate to East Africa. It was usually through the help and support of their new in-laws, along with that of other relatives and fellow-villagers, that these young migrants who had never gone beyond their own regional towns, were able to settle down in their new environment, as is shown in the following case study.[3]

Chunilal is a Patidar who is living in the United Kingdom. He was born in 1930. Chunilal describes his migration history as follows:

> Gordhanbhai, who later became my father-in-law, also a Patidar from our *gol* (marriage circle), was advised by his elder brother to go to Africa, because in their native village they did not have enough land and their financial position was not good. Besides, they had two unmarried sisters whose marriages were to be arranged for which dowry was to be organized.

Gordhanbhai's elder brother had written letters to his relatives and friends requesting them to help Gordhanbhai in getting a job and settling down there. During the first two years after his arrival Gordhanbhai worked in several firms in Mombassa. After that, he got a job in the civil service in Mombassa. In 1925, he asked for a transfer to Nairobi because it was a larger city and had a better climate. Immediately after settling down in Kenya he had started sending money back home for the maintenance of his elder brother's family and especially for the marriage of their two younger sisters.

In the meantime, Gordhanbhai also had one daughter and two sons. In 1951 the family came to the native village in Charotar for the marriage of the daughter who was the eldest child in Gordhanbhai's family.

> My family was one of the high-status families in our marriage circle. I was studying in the second year of the college. My family had quite some land, but by the time of my youth agriculture had become less productive and due to customary law of our Patel community the ancestral property had been divided over time resulting in small pieces of land. Therefore, I did not see much future in agriculture. Moreover, I was studying in the college but jobs were also not easily available in India. And I had heard from my friends and relatives that there were many opportunities in Africa. Therefore, I was looking for a chance to go to Africa. In the meantime a marriage proposal of Gordhanbhai's daughter came. Since I was interested in going to Africa, I readily accepted the proposal. My mother, who was a widow, was keen to extract some more dowry from Gordhanbhai in view of our deteriorating economic condition. But I persuaded her not to do so since I was getting an opportunity to go to Africa and the girl was also educated.

After my marriage I stayed back in India for two years to finish my studies and to get the permit to go to Africa. After receiving my permit, I went to Kenya in 1953. When I came to Kenya my father-in-law advised me to stay with his family in Nairobi before I would settle down comfortably. Although I did not like to be a *ghar-jamai*,[4] my father-in-law Gordhanbhai, persuaded me that while doing so I'll be able to save some money. He arranged for a job for me as a clerk in a law court. We got one son and one daughter. Over time, I regularly sent some money back home to my mother for the maintenance of my family. I also sent money for the repairs of our ancestral house. I used to receive many requests from different relatives for monetary help and I used to help them to buy property or to pay of their debts or to arrange social occasions like marriage, or even to support the education of their children.

During the colonial period and in the 1950s, there was only a very small trickle of Patidars to Britain. From the mid-1960s onwards, however, the pattern of migration of the selected Patidar households changed very quickly from East Africa to Britain. As a result of radical Africanization programmes in these countries and the fear that immigration restrictions would soon be implemented by the British government, many of these East African Indians left for Britain in a relatively short time-span. Between September 1967 and March 1968 alone, 12,000 South Asians from Kenya entered into Britain, while 29,000 Asians arrived in 1972 after being expelled from Uganda (Michaelson 1978/79, p. 351). Although a relatively prosperous minority of these so-called 'twice migrants' had already began to invest in Britain in the 1950s and early 1960s—mainly through the purchase of houses where young relatives could stay whilst studying (Michaelson 1978/79, p. 350)—most of those who migrated from Africa to Britain at the end of the 1960s, early 1970s, arrived practically empty-handed and were usually fully dependent on friends and relatives (Tambs-Lyche 1980, p. 41). The following narration of Manibhai illustrates this point:

In 1963, Kenya became independent and this was the turning-point in my life. At that time, I had three options before me: (i) to go back to India; (ii) to become a Kenyan citizen; or (iii) to become a British citizen. In those days most Indians in Kenya were thinking of returning to India. They thought that after independence of Kenya they had no future there, and they did not consider the UK as a good choice because their impression was that the climate there was not suitable to them. Nevertheless, some brave persons mustered courage to go to the UK from Kenya and they started sending favourable reports about the life in the UK through letters to their friends and relatives. This changed the minds of those who were living in Kenya and many of them decided to go to the UK instead of staying in Kenya or going back to India.

Although I had a permit to work in Kenya and I was not forced to leave Kenya, after hearing the news of better opportunities in the UK, I decided to go there in 1970. By this time, I had taken early retirement from my job though my wife was still working in Kenya. My children were also studying in Kenya and they were in the middle of their school year. Therefore, to explore the possibility of settlement in the UK, I decided to first go there alone.

When I went to the UK I was received by my relatives and Patel friends. I did not have any close relative in the UK, but that did not matter. In those days, all Patels were treating one another as relatives. One of my distant relatives, known to me from Kenya, came to pick me up from the Heathrow airport and took me to his house. I stayed with him for a week. After one week, I went to stay with another relative. After a few weeks, I went to live with another friend of mine. In those days, most of our friends were relatives and therefore there is a thin line between friends and relatives. And everyone was ready to help one another. And such frequent moving, though it caused some inconvenience, had some advantages also. Because you learned different things from the experiences of different persons. Moreover, everyone has some new piece of information or advice to give. That benefited me a lot. Besides, I did not become a burden on a single family for long. This was quite a common practice for many Patels who came from Kenya in the 1960s and early 1970s.

After four to five months I found a job and had an apartment of my own. In those days there was a shortage of manpower in the UK and jobs were easily available. I got a white-collar job as a clerk in a bank. After six months my family joined me in the UK. My wife got a job in the council and my children started studying here.

Transnational linkages

As a result of these patterns of migration, the Patels constitute one of the largest groups among the Gujarati Hindus in Britain. Not surprisingly 'Patel' is one of the most famous Indian surnames abroad along with 'Singh'. According to a conservative estimate of the membership of associations of all the marriage circles in Britain, there were about 30,000 Patels from central Gujarat living in Britain in the early 1990s, of which 90 per cent reside in London (Lyon and West 1995, p. 407).

A characteristic feature of the Patel community that we studied in London is that they remain attached to Indian culture and to their Gujarati background in terms of their social relations. Most of the older generation have retained their Patidar identity by organizing themselves on the basis of their village of origin and marriage circle (*gol*). These village-based associations and organizations of village circles in Britain bring out directories giving details of all the Patidar family members concerned. These directories are mostly used to help to arrange marriages. For this purpose, the associations also organize marriage-*melas*, in which young boys and girls publicly introduce themselves and try to find out suitable life-partners. Besides, the village associations and marriage circle associations of Patidars in Britain organize meetings to celebrate Nav Ratri, Diwali and other important Indian festivals, and have functions like dinner-and-dance parties, where they eat, drink, and dance to Hindi music till late in the night and early morning hours on weekends. Moreover, many Patels participate in religious activities, for which the Swaminarayan temple in North London is often a focal point. Although most of the active members in these associations belong to the older generations of Patidar migrants, many organizations also have youth committees in which youngsters are involved and encouraged to organize and participate in various activities.

Along with organizing social and religious events, members of the Patidar community in London have started making organized efforts to teach Gujarati to the younger generation. Children belonging to the second and third generation of migrants are mostly able to understand functional Gujarati, but they find it difficult to speak the language, and are often not able to read and write the Gujarati script. This problem, of course, is not confined to the Patel community in Britain. The Gujarati community as a whole has become more conscious about teaching Gujarati to their children. There are about 500 classes that teach Gujarati language all over Britain, often for two hours a week on Saturdays and Sundays. At the end of the 1990s, about one thousand to fifteen hundred students appeared in Gujarati language examinations each year.

On the whole, village life in Gujarat still has a profound effect on the first generation of Patidar migrants. They lived in the village during their formative years, where they studied and spent their childhood. Moreover, many of them grew up during the patriotic period of the national independence movement which made them even more conscious of being proud of Indian culture and heritage. The social, religious and cultural bonds with their home village and with other Patidar migrants from the same region, when they first lived in East Africa and later on in Britain, further cemented those ties with their village of origin. Therefore, the social identity of the first generation of Patidar migrants is deeply embedded in village life and the ties with their place of origin and with their relatives and friends in Gujarat are still quite powerful.

One of the indicators of social links between the Patidar migrants in Britain and their relatives in the villages in Gujarat are the various types of intense contacts that exist between the members of both groups. Letters are the main type of communication used by Gujarati households to contact their relatives in Britain, although phone calls are also an important way of keeping in touch. Telephone calls from India to Britain are usually very brief because of the cost and often only made in emergency situations or for very specific purposes. Patels from Britain do more often make a phone call to their family in the village; some even phone from Britain almost every week for a few minutes. During these calls information is exchanged about the well-being of relatives on both sides.

Navinbhai Bhupendrabhai Patel is 40 years old. He lives with his wife and their son in London where they have a grocery shop. Navinbhai was born and brought up in one of the selected villages and married a British citizen born in East Africa.

Navinbhai's father, his mother and his younger brother Yogesh and his family are still living in their ancestral house in the village. Almost every year, Navinbhai pays a visit to his family for about ten to fifteen days. Usually, he comes alone, leaving his wife behind in London to take care of their shop. In between his visits, Navinbhai keeps in regular contact with his relatives at home. At least once a week, Navinbhai makes a brief phone call to his father and his brother Yogesh. These calls are made at a fixed timing on a particular day of the week. Navinbhai especially uses telephone cards with a limited amount on it, which allows him to talk for a short while. During these brief conversations, the brothers exchange information about the health of their relatives on both sides, about the educational progress of the children of both brothers and their business undertakings. "Although our telephone conversations are very brief indeed, it gives us an opportunity to regularly keep in touch and to have the feeling that

Navinbhai and his family are not so far away", Yogesh told us after Navinbhai had made his weekly call.

Another important mode of contact between the households in Gujarat and their family members in Britain are the visits that relatives from Britain make to their home village. More than ninety per cent of the selected 313 households in the six villages had been visited by their relatives in Britain between 1993 and 1998. In total, 768 relatives had visited India, which comes to an average of 2.7 relatives per household, of which a substantial number visited India more than once during this five-year period. Most of these visits were relatively long: almost fifty per cent of the visitors stayed between one and three months, while the visits of nine per cent of the relatives from Britain lasted between four and six months. About forty per cent of the relatives who visited their home village stayed in India for less than a month.

In recent years, when many of the older migrants retired, a movement back home to India from Britain during winter has emerged. Among the older generation of Patidar migrants in Britain, there are quite a number who could be called 'international commuters'. These are Patidars from Britain who stay in India every winter for about one to five months. In most cases, they live in Gujarat in their own apartment or bungalow in one of the nearby towns or on the outskirts of their home village. Some of them have in practice returned to India, as they spend more time in their country of origin than in Britain. Although most of these people did return to spend their old age in India, a few of them came back because they no longer wanted to live with their family in Britain. Having returned to their village of origin, some of them realize, however, that they are no longer at home there either.

Shamalbhai is 72 years old and since 1994 has lived again in the village in which he was born in 1925. In 1953, at the age of 27 and already married, Shamalbhai left his native village. He was invited to come to Tanzania by his father's eldest brother's son whose family had been living there since the 1930s.

In 1956, Shamalbhai returned to his village to collect his wife and their three children. The highly unstable political situation around 1963 made them decide to bring their children back to Charotar and to leave them with Shamalbhai's relatives in his native village where they could attend the local schools. Although his wife stayed with their children for some months, she again joined her husband in Tanzania in 1964. Together, they lived and worked in Tanzania until 1973 with only one visit to their children in Charotar in 1969.

After their visit in 1973, his wife stayed in the village, while Shamalbhai returned again to Tanzania in 1974. From there he applied and was allowed to enter the United Kingdom in 1979. Within one year after his arrival in London, Shamalbhai called his wife and their three children to join him in Britain. Both Shamalbhai, his wife and their children were only able to get unskilled work during their early stay in Britain.

Shamalbhai recounted:

> I could only get a job in a factory. In Tanzania I had a big shop with assistants and drove around in a Jaguar car, but I had to leave almost all my property behind when I migrated to the UK and had to start again from scratch.

> I was not really happy in London. It was hard work for very low pay that my wife and I had to perform in those factories, but we did it for our children. By migrating to the UK we wanted to give them a better future, because they would not have good opportunities in India, being relatively low educated and without much property in the village. After my retirement in 1990, however, my wife and I started to visit India very regularly. In fact, we often used to stay several months per year in India. In 1994, we even returned and took up permanent residence again in my native village, because after my father's brother's daughter had left for the USA, there was no one left in the village to take care of my old father. We then built a new house on the outskirts of the village and since then we live here the whole year around, and only occasionally make a visit to the UK.

Although in the first instance, Shamalbhai returned to the village only because of his father, he visibly enjoys being part of the village life. Every day he makes his round through the village and on various evenings one can meet him in the village square, talking to old friends. On the other hand, however, he occupies a marginal position in his home village.

> Although I was born and brought up here, even after four years of my permanent return, I still do not feel that I am really part of the village society. We participate in various activities, but somehow we have difficulties to really mix with our relatives in the village and force ourselves to attend their gatherings. But to be honest, we used to have the same feeling when we were living in the UK, because I arrived there at the age of 55 and only worked there for about ten years.

After Shamalbhai left the room for a short while, his wife also started to express her views.

> Yes, we were also not at home in London, but at least we had our children and grandchildren nearby. I don't like it here at all and hardly leave our house. My whole life I have been able to live and adjust in different countries. I have lived in Charotar, in Tanzania and in London, but now that we are old, I sometimes feel that we do no longer feel at home anywhere and therefore better keep to ourselves inside our house.

As is to be expected, there are less visits by Indian relatives to Britain as compared to the number of visits from Patidar migrants to India. However, members of more than twenty per cent of the selected households made a visit to Britain between 1993 and 1998. In total, 128 members visited Britain in this period of five years which comes to an average of 1.6 relatives per household. This clearly indicates that there is a substantial number of household members from the villages who have visited Britain. These visits are often of a longer duration. Only eight per cent of the household members who visited Britain stayed there for less than a month. About 45 per cent of them stayed between one and three months, while the visits of 33 per cent lasted between four and six months, with the remaining 14 per cent staying in Britain for a period of more than half a year.

Although the selection of the households in the six villages was done on the basis of the existence of relatives in Britain, it turns out that 133 of the 157 selected case studies do not only have relatives abroad in Britain, but also outside Britain. In total this comes to 1,469 relatives with an average of 9.4 per household. With the rigorous immigration restrictions imposed, emigration to Britain decreased rapidly from the late 1970s, early 1980s onwards. Since then, the United States and Canada have become the most popular destination of Patidar migrants (Jain 1993; Helweg 1987 and 1990). This is confirmed by the findings from our study. Almost 75 per cent of the 1,469 relatives of the selected families in central Gujarat live in America, while almost 16 per cent live in East Africa.

One consequence of this widespread migration pattern of the Patidar community is that today there has come into being a category of people that we would describe as 'world citizens'. They are usually elder people who, although they have a residence in one country, often travel between UK, India, US, and East Africa throughout the year, staying in each country for a few months at a time. These people sometimes meet each other in different countries where they exchange information about relatives. There are even some cases of transnational holidays in which Patidar relatives from different parts of the world come together to spend their vacation by travelling to several countries. In the case presented below, however, the only one who is absent during these family gatherings is the one who lives in the home village.

Shantubhai is about 70 years old and a British Passport holder. After the death of his wife in London in 1987, Shantubhai moved back to his native village in Charotar. It was there that we met him for the first time. It was about six o'clock in the evening and Shantubhai was just on his way to the Swaminarayan temple at the entrance of the village. After he had paid his respect to the deity, Shantubhai went to the room at the back where he spends at least two evenings a week talking with other Patels from the village. To his surprise, it turned out that Gurubhai, an old friend of Shantubhai, was also present. Gurubhai lives in the US but Shantubhai and he have known each other for forty years, when both were staying in East Africa. Both of them went to the UK in the early 1970s. In the 1980s, two of Gurubhai's daughters got married to Patels from the US and settled there. It was through them that Gurubhai and his wife later on were able to migrate from the UK to America.

Over the years, Gurubhai and Shantubhai have been meeting each other at different places. In the past they regularly met in London at Shantubhai's home, whenever Gurubhai visited his two sons and their families. They also bumped into each other once in New Jersey, when Shantubhai paid a visit to one of his brothers there. More recently, they have been meeting every few years in Shantubhai's home village, which is also Gurubhai's wife's birthplace.

Shantubhai's family is also spread over many parts of the globe, following their early migration to East Africa. Today, two of Shantubhai's four brothers are in the UK, while two of his sisters and their descendants reside in the US. Moreover, one son of Shantubhai's third brother lives with his family in Tanzania. In fact, before Shantubhai's return to India, only one of Shantubhai's four brothers used to live in their native village, occupying the ancestral family home and looking after the small family plot.

"Although our family is spread over so many countries, we are still a closely related family", Shantubhai remarked. He continued:

> Every few years, we organise a tour somewhere in the world for which most members of our extended family come together from different parts of the world. Three years back, we made a tour through Europe and rented a coach, which took us to different European countries. In all, we were at that time about 30 relatives, both young and old. If all goes well, we are planning to organise a similar family tour to East Asia next year in which we would like to include Hong Kong, Singapore and Bangkok. We are already talking to a travel agent to organise such a tour and we expect that at least 20 of our relatives from the USA, UK and Africa will be present.

"Everyone will join", Shantubhai emphasized. A few days later, however, we were told by others that in fact not everyone of the family joins this 'tour of international migrants'. The one who is not able to join is the brother who has lived all his life in the village and took care of the ancestral property. Therefore, the international outing of this transnational family usually takes place without the 'representative' from the family's home village.

Different views

The foregoing brief account indicates that members of the Patidar community in London maintain frequent long-distance family linkages with their home region in India. Regular visits and frequent contacts keep many of the Patidar migrants in London well-linked to the villages in Gujarat and vice versa. As already hinted at in the case studies presented, however, these visits and contacts are not without problems. The following examples will show in more detail that there are sometimes differences of opinion between the Indian migrants in London and their relatives in Gujarat on the nature of their relationship and on the type of help rendered.

In many instances, the visits of the Patidar migrants to India and of their Indian relatives to Britain are related to marriages of one of their family members in Britain or India, mostly with a marriage partner from the other country. During the visits of the Patidar migrants to India, activities related to religion are also very common. During the last twenty-five years, the popularity of the Swaminarayan sect has increased among the Patels from Britain (Pocock 1976). Although many Patels from central Gujarat have been among the followers of the Swaminarayan sect for a long time already, the shift to the Akshar Pursottam 'branch' is a more recent phenomenon and one that is clearly related to the Patel community in Britain. During their visits to India, many relatives make tours to several temples in India, donate substantial amounts to local temples, and participate in rituals and gatherings in which they are often given special treatment in terms of a comfortable and prominent position. This emphasis on religion by the relatives from Britain, and the special 'VIP' treatment they receive in the temples in central Gujarat, is viewed by some local Patels with jealousy and ridiculed in private conversations.

In 1988, Mohanbhai retired from his clerical job in London, while his wife Vimlaben retired in 1991. Since then, the two of them have been visiting Gujarat annually every winter season for two to three months. In 1994, they bought their own apartment in the nearby city of Baroda.

During their stay in Gujarat, Mohanbhai and Vimlaben spend most of their time in Baroda and from there they also make trips to Charotar to visit friends and relatives in their native village. Alongside these social visits, they take the opportunity during their stay to visit temples in Gujarat and usually also make a tour of a few days to other religious places in India. Mohanbhai emphasizes his religious nature, and indicates that he regularly makes donations to local temples. "Also when I am in London", he told us, "I very often make visits to the temple. In London I am a member of the temple of Akshar Pursottam. Whenever we stay in Gujarat, we make it a point of going to the big temple of Akshar Pursottam in Gandhinagar".

During one of their trips to their native village, Mohanbhai and Vimlaben showed to some of their local relatives the photographs of the Yagna ritual in the village temple in which they had participated a few weeks before. While showing the photographs, Vimlaben pointed out several of her relatives and friends from the UK and US. They were in fact easily recognizable, because Vimlaben and the other women from the UK and US were making up the first row of the audience, sitting in chairs with their plates on a table in front of them, while all the other women from the village sat on the floor behind them.

Mohanbhai explained that Vimlaben and the other women from UK and US had been the honoured guests at the Yagna ritual in the village temple. While further elaborating on this, he took from his wallet a letter that he showed to us and his local relatives with some pride. It was a letter of recommendation from the Swaminarayan Mandir in London in which it was mentioned that Mohanbhai is a member of the Mandir in London and allowed to stay in any of their temples in Gujarat for two days with a maximum group of eight persons. "In this letter, the temples in Gujarat are requested to provide me with boarding and lodging, and to enable me to pray and to have conversations with the priests", Mohanbhai told us. "About two years ago, the Swaminarayan Mandir in London started to issue these letters in order to ensure that only genuine and honest persons can make use of the facilities of the temples in Gujarat. And because of this letter, I will get a special treatment during my stay in the temple", Mohanbhai added to his earlier remarks. "We will be given a clean private room furnished with a table and a chair, and air-conditioning if available. They will prepare not too spicy food for us and give us mineral water. This 'VIP treatment' is usually given to every NRI (Non-Resident Indian) who visits a temple in Gujarat", Mohanbhai told us before he and Vimlaben left the house to visit some of Mohanbhai's old school friends in the village.

Shortly after Mohanbhai and Vimlaben had left, their local relatives started to make some critical comments about what had been discussed before. One of Mohanbhai's cousin brothers remarked:

> This VIP treatment is given to the NRIs only because they donate in pounds or dollars instead of Indian rupees. Many of them were never very religious when they were staying in Africa or when they came to Britain. But now that they are retired, they suddenly have a need for Indian culture and rediscovered religion. However, many of them have already become too westernised. They are not even able to sit cross-legged on the floor for a long time and their stomachs can no longer stand our drinking water.

The other relatives present supported the cousin brother in their mild attempt to ridicule the NRIs emphasis on religion, but could at the same time also not hide their feelings of jealousy about the special treatment the NRIs are given in local temples.

Almost half of the 313 selected households in the villages have relatives in Britain who made investments in India between 1993 and 1998. By far the most important type of investment by these relatives from Britain are financial investments in bank and shares. Part of these investments are related to the various schemes that have been set up for NRIs by the Indian government over the past few years. Another important type of investment by the relatives from Britain is property. This includes farm land, residential plots, houses and apartments. Family members in the village are often asked to help their relatives in Britain to buy and afterwards to maintain the property. These investments in property of the Patel migrants from Britain partly create jealousy and some resentment among the local population who hold their investment behaviour responsible for the enormous increase in prices of real estate over the past few years.

Investment in business make up only a very small portion of the investments of the relatives from Britain, but they are certainly not completely absent. These productive investments of Patels from Britain are made in partnership with local Patels, some of them family members in the village or in one of the nearby towns. Actually, making capital investments in India is still not a major trend for the following reasons. First, the children of the first-generation migrants do not have long-term interest in India and therefore the first-generation of emigrants to the UK seem to have adopted Britain as their place of permanent residence, willingly or unwillingly. Second, the lack of political and economic stability back home in India also does not encourage them to make major capital investments in their homeland. Third, the bureaucratic red tape and corruption experienced by some of them in India also discourage them to make a determined effort to make long-term investments in their home region.

Finally, there are many Patels who emphasize that the lukewarm response to them by the Indian government in the early 1970s was more shocking than their sudden and unexpected expulsion from Uganda by Idi Amin. In those days the Indian government did not realize the importance of the Non-Resident Indians. Therefore, many of those who have settled down in the UK, after being expelled from Uganda, ironically interpret the term 'NRI', much trumpeted by the Indian government of late, as 'Non-Required Indians', and their bitterness is also reflected in their lack of enthusiasm in maintaining linkages back home in the form of investments in India.

For these reasons, there are no strong developmental linkages between the villages in Charotar and the Patel community in Britain, despite the size and frequency of monetary help and financial transfers of the Patel relatives from Britain. Many Patels in the villages express their negative views about the fact that migrants from Britain do not contribute as much to the development of their home village as they used to in the past. Although they indicate understanding of the economic problems faced by the Patels in Britain today, they strongly feel that they avoid their responsibilities by not contributing to the welfare of their home village.

Sureshbhai's family belongs to one of the economically most well-to-do families in the village. They own about 20 acres of land and have a large cold storage building along with one tile factory and several other undertakings. Sureshbhai's younger brother Mahendrabhai is a regional politician who is also quite active locally. Among other things, he is the chairman of the educational board and secretary of the village co-operative bank.

On various occasions, Sureshbhai and Mahendrabhai expressed criticism about the large-scale migration to the UK and US of members of the Patel community. "Not one of our direct relatives has migrated abroad", Sureshbhai used to say with some pride. "We are happy to live here and are not like all those Patels who do anything to be able to go abroad". Mahendrabhai adds to that:

And when they leave this village, they forget about their native place. In the past few years, there has hardly been any financial support from the Patels of our village who live in the UK. Until the 1960s, Patels who migrated to East Africa from our village used to regularly make donations to the educational board and village panchayat. It was because of these donations that our village was among the first in the area to have a high school. Since they migrated from East Africa to the UK, however, we have hardly received any donations from our fellow-villagers abroad. Even though they established a samaj from our village in London, this has not resulted in substantial support to the development of our village.

We realise that it is expensive to live in London, but as compared to Gujarat, the Patels in Britain hardly have any social obligations and therefore less expenses in this regard. I personally feel that Patels in the UK are only after money and obsessed with saving as much money as they can. They hardly care about relatives back home, but seem to have become misers who do not want to spend money on social obligations.

When they are in the UK, they don't think about the welfare or development of their native village, but when they visit their village, they start to emphasise that we are all part of the same village and samaj. They even expect us to treat them with the highest respect because they have come from abroad. But to be honest, I don't think the Patels in Britain from our village are part of our community anymore, they have become strangers to us, strangers who are no longer really concerned about the welfare of their native village.

Notwithstanding these negative views on the type of support rendered, in terms of financial assistance more than forty per cent of the selected households in Gujarat received some kind of monetary help from their relatives in Britain between 1993 and 1998. Most of this financial help and support is given to cover part of the maintenance of the family in the village, to pay for part of the repair costs of the house or to contribute to marriage expenses, religious rituals, or other social occasions of the family in central Gujarat.

As is to be expected, monetary help from the households in India to their relatives in Britain is almost non-existent, because the relatives back home are economically weak in comparison to their British counterparts, but it certainly is not totally absent. The existence of some kind of monetary help from Patidars in India to their relatives in Britain is a very interesting phenomenon, because it indicates a transfer of money resources from India to Britain. In most cases such monetary help to relatives in Britain is related to social matters. It may be mentioned here that among the Patidars of Central Gujarat there is a custom of distributing some money gifts among relatives on the occasions of marriage and death of some close relatives. Most of the monetary help given by the Indian relatives to their UK counterparts is of this nature.

Support to relatives in India is also provided during the visits by household members from India to Britain. Many of these household members helped their relatives in their shops or other businesses in London, while it has also become common for older people from India to help their children by taking care of their grandchildren at home while the parents are at work. However, there is also a drawback to these long-distance types of joint-family relations. In some cases, young relatives from India have to work extremely long hours in shops for meagre payment and are in that way exploited by their British relatives. Some elderly parents from India are almost treated as mere babysitters.

In several cases relations between relatives in Britain and their family members in the village in Gujarat have also become severely strained due to conflicts over property. Members of the village households are often of the opinion that they are entitled to the full ancestral property, because they looked after the family's property and often also after their parents and other elderly relatives in the village. The relatives in Britain, however, are sometimes of the opinion that they have a right to an equal share of the family's property, which they then will try to sell off.

Ramanbhai Patel lives in one of the selected villages in Gujarat. He has four brothers, two of them in India and two abroad. One of his brothers lives in Kenya and another brother went to the UK from Kenya. In the words of Ramanbhai:

> I was working as a clerk in a school in my village, I have two sons and two daughters, we had about 40 acres of land in the village, but most of it was taken away under the land reform act by the farmers who were tilling it. Even otherwise, agriculture was not very profitable and my salary was not very high. I had to support my family and my widow mother. My brother who is living in the UK sometimes sends money for my mother. Whenever he visits India and stays with us he does small repairs in our ancestral house which is a common property of all the four brothers. My two brothers who are living in India are also not very rich. We are a middle class family. Two of my brothers married with girls who were born in Kenya and therefore they could go there. But one of my brothers, who is still in Kenya, is not well-off, whereas the brother who went to the UK is relatively better-off. I am the only one living in the village, looking after my mother and ancestral property. I have to spend some money as per our customs on social occasions like birth, marriage, death, etc. of our relatives on behalf of my family. I have to do this because I am living in the village. Of course, those who are living outside the village later contribute to the expenses.
>
> However, when my children grew up I realized that it would be difficult for them in future to live a comfortable life in India. Therefore I requested my brother who is in the UK to invite my eldest son as visitor there and arrange his marriage with a girl who has a British passport. He did oblige me. He invited my eldest son to the UK in 1976 and within six months my brother arranged his marriage with a girl from *Chha Gaam* (one of the marriage circles) having British citizenship. Now my eldest son who is about 47 years old, is well settled in the UK having a candy shop and post office. After he settled down there comfortably, he started sending money to me. Out of this money I completely renovated my ancestral house, spending about ten lakh rupees. Later I also bought three taxis for my younger son. My younger son was working in a factory as a clerk. I asked him to take voluntary retirement and to start the transport business with these three taxis. Now we are relatively better off. We have built two houses on the outskirts of the village for both the

sons and I could also arrange marriages of my two daughters in good families. My younger son has a son and a daughter. Both of them go to English medium schools.

However, this does not mean that there are no tensions in Ramanbhai's family. As a matter of fact, as there is cooperation on the one hand in the family, there is conflict also on the other hand. For instance, Ramanbhai says:

> But what is the use of this prosperity? As my economic position improved, my brother started demanding his share in the ancestral house in which I am living and which I have rebuilt by spending a lot of money sent by my eldest son from the UK. And this has caused a considerable tension among the family of we four brothers. Now, I am economically better off but socially unhappy.

Conclusion

With worldwide improvements in communications, the ongoing relationships between the migrant and the home community is more efficient and more evident. In contrast to the ex-indentured populations, contemporary Patidar migrants have been able to maintain extensive ties with India. Marriage arrangements, kinship networks, property, remittances and religious affiliations keep many migrants well-linked to their places of origin. Contacts between the earlier migrants in East Africa and their home region were often maintained with an eye to a possible return of the migrant, as a result of which the home community acted as the focal point within the relationship.

However, based on information provided by the migrants in Greater London and their relatives in central Gujarat, it seems that over a period of time the orientation towards India of the Patidar emigrants has changed after going to the UK from East African countries. According to the views of the local Patidars in the villages, it appears that when the migrants were in East Africa they had a greater stake in maintaining strong ties with their relatives in India, perhaps because they thought that at some point in future they might come back to India for permanent settlement. In the perception of the local relatives, the subsequent migration from East Africa to Britain, however, has resulted in a change in this orientation towards India. The local relatives seem to be of the opinion that earlier, the migrants considered India as their motherland (*matru bhumi*) and a permanent shelter to which they always could return. After going to Britain, they have started to act as if India has become their wife's village (*sasru*) where they demand to be pampered and treated with extraordinary respect, and without reciprocity, as traditionally the Patidars have been expecting from their wife's family side.[5]

On the other hand, the first generation of Patidar migrants in Britain seems to be ambivalent towards their home region and their relatives in the native village. They are very much attached to Indian culture and depend emotionally on their social linkages with their relatives and friends in Gujarat. They want to be respected by their relatives and at the same time they criticize them on many occasions and are not always willing to accept the social obligations that are part of these linkages, or only do so very hesitantly.

To conclude, although migrants in Britain and their relatives in Gujarat should not be viewed as separate communities but be considered in the same unit of analysis, the findings of our study also indicate that they are neither to be seen as a homogenous transnational community (cf. Baumann 1996, p. 23). Social linkages keep many of the Patidar migrants in London well-linked to the villages in Gujarat and have resulted in a two-way flow of people, capital and ideas. These links are reinforced by frequent personal visits, continuous communication, and also by regular transfer of money and/or material goods. At the same time, however, these linkages between India and Britain are not without problems. Several of the cases showed that there are differences of opinion between the Indian migrants in London and their relatives in Gujarat on the nature of their relationship and on the type of help rendered. Therefore, these linkages between the Patidars in India and their migrant relatives in Britain have important consequences not only for the integration of the migrants in the host country, but also for the home area which is affected by the departure, return, money transfers, information and frequent contacts with the migrants abroad.

Notes

[1]   Following the pioneering study of R.H. Desai (1963) on the internal organization and adjustment of the Gujarati community in Britain, several studies have been conducted on various aspects of the Gujarati migrants in

Britain (see e.g. Lyon 1972/73; Tambs-Lyche 1975 and 1980; Pocock 1976; Michaelson 1978/79; Hahlo 1980; and Lyon and West 1995). For research on the Punjabi-speaking Sikhs that settled in Britain, see e.g. Aurora (1967); Marsh (1967); Beetham (1970); Ballard and Ballard (1977); R. Singh (1980); and Helweg (1986 and 1990).

2 For references to the migration process in studies on Gujarat, see e.g. Breman (1985, pp. 100–06), for references in studies on the Punjab, see e.g. Chadha (1986, pp. 31–32, 38). The studies by Helweg (1983 and 1989) and Ballard (1983) are among the few studies that focus on the impact of migration to Britain on the home region in India. Helweg's study concentrates on the Indian Punjab, while Ballard's study compares the consequences of migration in an area in the Indian Punjab and in Pakistan.

3 All names in the case studies presented in this paper are pseudonyms, an attempt to preserve some measure of anonymity.

4 *Ghar-jamai* means matrilocal rule of residence. This is considered beneath the dignity of a Patidar male since the Patidar community follows patrilocal rule of residence.

5 This feeling generally expressed by our local informants, was articulated by Prof. Bhikhu Parekh at a public lecture delivered at the meeting of the Viswa Gujarati Samaj held at Baroda on 2–4 January 1999.

References

Appleyard, R.T., 1991. *International Migration: Challenge for the Nineties*. Geneva: UNESCO.

Aurora, G.S. 1967. *The New Frontiersmen: Immigrants in the United Kingdom*. Bombay: Popular Prakashan.

Ballard, R. 1983. "The Context and Consequences of Migration: Jullundur and Mirpur Compared", *New Community* 11, no. 1/2, pp. 117–36.

Ballard, R. and C. Ballard. 1977. "The Sikhs: The Development of South Asian Settlements in Britain'. In *Between Two Cultures: Migrants and Minorities in Britain*, edited by T.L. Watson, pp. 21–57. Oxford: Oxford University Press.

Baumann, G. 1996. *Contesting Culture: Discourses of Identity in Multi-Ethnic London*. Cambridge Studies in Social and Cultural Anthropology. Cambridge: Cambridge University Press.

Beetham, D. 1970. *Transport and Turbans: A Comparative Study in Local Politics*. Oxford: Oxford University Press.

Breman, J. 1985. *Of Peasants, Migrants and Paupers: Rural Labour Circulation and Capitalist Production in West India*. Delhi: Oxford University Press.

Chadha, G.K. 1986. *The State and Rural Economic Transformation: The Case of Punjab 1950–85*. Delhi: Sage Publications.

Desai, M.B. 1948. *The Rural Economy of Gujarat*. Bombay: Oxford University Press.

Desai, R.H. 1963. *Indian Immigrants in Britain*. London: Oxford University Press for the Institute of Race Relations.

Dobbin, C. 1996. *Asian Entrepreneurial Minorities: Conjoint Communities in the Making of the World Economy, 1570–1940*. Richmond, Surrey: Curzon.

Hahlo, K.G. 1980. "Profile of a Gujarati Community in Bolton". *New Community* 8: 295–307.

Hardiman, D. 1981. *Peasant Nationalists of Gujarat: Kheda District 1917–1934*. Delhi: Oxford University Press.

Helweg, A.W. 1983. "Emigrant Remittances: Their Nature and Impact on a Punjabi Village": *New Community* 10, pp. 435–43.

———. 1986. *Sikhs in England*. Delhi: Oxford University Press.

———. 1987. "Why Leave India for America? A Case Study Approach to Understanding Migrant Behaviour". *International Migration* 25, pp. 165–78.

———. 1989. "Sikh Politics in India; The Emigrant Factor". In *The Sikh Diaspora; Migration and the Experience Beyond Punjab*, edited by N.G. Barrier and V.A. Dusenbery. Delhi: Chankaya Publication.

———. 1990, 'Sikh Identity in England: Its Changing Nature', in *Sikh History and Religion in the Twentieth Century*, edited by J.T. O'Connell et al. Delhi: Manohar Publications, pp. 356–75.

Jain, Prakash C. 1989. "Emigration and Settlement of Indians Abroad", *Sociological Bulletin* 30, no. 1: 155–68.

Jain, Ravindra K. 1993. *Indian Communities Abroad: Themes and Literature*. Delhi: Manohar Publications.

Lyon, M.H. 1972/73. "Ethnicity in Britain: The Gujarati Tradition". *New Community* 2, pp. 1–11.

Lyon, M.H. and B.J.M. West. 1995. "London Patels: Caste and Commerce", *New Community* 21, no. 3, pp. 399–419.

Marsh, P. 1967. *The Anatomy of a Strike*. London: Institute of Race Relations/ Oxford University Press.

Michaelson, M. 1978/79. "The Relevance of Caste amongst East African Gujaratis in Britain", *New Community* 7, pp. 350–60.

Pettigrew, J. 1977. "Socio-economic Background to the Emigration of Sikhs from Doaba", *Punjab Journal of Politics* 1, no. 1: 48–81.

Pocock, D.F. 1972. *Kanbi and Patidar: A Study of the Patidar Community of Gujarat*. Oxford: Clarendon.

———. 1976. "Preservation of the Religious Life: Hindu Immigrants in England". *Contributions to Indian Sociology* 10, no. 2, pp. 341–65.

Ram, S. 1989. *Indian Immigrants in Great Britain*. Delhi: Inter India Publications.

Rutten, M. 1995. *Farms and Factories: Social Profile of Large Farmers and Rural Industrialists in West India*. Delhi: Oxford University Press.

Singh, R. 1980. *The Sikh Community in Bradford*. Bradford: Bradford College.

Singh, P.A. Ghuman. 1994. *Coping with Two Cultures: British Asian and Indo-Canadian Adolescents*. Clevedon: Multilingual Matters.

Tambs-Lyche, H. 1975. "A Comparison of Gujarati Communities in London and the Midlands". *New Community* 4, pp. 349–56.

———. 1980. *London Patidars: A Case Study in Urban Ethnicity*. London: Routledge and Kegan Paul.

12

Framing 'the Other': A Critical Review of Vietnam War Movies and their Representation of Asians and Vietnamese

John Kleinen

We Were Soldiers (2002), the cinematic image of the first major clash between regular North Vietnamese and U.S. troops at Ia Drang in Southern Vietnam over three days in November 1965, is the Vietnam War version of *Saving Private Ryan* and *The Thin Red Line*. The director, writer and producer, Randall Wallace, depicts both American family values and dying soldiers. The movie is based on the book *We Were Soldiers Once…and Young* by the US commander in the battle, retired Lt Gen. Harold G. Moore (in a John Wayne-like performance by Mel Gibson). In the film, the US troops have little idea of what they face, are overrun, and suffer heavy casualties: the American GIs fight for their comrades, not for their fatherland. This narrow patriotism is accompanied by a new theme: the respect for the victims 'on the other side'. For the first time in the Hollywood tradition, we see fading shots of dying 'VC' and of their widows reading loved ones' diaries. This is not because the filmmaker was emphasizing 'love and peace' instead of 'war', but more importantly, Wallace seems to say, that war is noble.

Ironically, the popular Vietnamese actor, Don Duong, who plays the communist commander Nguyen Huu An, who led the Vietnamese People's Army to victory, has been criticized at home for tarnishing the image of Vietnamese soldiers. Don Duong has appeared in several foreign films and numerous Vietnamese-made movies about the War. He has also played a pedicab driver in the movie *Three Seasons* (2000) and a refugee camp translator in *Green Dragon* (2001), both directed by award-winning Vietnamese-American filmmaker Tony Bui. In these movies, he represents for the first time a genuine person, a belated portrayal by American filmmakers of Asians, or here Vietnamese, no longer as 'others'. His countrymen, through the official Army newspaper, see it differently and call him "a national traitor" (*Peoples' Army Daily* 18 September 2002).

My starting point is that visual media such as photographs, film and televison often have taken over from written texts the role of primary educator (Debord 1983; Ewen 1988; and Lutz and Collins 1993).

This contribution is about the way Western film culture helps to construct identities and worldviews by setting up the differences between 'us' and 'them': in this case, between 'the West' and the 'rest' who became the subject of European imperial expansion. What conceptions of Asia, and Vietnam, did these films and cultural practices construct? Vietnam war movies are a popular topic for social scientists (see Smith 1975; Adair 1981; Baker 1983; Auster and Quart 1988; Corrigan 1991; and Stora 1997). Except for some French and Vietnamese movies, I have chosen to discuss a number of 'orthodox' US-made films, which have already received extensive critical attention. The reason is simply that I have no direct access to the majority of hundreds of B-movies[1] (which do not differ much in their racial representation of Asians), but also because of the fact that the perspective I have chosen here is not so often taken. Most academic critics in the United States opted for the American side and seldom tried to see these films from an Asian, or in this case, Vietnamese, angle.

The best-known critical view on this discourse is Edward Said's *Orientalism*, whereby European and Western representations of Asians follow a set of stereotypes based on a Western-centred worldview, which is "capable of warping (distorting) the perspectives of reader and author equally" (1978, p. 13). Based on Foucault's idea about the linguistic apparatus as a means to express power and Gramsci's notion of cultural hegemony through which the elite maintain control over the masses, Said constructed a binary opposition between 'the West' or 'us' and 'the East' or the 'Other'. Although the term 'Orientalism' changed from a conservative and romantic approach in intellectual and political views on India, to many different kinds of representations in cultural texts, Said's coinage in 1978 created a new paradigm in the study of non-western societies and cultures. In the framework of Western domination of the non-western world, 'Orientalism' became the "corporate institution for dealing with the Orient by making statements about it, authorizing views of it, describing it, by teaching it, settling it, ruling it: in short Orientalism as a Western style for dominating, restructuring, and having authority over the Orient" (Said 1978, pp. 3, 222–24).

Said essentially outlines how the West, and in particular England and France, 'represented'—in effect created—something called 'the Orient'. This was nothing but a construct, however. What the West called the Orient never in fact existed except in the minds of Westerners. It was simply a tool that made Western subjugation of the region easily digestible. Hence, Said's book on Orientalism stands as one of the seminal texts on postcolonialism.

Its methodology has been applied by many authors to other recently decolonized or subjugated areas of the world (even including, in some cases, parts of Europe) and from different perspectives (see, for e.g, Lowe 1991, Frank 1998, Bernstein et al. 1997). In a second book, Said explores the relationship between culture and empire which he regards as a complicated "struggle over geography", embodied in the novel as "*the* esthetic object" which is important for the formation of imperial attitudes, references and experiences" (1993, pp. xii, 7; emphasis in original).

More recently, Said's work has come under criticism. Critics like Bernard Lewis (1982) and Aijaz Ahmad have tried to defend themselves against Said's accusation that the West simply invented 'the Orient', as well as Said's supposedly oversimplified dichotomy of 'East' and 'West'. Colonial reality was much more multifaceted than Said seems to suggest, these authors argue. The British author John MacKenzie (1995) points out that Said's polarization of 'the Other' or 'alterity' against 'us' and 'the West' itself was colonial discourse, while his notion of Western dominance and imperial hegemony as an unchallenged entity is unwarranted. McKenzie also points out that Said does not make any distinction between 'high art' and popular culture in which he has, according to his own words, little interest (see Sprinker 1992, p. 246). Apparently, Said sees more convergence than divergence between elite and popular culture, in particular in late Victorian and Edwardian times. Said's restrictions, however, limit 'Orientalism' (the book and the concept) to 'high culture' or 'great traditions', while film and other mass media like popular music, television, video, pulp fiction, comics, advertising, fashion, home design, and mass-produced food are not excluded. These fields belong to the broad domain of popular culture, which is generally referred to as mass culture.

High culture and low culture as it sometimes is understood belong nowadays nevertheless to a world economy that is no longer built on the assumption "(T)hat the original producers of a commodity necessarily control its consumption" (Appadurai 1983). Locality, Appadurai argues, is not taken for granted, but created, "deterritorialized" and "invented". He cites the transnational movement of Asian martial arts, as mediated by the Hollywood and Hong Kong film industries, as a rich case study that not only show long-cherished traditions, but also create new cultures of masculinity and violence (1990, p. 305).[2]

The Yellow Peril stereotype

The acceptance of Orientalism as a cultural tradition means, following Appadurai's argument, the acknowledgement of biological generalizations, cultural constructions, and racial and religious generalizations. Overt colonialist Orientalism has often used the racial stereotype of Asians in general, embedded in the expression the 'yellow peril' or 'the yellow hordes of coolies' to depict Japanese and Chinese migrants who came to the United States in the nineteenth century. Soon it collapsed into "one yellow horde" for those who came from Asia and became "a catchword signifying the 'yellow menace' to Western Christian civilization" (Marchetti 1993, p. 2; see also Isaacs 1958). American unions were major proponents of the 1882 Chinese Exclusion Act, the first racially exclusive US immigration policy targeting people from a single country. This policy of exclusion and hostility continued well into the twentieth century, beginning with the Boxer Rebellion, a "yellow threat" that menaced Western civilization.[3] While hostility to China declined somewhat during World War II as a result of its alliance in the war against Japan, the victory of Mao Tse-Dong and the Chinese Communist Party marked the beginning of the Cold War. Another fear came in the place of the 'Yellow Peril', 'the red menace'. Americans, and to a certain extent Europeans, were taught to fear the hundreds of millions of Red Chinese who were considered a threat to US security. During the Cold War, American attitudes toward China led to renewed racist portrayals of China and the Chinese as 'inscrutable', untrustworthy people, and ruthless killers.

Nowadays, shifting representations of Asian Americans as both model minorities and perilous yellow hordes are seen in phrases such as 'copy capitalists' (copying transistor radios and inundating the world with Toyotas and Hondas). Japan-bashing is an ongoing business, from time to time replaced by China-bashing: the approval of the Permanent Normal Trade Relations (PNTR) Act for China (May 24, 2000) sparked coast to coast protests from the American labour movement, which mounted its largest legislative campaign in years.[4] What was meant to be a strong anti-corporate and international solidarity stance against the World Trade Organization ended up in Cold War political jargon and racially offensive messages. And while the US Congress lashed out at Vietnam in recent years for its human rights record and suppression of religion, the same reaction was felt during the trade negotiations with Vietnam.

The most common portrayal of the 'yellow peril' stereotype in films, comic books and cartoons is the Fu Manchu character who embodies everything that Westerners feared: "Asian Mastery of Western knowledge and technique (denoted by his degrees from three European universities in chemistry, medicine, and physics); his access to mysterious Oriental 'occult' powers (to hypnotize victims); and his ability to "mobilize the yellow hordes" (Jun Xing 1998, p. 55). The sexual variant is depicted in E.M. Forster's *Passage to India* and other books of the period in which the 'white man's burden' turns into a passion to rule and whose females needs to be protected from Asians.[5] The fantasies of the Asian female who seduces the White male and the Asian male seducing the White female become an obsession for colonial governments which implemented policies to control the passions of

Europeans overseas. Cinematic representations of this abound, like Cecil B. Demille's *The Cheat* (1915), starring the Japanese actor Sessue Hayakawa, whose character tries to possess a white woman. A 1938 cinema version of Kipling's *Gunga Din* shows the title character as a subservient and unimposing anti-hero with openly racist undertones. But even long after decolonization, representations of the 'yellow peril' continue to flourish. In the *Year of the Dragon* (1985), a police inspector sees it as his mission to 'clean up' the dark, gang-controlled underworld of New York's Chinatown and 'rescues' his love interest, an Asian female newscaster, from her own culture (Marchetti 1993, p. 213). The Australian movie *Blood Oath* (1988) shows an Australian army officer at the end of WWII persecuting Japanese soldiers suspected of having committed war crimes. The suspects engaged in collective violence, but thanks to the civilizing efforts of the white man, they can be "de-orientalized" (Birch et al. 2001, p. 9). In most Vietnam war movies Vietnamese are reduced to stereotypes used for the Viet Cong, ARVN, the Saigon regime and almost any Asian who plays a role, in contrast to the individualistic white protagonists of the movie.

The Vietnam War through Vietnamese eyes?

The Vietnam War will be remembered as one where the international press, and the American press in particular, was given unprecedented access to American and South Vietnamese battlefields. Except on very rare occasions, no Western journalists were allowed by the Hanoi regime to report on their military activities. This one-sided news coverage often gave the South Vietnamese a 'bad press', and even sceptical reporters like David Halberstamm, Neil Sheehan and Stanley Karnow could easily point out instances of weaknesses and incompetence of the Army of the Republic of (South) Vietnam (ARVN).[6]

In Stanley Karnow's otherwise impressive *Vietnam: a Television History* (1982), the newsreel footage contrasts the American fighting men, and ARVN-soldiers and VC or People's Army forces. In many parts of the series, ARVN troops are shown in a negative or problematic way: as plunderers of corpses of killed 'VC'-troops, as assassins (e.g. the controversial photograph of the point blank shooting of a VC-suspect by police general Nguyen Ngoc Loan on February 1, during the Tet Offensive of 1968), or as auxilliary troops. This negative image of inept, poorly trained South Vietnamese soldiers and corrupt Vietnamese officials is a hallmark of nearly every Vietnam War movie. It started in the early 1950s and continued until the late 1970s. It even became a theme in the unsuccessful *Go Tell the Spartans* (1977), directed by Ted Post, who blamed the quagmire of the American involvement on the ill-advised Vietnamese troops (Auster 1988, p. 53–55).

Most historians now paint a more nuanced picture, pointing out that the South Vietnamese military structure, modelled along Western lines, was ill-fitted to fight a 'People's war' and too much reliance was placed on American logistical support (Bergerud 1991; Spector 1993; Clarke 1993). In retrospect, the important verdict on the ARVN was its proven ability to fight alone in difficult conditions. The image of an incompetent South Vietnamese army still haunts many Vietnamese migrants who seek to stress the many instances of heroism and determination shown by the ARVN in battle. The recent publication of McNamara's *In Retrospect: The Tragedy and Losses of Vietnam* again sparked heated debate within this community, reopening a wound that is yet to heal. Among the factors that might have hindered the performance of the ARVN, one aspect has been seldom mentioned, namely the specific conditions under which South Vietnamese troops had to fight compared to their North Vietnamese adversaries. The ARVN was seriously handicapped by a phenomenon called the 'family syndrome'.[7] After 1968's 'general mobilization', their wives and children, many of them housed in shantytowns near the military barracks or right within the army base, often accompanied South Vietnamese infantry soldiers. Recruitment often took place within the regions where the soldiers had their families or their homes. In military reports, the desertion problem was attributed to these 'dependants' and rated as the second highest on a list of nine contributing factors (Collins 1975, p. 60). In general the ARVN was plagued with low salaries and uncertain food supplies, and, until the late 1960s, ill-armed and ill-trained. Not surprisingly, many South Vietnamese soldiers were divided in their loyalties between duty and family when they far from their base camps and had to face a hardened North Vietnamese army, knowing that their kin were threatened. No doubt that the Northerners and their allies in the People's Liberation Armed Forces (PLAF) also faced the same hardships, but at least they had the assurance, at least in theory, that the 'homefront' was well looked after.

While the South Vietnamese army was often portrayed in an unflattering light, the People's Army of (North) Vietnam (PAVN) and its southern branch, the PLAF, better known in the West as the Viet Cong or VC, were often depicted as invincible troops who could take on the mighty American war machine. A rare exception is *The Siege of Firebase Gloria* (1988), starring Wings Hauser, R. Lee Ermey and the Philippino actor Robert Arevalo. The PLAF and its commanding officers, represented by Philippino-Vietnamese actors who speak (southern) Vietnamese, attack (in a highly unprobable version of a Vietnamese Dien Bien Phu), a remote American base during what is presented as their suicidal Tet Offensive in 1968.[8] The film shows atrocities only by the Vietnamese.

It took some seventeen years after the war ended for a northern writer like Bao Ninh, himself a veteran of some of the bloodiest battles in South Vietnam, to write about the darker side of the war from the victor's viewpoint. Bao Ninh's *Sorrow of War* (1991) gives ample evidence about the many ills that infected the northern army in the long years of fighting in the south: fear, cowardice, drug usage, brutality, self-doubt, and delusion. Bao Ninh's book is one of the few articulated counter-memories in modern Vietnamese literature also found in revisionist Vietnamese film (see Bradley 2001).

Cinema of the Vietnam War: Vietnamese and Western Perspectives

This review of the cinema of the Vietnam War era is, however, mainly concerned with American or Hollywood films about the war, even before the United States became directly involved. French movies about the First Indochina War have been analysed by Stora (1998; 2001), but I will deal extensively with those produced after 1955, when the French forces left Indochina. The main topic will be the portrayal of Asians in general, and Vietnamese in particular, in Western movies, concentrating primarily on the social, political and cultural meaning of these representations. Films produced in Vietnam before and after 1975 will be dealt with briefly, as long as they fit into the theme.

During the First and Second Indochina Wars, film production in both parts of Vietnam was limited because of material, organizational and budgetary constraints. Film production, then as now, is a high-risk business with no guaranteed income. French cinema had not established a Vietnamese branch, as the British had done in India. Consequently, those films that were produced were typically directed at the popular, commercial market. They were shown by Vietnam's first cinema chains, which were established by two French firms, Indochine Films et Cinema and Société des Cineastes de l'Indochine. A few Sino-Viet entrepreneurs also invested in building small, independent cinemas.

The bulk of the full-length features distributed in the Republic of Vietnam (1954–75) came mostly from foreign countries like France, the United States and India. In the North, equipment from the Soviet Union and the People's Republic of China was used to produce feature films and documentaries. A movie partly shot at Dien Bien Phu deserves special mention here. *Quyet chien, Quyet thang Dien Bien Phu* (Resolve to Fight, Resolve to Win: Dien Bien Phu), produced in 1954–55, was the first Vietnamese version of the battle by a Vietnamese crew, directed by Nguyen Tien Loi, Nguyen Hong Nghi and Nguyen Phu Can. The Russian director Roman Karmen, who worked with Joris Ivens and Ernest Hemingway in the Spanish Civil War, shot a version of the battle for an international audience, entitled *Vietnam on the Road to Victory*. In 1965, a commemorative version with a clear reference to the war effort in the South was released under the name *Chien Thang Dien Bien Phu* (Victory at Dien Bien Phu), by a certain Tran Viet.

The 1954 Vietnamese version is a mixture of (pre) battle scenes, footage from French directors (among them Pierre Schoendorffer) and re-enactments. Loi and Karmen worked closely together and used each other's images for their productions. The re-enactments show defeated soldiers, weeks later after the battle, in front of Karmen's cameras. They displayed remarkable fitness as they walk into captivity. The Vietnamese version of the victory was in line with the view of the Vietnamese Communist Party (here still named the Workers' Party), but the narrative and commentary impresses the contemporary viewer for its sober style and accuracy. The originality of the film lies in the verisimilitude of the images dating from this period.

Between 1956 and 1959 forty-five documentary films were released, which number doubled after the decision to 'liberate the South' was taken. Another forty feature films were produced from then until 1975.[9] Exceptions to the usual propagandist genre promoted by the North and the South are several high quality films made at the end of the 1950s. In *Chung Mot Dong Song* (On the Same River, 1959), the North Vietnamese cinematographers Nguyen Hong Nghi and Pham Hieu Dan used a Vietnamese version of Romeo and Juliet to depict the political division of their country. While the scenario was in line with the Party's decision to unify the country by force (May 1959), this first feature film of the DRV-film industry was exceptional in the way it presented personal emotions. There were no such nuances a year later, when all literary output and other mass media were explicitly devoted to mass mobilization and political propaganda. Individual revolutionary self-sacrifice in the 'War against the Americans', as the Vietnam War was coined in the North, was permitted in the war official narrative. *Vo Chuong A Phu* (The A Phu Couple) released in 1961, deals with the unhappy life of a couple belonging to the Meo minority. Happiness is brought by cadres of the Vietnamese Communist Pary, reinforcing the solidarity between the Vietnamese and other ethnic groups in the struggle to win the war. The same message is contained in *Lua Trung Tuyen* (Fire on the Middle Line) (1961) and *Mot Ngay Dau thu* (An Early Autumn) (1962), both set during the war with France, but clearly serving patriotic purposes for the next stage of the war.

In the South, independent film productions such as the films *Chung Toi Muon Song* (We Want to Live) and *Long Nhan Dao* (Human Compassion) were also possible until around 1964. As the war intensified, government institutions under the supervision of the Ministry of Information together with the ARVN became the most important suppliers of newsreels and films. Films became pivotal as part of the psychological warfare as was the case in the North (Sadoul 1963; Rouse 1986; Carlot 1994). Compared to the North, there were fewer feature films, probably because of the availability of foreign movies, high costs, and wartime conditions (for filmic traditions in post-war decolonization in Asia, see Dissanayake 1995).

Between 1939 and 1975, Western (French, American and British) movie companies, produced more than 150 'Vietnam' related feature films, of which more than half do not deal with the real Vietnam or Indochina, but only refers to the Vietnam experience, US counterculture, or the return of its veterans (Malo and Williams 1994). As American involvement increased, Hollywood remained reluctant to explore the subject, unlike French filmmakers during the first Indochina War. Between 1946 and 1954, France produced five movies in which the colony, and the effects of the war, played a sometimes modest role, including *Thérèse Raquin* (1953) by Marcel Carné and *Le Rendez-vous des Quais* (1953–55) by Paul Carpita. Carné's naturalist version of Emile Zola's novel follows the story of Thérèse (Simone Signoret) and her lover Laurent (Raf Valone), who kills her husband (Jacques Duby), and their final downfall. The most tragic part is played by a sailor (Roland Lesaffre) who had fought in Saigon in 1945–46 and whose war experiences made his re-adaptation to French society impossible. The movie contains therefore a coded reference to France's problems in Indochina. Explicit about the country's defeat at Dien Bien Phu is *Le Rendez-vous des Quais*, the French version of *Indonesia Calling!* (by Joris Ivens, 1946). The film portrays strikes in the port of Marseille where trade is paralysed by protests against France's involvement in Indochina. The director used a documentary approach to shoot real confrontations between riot police and strikers, actual scenes of wounded soldiers coming back from Indochina, and dockers refusing to load ships with weapons. Carpita showed a common strategy by politicians, police and employers to protect their own interests (Malo and Williams 1994, p. 493). The film was only showed once, in Paris, on 2 October 1955. It was seized by the police in Marseille and banned. The movie disappeared for 35 years. In 1989 the negative and copies were found. The film was restored and it received a general release in February 14, 1990, when it premiered on French television.[10]

While French moviemakers of the period did not take any interest in the Korean War, their interest in the Indochinese conflict was equally limited. Most of the productions date after the final departure of the French forces in April 1956 from Saigon. In the same year as Camus' *Mort en Fraude* (1957), Claude Bernard-Aubert authorized a typical 'war movie' with a lot of violence and a simple story line (*Patrouille de Choc*). A remake with equally low box office takings appeared in 1980, *Charlie Bravo*, but European audiences were already inundated by an influx of American movies about the war. During the sixties, when the war in Algeria haunted French politics, productions like *Fort du Fou* (1962) and *Les Parias de la Gloire* (1964) tried to glorify soldiers' companionship and personal bravery which borders anarchy. Needless to say, the Vietnamese as the eternal enemy are depicted in stereotypes as sinister Orientals.[11] Pierre Schoendoerffer's *La 317ème Section* (1964) is undoubtedly the most realistic and straightforward movie of the period. Filmed in Laos, an auxiliary platoon of Cambodian enlisted men under the leadership of *sous-lieutenant* Torrens (Bruno Cremer) is trying to fight their way to Dien Bien Phu to reinforce the beleaguered troops, but will arrive too late. The defeat is communicated by field radio. The Vietnamese and Laotian highlands take a heavy toll on the soldiers, most of whom do not survive, except for the commanding NCO and his deputy, a German soldier who looked back upon hardened battle experience in the Soviet Union. Schoendoerffer remade an American documentary version of the story of *La 317ème Section, The Anderson Platoon* (1968), a committed but non-political story about a black marine officer, Eugene S. James, who commands the 7th Marine Corps. These and other attempts to portray the war pose a striking contrast to the way Hollywood made 'Nam' a locality devoid of dates and names with no real, definable beginning or end.

Approximately one hundred Hollywood movies about the war were made between 1965, when the Marines landed at Da Nang and 1975, when the last American left. On the other hand, post-war movies tripled after the end of the war in 1975, numbering up to 300 US feature movies (Dittmar & Gene Michaud 1990). Another source taking the period between 1939 and 1992 into consideration details over 600 Vietnam War feature films including TV, pilot and short movies from the United States, Vietnam, France, Belgium, Australia, Hong Kong, South Africa, Great Britain and other countries (Malo and Williams 1995).

A few B-movies produced before 1965 showed that Indochina or Vietnam was a subject worth exploring. Samuel Fuller, famous for his Korean War movies, directed *China Gate* (1955), which was shot in a cartoon-like setting of a dangerous mission undertaken by soldiers of the French Foreign Legion out to destroy a secret Vietminh munitions dump.[12] However, the opening documentary footage with a picture of Ho Chi Minh is the only reference to Vietnam. The rest is a peculiar mix of anti-Communist adventure and a covert appeal for racial tolerance. The opening song by Nat King Cole, who also plays the close ally and friend of the chief protagonist, Johnny Brock/Gene Barry, refers to Fuller's attempt to combine a staunch anti-Communist movie with a plea for tolerance among the otherwise racially divided American public of the fifties. The main Asian characters are all played by white actors: Angie Dickinson who personifies the Eurasian saloon owner Lucky Legs, the 'dragon lady' in a slit (Chinese not Vietnamese) dress who leads the legionnaires to the hidden camp in return for having her son sent to the United States and the Viet Minh commander Major Cham [sic] (Lee Von

Cleef) who is Lucky Legs' secret lover. The interracial romance is peculiar and ambiguous because both parts are played by Caucasians. But even European viewers who, unlike many Americans at the time, not driven by a racial divide, were deemed not yet prepared for such a bond. In Marcel Camus' *Mort en Fraude*, the Vietnamese heroine who hides a Frenchman on the run in the village house of her father to protect him— in vain—from the white Saigon mafia, is the French-Vietnamese actress Anh Méchard (Delmeulle 1992). 'Métissage' becomes a marker for the representation of the 'Other' (see the chapter by Srilata Ravi). The representation of Indochina or as one critic labelled it—the feminization of the Other—became the theme of movies like *Indochine*, *The Lover* and even *Dien Bien Phu*, all released in 1992 (see Norindr 1996, pp. 131–55).[13]

Caucasian actors representing Asians, or for that matter Vietnamese, were common in the nineteen fifties and sixties. In one of the best-known films of the period, *The Quiet American* (1958), based on Graham Greene's famous book written three years earlier and directed by Joseph Manckiewicz, the actress Georgia Moll plays the part of Phuong, the Vietnamese girlfriend of the war-weary British foreign correspondent Fowler. On the surface, it is the story of a love triangle involving a naively destructive American secret agent, a cynical English journalist and a seemingly passive but quietly determined Vietnamese woman. The drama unfolds at various levels. In the book, the relationship between Fowler and the American CIA agent Pyle who came to Vietnam to create a 'third force', gets a personal undertone when Fowler finds his Vietnamese mistress the object of Pyle's affections. In the film, the ironic nature of the book is lost. The future American involvement in Vietnam against which Greene warns is replaced by a political plot driven by a shallow love triangle between the three protagonists and a clear message that the United States should be committed in Vietnam. The film's final dedication to "the people of the Republic of Vietnam and its president, Ngo Dinh Diem" makes the political message perfectly clear. The year is 1958, two years after the proposed free elections, pledged at the Geneva Conference, were buried forever. The first few years of the Ngo Dinh Diem regime did bring hope to those Vietnamese who were opposed to both Communism and colonialism south of the 17th parallel, particularly after the departure of the last French forces. Backed by American help to turn South Vietnam into a 'bastion of freedom' against Communism at the height of the Cold War, Diem embarked on a process of 'nation-building' by monopolizing political power, alienating many of his compatriots who would have liked a more liberal regime in opposition to the Communist alternative.

In the movie Audi Murphy, a hero of the Second World War, who starred in many films about 'his' own war, plays Pyle. Devoid of any US connection, Pyle becomes the active agent provocateur behind a plot to supply plastic bombs to a terrorist, third force Vietnamese general. Besides the role of the Japanese actor Yoko Tani, who plays the general, Vietnamese only figure as shadows (the sneaky Viet Minh) or as childish persons (ARVN soldiers in a watch tower; Phuong who seems only to be interested in her milkshake). Because the film is shot primarily in static close-ups of two people talking, there is almost no sense of the social and physical life of Saigon or Vietnam in the early fifties.[14]

In contrast to French movies of the war, *China Gate* and the *Quiet American* are striking examples of Hollywood's attempts to fit Vietnam into the spectrum of the Cold War commitments undertaken by the United States. In 1963 George Englund produced *The Ugly American*, based on the William J. Lederer and Eugene Burdick's novel, a belligerent Cold War book written to take the wind out of the pacifist Greene version on US intervention abroad. A thin disguised attempt to replace 'Vietnam' for the tiny kingdom of Sarkhan where an ex-OSS wartime officer and journalist-turned-ambassador MacWhite (Marlon Brando) tries to find a third way with a former guerilla leader, national hero, and personal friend Deong (played by the Japanese actor Eijo Okada, famous for his role as the Japanese lover in Alain Resnais' *Hiroshima Mon Amour* [1959]). In its genre, the film is a perfect illustration of the ambiguous Kennedy years of valiant idealism symbolized by the Peace Corps and a deep rooted mistrust of movements which did not follow the American way of political life. Compared to its near-namesake, *The Quiet American,* Englund's *The Ugly American* at least tries to communicate something of an Asian country by showing some characters who act beyond the usual clichés of "Orientals with an inscrutable and cunning nature" (Senator John Mitchell commenting on the Chinese Exclusion Act of 1882). Sarkhan's prime minister is Kwen Sai, a role played by Kukrit Pramoj, Thailand's Prime Minister in 1975–76. His fine acting and sophistication makes McWhite's body language in more than one sense 'uglier' than the maker of the movie intended. In a review of the film, Auster and Quart (1988) state that the *Ugly American* "tries to have it both ways in its depiction of the

Third World's desire for self-determination in a world dominated by the two power blocs. ... Therefore, ... the film is clearly pessimistic about the viability of the neutralist position" (p. 21). The film ends with a depiction of a non-committed home audience that is not interested in wise words about growing problems in developing countries. Unintentionally, *The Ugly American*, seems to be a premonition of what would happen in Cambodia after 1970, when a neutral country became involved in proxy wars and fell victim to a policy of auto-ethnocide, long after the Americans had left.

John Wayne's *The Green Berets* (1968) is probably the best example of this film genre on the other side of the Atlantic by its specific mode of address and correlated with specific audience segments. Wayne's earlier roles, e.g. in *The Alamo* brought him international fame. He took the unusual step of visiting Vietnam in 1967–68 and came to the conclusion that the US combat units in Vietnam were the best the Americans had ever fielded. Wayne believed that the media and the anti-war movement hid this fact from the American people, thus the aim of the film was to redress this imbalance. A critic wrote:

> What is so repugnant about "The Green Berets" is not its politics (nor even, politics apart, its total ineptitude purely as an adventure war movie) but the fact that, in spite of overwhelming evidence to the contrary, evidence that by the late 1960s had already filtered through to the US, its makers were still determined to reduce Vietnam to simple-minded Manichean antitheses: good guys vs. bad guys, cowboys vs. Indians, white men vs. "natives". (Adair 1981, p. 35).

The story is about a team of US Special Forces (the "Green Berets), led by Col. Mike Kirby (played by Wayne). The film opens at the John F. Kennedy Centre for Special Warfare at Fort Bragg, North Carolina, where a press conference is underway. Sgt Muldoon defends the US presence in Vietnam to the journalists. The critical comments by a journalist, George Beckwirth (played by David Janssen), provokes Kirby into challenging him to come to Vietnam with him to see for himself what the United States was doing there.

The dovish journalist is forced to re-evaluate his views as he sees for himself the true nature of the Viet Cong enemy who set bamboo booby traps, murder a village headman. Five of them rape the headman's daughter (her rape is coyly referred to as 'abuse'), and later forty [sic] rape his wife. The journalist abandons his anti-war stance and literally and figuratively takes up a rifle to defend himself. He is now eager to fight the barbaric enemy.

Stereotyping and clichés are so obvious in *The Green Berets*, that an enumeration would take several pages. It starts with the explicit link between the war in Vietnam and the war against Indians in the Westerns: the name above the US army camp is 'Dodge City'. The enemy is shown in black and white terms. Warfare is a way of 'cheating' because open battles and besieging camp are avoided by the guerrillas, but ruthless attacks in rough terrain and jungle fighting are preferred. Rape, torture, pillage, murder are the privileged fighting means, while America's Asian allies prefer to drink champagne, eat caviar and drive in limousines. No mention is made of American weapons and tactics: the use of napalm and defoliants, search-and-destroy missions, strategic hamlets, body counts, body bags, free-fire zones. There is no attempt to make war conditions in Vietnam 'realistic'. Filmed on location at Fort Benning, Georgia with a large supply of military weaponry there is no jungle, no humidity, the men do not sweat, and the trees are obviously pine trees.[15] The film ends with Kirby explaining to Hamchunk (a free combination of Vietnamese words?), an orphan, why the American cause in Vietnam is just. We see John Wayne walking off into the sunset at the South China Sea—in the East—a scene, which exemplifies the accurateness of the rest of the film.

Post-1975 Vietnam War Movies

The war in Vietnam, like that of other drawn-out conflicts, has its share of controversy, myths and legends, often emanating from those who fought the war themselves. The mythology has often been taken over by others, among them politicians, who have tried to rewrite history from their perspective. For most Americans, the Vietnam conflict is basically an American drama in which the Vietnamese only play second fiddle to heroic American generals and GIs having to fight 'with one hand tied behind their backs' by the politicians in Washington. Since the end of the war, there has been a growing popular view that its cause was just, but that the strategies and tactics of waging war were at fault, resulting in the disaster that would haunt America for years (Lewy 1978). Revisionist versions of the Vietnam War are manifold and the lessons derived from them are varied (see, for e.g., Turley 1986, pp. 189–99).

Generally, the reactions range from 'no more Vietnams' to President Bush's "spontaneous burst of pride" after the Gulf War ended with the Allies' victory: "By God, we've kicked the Vietnam Syndrome once and for all" (*Boston Globe*, 2 March 1991; Werner Luu 1993).

With the *Green Berets*, the chapter of an unproblematic representation of the Vietnam War closed for many years. Hollywood turned its interests into safer treatments of a conflict that became more unpopular on the home front by the month. 'Vietnam' played a role as a signal in the background or as a pretext for something different. As Auster and Quart (1988) remarked "film makers drew … toward black humour, irony, obliqueness, and ambiguity for a depiction of war—but not "the war" (Vietnam)—that would have some appeal to all shades of opinion" (p. 38). Films like *Easy Rider* (1969), *Taxi Driver* (1976) and *Dirty Harry* (1971), set the stage for alienated and paranoid Vietnam veterans. The dramatic end of the war in 1975 with the fall of Saigon and over 58,000 Americans killed, brought the veteran's pain and sorrow to the foreground and created a new theme for Hollywood. On the one hand, movies like *Coming Home* (1978) were warmly received by the anti-war movement, while a new tone was set by the release of Michael Cimino's *Deer Hunter* in the same year in which political amnesia, American ethnocentrism and racism predominated (Howard and Howard 1998, pp. 85–87). In the pivotal scene, Michael (Robert de Niro) and his friends are coerced by the 'Viet Cong' into playing Russian roulette against one another. Seldom have Orientalism and different variations of 'the yellow peril' been so brutally combined.[16]

Michael Cimino's depiction of a war (which he allegedly never participated in) would set the tone for a whole series of films in which the Vietnam veteran became the hunter-hero of the period. The painful symbolic representation of the memory of a lost war and the tensions of remembering and forgetting gave rise to many questions about the reasons why the war was fought and lost. The answer of many film-makers was in the framing of crude aesthetics and open racism: compared to films like *Uncommon Valor* (1983), *First Blood, Part II* (1985) and *Rambo III* (1988), or the *Missing in Action* series (1984 and 1985) *Deer Hunter* appeared sophisticated when it came to the depiction of 'the Other' (Budra 1990). The cinematic humiliation of the Vietnamese Communists and the successful liberation of MIAs remained for a while a leading theme. Important exceptions are *The Killing Fields* (1984), indirectly a film about the Vietnam War, and *Alamo Bay* (1985) on the plight of the Vietnamese boat people. Both films were directed by Europeans (Roland Joffe and Louis Malle) for American distributors.[17]

Although the 'Vietnam syndrome' played a leading role during the seventies and eighties on the imagination of film-makers and screenplay writers, there are some exceptions from the mainstream cinematographic remakes of the past. I will take four films as examples. These films tried to depict the war from the ordinary soldier's perspective and their makers showed a critical point of view towards the war effort. Orientalist themes persisted, however.

Platoon, directed by Oliver Stone in 1986, tells a war episode from the perspective of the soldier (grunt) and his unit or platoon. Filmed in Ilocos Norte in the Philippines (in real tropical jungle) by a British crew during the People's Revolution which ended the Marcos regime, the movie is based on Stone's own experiences of 15 months in Vietnam.[18] His alter ego, Chris Taylor (Charlie Sheen), 21 years old, arrives in Vietnam in September 1967, just a few months before the Tet Offensive of January 1968. The story is told with voice-overs but we actually see Taylor's arrival in Vietnam and his tour of duty. Marching through jungle and suffering from heat exhaustion, the platoon is ambushed by shadowy Viet Cong soldiers, which results in Taylor being injured. One of the suspenseful parts is the discovery of a North Vietnamese bunker complex and the death of three soldiers. This provides the pretext to take revenge on villagers nearby. The images that follow are strongly reminiscent of Ron Haerberle's photographs of the My Lai atrocities published in *Life*. What follows are scenes of rampage, murder and rape by soldiers in the platoon, which set the scene for a conflict between two competing sergeants who represent two hostile groups within the unit. In many reviews, the film is hailed as an anti-war movie, as a clever reflection on the divisions in US society about the war and as an antidote to revanchist patriotic caricatures like *Rambo*, but also as an answer to the metaphysically tinted *Apocalypse Now*. The 'realism' of the film is impressive in the way the foliage, climate and hostility of the environment of the Vietnamese highlands becomes tangible. The camera is always inside the jungle to give an impression of the soldiers' view of being surrounded by a hostile environment.[20] A British historian commented that *Platoon* "maintains straightforwardly that the US was 'guilty' in Vietnam" (without properly explaining how), but adds that "the grunts, with a few exceptions, were not themselves to blame" (James Porteus in Walsh and Aulich 1989, pp. 156–57). The central focus on American soldiers does not warrant the problem of the continuously disappearing Vietnamese. Even the ARVN troops who fought ostensibly for their freedom with US support do not get attention. The enemy ('Viet Cong' and the North Vietnamese Army (NVA)) remains hidden for most of the film and exists just off camera, hidden by jungle, as fleeting shadows, or corpses (500 NVA KIA, 22 wounded, as is dryly reported in the film). We see the face of a Vietnamese soldier only once as he bayonets a black soldier. In a voice-over we hear Charley Taylor/Charley Sheen saying, "I think now, looking back, we did not fight the enemy, we fought ourselves—and the enemy was in us..." (Hart 1998).

Auster and Quart (1988, p. 140) regard *Platoon* as Hollywood's total acceptance of the Vietnam War as a fit subject for film. In its wake followed *Hanoi Hilton* (1987), *Gardens of Stone* (1987), and *Full Metal Jacket* (1987). Stone went back to 'Vietnam' with *Born on the 4th of July* (1990) and his 'pro-Vietnamese' *Heaven and Earth* (1993).

Stanley Kubrick, the director of *2001: A Space Odyssey, Dr Strangelove* and *A Clockwork Orange*, was known for his depiction of violence. His film on the Vietnam War released in 1987, *Full Metal Jacket*, is based on the novel *The Short Timers* (1979) by Marine combatant correspondent Gustav Hasford, which was hailed in *Newsweek* as "extremely ugly" but "the best work of fiction about the Vietnam War" (Walter Clemons, quoted in Hillstrom and Hillstrom 1998, p. 125). Michael Herr, author of the widely praised *Dispatches*, contributed to the screenplay. Nearly half of the film is devoted to the harsh basic training experience of a platoon of Marine recruits. Two trainees with the names Joker (played by Mathew Modine) and Pyle (the very same name as Graham Greene's protagonist) play the central roles. The film is named after the type of bullet Pyle loads into his rifle to kill his cruel drilling instructor before he commits suicide.[20] *Full Metal Jacket* then follows Joker who moves to Vietnam as a Marine combat reporter to cover the Tet Offensive in Hue: "I wanted to meet people of an ancient and interesting culture and kill them", he tells people who ask him about his motives for joining the war effort.[21]

In the film, the strange architecture of what is meant to be the city of Hué in the film stems from 1930s buildings owned by British Gas in London's East End (which was bombed out during WW2 and further destroyed by Kubrick). The unit sweeps the city when a sniper hits one of the men, after which rescue attempts account for new casualties. The Marines finally infiltrate the hiding place of the Vietnamese attacker who turns out to be a Vietnamese woman. Heavily wounded, she begs Joker to kill her. He ultimately does, but his motives are not clear: was it out of compassion or just a desire for retribution?

Critics of the film reacted in a mixed way: some judged the characters "dehumanised, the audience desensitised and Vietnam depicted as a strange country" (Terrence Rafferty in *The Nation*, 1 August 1987); others saw it as an attempt "to attack male chauvinism of the gun-happy species" (Penelope Gilliat in *American Film*, September 1987, quoted in Hillstrom and Hillstrom 1998, p. 127). Apart from comments about Kubrick's attempt to grapple with the dilemmas of the Vietnam War and his penchant for the darker side of humanity, all critics focused upon the American characters in the film. The man who was shot first by the sniper is a black soldier nicknamed Eight Ball, who earlier had offered himself to a Vietnamese prostitute. The scene in which she figures is revealing not only because she is refusing him in broken French ("*too beaucoup*"), but also because of the comments of his buddies who press him to show his penis to her. Minutes later he is shot in the groin by what turns out to be a female gunner. All the clichés concerning women, in this case South Vietnamese women, and Vietnamese combatants, are used: the prostitutes speak broken English and French; their military pimps behave like quasi funny Kung-fu or sinister Fu Manchu characters, and the Viet Cong soldier who dies at the end of the film is shrouded in a mysterious light and begs first in an unintelligible language. Viet Nam and the Vietnamese are seen as the antithesis of something called 'civilization'. The Vietnamese are depicted as the 'Other', but Other in a specific way: as primitive in contrast to America's civilized technological, tall, clean-cut white boys. Within the realism of the primitive they are portrayed as the locus of sex, of death, and of sex-and-death (Christopher 1995).

What *Platoon* and *Full Metal Jacket* have in common is their uncompromising demonstration of the battlefield agonies of the common soldiers, whose images must be rescued from all those Vietnam films. While *Platoon* excels in realism, *Full Metal Jacket* betrays Kubrick's ambition to "explode the narrative structure of movies", as he remarked in an interview: "I want to do something earth-shaking" (*Newsweek*, 29 June 1987; quoted in Auster and Quart 1988, p. 142).

Olivier Stone's passion for Vietnam continued with the making of *Born on the Fourth of July* (1989). This movie has stars such as Tom Cruise, Willem Dafoe, Tom Berenger and Lili Taylor in a powerful depiction of the plight of Vietnam veterans. The screenplay is based on the eponymous novel by Ron Kovic, who was involved in the My Lai massacre. Kovic became a strong voice for the veterans in the US. The theme is that of some of the hurdles that Vietnam veterans endured after their homecoming. Like *Platoon*, the film won four Academy Awards. But again, Vietnam and the Vietnamese are just accessory subjects, as can be seen in the scene where a number of innocent villagers are slain in a sudden eruption of gunfire from the platoon Kovac is part of. They become a background against the drama that is unfolding: the accidental killing of a soldier by friendly fire. The film is shot in the Philippines and the Vietnamese characters were recruited from the population of Ilocos Norte. None of them plays an important role. This is in striking contrast with Stone's last film on Vietnam, which was hailed in the press as the first time 'Vietnam' was no longer a war, but a country. *Heaven and Earth*[22] (1993) is the story of a Vietnamese woman, who follows her great love (a US Army officer, played by Tommy Lee Jones) to America. The marriage breaks down, but the couple's two sons will have a bright future. Given Stone's reputation of mishandling female characters in his earlier films, this was a break with the past. The challenge, however, did not succeed in many ways, especially with the symbolic lead character (the Vietnamese-American actress Le Thi Hiep) and the loosely structured script. Detailing the life of Le Ly Hayslip (born Phung Thi Le Ly) as written in her two books *When Heaven and Earth Changed Places* (with Jay Wurts) and *Child of War, Woman of Peace* (with James Hayslip), this is a more conventionally structured movie. At the same time we are treated to the unique visual beauty of the Vietnamese countryside, if in a conventionally romanticized way, even during the war. American viewers received, probably for the first time, access to the minds of ordinary Vietnamese, albeit framed in a pro-Western, colonial, context.

The best illustration of cinematic Orientalist treatment of the Vietnam War is Francis Ford Coppola's famous movie, *Apocalypse Now* (1979). The film is based on Joseph Conrad's novel, *Heart of Darkness*, about the journey the Englishman Marlow makes to meet ivory hunter Kurtz at an upriver Congo company outpost. Against the pervading *mission civilisatrice* of the white man in the African darkness, the novel depicts the corruption of the white man by the alleged savagery of Africa, which increases as one travels upstream. The river becomes a metaphor for an 'implacable force' over which its traveller is pursuing a religious or mythological quest (Conrad 1971). The title of the movie refers in the first place to the last book of the New Testament (Revelations of St. John the Divine). One of the most important aspects of this revelation is of the 'last battle' (Armageddon Rev. 16.16) in which the forces of good and evil are set against each other prior to the final day of judgement. The suggestion seems to be that Vietnam was an apocalyptic moment for America: a struggle of good (democracy and capitalism) vs evil (communism) but the day of judgement however seems to have gone against the United States. The adding of the adverb 'Now' is a reference to the popular slogan 'Peace Now'. The film has two different endings. The TV version ends with an air strike on Kurtz's base; the 1979 cinematic version ends with Willard killing Kurtz with a machete, while Kurtz's followers ritually slaughter a water buffalo. The latest version released in 2000, entitled *Apocalypse Now Redux*, has an extra 53 minutes of previously unseen footage edited from the 1979 version and ends in the same way. The literature on this movie is exhaustive, which reflects its box office success (for an overview see Hillstrom and Hillstrom 1998; also Christopher 1995).

Kurtz (Marlon Brando) is a much decorated soldier and a rising star of the military establishment who becomes a dog soldier, fighting a private war with the assistance of Montagnard tribespeople against an unseen enemy (the North Vietnamese, the Viet Cong, or the Khmer Rouge?).[23] The US military send a Special Forces assassin, Capt. Willard (Martin Sheen) to find Kurtz and kill him. Willard travels upriver in a gunboat with a four-man crew to find Kurtz. Along the way the hunter reads the dossier prepared by military intelligence on Kurtz and discovers what he has become. The journey upriver enables Coppola to reveal the nature of the Vietnam war in a series of spectacular episodes: the long journey upriver on what seems to be the Mekong (which does not reach any major temple complex in Cambodia or Laos); the helicopter attack on a Vietnamese village (erroneously built on stilts);[24] the Angkor-style temple where Kurtz has his jungle empire, with a clear reference to James Frazer's *The Golden Bough*, which sees magic and religion as overlapping phenomena.[25] The theme of the *Golden Bough* prepares the viewer for the ritualized slaughter of a buffalo, which resembles closely the description by anthropologist Georges Condominas in *Nous avons Mangé le Forêt* (17–21 September 1949).[26]

There are a few historical references such as the American programme of assassinating suspected communist military and political village leaders during Operation Phoenix after the Tet Offensive in 1968. The sampan massacre refers to Lt Calley and the My Lai massacre of 1968. The massive air strikes refer to the illegal bombing of Cambodia during 1972. But there are also a number of historical fabrications which border on stereotypes of the yellow peril genre: body painted and 'carnivalesque' (the term is from Stora 1997, p. 216) mountain people who attack the Willard party with spears, bows and arrows (a faint reference to booby traps with sharpened bamboo spikes); the 'Viet Cong' did not hack off arms of inoculated children (compare the *Deer Hunter*'s references to POWs forced to play Russian roulette); these were not Mnong Gar montagnards (whose music is used) but played by Ifugao hill tribes from Banaue in the Philippines. The fuzzy geography which combines Nha Trang, Vung Tau and the estuary of the Trans Bassac (called Nung River) in one place (in reality the southern Philippines where the film was shot), dotted by jungle, instead of rice paddies, does not help much to uncover the historic reality of the war. But that is what Coppola apparently wanted: the lack of a precise geographical area gives rise to a phantasmagorical landscape, an underworld.

The movie attracted much criticism for depicting Vietnam as a madhouse where "the war was one bloody huge circus, with clowns, acrobats, fire-eaters and a big brass band" (Robert Hatch in *The Nation*, 25 August 1979, quoted in Hillstrom and Hillstrom 1998, p. 14) or a cartoon which "reduces the profound complexities of heart and mind to caricature, and in the end the audience can brush it all off with the explanation that it couldn't have been like that. And the audience is right, it couldn't and wasn't" (Ward Just in *Atlantic*, ibid., p. 14).[27]

According to Coppola, the recently released *Apocalypse Now Redux* is a film that is "more worrying, sometimes more amusing, more romantic too and whose historic perspective has become even stronger" Associated Press, 17 February 2001). A long monologue by a 'forgotten' French plantation owner who defends his threatened area against intruders is added to underline Coppola's bombastic view of history.

If the film claims to represent, in its director's phrase, "the moral dilemma of the Vietnam war", its current prolongation misses the point. Nevertheless, *Apocalypse Now* poses still as a seminal Vietnam movie despite its Orientalism.

Joseph Conrad's *Heart of Darkness* is cited at length on the first page of Edward Said's *Culture and Imperialism*. Conrad reveals the destruction of the Congo by Western powers as an embodiment of Western inhumanity (MacKenzie 1995, p. 14). But where Said seems to be disappointed by Conrad's lack of premonition of decolonization, Coppola does not even seem to bother to whom or what his hyperbolic Orientalist style is addressed. He is partly Willard and partly Kurtz in his kingdom: Hollywood's attempt to comprehend the war and finally to integrate it into the American imagination and psyche. The scene in which the Montagnard warriors bombard Willard's boat with little blunt arrows— a scene directly taken from Conrad's story—ends with the killing of the black captain. It suggests some link of primitiveness between two non-Western or non-American peoples. Or in the words of film critic Gilbert Adair:

> Vietnam (the war rather than the country) is no more than the heart of the darkness, and endless psychodrama, half Theatre of Cruelty, half Theatre of the Absurd, in which impulses normally lurking just below or intermittently bursting through the crust of civilization are given free rein. (…) And Kurtz's Cambodian enclave was doubtless intended to symbolize the very heart of the heart, the inner sanctum of America's collective unconscious" (1981, p. 155).

The temptation is great to study Vietnamese movies in search of its mirror image: Occidentalism,[28] a concept which at first posed as a positive Arab response to Edward Said's critique of Western Orientalism but which represents an objectification of the Occident in a similar way. Occidentalism is equally inflexible and relativist as its enemy. Or in the words of MacKenzie, Said's "identification of a monolithic and predominantly male-originated discourse, which equally subjects the West to 'Occidentalism'". Indeed, some movies made by Vietnamese filmmakers after 1975 clearly show signs of 'Occidentalism' portraying Europeans in a strange and cardboard-like way, but their depiction of the enemy in the form of officers and enlisted men of the ARVN forces is even more characteristic. The lack of Western actors especially in the North between 1954 and 1975 and in Vietnam after 1975 is the simplest explanation for this, while the socialist realist style is equally responsible for the reframing. The fierce reaction of the Vietnamese government to Don Duong's representation of a soldier of the victorious North Vietnamese Army in an American movie is understandable in the context of the commemoration of the war dead. As a result, this becomes a part of a state-sponsored project of memory of the 'just cause' of national liberation, rooted in a unilineal view on history. But this is a theme for another ongoing research interest (see e.g. Malarney 2001; Bradley 2001; Kleinen 1998, and Stora 1998).

Conclusions

By considering a variety of films, in chronological sequence, I have tried to underscore the representations of Asians, and especially Vietnamese, by Western American film-makers. While the themes changed from general war movies, through the depiction of bloodthirsty veterans and patriots towards the view of the victimized American servicemen, the representation of the Vietnamese did not change dramatically. Vietnamese soldiers and civilians are portrayed as cunning, cruel, even sadistic, ambivalent, and irresponsible. The landscape is mostly tropical, but also in terms of a paradox combining natural abundance and great fertility with poverty and disease (Arnold 2000, p. 7).

These articulations of latent and overt Orientalism in American movies about the Vietnam War are clear manifestations of a discourse which have had broader consequences for the way Asians and Vietnamese have been depicted. Where earlier movies showed a worldview in which the Asian participants are reduced to simple pawns in a chess game between the superpowers, the post-1975 'Vietnam syndrome' genre betrayed a stereotype, which reified the Vietnamese as devious and unchanging. Even those films considered to depict the war in more realistic terms, did not frame the Vietnamese in a new context. What changed was the manifest Orientalism, symbolized by the yellow peril, but the latent Orientalism of the so-called anti-war movies remained.

Current American and French cinematic production on Vietnam is not coming to terms with the past. The re-issued *Apocalypse Now Redux* is part of a 'cultural memorial' to remember the war in contradictory terms. *We were Soldiers* is not about the Vietnamese and 'their' war, but about 'us'. The Other remains an unknown Oriental.

Notes

1   See, for instance, the extremely useful overview of 600 cinematographic productions from more than 8 countries compiled by Jean-Jacques Malo and Tony Williams (1994).

2   The British historian David Arnold has contributed to the discussion with an elegant parallel of Orientalism as a cultural and political construction of the West by a new concept called 'tropicality'. The tropics was imagined and represented by "a landscape in which the power of nature dominated human existence and to no small degree determined its characteristics and quality". The construction of tropicality is closely linked to visual arts and literature, but also to scientific disciplines and technical specialities (Arnold 2000, p. 7).

3   See, for a European reception of the term, Bernd Soesemann, "Die sogenannte Hunnenrede Wilhelms II. Textkritische und interpretatorische Bemerkungen zur Ansprache des Kaisers vom 27 Juli 1900 in Bremerhaven", in *Historische Zeitschrift* 222 (1976), pp. 342–58.

4   See, for example, Kent Wong and Elaine Bernard, "Labour's Mistaken Anti-China Campaign", *New Labour Forum* (Fall / Winter 2000).

5   For instance, America's new Filipino subjects who are depicted in the famous poem as "your new-caught, sullen peoples / Half-devil and half-child".

6   A remarkable exception was the Australian war correspondent Neil Davis (1934–85) whose experiences with the ARVN differed strongly from those of his American colleagues. See *Front-line*, a documentary by David Bradbury, (Canberra: Ronin Films, 1979) and the impressive biography by Tim Bowden (1987). Davis's alter ego is fictionalized in Koch (1995). Another example is Pierre Schoendoerffer's *The Anderson Platoon* (French Broadcasting System, 1966–67). Director / Writer / Narrator Pierre Schoendoerffer depicts the day-to-day life of an army combat platoon in the Central Highlands / South Vietnamese combat zone. The men of the 1st Platoon Company "B" 12th "Chargers", 1st Cavalry Division, are commanded by a black Lieutenant, Joseph Anderson. Filmmaker Pierre Schoendoerffer had been a war correspondent, working as a cameraman for an army film unit at Dien Bien Phu.

7   The term is from Wiesner (1988). See also Nguyen Tien Hung and Jerrold L. Schecter 1986, p. 211; Spector 1993, p. 108.

8   The representation of the Vietnamese enemy is exceptional in the way they speak in southern dialect and are shown as fierce, but weak, soldiers. The Philippino Army was instrumental in providing material and allowing filming at Camp Aguinaldo in Manila. Eleven years before, Coppola received similar support for *Apocalypse Now*.

9   Figures taken from two 40th anniversary commemorative booklets, published by the Documentary and Scientific Film Studios (Hanoi) and Vietnam Feature Film (Hanoi and Ho Chi Minh city). See also Bradley 2001, p. 224 n. 16.

10 That Indochina still represented a trauma for France was demonstrated in 1984 when a six-part documentary series on Indochina directed by Henri de Turenne was shown on French public television. The documentary was the French version of Stanley Karnow's *Vietnam: A Television History*. Turenne's re-working created such an uproar that after the 3rd part, TV2, the television network, had to organize a live debate that turned out to be quite heated. In Holland, where I was responsible for the adaptation of the original 13-hour version into a 6-hour presentation, Vietnamese refugees threatened to protest in front of the broadcasting studio to show their assumed disapproval of what they termed "Hanoi's vision on Vietnamese history". After I had assured them that in the first part adaptations were made to show the broader coalition of nationalist forces during the colonial period, the protests were cancelled.

11 The film poster of *Patrouille de Choc* shows a grimacing Vietnamese soldier with a helmet, which points to the fact that the conflict is between two standing armies instead of a struggle between a guerilla force and an organized military unit. The title and the end of the story had to be changed due to censorship.

12 Other titles of this genre are *Saigon* (1947), *A Yank in Indo-China* (1952) with actor Harold Fong, *A Yank in Viet-Nam* (1963) with Vietnamese actors Kieu Chinh and Hoang Vinh Hoc, *Operation CIA* (Kieu Chinh again) and *Lost Command* (1965), starring Anthony Quinn and George Segal. A total of fifteen movies were produced before 1968 (see Adair 1981).

13 Norindr's critical reception of these movies is illuminating, but in the case of *Dien Bien Phu* he ignores Schoendorffer's earlier work and Mitterands' apologizing for the war (*un erreur*) when he visited Vietnam in 1993.

14 A second screen version of *The Quiet American* was released in September 2002, directed by Phillip Noyce and produced by Sydney Pollack. Fowler is played by Michael Caine, Pyle by Brendan Fraser, and Phuong for the first time by a Vietnamese actress, Hai Yen, a 19-year-old ballerina from Hanoi.

15 Markus Dunk, a journalist for the Mid-West newspaper *Express*, wrote on 30 August 2001: "According to newly released military documents, the Pentagon has repeatedly involved itself in the making of big-budget Hollywood movies—like the 1985 Tom Cruise vehicle *Top Gun*..., but also suggesting amendments, making alterations and occasionally rewriting history in exchange for its military cooperation ... The list of those films deemed by the

Pentagon unworthy of military support is equally revealing... Vietnam films as *Platoon, Full Metal Jacket,* and *Apocalypse Now* were rejected—one assumes because of their vehement opposition to the conflict. This created difficulties for *Apocalypse Now,* as director Francis Ford Coppola was forced to use helicopters and pilots from the Philippine army, who flew off regularly during filming to attack real-life rebel insurgents. Even films which seem to epitomize truth, justice and the American way have fallen foul of the military".

[16] Strong criticisms came from Gloria Emerson, John Pilger and other Vietnam War era reporters who denounced the Russian roulette scene as a lie (for an overview of reviews, some of which were positive, see Hillstrom and Hillstrom 1998, pp. 85–87).

[17] Minor exceptions are *The Boys in Company C* (1977), directed by Hong Kong director Raymond Chow and *Go Tell the Spartans* (1978) by Ted Post. Both display a moderate, even decent (the term is Adair's) treatment of the average war movie.

[18] *Platoon* is not his first 'Vietnam movie': in 1967 he made a short movie entitled *Last Year in Vietnam* while he was a film student of Martin Scorsese's (Dittmar and Michaud 1990, p. 124.)

[19] The use of veterans like Captain Dale Dye as technical advisor (and playing in the film) was necessary to show veterans how authentic the film was by including small things in the film that only those who had been there would know about. The video version announces that "All elements are packaged and bound like a Vietnam Veteran's scrapbook of his tour of duty". It includes photos of Stone in Vietnam together with photos of the actors and crew on location.

[20] A 7.62 mm high-velocity copper-jacketed bullet.

[21] In many war movies this cynicism is unheard of. In these films (e.g. John Wayne's *Iwo Jima*), it is clear who the enemy is (Asian and in uniform) and what 'victory' was (the taking of clearly defined territory such as Pacific islands held by the Japanese). So powerful have the images created by John Wayne of heroic US soldiers, that they influenced the thinking of young US troops in Vietnam, who had been brought up with Wayne movies on TV. Many imagined themselves to be Wayne-like heroes and the tragically inappropriate attempt by 19-year old soldiers to mimic the actor no doubt led to too many unnecessary deaths. In *Dispatches*, Michael Herr's most famous book about the Vietnam War, another myth is introduced: the fantasy-ritual of the gunfight, which was the leading theme of many Westerns (*High Noon*) on film and TV-series (*Gun Smoke*). *Full Metal Jacket* uses themes introduced in Herr (see Hellmann 1997, pp. 177–88).

[22] This should not be confused with the movie with the same name by Haruki Kadokawa, a student of Akira Kurosawa.

[23] The Kurtz figure is probably based upon Col. David Hackworth, the most decorated living American soldier who denounced his misconduct during the war and went into exile in Australia. He now runs a website on which he comments on American military issues. See his book *About Face* (Sydney: Pan, 1990).

[24] Filmed on location in Philippines during the anti-communist insurgency in the late seventies, helicopters from the Philippines air force figured in search and destroy mission scenes. From Coppola's wife Eleanor's accounts and *The Making of Apocalypse Now: Heart of Darkness*, we learn that these machines often disappeared from the film 'shoot' to shoot for real in jungle.

[25] The other book which Kurtz has as his bedside reading is Jesse L. Weston's *From Ritual to Romance* (1920) which was the source of much of Eliot's "The Wasteland" and its grail imagery. Among other things, Weston points out that British folk tradition is full of mock sacrifices; Coppola's film refers to the sacrifice of Kurtz by Willard. A *New York Times* critic calls the books examples of "speculative anthropology" (Scott 2001). See also an anthropologist's view on this matter (Verrips 2001).

[26] The use of Mnong Gar music in the movie, originally recorded by George Condominas for the UNESCO-label, is a clear reference to the book and Coppola's intellectual debt to anthropology.

[27] Ward Just quoted in Hillstrom and Hillstrom, 1998, p. 14. The same volume also has more positive reviews. Reviews of the film can also be found on the Internet, for example, <http://.tierranet.com/films/a.now>.

[28] According to Tønneson (1994, p. 8), the term was coined by Hasan Hanafi, leader of the Institute of Philosophy of the University of Cairo and a former researcher at the UN University in Tokyo.

References

Adair, Gilbert. 1981. *Vietnam on Film: From the Green Berets to Apocalypse Now*. London: Proteus.

Appadurai, Arjun. 1990. "Disjuncture and Difference in the Global Cultural Economy". In *Global Culture*, edited by M. Featherstone. London: SAGE.

Arnold, David. 2000. "Illusory Riches: Representations of the Tropical World, 1840–1950". *Singapore Journal of Tropical Geography* 21, no. 1 (March): 5–18.

Auster, Albert and Leonard Quart. 1988. *How the War was Remembered: Hollywood & Vietnam*. New York: Praeger.

Bernstein, Matthew and Gaylyn Studlar, eds. 1997. *Visions of the East: Orientalism in Film*. New Brunswick, N.J.: Rutgers University Press.

Bao Ninh. 1991. *Noi Buon Chien Tranh* [The Sorrow of War]. Hanoi: NXB. English version by Frank Palmos based on the translation from the Vietnamese by Vo

Bang Thanh and Phan Thanh Hao with Katherina Pierce. London: Secker and Warburg.

Bergerud, Eric M. 1991. *The Dynamics of Defeat. The Vietnam War in Hau Nghia Province*. Boulder: Westview Press.

Birch, David, Tony Schirato and Sanjay Srivastava. 2001. *Asia: Cultural Politics in the Global Age*. Crows Nest, NSW: Allen & Unwin.

Bowden, Tim. 1987. *One Crowded Hour: Neil Davis, Combat Cameraman 1934–1985*. Sydney: Collins.

Bradley, M.P. 2001. "Contests of Memory: Remembering and Forgetting War in the Contemporary Vietnamese Cinema". In *The Country of Memory. Remaking the Past in Late Socialist Vietnam,* by Ho Tai and Hue Tai. Berkeley: University of California Press.

Budra, Paul. 1990. "Rambo in the Garden: the POW Film as Pastoral". *Literature Film Quarterly* 18, no. 3: 188–93.

Carlot, John. 1994. "Vietnamese Cinema: First Views". In *Colonialism and Nationalism in Asian Cinema*, edited by Wimal Dissanayake, pp. 105–40. Bloomington and Indianapolis: Indiana University Press.

Christopher, Renny. 1995. *The Viet Nam War, the American War: Images and Representations in Euro-American and Vietnamese Exile Narratives*. Amherst: University of Massachusetts Press.

Clarke, Jeffrey. 1993. "Civil-Military Relations in South Vietnam and the American Advisory Effort". In *The Vietnam War: Vietnamese and American Perspectives,* by Jayne S. Werner and Luu Doan Huynh, pp. 165–98. New York: M.E. Sharpe.

Collins, James Lawton Jr. 1975. *The Development and Training of the South Vietnamese Army, 1950–1972*. Washington, D.C.: Department of the Army.

Corrigan, Timothy. 1991. *A Cinema without Walls: Movies and Culture after Vietnam*. New Brunswick: Rutgers University Press.

Conrad, Joseph. 1971. *Heart of Darkness: An Authoritative Text, Backgrounds and Sources, Criticism*, edited by Robert Kimbrough. New York: Norton.

Debord, Guy. 1983. *Society of the Spectacle*. Detroit: Black and Red.

Delmeulle, Frederic. 1992. "Fiction Cinematographique et Guerre d'Indochine". In *Cahiers de la Cinematheque,* pp. 63–72, numèro special: *Revue Histoire du Cinema* 483: 50–61.

Dissanayake, Wimal, ed. 1994. *Colonialism and Nationalism in Asian Cinema*. Bloomington: Indiana University Press.

Dittmar, Linda and Gene Michaud. 1990. *From Hanoi to Hollywood: The Vietnam War in American Film*. New Brunswick and London: Rutgers University Press.

Emerson, Gloria. 1976. *Winners and Losers*. New York: Random House.

Ewen, Stuart. 1988. *All Consuming Images: The Politics of Style in Contemporary Culture*. New York: Basis Books.

Faas, Horst and Tim Page, eds. 1997. *Requiem by the Photographers Who Died in Vietnam and Indochina*. New York: Random House.

Frank, A.G. 1998. *Reorient: Global Economy in the Asian Age*. Berkeley and London: University of California Press.

Hart, David. 1998. Responses to War: An Intellectual and Cultural History. <http://www.arts.adelaide.edu.au/personal/Dhart/ResponsesToWar/Art>.

Hellmann, John. 1997. "The Vietnam Film and American Memory". In *War and Memory in the Twentieth Century*, edited by Martin Evans and Ken Lunn, pp. 177–88.

Hillstrom, Kevin and Laurie Collier-Hillstrom. 1998. *The Vietnam Experience: A Concise Encyclopedia of American Literature, Songs and Films*. Westport, Connecticut and London: Greenwood Press.

Isaacs, Harold. 1958. *Images of Asia: American View of China and India*. New York: Harper Torch Books.

Jaehne, K. 1989. "Cinema in Vietnam. When the Shooting stopped...and the Filming Began". *Cineaste* X 11, no. 2: 32–37.

Karnow, Stanley. 1983. *Vietnam: A History*. New York: Viking.

Kleinen, John, and Cao Xuan Tu. 1998. "The Vietnam War Through Vietnamese Eyes: A Review of Literary Fiction and Cinema". *The Vietnam Review*, March, pp. 345–68.

Koch, Christopher. 1995. *Highways to a War*. Port Melbourne: Heinemann Australia.

Lewis, Bernard. 1982. "The Question of Orientalism". *New York Review of Books*, 24 June, pp. 49–56.

Lewy, Guenter. 1978. *America in Vietnam*. New York: Oxford University Press.

Lowe, Lisa. 1991. *Critical Terrains: French and British Orientalisms*. Ithaca: Cornell University Press.

Lutz, Catherine A. and Jane L. Collins. 1993. *Reading National Geographic*. Chicago: University of Chicago Press.

MacKenzie, John M. 1995. *Orientalism: History, Theory and the Arts*. Manchester: Manchester University Press.

Malarney, Shaun Kingsley. 2001. "'The Fatherland Remembers Your Sacrifice'. Commemorating War Dead in North Vietnam". In *The Country of Memory: Remaking the Past in Late Socialist Vietnam*, by Ho Tai and Hue Tai, pp. 46–76. Berkeley: University of California Press.

Malo, Jean-Jacques and Tony Williams, ed. 1994. *Vietnam War Films: Over 600 Feature, Made-For-TV, Pilot and Short Movies, 1939–1992, from the United States, Vietnam, France, Belgium, Australia*. Jefferson, N.C.: McFarland.

Marchetti, Gina. 1993. *Romance and the "Yellow Peril"*. Berkeley: University of California Press.

Moore, Harold G. and Joseph L. Galloway. 1992. *We Were Soldiers Once ... and Young: Ia Drang, the Battle that Changed the War in Vietnam*. New York: Random House.

Nepstad, Peter. 2000. Western Visions: Fu Manchu and the Yellow Peril. The Illuminated Lantern, <www.illuminatedlantern.com/fumanchu, www.mit.edu/21h.153j/www/aacinema/yellowperil.html.>.

Nguyen Tien Hung and Jerrold L. Schecter. 1986. *The Palace File*. New York: Harper & Row.

Rouse, S. 1986. "South Vietnam's Film Legacy". *Historical Journal of Film, Radio and Television* 6, no. 2: 212–23.

Sadoul, Georges. 1963. *Histoire du Cinema Mondial des Origines à nos Jours*. Paris: Flammarion.

Said, Edward. 1978. *Orientalism*. New York: Pantheon Books.

———. 1993. *Culture and Imperialism*. New York: Knopf.

Scott, A.O. 2001. "Aching Heart of Darkness". *New York Times*, 3 August 2001.

Spector, Ronald H. 1993. *After Tet*. New York: Vintage Books.

Sprinker, Michael. 1992. *Edward Said: A Critical Reader*. Oxford: Oxford University Press.

Stora, Benjamin. 1997. *Imaginaires de Guerre: Algenrie-Vietnam en France et aux Etats-Unis*. Paris: Editions La Decouverte.

———. 2001. La Guerre Française d'Indochine: Les Rares Images de Fiction d'une Guerre Oublièe. Paper presented at a symposium on Decolonisations, Loyalities and Nations: A History of Diminishing Choices, Maison Descartes, December 2001.

Tønnesson, Stein. 1994. "Orientalism and Universalism". *NIA Snytt-Asia Insights* 2: 4–10.

Turley, William. 1986. *The Second Indochina War. A Short Political and Military History, 1954–1975*. Boulder: Westview Press.

Verrips, J. 2001. "Golden Bough and Apocalypse Now: Another Fantasy". *Postcolonial Studies* 4 no. 3: 335–48.

Werner, Jayne S. and Luu Doan Huynh. 1993. *The Vietnam War: Vietnamese and American Perspectives*. New York: M.E. Sharpe.

Wiesner A. 1988. *Displaced Persons and Other War Victims in Vietnam, 1954–1975*. Westport, CT: Greenwood Press.

Walsh, Jeffrey and James Aulich, ed. 1989. *Vietnam Images: War and Representation*. New York: St. Martin's Press.

Xin, Jun. 1998. *Asian America through the Lens: History, Representations, and Identity*. Walnut Creek, CA: Altamira Press.

13

Métis, Métisse and Métissage: Representations and Self-Representations

Srilata Ravi

What does it mean to explore the boundaries and the ambiguities surrounding the notion of racial frontiers at a time when mixed race identity is more a norm than an exception? Clearly, the meanings of race and skin colour are mediated by language, religion, nationality and culture. Given the socially constructed character of race and the detrimental effects that these classifications have had on non-white peoples and especially on mixed race persons in the colonies, I would like to argue that a positive reconstruction of mixed race identities needs to be developed in postcolonial cultures.

Edouard Glissant, the Francophone Caribbean poet and writer, says that in today's world 'métissage' is operational as a rule. He adds that the 'single-root' (*racine unique*), purist definitions of racial identities have to be necessarily replaced by what he terms as *rhizome identities or relational identities*.[1] Glissant's theory of cultural creolization ('métissage'), is not some kind of vague humanism but an attempt to recover concealed histories by establishing a cross-cultural relationship in an egalitarian way:

> A l'identité-racine-unique qui était l'orgueil, la beauté, la somptuosité, mais aussi le mortuaire des cultures ataviques, nous tendons à substituer, non pas la non-identité, ni *l'identité-comme-ça*, celle qu'on choisit comme on veut, mais ce que j'appelle *l'identité relation, l'identité rhizome*. C'est l'identité ouverte sur l'autre…je peux changer en échangeant avec l'autre sans me perdre moi-même.[2]

> Instead of single root identities that was the pride, beauty, richness but also the death of atavistic cultures we would like to substitute not non-identities, nor indifferent identities that one chooses according to one's whims but one that I call identity–relation, identity–rhizome. It is the identity that opens on to the Other…I can change by exchanging with another without losing myself.

To Francoise Lionnet, feminist literary critic, renowned for her reading of Francophone women writers of African origin and her work on women's autobiographies, 'métissage' is an aesthetic concept to "illustrate the relationship between historical context and individual circumstances, the socio-cultural construction of race and gender and traditional genre theory, the cross-cultural linguistic mechanisms that allow a writer to generate polysemic meanings from deceptively simple or seemingly linear narrative techniques."[3]

The term 'métissage' is translated as cultural creolization by some cultural critics and others as cultural cross-breeding (I would personally prefer *cultural cross-braiding* which comes closest to the visual image contained in the term "métisse"). 'Métissage' as an extension of the word 'métis' encompassing the social, historical, cultural, racial, psychological and aesthetic issues that the word inspires does not have an exact cultural equivalent in English. More commonly used terms such as race-crossing, hybridization, miscegenation allude only to the biological aspects of the phenomenon. 'Métis' most often translated as half-breed, half-caste or mixed blood in English almost always carries a negative connotation because it seems to imply biological abnormalities and reduces human reproduction to animal breeding.[4] Linda Alcoff[5] in her chapter on "Mestizo Identity" uses the neutral hyphenated *mixed-race* to define the person but the nominalization of the hyphenated qualifier to designate the concept/implications would be linguistically awkward, I should think. Talking about recovering mixed-race identities or constructing the 'mestizo consciousness' would only concern some of the themes associated with 'métissage'.

In order to fully grasp the impact of Françoise Lionnet's and Edouard Glissant's valorisation of the word 'métissage' and its rather sophisticated usage by other cultural *gourous* and literary critics, this concept which has its roots in the historical realities of interracial unions has to be first understood in socio-political terms. Contemporary literary and cultural critics and writers like Anthony Appiah, Françoise Lionnet, Edouard Glissant and Maryse Condé perceive mixed race persons as valuable border crossers, negotiators and mediators not only between races but also between nations, cultures and linguistic communities. Such a vision is most definitely a positive definition and a viable alternative to the mixed person's usual representation/self-representation as lack, or as the tragically alienated figure. Too often the frustrations of self-negation and continual cultural collisions have produced a negative construction of the mestizo-consciousness. History also shows that such mixed-race persons have been exploited by the dominant to better control colonized subjects and the mixed race persons have themselves been reviled for their cooperation with the dominant communities.[6]

This paper will explore how 'métissage' is represented/self-represented in a variety of different Francophone discourses (colonial, literary and popular) set specifically in a Franco-Asian context. The first sections of this paper will be devoted to the literary and social construction of this term and its implication in Franco-Asian colonial and postcolonial cultures. I will then proceed to show how 'métissage' is reappropriated and rearticulated in contemporary discourse on pluri-racial identities. In these sections, the paper will examine the use of the term 'métissage' as reading practice by critics and an aesthetic tool by contemporary Franco-Asian 'métisse' writers. The main ideas examined in this paper are: métissage in French literature and culture; métissage as a social phenomenon in the colonies; métissage and postcolonial reconciliation; postcolonial francophone voices and literary métissage.

Métisse as Exotica in French Literature and Culture

In the French colonial context 'métis' ('métisse' is the feminine equivalent) constitutes a distinct but unstable racial category. It varies

according to the geography. In Canada, the term applies to a person of
French and native American descent only. In the late 18th century it
applied to persons of French and African descent in Senegal. In the
French Carribean, persons of mixed origin were also called Creoles,
mulâtres, cafres, cafrines.[7] In Indochina the term applied to persons of
French-Vietnamese descent. Irrespective of the geographical context,
the figure of the 'métisse' or woman of mixed race has always been
associated with the erotic and the exotic in French literature and popular
culture. In his study of Lafcadio Hearn's writings on the French
Caribbean, Jack Corzani[8] remarks that the writer's fascination for
women of colour was in fact a fascination for the 'métisse' or the 'sang
mêlée' and not the pure African. His writings are full of images of
"jambes dorés" and "torses basanés" vividly suggesting the mixed
colouring (bronze, coffee, gold) that the métisse, or mixed race woman
represents. While Lafcadio Hearn, like many others, laud the
primitivism and innocence of these 'women of colour', Corzani is
quick to note that the primitivism that the European finds attractive is
one that is bettered ("ameliorée") and not that which is really savage
and truly primitive. The métisse or "woman of mixed colours",
according to Corzani, attracts because she represents "domesticated
primitivism". Colour aesthetics and attraction for native innocence
added to the sexual fantasy that the métisse inspired in an inter-
relational context of political domination which was at the root of this
fascination:

> La fascination même exercée par la notion tient certainement à la
> dimension sexuelle qu'elle évoque: derrière le mot, c'est toujours, comme
> l'avait si bien ressenti Roger Bastide, l'étreinte des corps qui se profile,
> même si celle -si inscrit dans des rapports de domination. D'où sa
> puissance symbolique, et son extension métaphorique considérable
> puisque le terme a fini par désigner tous les phénomèmes de mélange ou
> de fusion affectant la réalité sociale métamorphorisés par le métissage
> étape par étape.[9]

> The very fascination that the word (métisse) exerts is due certainly to
> the sexual dimension that the word contains, Just like Roger Bastide
> had sensed it, the word conjures the embracing of bodies even if it in
> a inter-relational context of political domination. Its symbolic power
> and its metaphorical extension can therefore be understood, since the
> term succeeds in designating all the phenomena of mix and fusion
> affecting social realities that have been gradually transformed by
> métissage.

In his article "The Bananaia Song", Jean Louis Calvet points out that in French popular music, it is not the African but the 'métisse' that inspires the songwriters. From Henri Salvador, who laments the departure of his "doudou" to Julien Leclerc, who sings praises of his métisse, Melissa to Bernard Lavilliers ("Stand the Ghetto"), the image of the African as depicted in French songs is predominantly feminine and métisse.[10] The visual appeal that the aesthetics of métissage offers is not restricted to the coffee and golden complexions that the mixing of 'black' and 'white' races produces. It also applies to the representation of Asian women where the aesthetic/physical métissage is imagined in a confusion of stereotypical métisse colours. In Jean Hougron's *Asiates*, the Frenchman Bressan is seduced by the "golden arms" of his métisse mistress Pauline.

> Tandis qu'elle parlait, avec une confiance qui grandissait chaque jour, il détaillait son jeune corps, ses seins menus attachés haut, sa taille mince, ses bras ronds et dorés, couleurs d'abricot', (*La Nuit Indochinoise*, p. 393).

> While she spoke with a confidence that grew with each passing day, he made note of her young body...her round, golden arms, the color of apricot.

The visual imagery of the métisse is so deeply rooted in European imagination that to the first Frenchmen in Indochina, this physiological métissage is more imagined than real. In the first portraits of the Annamites by the French, it is the fantasized métissage of their physical traits that make these women attractive to them. Louis Lucien de Grammont, a Captain in the French army, in his observations on Cochinchina in 1864, paints a detailed physical portrait of the Annamite woman. He perceives a certain Europeanness in the oval form of the Annamite faces and more importantly he imagines the "exuberance characteristic of the Occidental races" in their "Mongolian" blood:

> La forme de leur visage se rapproche un peu de l'ovale européen...

> Au moral, elle est gaie , douce et rieuse. La Providence, par une heureuse anomalie a jeté dans ses veines, où circule le sang mongol, une étincelle de la vivacité de nos races occidentales. Elle est très féconde, excellente mère de famille et douée d'une activité infatigable.'[11]

Yet another novelist, Herbert Wild, describing his female protagonist from the Tonkin province of Indochina refers to the fact that her body resembles that of a beautiful European woman:

> Elle était grande, extrêmmement bien faite et pour qui n'eut point vu ses traits, l'impression eût été celui du corps d'une belle Européenne.[12]

To a large extent the women protagonists in the recent French films *Indochine* (Camille) and *The Lover* (the young Duras) perform the same functions as the métisse in exotic and colonial writings. The imagined/ reinforced physical métissage characterizing the onscreen representations of these women offers what Laura Mulvey calls scopophilic pleasure to their spectators. The films represent these women as métisse images, as exotic spectacles to be looked at, in order to centralize female subjectivity in the construction of filmic representation.[13] Both *Indochine* and *The Lover* position the female protagonists as privileged sites of desire by representing them as cultural métisses. As adopted child of a French mother and object of a Western male gaze (Jean Baptiste) in the first half of the film, Camille's Asian features 'cross-braid' with the Europeanness of her attire (Western dresses) and gait (the tango) to provide voyeuristic pleasure to the audience. When she dominates as the 'Red princess' in the second half, her métissage is erased in favour of a marked Indochinese identity and as such she is removed from the sphere of attraction and interaction.

Forms of cultural métissage are preferred to racial métissage in colonial cultures. Mixed-race unions are fantasized but as reality they are denigrated and even denied. Racial métissage, which is scorned in practice gives way to an appreciation of the ideal métisse, one who is European but born in the colonies like Eliane in the film *Indochine*[14] or the young Duras in *The Lover*.

The young Duras in the film *The Lover* played by Jane March appeals because of her métisse features. Duras's autobiographical novel refers to the slender wrists and thick long hair that the white adolescent girl possesses just like her Indochinese counterpart. The novel refers to the fact that the Chinese lover feels kinship with the French girl born and raised in the colonies because she bears a close resemblance to a girl from Indochina.[15] Duras's narrative subverts the stereotypical representation of a native woman subjected to the male European colonial gaze: it is the adolescent white European girl with Indochinese features who is subjected to the male Oriental gaze of the Chinese Lover. In the filmic transposition, however, it is the aesthetics of métissage that transforms Jane March into an erotic object for the film's Western audience.

Métissage in the colonies — social and legal status of the métis/métisse

Even if the Other inspired desire and fascination in the European as represented in colonial and exotic literatures and cultures, racial métissage and the actual union in the colonies was unthinkable since it was also synonymous of disorder and disintegration of values. Unbelievable though it may appear, colonization in Indochina favoured mixed unions at the beginning, according to Yvonne Knibiehler in *Les femmes au temps des colonies*. The native woman was to be considered as a trustworthy informant and interpreter ("une informatrice sûre") of the Other culture to initiate the "master" into the "local customs and languages" to "correct his blunders where necessary" and to facilitate the governing task of the colonial master.

> Le Blanc militaire ou civil, maître tout puissant et seigneur justicier de la population aux coutumes étranges, n'avait-il pas intérêt à avoir à ses côtés une informatrice sure, l'introduisant dans la vie locale, l'initiant aux mœurs et aux langues, corrigeant aux besoins ses maladresses.[16]

Mixed unions were permissible if local elites were involved but they were not allowed to flourish. In a report that the Governor General Louis Salaun made in 1902, he stated that a couple of mixed unions had been celebrated between well known families.[17] He added however, that temporary unions between young Frenchmen and locals were less favoured. He observed benevolently that children born out these unions were either taken care of by the mother or by the father who would give them a European education. The abandoned ones were taken over by the missionaries of Saint Enfance who looked after their survival and education.[18] In order to discourage such cross-racial unions, the French government in Indochina simplified marriage procedures for French couples. Interestingly, Governor General Louis Salaun who lauded the cultural and interracial harmony present in the colonies, affirmed at the same time that the presence of French women in the colonies was important to redress the morality of the French men.[19] Very soon, a strong and powerful inverse current denouncing mixed unions becomes the order of the day. Such unions were seen as the source of all evils and a new morality was introduced. Métissage that was ideologically accepted in 'pre-colonial' and 'early colonial era' became a colonial burden in the late 19th century.

> Le metissage accepté à l'age classique était devenue à la fin du XIXe le fardeau de la honte du colonisateur.[20]

> Métissage accepted in the classical period had become the burden and shame of the colonizer at the end of the nineteeth century.

In order to perpetuate the French race (in the purist sense of the word) and to deter French men from falling prey to exotic relationships ("détourner les coloniaux des amours exotiques"), colonial administrators felt that French women had to be brought into the colonies to play the role of wife-mothers ("épouses-mères").

> Si l'on voulait détourner les coloniaux des amours exotiques il fallait leur donner des partenaires de chez eux, si l'on voulait qu'ils perpetuent la race française et qu'ils en affirment à travers le monde l'évidente suprématie, il fallait leur procurer les épouses mères.[21]

In her chapter entitled "Enfants de la colonie: bâtards raciaux, bâtards sociaux"[22], Emmannuelle Saada suggests that a historical study of métissage in the colonies is important to understand the problems of immigration in France today, and notes that between 1890 and 1959, "le problème du métissage dans les colonies" was of prime social importance. Métissage problematized the frontiers between colonizer and colonized, provoking a series of debates on who was native and who was French.[23] Métis children, unclaimed by their fathers, were at the heart of this problem. Between 1900 and 1950, legal debates concerning the status of these children were very common. Children born out of wedlock (French with native woman) or raised by the father outside of marriage were never considered problematic, they were considered French by the colonial society ("français par filiation"). Those abandoned by the father were more numerous. They were legally natives and were rejected by both the native and colonial society. Kim Lefevre's (1989) autobiographical reminiscences of her childhood and adolescence spent in a Vietnamese milieu accentuate the poignancy of the situation of the métisse in Indochinese society even as late as the 1940s and 1950s.

> Tout en moi heurtait mes proches; mon physique de métisse, mon caractère imprévu, difficile à comprendre, si peu vietnamien en un mot. ... Je n'ai gardé aucun souvenir des première années de ma vie, hormis ce sentiment très tôt ressenti d'être partout déplacée, étrangère.[24]

> Everything in me bothered my family, my physical traits of a cross breed, my unpredictable character, difficult to understand, in short hardly Vietnamese... I have not retained any memories of the first years of my life except that initial sentiment of being displaced and of being a foreigner.

Acutely conscious that she does not possess the kind of beauty so praised by the French poets, Kim finds herself too métisse to please the Vietnamese and too Vietnamese to fit in the French society in the colonies.[25] Made to feel very conscious of her métissage as a physical deformity in the Vietnamese milieu she was being brought up in, she is further denounced as immoral ("métisse, immorale et folle") when a French instructor in her school involves her in an extramarital affair.[26]

In actual fact, in 1928 the social problem of abandoned métis children was deemed to have been solved when a law was passed stating that métis children born of unknown parents were French citizens. The law was first passed in Indochina and later in western and Equatorial Africa. Emmannuelle Saada argues that jurists, anthropologists and colonial administrators contributed to a social construction of métis and métissage that further isolated them[27] in colonial society. Race, citizenship and family status entered into the codification of the métis identity and the word race entered for the first time in a judicial document in this context.

> Ce sont donc les relations entre race, citoyenneté et status familial qu'engagent les codifications de l'identité métisse.[28]

> The métis identity was thus codified in terms of the relation between race, citizenship and family status.

Such a law made sense in colonies where there was *indigénat* because the distinction citizen/local had to be maintained. Racial difference added to legal differences to contribute to the social problem of métissage in colonies like Indochina, Western and Equatorial Africa, and New Caledonia. In Guadeloupe, Martinique, Tahiti, Senegal, etc, where locals got citizenship automatically, archives and administrative documents make rare references to métissage and differences in colour (only personal and private documents make references as mentioned earlier). In Algeria, métissage is rarely mentioned because there were less mixed unions (due to religious reasons).

Anthropologists were troubled and obsessed with the 'métis' question. Métissage questioned anthropology's main objectives which is to treat different races as finite unities. Colonial ethnography viewed the métis as unstable physically since he/she was torn between two heredities, psychologically unstable because he/she had contradictory instincts and socially unstable since as a rejected category they were potentially criminal. Gradually, the figure of the ungovernable métis was imported from the colonies to describe the dangers of immigration in the metropolis. Since what the métis lacks is a family and the support that he ought to get from it, the State become 'un père protecteur' to make up for the father who had failed in his responsibilities. In 1890 orphanages for abandoned métis were founded to train and look after them and were soon made public institutions. But, by segregating the métis children from 'normal' children, this philanthropic action contributed to the racialization of the colonial society and the social visibility of métis children increased.

> ...Ce sont ces institutions charitables qui vont les premières porter la question du statut juridique de ces metis devant les tribunaux qu'on leur reconnaisse la qualité de français du fait de leur appartenance à la race française.[29]

> ...These charitable institutions were the first to raise the question of the legal status of métis children in the courts in order that they be recognized as French by their "appendage" to the French race.

However, in the eyes of the colonial administrators, métis children were more than just mixed-race/hybrid children, they were illegitimate.

> Cela non pas tant parce qu'il produit des êtres racialement indéterminés mais parce qu'il fait grossir dans les faubourgs des metropoles de l'Empire une population d'enfants illegitimes, parias de la societé coloniale comme de la societé colonisée et leaders potentiels de mouvements de rebellions contre ces pères qui les ont abandonnés.[30]

The administrators considered métissage to be both a social (moral depravity) and a political problem. They feared that the métis, rejected by both colonial and local societies (*parias de la societé coloniale comme de la societé colonisée*) would at a later stage become potential leaders of a rebellious cause against France in a symbolic fight against the father who had abandoned them (*et leaders potentiels de mouvements de rebellions contre ces pères qui les ont abandonnés*):

> La dimension raciale intervient dans le traitement administratif du problème des métis dans la mesure où la notion de race n'est pas une pure catégorie biologique et se construit en lien avec des normes de comportement sexuel et d'organisation domestique. Qu'ils soient issus de relations passagères ou non, les métis sont la preuve vivante de la déchéance de certains français qui se sont indigéneisés—on dit parfois plus violemment bougnoulisés—et en cela ils représentent une menace pour le prestige des colonisateurs auprès des indigènes.[31]

The métis was seen as living proof of the depravity of those French who had gone native and thus threatened the prestigious status of the colonizer (*les metis sont la preuve vivante de la déchéance de certains français qui se sont indigéneisés... et en cela ils représentent une menace pour le prestige des colonisateurs...*). The racial dimension become an integral part of the administrative solution to the problem since the concept of race was not merely seen as a biological category but also a reflection of social and moral behaviour (*... la notion de race n'est pas une pure catégorie biologique et se construit en lien avec des normes de comportement sexuel et d'organisation domestique*).

In contrast to the paternalistic and high moralistic rhetoric of official documents, there is ample evidence of the double standards and ambiguities surrounding the norms of morality and charity in the colonies. Novelist Duras makes a mention of one such school for half-castes in her autobiographical masterpiece *The Lover*. The young Duras is obliged to attend such a school because she is a low caste 'European' not because of racial métissage but because of her impoverished social status. She attends a state-run school responsible for transforming abandoned métisses into respectable French women. Ironically, the young Duras flaunts the social norms concerning interracial unions under the very noses of those who were attempting to rehabilitate the products of French immorality by having an affair with the rich Chinaman from Cholon...

In 1889 the *Code de la Nationalité* gave access to French citizenship according to *droit du sang and droit du sol* (*enfants nés de parents étrangers en France deviennent Français à sa majorité*): This law was also applicable to French soil overseas in the colonies. In this context, métissage becomes problematic. The status of the 'métis reconnus' was less of a problem to the jurists than it was to the colonial administrators.[32] The *Code* recognized as French citizens all those children born out of marriage between a French father and a local. Abandoned children posed a problem. The law in 1889 claimed that children born of unknown parents on French soil were also French and this was made clear in 1897. Colonial administration could not however accept the fact that all abandoned local children could be thus assimilated into the community of French citizens. Thus the *Code de la Nationalité* was subverted in the colonies. To solve the debate it was decided that what had to be proven was not just the parentage (filiation déterminée) but also French connections (filiation collective). The Hanoi court in 1926 pronounced a new law on the definition of métissage for the purposes of accordance of citizenship where race was included in the judicial document.

> La preuve de la race peut être faite par tous modes de preuves, preuves par écrits, preuves par témoins, preuves par simples presumptions, notamment par l'aspect physique de l'enfant...la possesion de l'état, prévue par le code civil à propos de filiation légitime...peut être admise pour établir la race dudit enfant.
>
> Il resulte des constations faites par la Cour...que V.est de race mixte...La Cour a constaté qu'il réunissait sans aucun doute possible des caractères physiques du métis européen-annamite; d'autre part il a reçu une instruction et une éducation françaises et a toujours vécu dans un milieu européen...[33]

Acquiring French citizenship meant proving a cultural and physiological connection (*aspect physique*) to the French race. The fact that the métis had received French instruction and has lived in a European milieu (*...d'autre part il a reçu une instruction et une éducation françaises et a toujours vécu dans un milieu européen...*) contributed to judging his case favourably proving that racial and cultural logic were perceived as complimentary to colonial logic. A series of such laws from 1928 in Indochina regularized the legal position of the abandoned métis but in society they became even more socially visible as different, and more importantly, inferior citizens.

Kim Lefevre's story *La Metisse Blanche* provides another dimension and displays the ambiguities of the system. Kim was abandoned by her father but not by her mother, who tries her best to give her a normal childhood despite rejection by her own Vietnamese milieu. However, Kim's mother is forced to send her to an orphanage run by missionaries. In order to do so she had to renounce her maternal rights so that her métisse daughter could be brought up as a French citizen. In an ironic turn of events in 1946, when trouble was brewing in French Indochina, with Ho Chi Minh in Hanoi, the Sisters appeal to the families to recall their children so that the métis numbers to be repatriated to France would be reduced...[34]

In Philippe Franchini's autobiographical narrative *Continental Saigon*, he relates the life of a métis, legal offspring of a rich hotelier and owner of The Continental, the most celebrated hotel in colonial Saigon. From young Philippe's observations we learn that métissage codified by jurists and controlled by administrators was still a social taboo even in well-to-do milieus. He observes with some degree of embarrassment that the métis always chose the French camp in public life such as sports meets. Philippe Franchini's social status gained him entry into the exclusive Cercle Sportif de Saigon but he was not spared taunting receptions and unwelcome remarks. Acutely conscious of his physical weakness compared to the physical strength of the French, he believes that the more beautiful métisses have an easier time. Both Kim in *Metisse Blanche* and Philippe in *Continental Saigon* are haunted by the physical aspect of their métissage more than anything else. Self-representation contradicts the dominant representation of the métis/métisse in popular French imagination. As we have already observed, it is the physical aspect of the métisse that appeals to popular European aesthetics and lyricism in the nineteenth century.

By and large fiction on Indochina written between the wars and before represents the métis and métisse as societal rejects or 'the white man's sin'. Henri Copin (1996) in his analysis of the image of the métisse observes that the métisse as femme fatale is the most common representation.[35] He summarizes what he calls the "drame métis" (the métis tragedy) firstly in terms of rejection by the father, secondly in terms of the emotional distancing from an Annamite mother who is destined to return to her traditional roots, and thirdly as object of the humiliating gaze of society. The child métisse begins by hating herself because she never hears anything remotely positive being said to describe her. The story of *Confidences d'une Métisse* (1926) by Clotilde Chivas Baron is a fictional autobiography of a métisse who takes revenge on her French father for abandoning her and for marrying her mother to a small time French civil servant. Humiliated, Jeannie becomes the mistress of one of her father's partners and fiancé of her half sister. She travels to Paris where she becomes a dancer. On her return to Indochina she finds herself on the same ship as her father, whom she seduces first before revealing her identity. The narrative concludes with the death of both Jeannie and her French father. The book written in 1926 is not a socio-critical study. In fact the socio-political realities are camouflaged by foregrounding the psychological in the narrative: The book begins with: "I am a proud woman humiliated by life…" The epilogue takes on a very ambivalent note of representing the story as a conflict between cultures rather than foregrounding the power relations as origin of the tragic situation of the métisse. Henry Copin (the literary critic), like Chivas Baron (the writer) almost 70 years before him, seems to concentrate on the more apolitical, ahistorical issues like the psychological aspects of the métisse tragedy. In Jeannie's death Copin, like Chivas-Baron before him, sees failure and further isolation, whereas the act of revenge (Jeannie's seduction of her father), is a literalization of the violence that French Indochina's métis tragedy has generated.

Postcolonial 'métissage' and reconciliation

Métis characters like Étienne, son of Camille and Jean Baptiste in *Indochine* (1992), and Kim in the comic book *Les Oubliés d'Annam* (2000) have been re-deployed by contemporary European authors, this time to literalize the act of postcolonial reconciliation. Camille the adopted Vietnamese daughter of the French woman Eliane in *Indochine* takes up the cause of the Vietnamese communists against French colonial rule. Camille's 'betrayal' can be seen to signify the failure of France's 'assimilationist' policies in the colonies but Eliane the Asiate's continued commitment to her adopted métis grandchild and Étiennes' acknowledgement of Eliane as his only mother, dramatized against the backdrop of the Geneva accords, contribute on one hand to represent postcolonial Franco-Indochinese reconciliation and on the other to reinforcing the image of France: *mère protectrice* (mother-protector) despite historical realities… At another level of métissage aesthetics, Eliane the European born and raised in Indochina represents the perfectly acceptable cultural métisse. The last shots of an older 'post-colonial' Eliane in chic Vietnamese-style clothes reinforce the visual aesthetics of her cultural métissage.

The comic book *Les Oubliés d'Annam* (2000) uses métissage to re-explore France's colonial past. French soldier Joubert deserts the French army in Indochina to marry a Vietnamese woman and to join the liberationist forces. *Les Oubliés d'Annam* is the story of how a French journalist unravels the anticolonial stand of a French colonial. He contributes to constructing a reconciliation between present-day France and its colonial past by helping to bring the métisse Kim Chi to France and reuniting her with her French grandmother. The actual 'emotional' reconciliation is represented in a full page (non-verbal) sequence of pictures. The presence and acceptance of the métisse in France by the French grandmother is a strong statement of cultural appeasement even as the plot continues to struggle with partisans and ghosts of a colonial past in the historical present.[36]

Postcolonial Francophone Voices and Literary Métissage

Exploring the linguistic origins and associated socio-political connotations of the term, 'métissage' permits one to understand the reappropriation of this term in contemporary discourse on pluri-racial identities, and the use of the term 'métissage' as reading practice by critics and as an aesthetic tool by contemporary 'métisse' writers. For the purposes of studying interracial relations, the word 'métis' is useful since it derives from the Latin *mixtus*, originally referring to cloth made of two fibres where the woof is in flax and the warp in cotton. This association erases all sexual connotations and biological allusion that the historical references to métissage could represent. It also does away with connotations regarding pedigree that the association cross-breed would suggest. Interestingly, its Greek homonym *métis* (a cunning intelligence) is also a figure of a function of a power (a form of techne that cannot be subsumed under a single identifiable system of diametric dichotomies). This reference enhances the importance of the use of métissage as a liberationist technique by contemporary métisse writers.

Since the seventies, Francophone women's voices have been announcing innovative writing strategies. Linda Lê, like Kim Lefevre, Assia Djebar and Leila Sebbar, all cultural or racial métisses, use métissage as a concept and practice in order to articulate new visions of themselves to bypass ancient symmetries and dichotomies. Françoise Lionnet suggests that "métissage is a site of undecidability and indeterminacy, where solidarity becomes the fundamental principal of political action against hegemonic languages."[37]

In Linda Lê's *Calomnies* (1993), the author uses métissage as a liberating strategy to celebrate her narrator's 'mestizo consciousness'. The novel alternates regularly between two narrative points of view, that of the uncle (doubly dislocated, in Corrèze and in an asylum) and that of the niece—doubly exiled between two spaces of origin/ Father(lands). The novel maintains ambiguity and ambivalence at all levels: plot, characterization and setting. The plot is centred upon a letter received by the uncle from his niece. The niece has requested him to reveal to her the details of her real father (the foreigner). She has learnt from her mother that her husband was not the narrator's real father but had claimed her as his own even after knowing that she was the offspring of his wife's affair with a foreign soldier. The niece, who is in exile in France, contacts her uncle, who has been sent away from *le Pays* and isolated in an asylum in Corrèze. The plot brings into play the various binaries that operate in such a situation: centre/margin; colonizer/colonized, home/abroad, loyalty/betrayal, etc. But instead of reinforcing the divide, the text blurs these divisions.

In order to assume her identity the niece has to make a choice between two narrative spaces that her double denomination produces "celui d'un livre charmeur (that of the foreigner father) et "celui d'un livre austere" (that of her Vietnamese father). The double narration translates the connection that the narrative finally establishes between "se consacrer à la folie" and, "se consacrer à l'écriture". The 'mad' uncle submits to the dominant discourse of reason (by learning to read and write) and no longer assumes his madness (freedom), while the niece eventually gives up her attachments (to her fathers/fatherlands/spaces of difference) in order to be free of any restraints (she gives herself to madness—"se consacrer à la folie").

The "Conseiller", a French character in the book, suggests that the narrator rewrite her story to sensationalize it in terms of a foreign father that she had never known, but Ricin, her partner, advises her to cultivate her marginal space: "Reste métèque—cultive des marges..." (*Calomnies*, p. 33). She has to decide between integration/assimilation and the border zones of hybridity. In the end her refusal to read her uncle's version of her life symbolizes her rejection of her French connection.

Her mother had offered her the possibility of freeing herself from the tyranny of tradition (represented by her Vietnamese father, the 'raté'), and from the confines of *le Pays* to accede to another enclosed space (designated by the biological father, the 'séducteur'—France), "Grace à sa mère elle pourrait s'offrir un autre père" (*Calomnies*, p. 54). She had the opportunity to rewrite her space of identity by replacing one father (land) for another, one place for another, as if the borders between the two were static and well-defined. In France, she little realizes that she has been playing the role of a well assimilated model immigrant till she decides to reject both her origins and stay 'métèque'. The double location and double identity restrict her freedom so she decides to live in the margins.

> Je suis un étranger ici—je suis un étranger là bas. (*Calomnies*, p. 32)
> I am a stranger here—I am a stranger there.

In *Calomnies*, France as well as *Le Pays* as two distinct enclosed spaces are perceived as societal sites of repression and the state of madness is viewed as a psychological space of liberty and expression. It represents non-assimilation and freedom to live in the border zone. The narrative thwarts the binary hierarchy of the centre and the margin: the margin refuses its place as the Other and the boundaries of the centre are demystified. Linda Lê's *Calomnies* shows that space in the margin is a site of creativity and power, where the self can be recovered by erasing the category colonizer/colonized.[38] Choosing the margin as a space of radical openness suggests that one can move beyond binary oppositions of race, gender and class. Assimilation, imitation or assuming the role of the radical exotic are often the choices foisted by liberal modernist discourse on activist colonized subjects. *Calomnies* proposes a space that is in between, interconnected and simultaneously central and marginal. Linda Lê proposes a 'logique métisse' that permits her to live her metissage in an original beneficial and liberating way.

Kim Lefevre in *Le Retour à la Saison des Pluies* (1990), her sequel to *Métisse Blanche*, brings herself to reappropriate her métissage to construct her mixed-race consciousness in a positive light. Returning to Vietnam and revisiting her home that she had abandoned thirty years earlier has shown Kim the way to find the means to survive her present and to live her racial and cultural métissage:

> Dans cette remontée vers l'amont où presque rien de ce qui fut ne subsiste, ma famille est mon point de repère, le cordon qui m'attache à ce pays où

je suis née. Elle est mon passé vivant, le trait d'union entre ce que j'étais et ce que je suis.[39]

Going back in time, where almost nothing that was exists any longer, my family is my only reference point, the cord that attaches me to the country where I was born. It is my living past, the bridge between what I was and what I am.

Kim's past is both living (her surviving family in Vietnam) and dead, (the rejection of her 'original home' in Vietnam. Her present/'ma France' is both present located in language: "Je suis française par la langue", and historical past since she is the daughter of a *colon*. For Lefevre, a racial and cultural métisse, it is the 'mé-tissage' (cross-braiding) of two different space-time compresses that provide her with the tools for emancipation.

Kim's 'parole métèque' is an act that puts the Self into position to take a stand in present time and not in a geographically limited space. Her language is her emplacement that permits her to live her "métissage" in a dynamic space-time frame. By appropriating the *territoire du colon* (land of the colonizer) as *ma France* (my France) only to claim linguistic citizenship, her 'emplacement' makes her a stranger to the geographical spaces of both Vietnam and France. However, when she lives her métissage in the margins and her choice is geographical, linguistic as well as political.

To write in French is thus also to transform French into a language that become's the writer's own: French is appropriated, made into a vehicle to express a hybrid, heteroglot universe. The creative act of taking possession of a language gives rise to a kind of linguistic métissage visible in many francophone works.[40]

Conclusion

Métissage as an aesthetic concept encompasses biology and history, anthropology and philosophy, linguistics, and literature. The cultural or racial métis/métisse is neither a mere apology of colonization nor a site of unproblematic multiculturalism. Métissage represents a colonial encounter that in its violence created hybridization which cannot be erased. Glissant, while defining a positive construction of creolization and mixed-race identities in philosophical terms, is not unaware of the economic dimensions of this problem. He cautions however that creolization is not "un étendard libérateur", a banner for revolt, in all contexts. Economic aid has to be given first in some cases so that underprivileged populations can first re-discover their dignity. Inclusivity and mutability would be the main characteristics of métissage as articulated by Glissant, Condé, Lionnet and Alcoff, a métissage which is a *conscious* articulation of mixed identities, allegiances and traditions. It is only this consciousness that can argue for a positive construction of the mixed-race identity.

In conclusion, I would like quote Maryse Condé who expands on Glissant's idea of métissage. She claims that at the end of the 20th century we have all become métis. The challenge is to accept this fact and to integrate that pluriculturalism into our lives, that which some writers have integrated into their texts:

> On l'aura compris, pour moi qui ne crois plus guère à la race, le métissage n'est pas une question d'ethnicité. De sang. Comme on dit aux Antilles, de "peaux chappées" et de bons cheveux. Il s'ancre au plus profond. Dans la culture. Aucune culture n'est pure. Nous avons tendance à réduire la nôtre parce que nous mythologisons une part, toujours la même, de notre histoire: l'arrachement à la matrice africaine, le Middle passage. Nous arrêtons bien volontiers au système de plantations. Nous nous accrochons à l'Oralité et mythifions le Conteur. Nous ne voulons pa reconnaître que pour le meilleur et pour le pire, la colonisation a signalé notre entrée dans ce qu'il est convenu d'appeler la modernité. Les migrations, l'évolution du monde dans lequel nous vivons ont fait le reste. Ainsi qu'une bonne majorité des êtres humains, en cette fin du 20ème siècle, nous sommes devenus des métis. Le défi consiste à accepter ce fait et à intégrer ce pluriculturalisme dans nos existences, ce que certains écrivains ont déjà accepté et intégré dans leur texte.[41]

> One would have understood, that I, who no longer believes in race, do not see métissage as an ethnic issue... It is anchored deeper. In culture. No culture is pure. We tend to mythologize ours...Wrenched from the African matrix, the Middle passage. We stop willingly with the plantations. We believe in Orality and we mythify the Storyteller. We do not want to recognize that colonization has heralded our entry into what is said to be modernity. Migrations and the evolution of the world in which we live have done the rest. Thus like the majority of human beings in the 20th century we have become métis. The challenge is to accept the fact and to integrate this pluriculturalism into our lives...

Notes

1   See Edouard Glissant, "Métissage et créolisation", in *Discours sur le métissage, Identités métisses: En quête d'Ariel,* edited by Sylvie Kandé (Paris: Harmattan, 1999), pp. 50–52.

2   Ibid., p. 52. The translation that follows this passage is mine.

3   See Françoise Lionnet, "The Politics and Aesthetics of Métissage", in *Women, Autobiography and Gender,* edited by Sidonie Smith and Julia Watson (Madison: University of Wisconsin Press, 1998), pp. 334.

4   The word mulatto suggesting a reference to the animal world is used sometimes. Lionnet (op. cit., p. 327) wonders if the Anglo-American consciousness can accommodate miscegenation positively through language? I am not suggesting here that the word metis/metisse is devoid of negative connotations in the French/Francophone context. The paper will be looking at some of the negative articulations of the term.

5   Linda Alcoff, "Mestizo Identity", in *The Idea of Race,* edited by R. Bernasconi and Tommy L. Lott (Indianapolis/Cambridge: Hackett Publishing, 2000), pp. 139–60.

6   See Alcoff in *The Idea of Race,* p. 159.

7   See Lionnet op. cit., p. 327. Creoles were more white and cafres were more black. Confusion was bound to occur as the word Creoles also referred to Europeans born in the Carribean. Europeans born and raised in Indochina were called 'Asiates'.

8   See Jack Corzani, "Lafcadio Hearn aux Antilles: Les dessous de l'esthétisme colonial" in *Notre librarie* 91, special issue on "Images du Noir dans la Littérature Coloniale: De la conquête coloniale à nos jours", pp. 77, 79. Lafcadio Hearn is better known for his writings on Japan.

9   See Jean Luc Bonniol, "Le métissage entre social et biologique. L'exemple des Antilles de colonisation française, in *Discours sur le métissage, Identités métisses: En quête d'Ariel,* edited by Sylvie Kandé (Paris: Harmattan, 1999), p. 56. The translation is mine.

10 See Jean Calvet, *Notre librarie* 91, p. 124. "Mais si nous tentons de cerner aujourd'hui l'image du noir dans la chanson française, une évidence s'impose: ce n'est pas le noir que nous rencontrons, c'est plutôt la noire. Et souvent la métisse."

    See also Yao Amela, "Quelques Grands Auteurs", in *Notre Librairie* 90, pp. 40–47, which explores images of women of colour in the poems of Baudelaire. With his collection of poems *Fleurs du Mal,* Baudelaire launched a new sense of visual and lyrical aestheticism dominated by images of women of colour in 'languorous Asia' and 'burning Africa'. The visual fascination for the metisse is replayed in a recent Mathieu Kassowitz film (*Café au lait-Metisse*) that dramatizes a love triangle between a metisse, a rich Jew and a Frenchman.

[11] See L. L de Grammont, "Section V, 'Sous Le Gouvernement des Amiraux'", in *L'Indochine par les Français*, edited by Ajalbert (1931), p. 114.

[12] See Herbert Wild, "Section VII, 'L'Union Indochinoise'", in *L'Indochine par les Français*, op. cit., p. 237.

[13] See Panivong Norindr, "Filmic Memorials, Colonial Blues", *Phantasmatic Indochina* (Chapel Hill: Duke University Press, 1996), pp. 137–38. See also Laura Mulvey, "Visual Pleasure and Narrative Cinema", in *Critical and Cultural Theory Reader*, edited by Antony Easthope and Kate McGowan (Buckingham: Open University Press, 1992).

[14] "Le thème de l'union mixte, du métissage est sans doute le plus fréquent de la littérature coloniale et renvoie donc à une réalité que les auteurs s'évertuent à nier ou à dénigrer tout en—et c'est là que se situe le paradoxe—le fantasmant, et cela à plusieurs niveaux. Mais le métissage biologique faisant l'objet d'une répulsion bien trop forte ce métis idéal se réalise dans la figure de la Créole blanche, dont la naissance sur un sol indianisé garantit un métissage naturel, inné, qui ne serait pas le résultat d'une mésalliance", Valérie Paüs, Des Indianités dans la Littérature Coloniale de l'Océan Indie, Mémoire de D.E.A. 1999 sous la direction du Professeur M. Marimoutou (C.) <http://www.dodille.com/rdos/paus/indianites.htm>, accessed 19 Nov 2001. In his reading of Marius-Ary Leblond's "Moutousami Mauricien" and Clément Charoux's *Ameenah*, Valérie Paüs claims that "De manière générale les sociétés occidentales ont toujours refusé le métissage, synonyme souvent de trouble, de désordre et de confusion. Le romancier colonial semble partager cette opinion et le discours colonial, diabolisant le métissage, le montre clairement".

[15] *The Lover*, p. 98.

[16] Yvonne Knibiehler, *La femme au temps des colonies* (Paris: Stock, 1985), pp. 69–70.

[17] Louis Salaun, *L'Indochine* (Paris: Imprimerie Nationale, 1902), p. 385.

[18] Salaun (1902), p. 385.

[19] See Salaun (1902), p. 386, for the prescribed role of Frenchwomen in the colonies.

[20] Knibielher (1985), p. 77.

[21] Knibielher (1985), p. 79 The author suggests that perhaps European women who were more in number and established on colonial territory may have introduced such ideas in order to monopolize their men.

[22] Emmannuelle Saada, "Enfants de la colonie: batards raciaux, batards sociaux", in *Discours sur le métissage, Identités métisses: En quête d'Ariel*, edited by Sylvie Kandé (Paris: Harmattan, 1999), pp. 75–96.

[23] See also Anne Laura Stoler, *Race and the Education of Desire* (Durham: Duke University Press, 1995) and *Tensions of the Empire—Colonial Cultures in a Bourgeois World*, edited by Frederic Cooper and Anne Laura Stoler (Berkeley: University of California Press, 1997).

[24] See *Metisse Blanche*, pp. 14–15.

[25] *Metisse Blanche,* p. 138.

[26] *Metisse Blanche,* p. 264.

[27] Anne Stoler, "Rethinking Colonial Categories: European Communities and the Boundaries of Rule, in *Comparative Studies in History and Society* 31, no. 1 (1989), pp. 134–61; and "Sexual Affronts and Racial Frontiers: European Identities and the Cultural Politics of Exclusion in Colonial Southeast Asia", *Comparative Studies in History and Society* 34, no. 3 (1992), pp. 514–51.

[28] Saada (1999), op. cit. n. 22, p. 81.

[29] Ibid., p. 88.

[30] Ibid., p. 89.

[31] Ibid., p. 89.

[32] Ibid., p. 91.

[33] Ibid., p. 93. According to Emannuelle Saada, colonial history shows that race was a complex construction of biology and culture. She also claims that the colonial era, far from being an era of clear and distinct identities, was also an era of shifting ambiguities. "L'analyse historique dela question des métis montre bien que l'ère colonial loin d'être le moment des identités claires et distinctes, était déjà constamment travaillée par les mouvements, les ambiguités et les chevauchements identitaires qui ont provoqué un immense travail collectif de codification". Ibid., pp. 95–96.

[34] *Metisse Blanche,* pp. 72–73.

[35] See Henri Copin, *L'Indochine dans la littérature française des vingt à 1954: Exotisme et altérité* (Paris: L'Harmattan, 1996), pp. 224–40.

[36] See Mark Mackinney, "Metissage in Postcolonial Comics", in *Postcolonial Cultures and Literatures in France,* edited by Hargreaves and McKinney (London and New York: Routledge, 1997), p. 177.

[37] Lionnet 1998, p. 326.

[38] For a more detailed analysis of the novel see Ravi, "Towards a Progressive Sense of Space—Linda Le's Calomnies", in *Géopolitique et Mondialisation, coll. Frontières, Presses de l'Université de Paris-Sorbonne,* no. 10, 2003, pp. 55–68.

[39] *Le Retour à la Saison des Pluies* (1990), p. 221.

[40] See Françoise Lionnet, "Logiques Metisses: Cultural Appropriations and Postcolonial Representations", in *Postcolonial Subjects: Francophone Woman Writers,* edited by Green et al. (1997), p. 326.

[41] Maryse Conde, "Le Métissage du texte" in Kandé 1999, p. 217.

References

Ajalbert, Jean, ed. 1931. *L'Indochine par les Français.* Paris: Gallimard.

Bernasconi, K., and Tommy L. Lott, eds. 2000. *The Idea of Race.* Indianapolis/ Cambridge: Hackett Publishing.

Bernstein, Mathew and Gaylyn Studlar, eds. 1997. *Visions of the East—Orientalism in Film.* London: I.B. Tauris.

Chivas-Baron, Clotilde. 1926. *Confidences de Métisse.* Paris: Fasquelle.

Cooper, Frederic and Anne Laura Stoler, eds. 1997. *Tensions of the Empire—Colonial Cultures in a Bourgeois World*. Berkeley: University of California Press.

Copin, Henri. 1996. *L'Indochine dans la Literature Française des Vingt à 1954: Exotisme et Altérité*. Paris: L'Harmattan.

Devine, Jeremy M. 1995. *Vietnam at 24 Frames a Second*. Jefferson, North Carolina: McFarland.

Donadey, Anne. 2001. *Recasting Postcolonialism: Women Writing between Two Worlds*, Portsmouth: Heinmann.

Duras, Margeurite. 1985. *The Lover*. Translated by Barbara Bray. New York: Pantheon Books.

Franchini, Philippe. 1995. *Continental Saigon*. Paris: Ed Métailié.

Green, Mary Jean, Karen Gould, Micheline Rice-Maximin, Keith L. Walker and Jack A. Yeager, eds. 1996. *Postcolonial Subjects: Francophone Women Writers*. Minneapolis: University of Minnesota Press.

Hargreaves, Alec G. and Mark McKinney, eds. 1997. *Postcolonial Cultures and Literatures in France*. London and New York: Routledge.

Hougron, Jean. 1989. *La Nuit Indochinoise*. Paris: Editions Rober Laffont.

Kandé, Sylvie, ed. 1999. *Discours sur le Métissage, Identités Métisses: En quête d'Ariel*. Paris: L'Harmattan.

Knibiehler, Yvonne. 1985. *Les Femmes dans les Colonies*. Paris: Stock.

Lax, Christian Lacroix and Frank Giroud. 2000. *Les Oubliés d'Annam*. Marcinelle, Belgium: Dupuis.

Lê, Linda. 1993. *Calomnies*. Paris: Christian Bourgeois Éditeur.

Lefèvre, Kim. 1995. *Le Retour à la Saison des Pluies*. Paris: Éditions de l'Aube. [First édition: Bernard Barrault, 1990].

———. 1989. *Metisse Blanche*. Paris: Éditions Barrault. [Second edition, Paris: Flammarion (J'au lu), 1990].

Lionnet, Françoise. 1989. *Autobiographical Voices: Race, Gender, Self-portraiture*. Ithaca: Cornell University Press.

Notre librairie 90. 1987. Images du Noir dans la Littérature Coloniale: Du Moyen Age à la conquête coloniale, Oct–Dec.

Notre librarie 91. 1988. Images du Noir dans la Littérature Coloniale: De la conquête coloniale à nos jours, Jan–Feb.

Salaun, Louis. 1902. *L'Indochine*. Paris: Imprimerie Nationale.

Sherzer, Dina, ed. 1996. *Cinema Colonialism and Postcolonialism*. Austin: University of Texas Press.

Stoler, Laura Anne. 1995. *Race and the Education of Desire*. Durham: Duke University Press.

Films

Indochine, directed by Régis Wargnier; screenplay, Catherine Cohen, Louis Gardel, Erik Orsenna. 1992.

The Lover, directed by Jean Jacques Annaud. 1992.

About the Contributors

Syed Farid Alatas is Associate Professor at the Department of Sociology, National University of Singapore. His book *Democracy and Authoritarianism: The Rise of the Post-Colonial State in Indonesia and Malaysia* is published by Macmillan (1997). His recent articles include "The Study of the Social Sciences in Developing Societies: Towards an Adequate Conceptualization of Relevance" (with Vineeta Sinha); "Teaching Classical Sociological Theory in Singapore: The Context of Eurocentrism; "Islam, Ilmu-Ilmu Sosial dan Masyarakat Sipil", *Antropologi Indonesia* 25; and "Eurocentrism and the Role of the Human Sciences in the Dialogue Among Civilizations", *The European Legacy* 7. He is currently working on a second book in the area of the philosophy and sociology of social science and on another project on Muslim ideologies and utopias.

Gregory K. Clancey teaches in the Department of History at the National University of Singapore. His research is primarily on the cultural history of modern Japanese science, but he also writes about architecture, natural disaster, and the politics of emergency. He has co-edited *Historical Perspectives on East Asian Science, Technology, and Medicine* (Singapore: Singapore University Press & World Scientific, 2002) and *Major Problems in the History of American Technology* (Boston: Houghton-Mifflin, 1998). He is currently writing a book about the science, culture and politics of earthquakes in Meiji Japan.

Beng-Lan Goh is Assistant Professor at the Southeast Asian Studies Program, National University of Singapore. She is a cultural anthropologist working on the issue of postcolonial modernity and urbanism in Southeast Asia. She is the author of *Modern Dreams: An Enquiry into Power, Cultural Difference and the Cityscape in Contemporary*

Urban Malaysia (Ithaca: Cornell Southeast Asia Program Publications, 2002).

John Kleinen is Senior Lecturer in Anthropology at the University of Amsterdam. He is a former SSRC representative in Hanoi collaborating with the National Centre for Social Sciences and Humanities. He has extensively researched rural villages, fisheries and integrated coastal zone management in Vietnam, and Vietnamese migrants in Europe. His previous publications include *Vietnam* (1989), *Facing the Future, Reviving the Past* (1999), *Vietnamese Society in Transition* (edited, 2001). He is also part of the Maritime Anthropology Research Unit.

Van Nguyen-Marshall is Assistant Professor of History at Trent University, where she teaches the histories of East Asia and Southeast Asia. Nguyen-Marshall's research interest lies in modern Vietnamese history, with a particular focus on social and cultural issues. Her doctoral dissertation examines elite discourses on poverty and charity in French colonial Vietnam. She is presently researching the organization and meanings of Vietnamese mutual-aid societies in early twentieth-century Vietnam.

Henk Schulte Nordholt is Associate Professor of Anthropology at the University of Amsterdam and IIAS Professor of Asian History at Erasmus University Rotterdam. He coordinates a research programme on modern Indonesia at the KITLV in Leiden. His research interests are Balinese history, the anthropology of colonialism, and political violence. Recent publications include *The Spell of Power: A History of Balinese Politics 1650-1940* (1996); (edited) *Outward Appearances: Dressing State and Society in Indonesia* (1997); (edited with I. Abdullah) *Indonesia: In Search of Transition* (2002); *Kriminalitas, Modernitas dan Identitas dalam Sejarah Indonesia* (2002); *Indonesia in Transition: Work in Progress* (edited with Gusti Asnan, 2003).

Pravin J. Patel, Vice-Chancellor of Sardar Patel University, Gujarat, is a sociologist, and did his post-doctoral research at Columbia University. He has held several important positions in the M.S. University of Baroda, Vadodara, and won several awards and honours including a Fulbright Fellowship, Charles Wallace Fellowship and UGC Visiting Professorships/Fellowships at many universities of India. He is on the editorial boards of several academic journals including the British Sociological Society's *Work, Employment and Society.*

Maurizio Peleggi is Assistant Professor of History at the National University of Singapore and is the author of *The Politics of Ruins and the Business of Nostalgia* (Bangkok: White Lotus, 2002) and *Lords of Things: The Fashioning of the Siamese Monarchy's Modern Image* (Honolulu: University of Hawai'i Press, 2002). He is currently working on a social and cultural history of modern Thailand to be published by Reaktion Books in 2006.

Srilata Ravi (formerly of the National University of Singapore) is currently teaching in European Languages and Studies at the University of Western Australia. Her main research interests are in twentieth century French and Francophone literatures, travel literature and postcolonial studies. She is the author of *L'Inde Romancée: L'Inde dans le genre Romanesque français depuis 1947* (1997) and has published several articles in major international journals on gender, place and identity in colonial and postcolonial fiction in French.

Mario Rutten is Professor of Comparative Sociology of Asia at the University of Amsterdam, and Director of Asian Studies in Amsterdam. He has extensive research experience on rural entrepreneurship and labour relations in India, Indonesia and Malaysia, and on Indian migrants in Europe. His previous publications include *Farms and Factories* (1995), *Small Business Entrepreneurs in Asia and Europe* (co-edited, 1997), *Development and Deprivation in Gujarat* (co-edited, 2002) and *Rural Capitalists in Asia* (2003).

Satish Saberwal taught Sociology at the Centre for Historical Studies, Jawaharlal Nehru University, New Delhi. He conducted fieldwork in central Kenya (1963–64) and in a Punjabi industrial town (1969, 1989). His current interests are the social backdrop to the 1947 partition of the Indian subcontinent, and the evolution of the Chinese society. Recent publications include *Wages of Segmentation: Comparative Historical Studies on Europe and India* (1995); *Roots of Crisis: Interpreting Contemporary Indian Society* (1996); *Social Conflict* (co-edited, 1996); and *Rules, Laws, Constitutions* (co-edited, 1998).

Vineeta Sinha is Assistant Professor at the Department of Sociology, National University of Singapore. Her research interests include the critique of concepts and categories in the social sciences, the history of the social sciences, sociological and anthropological theory, sociology and anthropology of religion, the Hindu diaspora and the political economy of health care in medically plural societies. Her teaching areas include courses in classical sociological theory, and the sociology of religion, everyday life, and food. Some recent publications are "Merging Different Sacred Spaces: Enabling Religious Encounters through Pragmatic Utilisation of Space?", "Decentring Social Sciences in Practice through Individuals Actions and Choices", and "Teaching Classical Theory in Singapore: The Context of Eurocentrism".